Also by Bruno Bettelheim

*Love Is Not Enough: The Treatment of Emotionally
    Disturbed Children* (1950)
Symbolic Wounds: Puberty Rites and the Envious Male (1954)
*Truants from Life: The Rehabilitation of Emotionally
    Disturbed Children* (1955)
The Informed Heart: Autonomy in a Mass Age (1960)
Paul and Mary: Two Cases from Truants from Life (1961)
Dialogues with Mothers (1962)
Co-author (with M. B. Janowitz): *Social Change
    and Prejudice* (1964)
The Empty Fortress (1967)
Children of the Dream (1969)
A Home for the Heart (1974)

THE USES OF
ENCHANTMENT

THE USES OF ENCHANTMENT

The Meaning and Importance
of Fairy Tales

Bruno Bettelheim

Alfred A. Knopf
New York   1976

THIS IS A BORZOI BOOK
PUBLISHED BY ALFRED A. KNOPF, INC.

Portions of this book originally appeared in *The New Yorker*.

Library of Congress Cataloging in Publication Data

Bettelheim, Bruno.   The uses of enchantment.

Bibliography: p.
Includes index.
1. Fairy tales—History and criticism. 2. Psychoanalysis.
3. Folklore and children. I. Title.
GR550.B47   398'.45   75-36795
ISBN 0-394-49771-6

Manufactured in the United States of America
First Edition

CONTENTS

ACKNOWLEDGMENTS

Many people were involved in the creation of fairy tales. Many people also contributed to the writing of this book. Foremost were the children, whose responses made me aware of the importance of fairy stories in their lives; and psychoanalysis, which permitted me access to the stories' deeper meaning. It was my mother who opened to me the magic world of fairy tales; without her influence this book would not have been written. In writing it, I received helpful suggestions from friends who took a kind interest in my efforts. For their suggestions I am grateful to Marjorie and Al Flarsheim, Frances Gitelson, Elizabeth Goldner, Robert Gottlieb, Joyce Jack, Paul Kramer, Ruth Marquis, Jacqui Sanders, Linnea Vacca, and many others.

Joyce Jack edited the manuscript; it is thanks to her patient and extremely sensitive efforts that it has assumed its present form. I was fortunate to find in Robert Gottlieb the rare publisher who combines finely perceptive and therefore most encouraging understanding with the sound critical attitude which makes him the most desirable final editor an author could wish for.

Last, but certainly not least, I wish to acknowledge gratefully the generous support of the Spencer Foundation, which made it possible for me to write this book. The sympathetic understanding and the friendship of its president, H. Thomas James, provided much-appreciated encouragement for my undertaking.

THE USES OF
ENCHANTMENT

INTRODUCTION:
THE STRUGGLE FOR MEANING

If we hope to live not just from moment to moment, but in true consciousness of our existence, then our greatest need and most difficult achievement is to find meaning in our lives. It is well known how many have lost the will to live, and have stopped trying, because such meaning has evaded them. An understanding of the meaning of one's life is not suddenly acquired at a particular age, not even when one has reached chronological maturity. On the contrary, gaining a secure understanding of what the meaning of one's life may or ought to be —this is what constitutes having attained psychological maturity. And this achievement is the end result of a long development: at each age we seek, and must be able to find, some modicum of meaning congruent with how our minds and understanding have already developed.

Contrary to the ancient myth, wisdom does not burst forth fully developed like Athena out of Zeus's head; it is built up, small step by small step, from most irrational beginnings. Only in adulthood can an intelligent understanding of the meaning of one's existence in this world be gained from one's experiences in it. Unfortunately, too many parents want their children's minds to function as their own do—as if mature understanding of ourselves and the world, and our ideas about the meaning of life, did not have to develop as slowly as our bodies and minds.

Today, as in times past, the most important and also the most difficult task in raising a child is helping him to find meaning in life. Many growth experiences are needed to achieve this. The child, as he develops, must learn step by step to understand himself better; with this he becomes more able to understand others, and eventually can relate to them in ways which are mutually satisfying and meaningful.

To find deeper meaning, one must become able to transcend the narrow confines of a self-centered existence and believe that one will make a significant contribution to life—if not right now, then at some future time. This feeling is necessary if a person is to be satisfied with himself and with what he is doing. In order not to be at the mercy of the vagaries of life, one must develop one's inner resources, so that one's emotions, imagination, and intellect mutually support and enrich one another. Our positive feelings give us the strength to develop our rationality; only hope for the future can sustain us in the adversities we unavoidably encounter.

As an educator and therapist of severely disturbed children, my main task was to restore meaning to their lives. This work made it obvious to me that if children were reared so that life was meaningful to them, they would not need special help. I was confronted with the problem of deducing what experiences in a child's life are most suited to promote his ability to find meaning in his life; to endow life in general with more meaning. Regarding this task, nothing is more important than the impact of parents and others who take care of the child; second in importance is our cultural heritage, when transmitted to the child in the right manner. When children are young, it is literature that carries such information best.

Given this fact, I became deeply dissatisfied with much of the literature intended to develop the child's mind and personality, because it fails to stimulate and nurture those resources he needs most in order to cope with his difficult inner problems. The preprimers and primers from which he is taught to read in school are designed to teach the necessary skills, irrespective of meaning. The overwhelming bulk of the rest of so-called "children's literature" attempts to entertain or to inform, or both. But most of these books are so shallow in substance that little of significance can be gained from them. The acquisition of skills, including the ability to read, becomes devalued when what one has learned to read adds nothing of importance to one's life.

We all tend to assess the future merits of an activity on the basis of what it offers now. But this is especially true for the child, who, much more than the adult, lives in the present and, although he has anxieties about his future, has only the vaguest notions of what it may require or be like. The idea that learning to read may enable one later to enrich one's life is experienced as an empty promise when the stories the child listens to, or is reading at the moment, are vacuous. The worst feature of these children's books is that they cheat the child of what he ought to gain from the experience of literature: access to deeper meaning, and that which is meaningful to him at his stage of development.

For a story truly to hold the child's attention, it must entertain him and arouse his curiosity. But to enrich his life, it must stimulate his imagination; help him to develop his intellect and to clarify his emotions; be attuned to his anxieties and aspirations; give full recognition to his difficulties, while at the same time suggesting solutions to the problems which perturb him. In short, it must at one and the same time relate to all aspects of his personality—and this without ever belittling but, on the contrary, giving full credence to the seriousness of the child's predicaments, while simultaneously promoting confidence in himself and in his future.

In all these and many other respects, of the entire "children's literature"—with rare exceptions—nothing can be as enriching and satisfying to child and adult alike as the folk fairy tale. True, on an overt level fairy tales teach little about the specific conditions of life in modern mass society; these tales were created long before it came into being. But more can be learned from them about the inner problems of human beings, and of the right solutions to their predicaments in any society, than from any other type of story within a child's comprehension. Since the child at every moment of his life is exposed to the society in which he lives, he will certainly learn to cope with its conditions, provided his inner resources permit him to do so.

Just because his life is often bewildering to him, the child needs even more to be given the chance to understand himself in this complex world with which he must learn to cope. To be able to do so, the child must be helped to make some coherent sense out of the turmoil of his feelings. He needs ideas on how to bring his inner house into order, and on that basis be able to create order in his life. He needs —and this hardly requires emphasis at this moment in our history— a moral education which subtly, and by implication only, conveys to him the advantages of moral behavior, not through abstract ethical concepts but through that which seems tangibly right and therefore meaningful to him.

The child finds this kind of meaning through fairy tales. Like many other modern psychological insights, this was anticipated long ago by poets. The German poet Schiller wrote: "Deeper meaning resides in the fairy tales told to me in my childhood than in the truth that is taught by life." (*The Piccolomini*, III, 4.)

Through the centuries (if not millennia) during which, in their retelling, fairy tales became ever more refined, they came to convey at the same time overt and covert meanings—came to speak simultaneously to all levels of the human personality, communicating in a manner which reaches the uneducated mind of the child as well as that of the sophisticated adult. Applying the psychoanalytic model of the human personality, fairy tales carry important messages to the conscious, the preconscious, and the unconscious mind, on whatever level each is functioning at the time. By dealing with universal human problems, particularly those which preoccupy the child's mind, these stories speak to his budding ego and encourage its development, while at the same time relieving preconscious and unconscious pressures. As the stories unfold, they give conscious credence and body to id pressures and show ways to satisfy these that are in line with ego and superego requirements.

But my interest in fairy tales is not the result of such a technical analysis of their merits. It is, on the contrary, the consequence of asking myself why, in my experience, children—normal and abnormal alike, and at all levels of intelligence—find folk fairy tales more satisfying than all other children's stories.

The more I tried to understand why these stories are so successful at enriching the inner life of the child, the more I realized that these tales, in a much deeper sense than any other reading material, start where the child really is in his psychological and emotional being. They speak about his severe inner pressures in a way that the child unconsciously understands, and—without belittling the most serious inner struggles which growing up entails—offer examples of both temporary and permanent solutions to pressing difficulties.

When a grant from the Spencer Foundation provided the leisure to study what contributions psychoanalysis can make to the education of children—and since reading and being read to are essential means of education—it seemed appropriate to use this opportunity to explore in greater detail and depth why folk fairy tales are so valuable in the upbringing of children. My hope is that a proper understanding of the unique merits of fairy tales will induce parents and teachers to assign them once again to that central role in the life of the child they held for centuries.

Fairy Tales and the Existential Predicament

In order to master the psychological problems of growing up—overcoming narcissistic disappointments, oedipal dilemmas, sibling rivalries; becoming able to relinquish childhood dependencies; gaining a feeling of selfhood and of self-worth, and a sense of moral obligation

—a child needs to understand what is going on within his conscious self so that he can also cope with that which goes on in his unconscious. He can achieve this understanding, and with it the ability to cope, not through rational comprehension of the nature and content of his unconscious, but by becoming familiar with it through spinning out daydreams—ruminating, rearranging, and fantasizing about suitable story elements in response to unconscious pressures. By doing this, the child fits unconscious content into conscious fantasies, which then enable him to deal with that content. It is here that fairy tales have unequaled value, because they offer new dimensions to the child's imagination which would be impossible for him to discover as truly on his own. Even more important, the form and structure of fairy tales suggest images to the child by which he can structure his daydreams and with them give better direction to his life.

In child or adult, the unconscious is a powerful determinant of behavior. When the unconscious is repressed and its content denied entrance into awareness, then eventually the person's conscious mind will be partially overwhelmed by derivatives of these unconscious elements, or else he is forced to keep such rigid, compulsive control over them that his personality may become severely crippled. But when unconscious material *is* to some degree permitted to come to awareness and worked through in imagination, its potential for causing harm—to ourselves or others—is much reduced; some of its forces can then be made to serve positive purposes. However, the prevalent parental belief is that a child must be diverted from what troubles him most: his formless, nameless anxieties, and his chaotic, angry, and even violent fantasies. Many parents believe that only conscious reality or pleasant and wish-fulfilling images should be presented to the child—that he should be exposed only to the sunny side of things. But such one-sided fare nourishes the mind only in a one-sided way, and real life is not all sunny.

There is a widespread refusal to let children know that the source of much that goes wrong in life is due to our very own natures—the propensity of all men for acting aggressively, asocially, selfishly, out of anger and anxiety. Instead, we want our children to believe that, inherently, all men are good. But children know that *they* are not always good; and often, even when they are, they would prefer not to be. This contradicts what they are told by their parents, and therefore makes the child a monster in his own eyes.

The dominant culture wishes to pretend, particularly where children are concerned, that the dark side of man does not exist, and professes a belief in an optimistic meliorism. Psychoanalysis itself is viewed as having the purpose of making life easy—but this is not what its founder intended. Psychoanalysis was created to enable man to accept the problematic nature of life without being defeated by it, or giving in to escapism. Freud's prescription is that only by struggling courageously against what seem like overwhelming odds can man succeed in wringing meaning out of his existence.

This is exactly the message that fairy tales get across to the child in manifold form: that a struggle against severe difficulties in life is unavoidable, is an intrinsic part of human existence—but that if one does not shy away, but steadfastly meets unexpected and often unjust hardships, one masters all obstacles and at the end emerges victorious.

Modern stories written for young children mainly avoid these existential problems, although they are crucial issues for all of us. The child needs most particularly to be given suggestions in symbolic form about how he may deal with these issues and grow safely into maturity. "Safe" stories mention neither death nor aging, the limits to our existence, nor the wish for eternal life. The fairy tale, by contrast, confronts the child squarely with the basic human predicaments.

For example, many fairy stories begin with the death of a mother or father; in these tales the death of the parent creates the most agonizing problems, as it (or the fear of it) does in real life. Other stories tell about an aging parent who decides that the time has come to let the new generation take over. But before this can happen, the successor has to prove himself capable and worthy. The Brothers Grimm's story "The Three Feathers" begins: "There was once upon a time a king who had three sons. . . . When the king had become old and weak, and was thinking of his end, he did not know which of his sons should inherit the kingdom after him." In order to decide, the king sets all his sons a difficult task; the son who meets it best "shall be king after my death."

It is characteristic of fairy tales to state an existential dilemma briefly and pointedly. This permits the child to come to grips with the problem in its most essential form, where a more complex plot would confuse matters for him. The fairy tale simplifies all situations. Its figures are clearly drawn; and details, unless very important, are eliminated. All characters are typical rather than unique.

Contrary to what takes place in many modern children's stories, in fairy tales evil is as omnipresent as virtue. In practically every fairy tale good and evil are given body in the form of some figures and their actions, as good and evil are omnipresent in life and the propensities for both are present in every man. It is this duality which poses the moral problem, and requires the struggle to solve it.

Evil is not without its attractions—symbolized by the mighty giant or dragon, the power of the witch, the cunning queen in "Snow White"—and often it is temporarily in the ascendancy. In many fairy tales a usurper succeeds for a time in seizing the place which rightfully belongs to the hero—as the wicked sisters do in "Cinderella." It is not that the evildoer is punished at the story's end which makes immersing oneself in fairy stories an experience in moral education, although this is part of it. In fairy tales, as in life, punishment or fear of it is only a limited deterrent to crime. The conviction that crime does not pay is a much more effective deterrent, and that is why in fairy tales the bad person always loses out. It is not the fact that virtue wins out at the end which promotes morality, but that the hero is most attractive to the child, who identifies with the hero in all his struggles. Because of this identification the child imagines that he suffers with the hero his trials and tribulations, and triumphs with him as virtue is victorious. The child makes such identifications all on his own, and the inner and outer struggles of the hero imprint morality on him.

The figures in fairy tales are not ambivalent—not good and bad at the same time, as we all are in reality. But since polarization dominates the child's mind, it also dominates fairy tales. A person is either good or bad, nothing in between. One brother is stupid, the other is clever. One sister is virtuous and industrious, the others are vile and lazy. One is beautiful, the others are ugly. One parent is all good, the other evil. The juxtaposition of opposite characters is not for the purpose of stressing right behavior, as would be true for cautionary tales. (There are some amoral fairy tales where goodness or badness, beauty or ugliness play no role at all.) Presenting the polarities of character permits the child to comprehend easily the difference between the two, which he could not do as readily were the figures drawn more true to life, with all the complexities that characterize real people. Ambiguities must wait until a relatively firm personality has been established on the basis of positive identifications. Then the child has a basis for understanding that there are great differences between people, and that therefore one has to make choices about who one wants to be. This basic decision, on which all later personality development will build, is facilitated by the polarizations of the fairy tale.

Furthermore, a child's choices are based, not so much on right versus wrong, as on who arouses his sympathy and who his antipathy.

The more simple and straightforward a good character, the easier it is for a child to identify with it and to reject the bad other. The child identifies with the good hero not because of his goodness, but because the hero's condition makes a deep positive appeal to him. The question for the child is not "Do I want to be good?" but "Who do I want to be like?" The child decides this on the basis of projecting himself wholeheartedly into one character. If this fairy-tale figure is a very good person, then the child decides that he wants to be good, too.

Amoral fairy tales show no polarization or juxtaposition of good and bad persons; that is because these amoral stories serve an entirely different purpose. Such tales or type figures as "Puss in Boots," who arranges for the hero's success through trickery, and Jack, who steals the giant's treasure, build character not by promoting choices between good and bad, but by giving the child the hope that even the meekest can succeed in life. After all, what's the use of choosing to become a good person when one feels so insignificant that he fears he will never amount to anything? Morality is not the issue in these tales, but rather, assurance that one can succeed. Whether one meets life with a belief in the possibility of mastering its difficulties or with the expectation of defeat is also a very important existential problem.

The deep inner conflicts originating in our primitive drives and our violent emotions are all denied in much of modern children's literature, and so the child is not helped in coping with them. But the child is subject to desperate feelings of loneliness and isolation, and he often experiences mortal anxiety. More often than not, he is unable to express these feelings in words, or he can do so only by indirection: fear of the dark, of some animal, anxiety about his body. Since it creates discomfort in a parent to recognize these emotions in his child, the parent tends to overlook them, or he belittles these spoken fears out of his own anxiety, believing this will cover over the child's fears.

The fairy tale, by contrast, takes these existential anxieties and dilemmas very seriously and addresses itself directly to them: the need to be loved and the fear that one is thought worthless; the love of life, and the fear of death. Further, the fairy tale offers solutions in ways that the child can grasp on his level of understanding. For example, fairy tales pose the dilemma of wishing to live eternally by occasionally concluding: "If they have not died, they are still alive." The other ending—"And they lived happily ever after"—does not for a moment fool the child that eternal life is possible. But it does indicate that which alone can take the sting out of the narrow limits of our time on this earth: forming a truly satisfying bond to another. The tales teach that when one has done this, one has reached the ultimate in emotional security of existence and permanence of relation available to man; and this alone can dissipate the fear of death. If one has found true adult love, the fairy story also tells, one doesn't need to wish for eternal life. This is suggested by another ending found in fairy tales: "They lived for a long time afterward, happy and in pleasure."

An uninformed view of the fairy tale sees in this type of ending an unrealistic wish-fulfillment, missing completely the important message it conveys to the child. These tales tell him that by forming a true interpersonal relation, one escapes the separation anxiety which haunts him (and which sets the stage for many fairy tales, but is always resolved at the story's ending). Furthermore, the story tells, this ending is not made possible, as the child wishes and believes, by holding on to his mother eternally. If we try to escape separation anxiety and death anxiety by desperately keeping our grasp on our parents, we will only be cruelly forced out, like Hansel and Gretel.

Only by going out into the world can the fairy-tale hero (child) find himself there; and as he does, he will also find the other with whom he will be able to live happily ever after; that is, without ever again having to experience separation anxiety. The fairy tale is future-oriented and guides the child—in terms he can understand in both his conscious and his unconscious mind—to relinquish his infantile dependency wishes and achieve a more satisfying independent existence.

Today children no longer grow up within the security of an extended family, or of a well-integrated community. Therefore, even more than at the times fairy tales were invented, it is important to provide the modern child with images of heroes who have to go out into the world all by themselves and who, although originally ignorant of the ultimate things, find secure places in the world by following their right way with deep inner confidence.

The fairy-tale hero proceeds for a time in isolation, as the modern child often feels isolated. The hero is helped by being in touch with primitive things—a tree, an animal, nature—as the child feels more in touch with those things than most adults do. The fate of these heroes convinces the child that, like them, he may feel outcast and abandoned in the world, groping in the dark, but, like them, in the course of his life he will be guided step by step, and given help when it is needed. Today, even more than in past times, the child needs the reassurance offered by the image of the isolated man who nevertheless is capable of achieving meaningful and rewarding relations with the world around him.

The Fairy Tale: A Unique Art Form

While it entertains the child, the fairy tale enlightens him about himself, and fosters his personality development. It offers meaning on so many different levels, and enriches the child's existence in so many ways, that no one book can do justice to the multitude and diversity of the contributions such tales make to the child's life.

This book attempts to show how fairy stories represent in imaginative form what the process of healthy human development consists of, and how the tales make such development attractive for the child to engage in. This growth process begins with the resistance against the parents and fear of growing up, and ends when youth has truly found itself, achieved psychological independence and moral maturity, and no longer views the other sex as threatening or demonic, but is able to relate positively to it. In short, this book explicates why fairy tales make such great and positive psychological contributions to the child's inner growth.

The delight we experience when we allow ourselves to respond to a fairy tale, the enchantment we feel, comes not from the psychological meaning of a tale (although this contributes to it) but from its literary qualities—the tale itself as a work of art. The fairy tale could not have its psychological impact on the child were it not first and foremost a work of art.

Fairy tales are unique, not only as a form of literature, but as works of art which are fully comprehensible to the child, as no other form of art is. As with all great art, the fairy tale's deepest meaning will be different for each person, and different for the same person at various moments in his life. The child will extract different meaning from the same fairy tale, depending on his interests and needs of the moment. When given the chance, he will return to the same tale when he is ready to enlarge on old meanings, or replace them with new ones.

As works of art, fairy tales have many aspects worth exploring in addition to the psychological meaning and impact to which this book is devoted. For example, our cultural heritage finds expression in fairy tales, and through them is communicated to the child's mind.* An-

*One example may illustrate: In the Brothers Grimm's story "The Seven Ravens," seven brothers disappear and become ravens as their sister enters life. Water has to be fetched from the well in a jug for the girl's baptism, and the loss of the jug is the fateful event which sets the stage for the story. The ceremony of baptism also heralds

other volume could detail the unique contribution fairy tales can and do make to the child's moral education, a topic which is only touched on in the pages which follow.

Folklorists approach fairy tales in ways germane to their discipline; linguists and literary critics examine their meaning for other reasons. It is interesting to observe that, for example, some see in the motif of Little Red Riding Hood's being swallowed by the wolf the theme of night devouring the day, of the moon eclipsing the sun, of winter replacing the warm seasons, of the god swallowing the sacrificial victim, and so on. Interesting as such interpretations are, they seem to offer little to the parent or educator who wants to know what meaning a fairy story may have to the child, whose experience is, after all, quite far removed from interpretations of the world on the basis of concerns with nature or celestial deities.

Fairy tales also abound in religious motifs; many Biblical stories are of the same nature as fairy tales. The conscious and unconscious associations which fairy tales evoke in the mind of the listener depend on his general frame of reference and his personal preoccupations. Hence, religious persons will find in them much of importance that is not mentioned here.

Most fairy tales originated in periods when religion was a most important part of life; thus, they deal, directly or by inference, with religious themes. The stories of *The Thousand and One Nights* are full of references to Islamic religion. A great many Western fairy tales have religious content; but most of these stories are neglected today and unknown to the larger public just because, for many, these religious themes no longer arouse universally and personally meaningful associations. The neglect of "Our Lady's Child," one of the most beautiful stories of the Brothers Grimm, illustrates this. It begins ex-

---

the beginning of a Christian existence. It is possible to view the seven brothers as representing that which had to disappear for Christianity to come into being. If so, they represent the pre-Christian, pagan world in which the seven planets stood for the sky gods of antiquity. The newborn girl is then the new religion, which can succeed only if the old creed does not interfere with its development. With Christianity, the brothers who represent paganism become relegated to darkness. But as ravens, they dwell in a mountain at the end of the world, and this suggests their continued existence in a subterranean, subconscious world. Their return to humanity occurs only because the sister sacrifices one of her fingers, and this conforms to the Christian idea that only those who are willing to sacrifice that part of their body which prevents them from reaching perfection, if the circumstance requires it, will be allowed to enter heaven. The new religion, Christianity, can liberate even those who remained at first arrested in paganism.

actly like "Hansel and Gretel": "Hard by a great forest dwelt a wood-cutter with his wife." As in "Hansel and Gretel," the couple are so poor that they can no longer feed themselves and their three-year-old daughter. Moved by their distress, the Virgin Mary appears to them and offers to take care of the little girl, whom she takes with her to heaven. The girl lives a wonderful life there until she reaches the age of fourteen. At this time, much as in the very different tale of "Blue-beard," the Virgin entrusts the girl with the keys to thirteen doors, twelve of which she may open, but not the thirteenth. The girl cannot resist this temptation; she lies about it, and in consequence has to return to earth, mute. She undergoes severe ordeals and is about to be burned at the stake. At this moment, as she desires only to confess her misdeed, she regains her voice to do so, and is granted by the Virgin "happiness for her whole life." The lesson of the story is: a voice used to tell lies leads us only to perdition; better we should be de-prived of it, as is the heroine of the story. But a voice used to repent, to admit our failures and state the truth, redeems us.

Quite a few of the Brothers Grimm's other stories contain or begin with religious allusions. "The Old Man Made Young Again" starts: "At the time when our Lord still walked the earth, he and St. Peter stopped one evening at a smith's house. . . ." In another story, "The Poor Man and the Rich Man," God, like any other fairy-tale hero, is tired from walking. That story begins: "In olden times, when the Lord himself still used to walk about on this earth amongst men, it once happened that he was tired and overtaken by the darkness before he could reach an inn. Now there stood on the road before him two houses facing each other. . . ." But important and fascinating as these religious aspects of fairy stories are, they remain beyond the scope and purpose of this book, and so are left unexamined here.

Even given this book's relatively restricted purpose, that of suggest-ing why fairy tales are so meaningful to children in helping them cope with the psychological problems of growing up and integrating their personalities, some serious but necessary limitations have had to be accepted.

The first of these lies in the fact that today only a small number of fairy tales are widely known. Most of the points made in this book could have been illustrated more vividly if some of the more obscure fairy stories could have been referred to. But since these tales, though once familiar, are presently unknown, it would have been necessary to reprint them here, making for a book of unwieldy size. Therefore the decision was made to concentrate on a few still-popular fairy stories, to show some of their underlying meanings, and how these may relate to the child's growing-up problems, to our understanding of ourselves and of the world. And the second part of the book, rather than striving for an exhaustive completeness that is beyond reach, examines some well-known favorites in some detail, for the meaning and pleasure that may be gained from them.

If this book had been devoted to only one or two tales, it would have been possible to show many more of their facets, although even then complete probing of their depths would not have been achieved; for this, each story has meanings on too many levels. Which story is most important to a particular child at a particular age depends entirely on his psychological stage of development, and the problems which are most pressing to him at the moment. While in writing the book it seemed reasonable to concentrate on a fairy tale's central meanings, this has the shortcoming of neglecting other aspects which might be much more significant to some individual child because of problems he is struggling with at the time. This, then, is another necessary limitation of this presentation.

For example, in discussing "Hansel and Gretel," the child's striving to hold on to his parents even though the time has come for meeting the world on his own is stressed, as well as the need to transcend a primitive orality, symbolized by the children's infatuation with the gingerbread house. Thus, it would seem that this fairy tale has most to offer to the young child ready to make his first steps out into the world. It gives body to his anxieties, and offers reassurance about these fears because even in their most exaggerated form—anxieties about being devoured—they prove unwarranted: the children are victorious in the end, and a most threatening enemy—the witch—is utterly defeated. Thus, a good case could be made that this story has its greatest appeal and value for the child at the age when fairy tales begin to exercise their beneficial impact, that is, around the age of four or five.

But separation anxiety—the fear of being deserted—and starvation fear, including oral greediness, are not restricted to a particular period of development. Such fears occur at all ages in the unconscious, and thus this tale also has meaning for, and provides encouragement to, much older children. As a matter of fact, the older person might find it considerably more difficult to admit consciously his fear of being deserted by his parents, or to face his oral greed; and this is even more reason to let the fairy tale speak to his unconscious, give body to his unconscious anxieties, and relieve them, without this ever coming to conscious awareness.

Other features of the same story may offer much-needed reassurance and guidance to an older child. In early adolescence a girl had been fascinated by "Hansel and Gretel," and had derived great comfort from reading and rereading it, fantasizing about it. As a child, she had been dominated by a slightly older brother. He had, in a way, shown her the path, as Hansel did when he put down the pebbles which guided his sister and himself back home. As an adolescent, this girl continued to rely on her brother; and this feature of the story felt reassuring. But at the same time she also resented the brother's dominance. Without her being conscious of it at the time, her struggle for independence rotated around the figure of Hansel. The story told her unconscious that to follow Hansel's lead led her back, not forward, and it was also meaningful that although Hansel was the leader at the story's beginning, it was Gretel who in the end achieved freedom and independence for both, because it was she who defeated the witch. As an adult, this woman came to understand that the fairy tale had helped her greatly in throwing off her dependence on her brother, as it had convinced her that an early dependence on him need not interfere with her later ascendancy. Thus, a story which for one reason had been meaningful to her as a young child provided guidance for her at adolescence for a quite different reason.

The central motif of "Snow White" is the pubertal girl's surpassing in every way the evil stepmother who, out of jealousy, denies her an independent existence—symbolically represented by the stepmother's trying to see Snow White destroyed. The story's deepest meaning for one particular five-year-old, however, was far removed from these pubertal problems. Her mother was cold and distant, so much so that she felt lost. The story assured her that she need not despair: Snow White, betrayed by her stepmother, was saved by males—first the dwarfs and later the prince. This child, too, did not despair because of the mother's desertion, but trusted that rescue would come from males. Confident that "Snow White" showed her the way, she turned to her father, who responded favorably; the fairy tale's happy ending made it possible for this girl to find a happy solution to the impasse in living into which her mother's lack of interest had projected her. Thus, a fairy tale can have as important a meaning to a five-year-old as to a thirteen-year-old, although the personal meanings they derive from it may be quite different.

In "Rapunzel" we learn that the enchantress locked Rapunzel into the tower when she reached the age of twelve. Thus, hers is likewise the story of a pubertal girl, and of a jealous mother who tries to prevent her from gaining independence—a typical adolescent problem, which finds a happy solution when Rapunzel becomes united with her prince. But one five-year-old boy gained quite a different reassurance from this story. When he learned that his grandmother, who took care of him most of the day, would have to go to the hospital because of serious illness—his mother was working all day, and there was no father in the home—he asked to be read the story of Rapunzel. At this critical time in his life, two elements of the tale were important to him. First, there was the security from all dangers in which the substitute mother kept the child, an idea which greatly appealed to him at that moment. So what normally could be viewed as a representation of negative, selfish behavior was capable of having a most reassuring meaning under specific circumstances. And even more important to the boy was another central motif of the story: that Rapunzel found the means of escaping her predicament in her own body—the tresses on which the prince climbed up to her room in the tower. That one's body can provide a lifeline reassured him that, if necessary, he would similarly find in his own body the source of his security. This shows that a fairy tale—because it addresses itself in the most imaginative form to essential human problems, and does so in an indirect way—can have much to offer to a little boy even if the story's heroine is an adolescent girl.

These examples may help to counteract any impression made by my concentration here on a story's main motifs, and demonstrate that fairy tales have great psychological meaning for children of all ages, both girls and boys, irrespective of the age and sex of the story's hero. Rich personal meaning is gained from fairy stories because they facilitate changes in identification as the child deals with different problems, one at a time. In the light of her earlier identification with a Gretel who was glad to be led by Hansel, the adolescent girl's later identification with a Gretel who overcame the witch made her growth toward independence more rewarding and secure. The little boy's first finding security in the idea of being kept within the safety of the tower permitted him later on to glory in the realization that a much more dependable security could be found in what his body had to offer him, by way of providing him with a lifeline.

As we cannot know at what age a particular fairy tale will be most important to a particular child, we cannot ourselves decide which of the many tales he should be told at any given time or why. This only the child can determine and reveal by the strength of feeling with which he reacts to what a tale evokes in his conscious and unconscious mind. Naturally a parent will begin by telling or reading to his child a tale the parent himself or herself cared for as a child, or cares for now. If the child does not take to the story, this means that its motifs or themes have failed to evoke a meaningful response at this moment in his life. Then it is best to tell him another fairy tale the next evening. Soon he will indicate that a certain story has become important to him by his immediate response to it, or by his asking to be told this story over and over again. If all goes well, the child's enthusiasm for this story will be contagious, and the story will become important to the parent too, if for no other reason than that it means so much to the child. Finally there will come the time when the child has gained all he can from the preferred story, or the problems which made him respond to it have been replaced by others which find better expression in some other tale. He may then temporarily lose interest in this story and enjoy some other one much more. In the telling of fairy stories it is always best to follow the child's lead.

Even if a parent should guess correctly why his child has become involved emotionally with a given tale, this is knowledge best kept to oneself. The young child's most important experiences and reactions are largely subconscious, and should remain so until he reaches a much more mature age and understanding. It is always intrusive to interpret a person's unconscious thoughts, to make conscious what he wishes to keep preconscious, and this is especially true in the case of a child. Just as important for the child's well-being as feeling that his parent shares his emotions, through enjoying the same fairy tale, is the child's feeling that his inner thoughts are not known to his parent until he decides to reveal them. If the parent indicates that he knows them already, the child is prevented from making the most precious gift to his parent of sharing with him what until then was secret and private to the child. And since, in addition, a parent is so much more powerful than a child, his domination may appear limitless—and hence destructively overwhelming—if he seems able to read the child's secret thoughts, know his most hidden feelings, even before the child himself has begun to become aware of them.

Explaining to a child why a fairy tale is so captivating to him destroys, moreover, the story's enchantment, which depends to a considerable degree on the child's not quite knowing why he is delighted by it. And with the forfeiture of this power to enchant goes also a loss of the story's potential for helping the child struggle on his own, and master all by himself the problem which has made the story meaningful to him in the first place. Adult interpretations, as correct as they may be, rob the child of the opportunity to feel that he, on his own, through repeated hearing and ruminating about the story, has coped successfully with a difficult situation. We grow, we find meaning in life, and security in ourselves by having understood and solved personal problems on our own, not by having them explained to us by others.

Fairy-tale motifs are not neurotic symptoms, something one is better off understanding rationally so that one can rid oneself of them. Such motifs are experienced as wondrous because the child feels understood and appreciated deep down in his feelings, hopes, and anxieties, without these all having to be dragged up and investigated in the harsh light of a rationality that is still beyond him. Fairy tales enrich the child's life and give it an enchanted quality just because he does not quite know how the stories have worked their wonder on him.

This book has been written to help adults, and most especially those with children in their care, to become more fully aware of the importance of such tales. As has already been pointed out, innumerable interpretations besides those suggested in the text that follows may be pertinent; fairy tales, like all true works of art, possess a multifarious richness and depth that far transcend what even the most thorough discursive examination can extract from them. What is said in this book should be viewed as illustrative and suggestive merely. If the reader is stimulated to go beyond the surface in his own way, he will extract ever more varied personal meaning from these stories, which will then also become more meaningful to the children he may tell them to.

Here, however, one especially crucial limitation must be noted: The true meaning and impact of a fairy tale can be appreciated, its enchantment can be experienced, only from the story in its original form. Describing the significant features of a fairy tale gives as little feeling for what it is all about as the listing of the events of a poem does for its appreciation. Such a description of main features, however, is all that a book like this one can provide, short of actually reprinting the stories. Since most of these fairy tales are readily available elsewhere, the hope is that this book will be read in conjunction with a re-reading of the tales discussed.* Whether it is "Little Red Riding Hood," "Cinderella," or any other fairy tale, only the story itself permits an appreciation of its poetic qualities, and with it an understanding of how it enriches a responsive mind.

*The versions of the fairy tales discussed in this book are referred to in the Notes at the end of the book.

Part One

A POCKETFUL
OF MAGIC

LIFE DIVINED
FROM THE INSIDE

"Little Red Riding Hood was my first love. I felt that if I could have married Little Red Riding Hood, I should have known perfect bliss." This statement by Charles Dickens indicates that he, like untold millions of children all over the world throughout the ages, was enchanted by fairy tales. Even when world-famous, Dickens acknowledged the deep formative impact that the wondrous figures and events of fairy tales had had on him and his creative genius. He repeatedly expressed scorn for those who, motivated by an uninformed and petty rationality, insisted on rationalizing, bowdlerizing, or outlawing these stories, and thus robbed children of the important contributions fairy tales could make to their lives. Dickens understood that the imagery of fairy tales helps children better than anything else in their most difficult and yet most important and satisfying task: achieving a more mature consciousness to civilize the chaotic pressures of their unconscious.[1]

Today, as in the past, the minds of both creative and average children can be opened to an appreciation of all the higher things in life by fairy tales, from which they can move easily to enjoying the greatest works of literature and art. The poet Louis MacNeice, for example, tells that "Real fairy stories always meant much to me as a person, even when I was at a public school where to admit this meant losing face. Contrary to what many people say even now, a fairy story, at least of the classical folk variety, is a much more solid affair than the average naturalistic novel, whose hooks go little deeper than a gossip column. From folk tales and sophisticated fairy tales such as Hans Andersen's or Norse mythology and stories like the *Alice* books and *Water Babies* I graduated, at about the age of twelve, to the *Faerie*

Queene."[2] Literary critics such as G. K. Chesterton and C. S. Lewis felt that fairy stories are "spiritual explorations" and hence "the most life-like" since they reveal "human life as seen, or felt, or divined from the inside."[3]

Fairy tales, unlike any other form of literature, direct the child to discover his identity and calling, and they also suggest what experiences are needed to develop his character further. Fairy tales intimate that a rewarding, good life is within one's reach despite adversity—but only if one does not shy away from the hazardous struggles without which one can never achieve true identity. These stories promise that if a child dares to engage in this fearsome and taxing search, benevolent powers will come to his aid, and he will succeed. The stories also warn that those who are too timorous and narrow-minded to risk themselves in finding themselves must settle down to a humdrum existence—if an even worse fate does not befall them.

Past generations of children who loved and felt the importance of fairy tales were subjected to the scorn only of pedants, as happened to MacNeice. Today many of our children are far more grievously bereaved—because they are deprived of the chance to know fairy stories at all. Most children now meet fairy tales only in prettified and simplified versions which subdue their meaning and rob them of all deeper significance—versions such as those on films and TV shows, where fairy tales are turned into empty-minded entertainment.

Through most of man's history, a child's intellectual life, apart from immediate experiences within the family, depended on mythical and religious stories and on fairy tales. This traditional literature fed the child's imagination and stimulated his fantasizing. Simultaneously, since these stories answered the child's most important questions, they were a major agent of his socialization. Myths and closely related religious legends offered material from which children formed their concepts of the world's origin and purpose, and of the social ideals a child could pattern himself after. These were the images of the unconquered hero Achilles and wily Odysseus; of Hercules, whose life history showed that it is not beneath the dignity of the strongest man to clean the filthiest stable; of St. Martin, who cut his coat in half to clothe a poor beggar. It is not just since Freud that the myth of Oedipus has become the image by which we understand the ever new but age-old problems posed to us by our complex and ambivalent feelings about our parents. Freud referred to this ancient story to make us aware of the inescapable cauldron of emotions which every child, in his own way, has to manage at a certain age.

In the Hindu civilization, the story of Rama and Sita (part of the *Ramayana*), which tells of their peaceable courage and their passionate devotion to each other, is the prototype of love and marriage relationships. The culture, moreover, enjoins everyone to try to relive this myth in his or her own life; every Hindu bride is called Sita, and as part of her wedding ceremony she acts out certain episodes of the myth.

In a fairy tale, internal processes are externalized and become comprehensible as represented by the figures of the story and its events. This is the reason why in traditional Hindu medicine a fairy tale giving form to his particular problem was offered to a psychically disoriented person, for his meditation. It was expected that through contemplating the story the disturbed person would be led to visualize both the nature of the impasse in living from which he suffered, and the possibility of its resolution. From what a particular tale implied about man's despair, hopes, and methods of overcoming tribulations, the patient could discover not only a way out of his distress but also a way to find himself, as the hero of the story did.

But the paramount importance of fairy tales for the growing individual resides in something other than teachings about correct ways of behaving in this world—such wisdom is plentifully supplied in religion, myths, and fables. Fairy stories do not pretend to describe the world as it is, nor do they advise what one ought to do. If they did, the Hindu patient would be induced to follow an imposed pattern of behavior—which is not just bad therapy, but the opposite of therapy. The fairy tale is therapeutic because the patient finds his *own* solutions, through contemplating what the story seems to imply about him and his inner conflicts at this moment in his life. The content of the chosen tale usually has nothing to do with the patient's external life, but much to do with his inner problems, which seem incomprehensible and hence unsolvable. The fairy tale clearly does not refer to the outer world, although it may begin realistically enough and have everyday features woven into it. The unrealistic nature of these tales (which narrow-minded rationalists object to) is an important device, because it makes obvious that the fairy tales' concern is not useful information about the external world, but the inner processes taking place in an individual.

In most cultures, there is no clear line separating myth from folk or fairy tale; all these together form the literature of preliterate societies. The Nordic languages have only one word for both: *saga*. German has retained the word *Sage* for myths, while fairy stories are called *Märchen*. It is unfortunate that both the English and French names for these stories emphasize the role of fairies in them—because in most, no fairies appear. Myths and fairy tales alike attain a definite form only when they are committed to writing and are no longer subject to continuous change. Before being written down, these stories were either condensed or vastly elaborated in the retelling over the centuries; some stories merged with others. All became modified by what the teller thought was of greatest interest to his listeners, by what his concerns of the moment or the special problems of his era were.

Some fairy and folk stories evolved out of myths; others were incorporated into them. Both forms embodied the cumulative experience of a society as men wished to recall past wisdom for themselves and transmit it to future generations. These tales are the purveyors of deep insights that have sustained mankind through the long vicissitudes of its existence, a heritage that is not revealed in any other form as simply and directly, or as accessibly, to children.

Myths and fairy tales have much in common. But in myths, much more than in fairy stories, the culture hero is presented to the listener as a figure he ought to emulate in his own life, as far as possible.

A myth, like a fairy tale, may express an inner conflict in symbolic form and suggest how it may be solved—but this is not necessarily the myth's central concern. The myth presents its theme in a majestic way; it carries spiritual force; and the divine is present and is experienced in the form of superhuman heroes who make constant demands on mere mortals. Much as we, the mortals, may strive to be like these heroes, we will remain always and obviously inferior to them.

The figures and events of fairy tales also personify and illustrate inner conflicts, but they suggest ever so subtly how these conflicts may be solved, and what the next steps in the development toward a higher humanity might be. The fairy tale is presented in a simple, homely way; no demands are made on the listener. This prevents even the smallest child from feeling compelled to act in specific ways, and he is never made to feel inferior. Far from making demands, the fairy tale reassures, gives hope for the future, and holds out the promise of a happy ending. That is why Lewis Carroll called it a "love-gift" —a term hardly applicable to a myth.*

*Child of the pure unclouded brow
And dreaming eyes of wonder!
Though time be fleet, and I and thou

Obviously, not every story contained in a collection called "Fairy Tales" meets these criteria. Many of these stories are simply diversions, cautionary tales, or fables. If they are fables, they tell by means of words, actions, or events—fabulous though these may be—what one ought to do. Fables demand and threaten—they are moralistic— or they just entertain. To decide whether a story is a fairy tale or something entirely different, one might ask whether it could rightly be called a love-gift to a child. That is not a bad way to arrive at a classification.

To understand how a child views fairy tales, let us consider as examples the many fairy stories in which a child outwits a giant who scares him or even threatens his life. That children intuitively understand what these "giants" stand for is illustrated by the spontaneous reaction of a five-year-old.

Encouraged by discussion about the importance fairy tales have for children, a mother overcame her hesitation about telling such "gory and threatening" stories to her son. From her conversations with him, she knew that her son already had fantasies about eating people, or people getting eaten. So she told him the tale of "Jack the Giant Killer."[4] His response at the end of the story was: "There aren't any such things as giants, are there?" Before the mother could give her son the reassuring reply which was on her tongue—and which would have destroyed the value of the story for him—he continued, "But there are such things as grownups, and they're like giants." At the ripe old age of five, he understood the encouraging message of the story: although adults can be experienced as frightening giants, a little boy with cunning can get the better of them.

This remark reveals one source of adult reluctance to tell fairy stories: we are not comfortable with the thought that occasionally we look like threatening giants to our children, although we do. Nor do we want to accept how easy they think it is to fool us, or to make fools of us, and how delighted they are by this idea. But whether or not we tell fairy tales to them, we *do*—as the example of this little boy proves —appear to them as selfish giants who wish to keep to ourselves all the wonderful things which give us power. Fairy stories provide reassur-

---

Are half a life asunder,
Thy loving smile will surely hail
The love-gift of a fairy-tale.
    C. L. Dodgson (Lewis Carroll), in *Through the Looking-Glass*

ance to children that they can eventually get the better of the giant —i.e., they can grow up to be like the giant and acquire the same powers. These are "the mighty hopes that make us men."[5]

Most significantly, if we parents tell such fairy stories to our children, we can give them the most important reassurance of all: that we approve of their playing with the idea of getting the better of these giants. Here reading is not the same as being told the story, because while reading alone the child may think that only some stranger—the person who wrote the story or arranged the book—approves of outwitting and cutting down the giant. But when his parents *tell* him the story, a child can be sure that they approve of his retaliating in fantasy for the threat which adult dominance entails.

"THE FISHERMAN
AND THE JINNY"

FAIRY TALE COMPARED TO FABLE

One of the *Arabian Nights* tales, "The Fisherman and the Jinny," gives an almost complete rendering of the fairy-tale motif which features a giant in conflict with an ordinary person.[6] This theme is common to all cultures in some form, since children everywhere fear and chafe under the power adults hold over them. (In the West, the theme is best known in the form exemplified by the Brothers Grimm's story "The Spirit in the Bottle.") Children know that, short of doing adults' bidding, they have only one way to be safe from adult wrath: through outwitting them.

"The Fisherman and the Jinny" tells how a poor fisherman casts his net into the sea four times. First he catches a dead jackass, the second time a pitcher full of sand and mud. The third effort gains him less than the preceding ones: potsherds and broken glass. The fourth time around, the fisherman brings up a copper jar. As he opens it, a huge cloud emerges, which materializes into a giant Jinny (genie) that threatens to kill him, despite all the fisherman's entreaties. The fisherman saves himself with his wits: he taunts the Jinny by doubting aloud that the huge Jinny could ever have fitted into such a small vessel; thus he induces the Jinny to return into the jar to prove it. Then the fisherman quickly caps and seals the jar and throws it back into the ocean.

In other cultures the same motif may appear in a version where the evil figure materializes as a big, ferocious animal which threatens to devour the hero, who, except for his cunning, is in no way a match for this adversary. The hero then reflects aloud that it must be easy for such a powerful spirit to take the form of a huge creature, but that it could not possibly turn itself into a little animal, such as a mouse or a bird. This appeal to the vanity of the spirit spells its doom. To show that nothing is impossible to it, the evil spirit transforms itself into the tiny animal, which is then easily vanquished by the hero.[7]

The story of "The Fisherman and the Jinny" is richer in hidden messages than other versions of this fairy-tale motif, as it contains significant details not always found in other renderings. One feature is an account of how the Jinny came to be so ruthless as to wish to kill the person who sets him free; another feature is that three unsuccessful attempts are finally rewarded on the fourth try.

According to adult morality, the longer an imprisonment lasts, the more grateful the prisoner should be to the person who liberates him. But this is not how the Jinny describes it: As he sat confined in the bottle during the first hundred years, he "said in my heart, 'Whoso shall release me, him will I enrich for ever and ever.' But the full century went by, and when no one set me free, I entered upon the second five score saying: 'Whoso shall release me, for him I will open the hoards of the earth.' Still no one set me free, and thus four hundred years passed away. Then quoth I, 'Whoso shall release me, for him will I fulfill three wishes.' Yet no one set me free. Thereupon I waxed wroth with exceeding wrath and said to myself, 'Whoso shall release me from this time forth, him will I slay. . . .' "

This is exactly how a young child feels when he has been "deserted." First he thinks to himself how happy he will be when his mother comes back; or when sent to his room, how glad he will be when permitted to leave it again, and how he will reward Mother. But as time passes, the child becomes angrier and angrier, and he fantasizes the terrible revenge he will take on those who have deprived him. The fact that, in reality, he may be very happy when reprieved does not change how his thoughts move from rewarding to punishing those who have inflicted discomfort on him. Thus, the way the Jinny's thoughts evolve gives the story psychological truth for a child.

An example of this progression of feelings was shown by a three-year-old boy whose parents had gone abroad for several weeks. The boy had been speaking quite well before his parents' departure, and continued to do so with the woman taking care of him and with others. But on his parents' return, he wouldn't say a word to them or anybody else for two weeks. From what he had told his caretaker, it was clear that during the first few days of his parents' absence he had looked forward with great anticipation to their return. By the end of the first week, however, he began to talk about how angry he was that they had left him, and how he would get even with them on their return. A week later, he refused even to speak about his parents, and became violently angry at anyone who mentioned them. When his mother and father did finally arrive, he silently turned away from them. Despite all efforts to reach him, the boy remained frozen in his rejection. It took several weeks of compassionate understanding of his predicament on the part of his parents before the boy could become his old self again. It seems clear that as time passed, the child's anger had increased until it became so violent and overwhelming as to make him fear that if he let himself go, he would destroy his parents or be destroyed in retaliation. His refusal to talk was his defense: his way of protecting both himself and his parents against the consequences of his towering rage.

There is no way to know whether in the original language of "The Fisherman and the Jinny" there is a saying similar to ours about "bottled-up" feelings. But the image of confinement in a bottle was as apt then as it is for us now. In some form, every child has experiences similar to those of the three-year-old boy, though usually in less extreme form and without overt reactions like his. On his own, the child does not know what has happened to him—all he knows is that he *has* to act this way. Efforts to help such a child understand rationally will not affect the child, and will leave him defeated to boot, since he does not yet think rationally.

If you tell a small child that a little boy became so angry at his parents that he didn't talk to them for two weeks, his reaction will be: "That's stupid!" If you try to explain why the boy didn't speak for two weeks, your listening child feels even more that to act this way is stupid—now, not only because he considers the action foolish, but also because the explanation does not make sense to him.

A child cannot consciously accept that his anger may make him speechless, or that he may wish to destroy those on whom he depends for his existence. To understand this would mean he must accept the fact that his own emotions may so overpower him that he does not have control over them—a very scary thought. The idea that forces may reside within us which are beyond our control is too threatening to be entertained, and not just by a child.*

Action takes the place of understanding for a child, and this becomes increasingly true the more strongly he feels. A child may have learned to *say* otherwise under adult guidance, but as he really sees it, people do not cry because they are sad; they just cry. People do not hit out and destroy, or stop talking because they are angry; they just do these things. A child may have learned he can placate adults by explaining his action thus: "I did it because I am angry"—but that does not change the fact that the child does not experience anger as anger, but only as an impulse to hit, to destroy, to keep silent. Not before puberty do we begin to recognize our emotions for what they are without immediately acting on them, or wishing to do so.

The child's unconscious processes can become clarified for him only through images which speak directly to his unconscious. The images evoked by fairy tales do this. As the child does not think, "When Mother comes back, I'll be happy" but "I'll give her something," so the Jinny said to himself, "Whoever will release me, I'll enrich." As the child does not think, "I'm so angry I could kill this person" but "When I see him, I'll kill him," so the Jinny says "I'll slay whoever releases me." If a *real* person is said to think or act this way, that idea arouses too much anxiety to permit understanding. But the child knows that the Jinny is an imaginary figure, so he can afford to recognize what motivates the Jinny, without being forced to make a direct application to himself.

As the child spins fantasies around the story—and unless he does, the fairy tale loses most of its impact—he slowly becomes familiar with how the Jinny responds to frustration and incarceration, an important step toward becoming acquainted with parallel reactions in himself. Since it is a fairy tale out of never-never-land which presents the child with these images of behaving, he can swing back and forth in his own mind between "It's true, that's how one acts and reacts" and "It's all untrue, it's just a story," depending on how ready he is to recognize these processes in himself.

*How upsetting it is for a child to think that, unbeknownst to him, powerful processes are going on within him may be illustrated by what happened to one seven-year-old when his parents tried to explain to him that his emotions had carried him away to do things of which they—and he—severely disapproved. The child's reaction was: "You mean there is a machine in me that ticks away all the time and at any moment may explode me?" From then on, this boy lived for a time in real terror of impending self-destruction.

Most important of all, since the fairy tale guarantees a happy outcome, the child need not fear permitting his unconscious to come to the fore in line with the story's content, because he knows that, whatever he may find out, he'll "live happily ever after."

The fantastic exaggerations of the story, such as being "bottled up" for centuries, make reactions plausible and acceptable where situations presented more realistically, such as a parent's absence, would not. To the child, the parent's absence seems an eternity—a feeling that remains unaffected by Mother's truthful explanation that she was gone for only half an hour. So the fairy tale's fantastic exaggerations give it the ring of psychological truth—while realistic explanations seem psychologically untrue, however true to fact.

"The Fisherman and the Jinny" illustrates why the simplified and bowdlerized fairy tale loses all value. Looking at the story from the outside, it would seem unnecessary to have the Jinny's thought undergo such changes from wishing to reward the person who will set him free to deciding to punish him. The story could be told as just an evil Jinny wishing to kill his liberator, who, although only a weak human, nevertheless manages to outsmart the powerful spirit. But in this simplified form it becomes just a scary tale with a happy ending, without psychological truth to it. It is the Jinny's change from wishing-to-reward to wishing-to-punish which permits the child to empathize with the story. Since the story so truthfully describes what went on in the Jinny's mind, the idea that the fisherman may be able to outwit the Jinny also attains veracity. It is the elimination of such seemingly insignificant elements which makes fairy tales lose their deeper meaning, and thus makes them uninteresting to the child.

Without being conscious of it, the child rejoices in the fairy tale's warning to those who hold the power to "bottle him up." There are plenty of modern children's stories in which a child outwits an adult. But because they are too direct, these stories do not offer relief in imagination from always having to live under the sway of adult power; or else they scare the child, whose security rests on the adult being more accomplished than he, and able to protect him reliably.

This is the value of outsmarting a Jinny or a giant, as opposed to doing the same to an adult. If the child is told he can get the better of somebody like his parents, this does offer a pleasurable thought, but at the same time it creates anxiety, because if that is possible, then the child might not be adequately protected by such gullible people. But since a giant is an imaginary figure, the child can fantasize outsmarting him to the degree of being able not only to overpower but to destroy him, and still retain real grownup people as protectors.

The fairy story "The Fisherman and the Jinny" has several advantages over those of the Jack ("Jack the Giant Killer," "Jack and the Beanstalk") cycle. Since the fisherman is not only an adult but, as we are told, the father of children, the child is told implicitly by the story that his parent may feel threatened by powers stronger than he, but is so clever that he overcomes them. According to this tale, the child can truly have the best of both worlds. He can cast himself in the role of the fisherman and imagine himself getting the better of the giant. Or he can cast his parent in the role of the fisherman, and imagine himself as a spirit that can threaten his parent, while being assured that the same parent will win out.

A seemingly insignificant but important feature of "The Fisherman and the Jinny" is that the fisherman has to experience three defeats before he catches the vessel with the Jinny in it. Although it would be simpler to begin the story with the netting of the fateful bottle, this element tells the child without any moralizing that one cannot expect success with the first, or even the second or the third try. Things are not quite so easy to accomplish as one may imagine or wish. To a less persistent person, the fisherman's first three catches would suggest giving up because each effort leads only to worse things. That one must *not* give up, despite initial failure, is such an important message for children that many fables and fairy tales contain it. The message is effective as long as it is delivered not as a moral or demand, but in a casual way which indicates that this is how life is. Further, the magic event of overpowering the giant Jinny does not take place without effort or cunning; these are good reasons to sharpen one's mind and continue one's efforts, whatever the task may be.

Another detail in this story that may likewise seem insignificant, but whose elimination would similarly weaken the story's impact, is the parallel made between the four efforts of the fisherman which are finally crowned by success, and the four steps in the increasing anger of the Jinny. This juxtaposes the maturity of the parent-fisherman and the immaturity of the Jinny, and addresses the crucial problem which life early presents to all of us: whether to be governed by our emotions or by our rationality.

To put the conflict into psychoanalytic terms, it symbolizes the difficult battle we all have to struggle with: should we give in to the pleasure principle, which drives us to gain immediate satisfaction of our wants or to seek violent revenge for our frustrations, even on those who have nothing to do with them—or should we relinquish living by such impulses and settle for a life dominated by the reality principle, according to which we must be willing to accept many frustrations in order to gain lasting rewards? The fisherman, by not permitting his disappointing catches to deter him from continuing his efforts, chose the reality principle, which finally gained him success.

The decision about the pleasure principle is so important that many fairy tales and myths try to teach it. To illustrate the direct, didactic way a myth deals with this crucial choice compared to the gentle, indirect, undemanding, and therefore psychologically more effective way in which fairy tales convey this message, let us consider the myth of Hercules.[8]

In the myth, we are told that for Hercules "the time had come when it was to be seen whether he would use his gifts for good or for evil. Hercules left the shepherds and went to a solitary region to consider what his course in life should be. As he sat pondering, he saw two women tall in stature coming toward him. One was beautiful and noble, of modest mien. The other was full-bosomed and seductive and carried herself arrogantly." The first woman, the tale continues, is Virtue; the second is Pleasure. Each woman offers promises for Hercules' future if he chooses the path she suggests as his life's course.

Hercules at the crossroads is a paradigmatic image because we all, like him, are enticed by the vision of eternal easy enjoyment where we "will reap the fruits of another's labor and refuse nothing that could bring profit," as promised by "Idle Pleasure, camouflaged as Permanent Happiness." But we also are beckoned by Virtue and its "long and hard way to satisfaction," which tells "that nothing is granted to man without effort and toil" and that "if you would be held in esteem by a city, you must render it services; if you would harvest, you must sow."

The difference between myth and fairy tale is highlighted by the myth telling us directly that the two women speaking to Hercules are "Idle Pleasure" and "Virtue." Similar to figures in a fairy tale, these two women are embodiments of the conflicting inner tendencies and the thoughts of the hero. In this myth the two are described as alternatives, although it is clearly implied that in fact they are not—between Idle Pleasure and Virtue, we must choose the latter. The fairy tale never confronts us so directly, or tells us outright how we must choose. Instead, the fairy tale helps children to develop the desire for a higher consciousness through what is implied in the story. The fairy tale convinces through the appeal it makes to our imagination and the attractive outcome of events, which entices us.

Photo by Steve Koke

FAIRY TALE
VERSUS MYTH

OPTIMISM VERSUS PESSIMISM

Plato—who may have understood better what forms the mind of man than do some of our contemporaries who want their children exposed only to "real" people and everyday events—knew what intellectual experiences make for true humanity. He suggested that the future citizens of his ideal republic begin their literary education with the telling of myths, rather than with mere facts or so-called rational teachings. Even Aristotle, master of pure reason, said: "The friend of wisdom is also a friend of myth."

Modern thinkers who have studied myths and fairy tales from a philosophical or psychological viewpoint arrive at the same conclusion, regardless of their original persuasion. Mircea Eliade, for one, describes these stories as "models for human behavior [that,] by that very fact, give meaning and value to life." Drawing on anthropological parallels, he and others suggest that myths and fairy tales were derived from, or give symbolic expression to, initiation rites or other *rites de passage*—such as a metaphoric death of an old, inadequate self in order to be reborn on a higher plane of existence. He feels that this is why these tales meet a strongly felt need and are carriers of such deep meaning.[9]*

Other investigators with a depth-psychological orientation emphasize the similarities between the fantastic events in myths and fairy

*Eliade, who is influenced in these views by Saintyves, writes: "It is impossible to deny that the ordeals and adventures of the heroes and heroines of fairy tales are almost always translated into initiatory terms. Now this to me seems of the utmost importance: from the time—which is so difficult to determine—when fairy tales took shape as such, men, both primitive and civilized alike, have listened to them with a pleasure susceptible of indefinite repetition. This amounts to saying that initiatory scenarios—even camouflaged, as they are in fairy tales—are the expression of a psychodrama that answers a deep need in the human being. Every man wants to experience certain perilous situations, to confront exceptional ordeals, to make his way into the Other World—and he experiences all this, on the level of his imaginative life, by hearing or reading fairy tales."

tales and those in adult dreams and daydreams—the fulfillment of wishes, the winning out over all competitors, the destruction of enemies—and conclude that one attraction of this literature is its expression of that which is normally prevented from coming to awareness.[10]

There are, of course, very significant differences between fairy tales and dreams. For example, in dreams more often than not the wish fulfillment is disguised, while in fairy tales much of it is openly expressed. To a considerable degree, dreams are the result of inner pressures which have found no relief, of problems which beset a person to which he knows no solution and to which the dream finds none. The fairy tale does the opposite: it projects the relief of all pressures and not only offers ways to solve problems but promises that a "happy" solution will be found.

We cannot control what goes on in our dreams. Although our inner censorship influences what we may dream, such control occurs on an unconscious level. The fairy tale, on the other hand, is very much the result of common conscious and unconscious content having been shaped by the conscious mind, not of one particular person, but the consensus of many in regard to what they view as universal human problems, and what they accept as desirable solutions. If all these elements were not present in a fairy tale, it would not be retold by generation after generation. Only if a fairy tale met the conscious and unconscious requirements of many people was it repeatedly retold, and listened to with great interest. No dream of a person could arouse such persistent interest unless it was worked into a myth, as was the story of the pharaoh's dreams as interpreted by Joseph in the Bible.

There is general agreement that myths and fairy tales speak to us in the language of symbols representing unconscious content. Their appeal is simultaneously to our conscious and unconscious mind, to all three of its aspects—id, ego, and superego—and to our need for ego-ideals as well. This makes it very effective; and in the tales' content, inner psychological phenomena are given body in symbolic form.

Freudian psychoanalysts concern themselves with showing what kind of repressed or otherwise unconscious material underlies myths and fairy tales, and how these relate to dreams and daydreams.[11]

Jungian psychoanalysts stress in addition that the figures and events of these stories conform to and hence represent archetypical psychological phenomena, and symbolically suggest the need for gaining a higher state of selfhood—an inner renewal which is achieved as personal and racial unconscious forces become available to the person.[12]

There are not only essential similarities between myths and fairy tales; there are also inherent differences. Although the same exemplary figures and situations are found in both and equally miraculous events occur in both, there is a crucial difference in the way these are communicated. Put simply, the dominant feeling a myth conveys is: this is absolutely unique; it could not have happened to any other person, or in any other setting; such events are grandiose, awe-inspiring, and could not possibly happen to an ordinary mortal like you or me. The reason is not so much that what takes place is miraculous, but that it is described as such. By contrast, although the events which occur in fairy tales are often unusual and most improbable, they are always presented as ordinary, something that could happen to you or me or the person next door when out on a walk in the woods. Even the most remarkable encounters are related in casual, everyday ways in fairy tales.

An even more significant difference between these two kinds of story is the ending, which in myths is nearly always tragic, while always happy in fairy tales. For this reason, some of the best-known stories found in collections of fairy tales don't really belong in this category. For example, Hans Christian Andersen's "The Little Match Girl" and "The Steadfast Tin Soldier" are beautiful but extremely sad; they do not convey the feeling of consolation characteristic of fairy tales at the end. Andersen's "The Snow Queen," on the other hand, comes quite close to being a true fairy tale.

The myth is pessimistic, while the fairy story is optimistic, no matter how terrifyingly serious some features of the story may be. It is this decisive difference which sets the fairy tale apart from other stories in which equally fantastic events occur, whether the happy outcome is due to the virtues of the hero, chance, or the interference of supernatural figures.

Myths typically involve superego demands in conflict with id-motivated action, and with the self-preserving desires of the ego. A mere mortal is too frail to meet the challenges of the gods. Paris, who does the bidding of Zeus as conveyed to him by Hermes, and obeys the demand of the three goddesses in choosing which shall have the apple, is destroyed for having followed these commands, as are untold other mortals in the wake of this fateful choice.

Try as hard as we may, we can never live up fully to what the superego, as represented in myths by the gods, seems to require of us. The more we try to please it, the more implacable its demands. Even when the hero does not know that he gave in to the proddings of his id, he is still made to suffer horribly for it. When a mortal incurs the displeasure of a god without having done anything wrong, he is destroyed by these supreme superego representations. The pessimism of myths is superbly exemplified in that paradigmatic myth of psychoanalysis, the tragedy of Oedipus.

The myth of Oedipus, particularly when well performed on the stage, arouses powerful intellectual and emotional reactions in the adult—so much so, that it may provide a cathartic experience, as Aristotle taught all tragedy does. After watching Oedipus, a viewer may wonder why he is so deeply moved; and in responding to what he observes as his emotional reaction, ruminating about the mythical events and what these mean to him, a person may come to clarify his thoughts and feelings. With this, certain inner tensions which are the consequence of events long past may be relieved; previously unconscious material can then enter one's awareness and become accessible for conscious working through. This can happen if the observer is deeply moved emotionally by the myth, and at the same time strongly motivated intellectually to understand it.

Vicariously experiencing what happened to Oedipus, what he did and what he suffered, may permit the adult to bring his mature understanding to what until then had remained childish anxieties, preserved intact in infantile form in the unconscious mind. But this possibility exists only because the myth refers to events which happened in the most distant times, as the adult's oedipal longings and anxieties belong to the dimmest past of his life. If the underlying meaning of a myth were spelled out and presented as an event that could have happened in the person's adult conscious lifetime, then this would vastly increase old anxieties, and result in deeper repression.

A myth is not a cautionary tale like a fable which, by arousing anxiety, prevents us from acting in ways which are described as damaging to us. The myth of Oedipus can never be experienced as warning us not to get caught in an oedipal constellation. If one is born and raised as a child of two parents, oedipal conflicts are inescapable.

The oedipus complex is the crucial problem of childhood—unless a child remains fixated at an even earlier stage of development, such as the oral stage. A young child is completely caught up in oedipal conflicts as the inescapable reality of his life. The older child, from about age five on, is struggling to extricate himself by partly repressing the conflict, partly solving it by forming emotional attachments to others besides his parents, and partly sublimating it. What such a child needs least of all is to have his oedipal conflicts activated by such a myth. Suppose that the child still actively wishes, or has barely repressed the desire, to rid himself of one parent in order to have the other exclusively; if he is exposed—even though only in symbolic form—to the idea that by chance, unknowingly, one may murder a parent and marry the other, then what the child has played with only in fantasy suddenly assumes gruesome reality. The consequence of this exposure can only be increased anxiety about himself and the world.

A child not only dreams about marrying his parent of the other sex, but actively spins fantasies around it. The myth of Oedipus tells what happens if that dream becomes reality—and still the child cannot yet give up wishful fantasies of marrying the parent at some future time. After hearing the myth of Oedipus, the conclusion in the child's mind could only be that similar horrible things—the death of a parent and mutilation of himself—will happen to him.

At this age, from four until puberty, what the child needs most is to be presented with symbolic images which reassure him that there is a happy solution to his oedipal problems—though he may find this difficult to believe—provided that he slowly works himself out of them. But reassurance about a happy outcome has to come first, because only then will the child have the courage to labor confidently to extricate himself from his oedipal predicament.

In childhood, more than in any other age, all is becoming. As long as we have not yet achieved considerable security within ourselves, we cannot engage in difficult psychological struggles unless a positive outcome seems certain to us, whatever the chances for this may be in reality. The fairy tale offers fantasy materials which suggest to the child in symbolic form what the battle to achieve self-realization is all about, and it guarantees a happy ending.

Mythical heroes offer excellent images for the development of the superego, but the demands they embody are so rigorous as to discourage the child in his fledgling strivings to achieve personality integration. While the mythical hero experiences a transfiguration into eternal life in heaven, the central figure of the fairy tale lives happily ever after on earth, right among the rest of us. Some fairy tales conclude with the information that if perchance he has not yet died, the hero may be still alive. Thus, a happy though ordinary existence is projected by fairy tales as the outcome of the trials and tribulations involved in the normal growing-up process.

True, these psychosocial crises of growing up are imaginatively embroidered and symbolically represented in fairy tales as encounters with fairies, witches, ferocious animals, or figures of superhuman intelligence or cunning—but the essential humanity of the hero, despite his strange experiences, is affirmed by the reminder that he will have to die like the rest of us. Whatever strange events the fairy-tale hero experiences, they do not make him superhuman, as is true for the mythical hero. This real humanity suggests to the child that, whatever the content of the fairy tale, it is but fanciful elaborations and exaggerations of the tasks he has to meet, and of his hopes and fears.

Though the fairy tale offers fantastic symbolic images for the solution of problems, the problems presented in them are ordinary ones: a child's suffering from the jealousy and discrimination of his siblings, as is true for Cinderella; a child being thought incompetent by his parent, as happens in many fairy tales—for example, in the Brothers Grimm's story "The Spirit in the Bottle." Further, the fairy-tale hero wins out over these problems right here on earth, not by some reward reaped in heaven.

The psychological wisdom of the ages accounts for the fact that every myth is the story of a particular hero: Theseus, Hercules, Beowulf, Brunhild. Not only do these mythical characters have names, but we are also told the names of their parents, and of the other major figures in a myth. It just wouldn't do to name the myth of Theseus "The Man Who Slew the Bull," or that of Niobe "The Mother Who Had Seven Daughters and Seven Sons."

The fairy tale, by contrast, makes clear that it tells about everyman, people very much like us. Typical titles are "Beauty and the Beast," "The Fairy Tale of One Who Went Forth to Learn Fear." Even recently invented stories follow this pattern—for example, "The Little Prince," "The Ugly Duckling," "The Steadfast Tin Soldier." The protagonists of fairy tales are referred to as "a girl," for instance, or "the youngest brother." If names appear, it is quite clear that these are not proper names, but general or descriptive ones. We are told that "Because she always looked dusty and dirty, they called her Cinderella," or: "A little red cap suited her so well that she was always called 'Little Red Cap.' " Even when the hero is given a name, as in the Jack stories, or in "Hansel and Gretel," the use of very common names makes them generic terms, standing for any boy or girl.

This is further stressed by the fact that in fairy stories nobody else has a name; the parents of the main figures in fairy tales remain nameless. They are referred to as "father," "mother," "stepmother," though they may be described as "a poor fisherman" or "a poor woodcutter." If they are "a king" and "a queen," these are thin disguises for father and mother, as are "prince" and "princess" for boy and girl. Fairies and witches, giants and godmothers remain equally unnamed, thus facilitating projections and identifications.

Mythical heroes are of obviously superhuman dimensions, an aspect which helps to make these stories acceptable to the child. Otherwise the child would be overpowered by the implied demand that he emulate the hero in his own life. Myths are useful in forming not the total personality, but only the superego. The child knows that he cannot possibly live up to the hero's virtue, or parallel his deeds; all he can be expected to do is emulate the hero to some small degree; so the child is not defeated by the discrepancy between this ideal and his own smallness.

The real heroes of history, however, having been people like the rest of us, impress the child with his own insignificance when compared with them. Trying to be guided and inspired by an ideal that no human can fully reach is at least not defeating—but striving to duplicate the deeds of actual great persons seems hopeless to the child and creates feelings of inferiority: first, because one knows one cannot do so, and second, because one fears others might.

Myths project an ideal personality acting on the basis of superego demands, while fairy tales depict an ego integration which allows for appropriate satisfaction of id desires. This difference accounts for the contrast between the pervasive pessimism of myths and the essential optimism of fairy tales.

"THE THREE
LITTLE PIGS"

PLEASURE PRINCIPLE
VERSUS REALITY PRINCIPLE

The myth of Hercules deals with the choice between following the pleasure principle or the reality principle in life. So, likewise, does the fairy story of "The Three Little Pigs."[13]

Stories like "The Three Little Pigs" are much favored by children over all "realistic" tales, particularly if they are presented with feeling by the storyteller. Children are enraptured when the huffing and puffing of the wolf at the pig's door is acted out for them. "The Three Little Pigs" teaches the nursery-age child in a most enjoyable and dramatic form that we must not be lazy and take things easy, for if we do, we may perish. Intelligent planning and foresight combined with hard labor will make us victorious over even our most ferocious enemy—the wolf! The story also shows the advantages of growing up, since the third and wisest pig is usually depicted as the biggest and oldest.

The houses the three pigs build are symbolic of man's progress in history: from a lean-to shack to a wooden house, finally to a house of solid brick. Internally, the pigs' actions show progress from the id-dominated personality to the superego-influenced but essentially ego-controlled personality.

The littlest pig builds his house with the least care out of straw; the second uses sticks; both throw their shelters together as quickly and effortlessly as they can, so they can play for the rest of the day. Living in accordance with the pleasure principle, the younger pigs seek immediate gratification, without a thought for the future and the dangers of reality, although the middle pig shows some growth in trying to build a somewhat more substantial house than the youngest.

Only the third and oldest pig has learned to behave in accordance with the reality principle: he is able to postpone his desire to play, and instead acts in line with his ability to foresee what may happen in the future. He is even able to predict correctly the behavior of the wolf —the enemy, or stranger within, which tries to seduce and trap us; and therefore the third pig is able to defeat powers both stronger and more ferocious than he is. The wild and destructive wolf stands for all asocial, unconscious, devouring powers against which one must learn to protect oneself, and which one can defeat through the strength of one's ego.

"The Three Little Pigs" makes a much greater impression on children than Aesop's parallel but overtly moralistic fable of "The Ant and the Grasshopper." In this fable a grasshopper, starving in winter, begs an ant to give it some of the food which the ant had busily collected all summer. The ant asks what the grasshopper was doing during the summer. Learning that the grasshopper sang and did not work, the ant rejects his plea by saying, "Since you could sing all summer, you may dance all winter."

This ending is typical for fables, which are also folk tales handed down from generation to generation. "A fable seems to be, in its genuine state, a narrative in which beings irrational, and sometimes inanimate, are, for the purpose of moral instruction, feigned to act and speak with human interests and passions" (Samuel Johnson). Often sanctimonious, sometimes amusing, the fable always explicitly states a moral truth; there is no hidden meaning, nothing is left to our imagination.

The fairy tale, in contrast, leaves all decisions up to us, including whether we wish to make any at all. It is up to us whether we wish to make any application to our life from a fairy tale, or simply enjoy the fantastic events it tells about. Our enjoyment is what induces us to respond in our own good time to the hidden meanings, as they may relate to our life experience and present state of personal development.

A comparison of "The Three Little Pigs" with "The Ant and the Grasshopper" accentuates the difference between a fairy tale and a fable. The grasshopper, much like the little pigs and the child himself, is bent on playing, with little concern for the future. In both stories the child identifies with the animals (although only a hypocritical prig can identify with the nasty ant, and only a mentally sick child with the wolf); but after having identified with the grasshopper, there is no hope left for the child, according to the fable. For the grasshopper beholden to the pleasure principle, nothing but doom awaits; it is an "either/or" situation, where having made a choice once settles things forever.

But identification with the little pigs of the fairy tale teaches that there are developments—possibilities of progress from the pleasure principle to the reality principle, which, after all, is nothing but a modification of the former. The story of the three pigs suggests a transformation in which much pleasure is retained, because now satisfaction is sought with true respect for the demands of reality. The clever and playful third pig outwits the wolf several times: first, when the wolf tries three times to lure the pig away from the safety of home by appealing to his oral greed, proposing expeditions to where the two would get delicious food. The wolf tries to tempt the pig with turnips which may be stolen, then with apples, and finally with a visit to a fair.

Only after these efforts have come to naught does the wolf move in for the kill. But he has to enter the pig's house to get him, and once more the pig wins out, for the wolf falls down the chimney into the boiling water and ends up as cooked meat for the pig. Retributive justice is done: the wolf, which has devoured the other two pigs and wished to devour the third, ends up as food for the pig.

The child, who throughout the story has been invited to identify with one of its protagonists, is not only given hope, but is told that through developing his intelligence he can be victorious over even a much stronger opponent.

Since according to the primitive (and a child's) sense of justice only those who have done something really bad get destroyed, the fable seems to teach that it is wrong to enjoy life when it is good, as in summer. Even worse, the ant in this fable is a nasty animal, without any compassion for the suffering of the grasshopper—and this is the figure the child is asked to take for his example.

The wolf, on the contrary, is obviously a bad animal, because it wants to destroy. The wolf's badness is something the young child recognizes within himself: his wish to devour, and its consequence—the anxiety about possibly suffering such a fate himself. So the wolf is an externalization, a projection of the child's badness—and the story tells how this can be dealt with constructively.

The various excursions in which the oldest pig gets food in good ways are an easily neglected but significant part of the story, because they show that there is a world of difference between eating and devouring. The child subconsciously understands it as the difference between the pleasure principle uncontrolled, when one wants to devour all at once, ignoring the consequences, and the reality principle, in line with which one goes about intelligently foraging for food. The mature pig gets up in good time to bring the goodies home before the wolf appears on the scene. What better demonstration of the value of acting on the basis of the reality principle, and what it consists of, than the pig's rising very early in the morning to secure the delicious food and, in so doing, foiling the wolf's evil designs?

In fairy tales it is typically the youngest child who, although at first thought little of or scorned, turns out to be victorious in the end. "The Three Little Pigs" deviates from this pattern, since it is the oldest pig who is superior to the two little pigs all along. An explanation can be found in the fact that all three pigs are "little," thus immature, as is the child himself. The child identifies with each of them in turn and recognizes the progression of identity. "The Three Little Pigs" is a fairy tale because of its happy ending, and because the wolf gets what he deserves.

While the child's sense of justice is offended by the poor grasshopper having to starve although it did nothing bad, his feeling of fairness is satisfied by the punishment of the wolf. Since the three little pigs represent stages in the development of man, the disappearance of the first two little pigs is not traumatic; the child understands subconsciously that we have to shed earlier forms of existence if we wish to move on to higher ones. In talking to young children about "The Three Little Pigs," one encounters only rejoicing about the deserved punishment of the wolf and the clever victory of the oldest pig—not grief over the fate of the two little ones. Even a young child seems to understand that all three are really one and the same in different stages—which is suggested by their answering the wolf in exactly the same words: "No, no, not by the hair of my chinni-chin-chin!" If we survive in only the higher form of our identity, this is as it should be.

"The Three Little Pigs" directs the child's thinking about his own development without ever telling what it ought to be, permitting the child to draw his own conclusions. This process alone makes for true maturing, while telling the child what to do just replaces the bondage of his own immaturity with a bondage of servitude to the dicta of adults.

THE CHILD'S NEED
FOR MAGIC

Myths and fairy stories both answer the eternal questions: What is the world really like? How am I to live my life in it? How can I truly be myself? The answers given by myths are definite, while the fairy tale is suggestive; its messages may imply solutions, but it never spells them out. Fairy tales leave to the child's fantasizing whether and how to apply to himself what the story reveals about life and human nature.

The fairy tale proceeds in a manner which conforms to the way a child thinks and experiences the world; this is why the fairy tale is so convincing to him. He can gain much better solace from a fairy tale than he can from an effort to comfort him based on adult reasoning and viewpoints. A child trusts what the fairy story tells, because its world view accords with his own.

Whatever our age, only a story conforming to the principles underlying our thought processes carries conviction for us. If this is so for adults, who have learned to accept that there is more than one frame of reference for comprehending the world—although we find it difficult if not impossible truly to think in any but our own—it is exclusively true for the child. His thinking is animistic.

Like all preliterate and many literate people, "the child assumes that his relations to the inanimate world are of one pattern with those to the animate world of people: he fondles as he would his mother the pretty thing that pleased him; he strikes the door that has slammed on him."[14] It should be added that he does the first because he is convinced that this pretty thing loves to be petted as much as he does; and he punishes the door because he is certain that the door slammed deliberately, out of evil intention.

As Piaget has shown, the child's thinking remains animistic until the age of puberty. His parents and teachers tell him that things cannot feel and act; and as much as he may pretend to believe this to please these adults, or not to be ridiculed, deep down the child knows better. Subjected to the rational teachings of others, the child only buries his "true knowledge" deeper in his soul and it remains untouched by rationality; but it can be formed and informed by what fairy tales have to say.

To the eight-year-old (to quote Piaget's examples), the sun is alive because it gives light (and, one may add, it does that because it wants to). To the child's animistic mind, the stone is alive because it can move, as it rolls down a hill. Even a twelve-and-a-half-year-old is convinced that a stream is alive and has a will, because its water is flowing. The sun, the stone, and the water are believed to be inhabited by spirits very much like people, so they feel and act like people.[15]

To the child, there is no clear line separating objects from living things; and whatever has life has life very much like our own. If we do not understand what rocks and trees and animals have to tell us, the reason is that we are not sufficiently attuned to them. To the child trying to understand the world, it seems reasonable to expect answers from those objects which arouse his curiosity. And since the child is self-centered, he expects the animal to talk about the things which are really significant to him, as animals do in fairy tales, and as the child himself talks to his real or toy animals. A child is convinced that the animal understands and feels with him, even though it does not show it openly.

Since animals roam freely and widely in the world, how natural that in fairy tales these animals are able to guide the hero in his search which takes him into distant places. Since all that moves is alive, the child can believe that the wind can talk and carry the hero to where he needs to go, as in "East of the Sun and West of the Moon."[16] In animistic thinking, not only animals feel and think as we do, but even stones are alive; so to be turned into stone simply means that the being has to remain silent and unmoving for a time. By the same reasoning, it is entirely believable when previously silent objects begin to talk, give advice, and join the hero on his wanderings. And since everything is inhabited by a spirit similar to all other spirits (namely, that of the child who has projected his spirit into all these things), because of this inherent sameness it is believable that man can change into animal, or the other way around, as in "Beauty and the Beast" or "The Frog King."[17] Since there is no sharp line drawn between living and dead things, the latter, too, can come to life.

When, like the great philosophers, children are searching for the solutions to the first and last questions—"Who am I? How ought I to deal with life's problems? What must I become?"—they do so on the basis of their animistic thinking. But since the child is so uncertain of what his existence consists, first and foremost comes the question "Who am I?"

As soon as a child begins to move about and explore, he begins to ponder the problem of his identity. When he spies his mirror image, he wonders whether what he sees is really he, or a child just like him standing behind this glassy wall. He tries to find out by exploring whether this other child is really, in all ways, like him. He makes faces, turns this way or that, walks away from the mirror and jumps back in front of it to ascertain whether this other one has moved away or is still there. Though only three years old, the child is already up against the difficult problem of personal identity.

The child asks himself: "Who am I? Where did I come from? How did the world come into being? Who created man and all the animals? What is the purpose of life?" True, he ponders these vital questions not in the abstract, but mainly as they pertain to him. He worries not whether there is justice for individual man, but whether *he* will be treated justly. He wonders who or what projects him into adversity, and what can prevent this from happening to him. Are there benevolent powers in addition to his parents? Are his parents benevolent powers? How should he form himself, and why? Is there hope for him, though he may have done wrong? Why has all this happened to him? What will it mean for his future? Fairy tales provide answers to these pressing questions, many of which the child becomes aware of only as he follows the stories.

From an adult point of view and in terms of modern science, the answers which fairy stories offer are fantastic rather than true. As a matter of fact, these solutions seem so incorrect to many adults—who have become estranged from the ways in which young people experience the world—that they object to exposing children to such "false" information. However, realistic explanations are usually incomprehensible to children, because they lack the abstract understanding required to make sense of them. While giving a scientifically correct answer makes adults think they have clarified things for the child, such explanations leave the young child confused, overpowered, and intellectually defeated. A child can derive security only from the conviction that he understands now what baffled him before—never from being given facts which create *new* uncertainties. Even as the child accepts such an answer, he comes to doubt that he has asked the right question. Since the explanation fails to make sense to him, it must apply to some unknown problem—not the one he asked about.

It is therefore important to remember that only statements which are intelligible in terms of the child's existing knowledge and emotional preoccupations carry conviction for him. To tell a child that the earth floats in space, attracted by gravity into circling around the sun, but that the earth doesn't fall to the sun as the child falls to the ground, seems very confusing to him. The child knows from his experience that everything has to rest on something, or be held up by something. Only an explanation based on that knowledge can make him feel he understands better about the earth in space. More important, to feel secure on earth, the child needs to believe that this world is held firmly in place. Therefore he finds a better explanation in a myth that tells him that the earth rests on a turtle, or is held up by a giant.

If a child accepts as true what his parents tell him—that the earth is a planet held securely on its path by gravity—then the child can only imagine that gravity is a string. Thus the parents' explanation has led to no better understanding or feeling of security. It requires considerable intellectual maturity to believe that there can be stability to one's life when the ground on which one walks (the firmest thing around, on which everything rests) spins with incredible speed on an invisible axis; that in addition it rotates around the sun; and furthermore hurtles through space with the entire solar system. I have never yet encountered a prepubertal youngster who could comprehend all these combined movements, although I have known many who could repeat this information. Such children parrot explanations which according to their own experience of the world are lies, but which they must believe to be true because some adult has said so. The consequence is that children come to distrust their own experience, and therefore themselves and what their minds can do for them.

In the fall of 1973, the comet Kohoutek was in the news. At that time a competent science teacher explained the comet to a small group of highly intelligent second- and third-graders. Each child had carefully cut out a paper circle and had drawn on it the course of the planets around the sun; a paper ellipse, attached by a slit to the paper circle, represented the course of the comet. The children showed me the comet moving along at an angle to the planets. When I asked them, the children told me that they were holding the comet in their hands, showing me the ellipse. When I asked how the comet which they were holding in their hands could also be in the sky, they were all nonplussed.

In their confusion, they turned to their teacher, who carefully explained to them that what they were holding in their hands, and had so diligently created, was only a model of the planets and the comet. The children all agreed that they understood this, and would have repeated it if questioned further. But whereas before they had regarded proudly this circle-cum-ellipse in their hands, they now lost all interest. Some crumpled the paper up, others dropped the model in the wastepaper basket. When the pieces of paper had been the comet to them, they had all planned to take the model home to show their parents, but now it no longer had meaning for them.

In trying to get a child to accept scientifically correct explanations, parents all too frequently discount scientific findings of how a child's mind works. Research on the child's mental processes, especially Piaget's, convincingly demonstrates that the young child is not able to comprehend the two vital abstract concepts of the permanence of quantity, and of reversibility—for instance, that the same quantity of water rises high in a narrow receptacle and remains low in a wide one; and that subtraction reverses the process of addition. Until he can understand abstract concepts such as these, the child can experience the world only subjectively.[18]

Scientific explanations require objective thinking. Both theoretical research and experimental exploration have shown that no child below school age is truly able to grasp these two concepts, without which abstract understanding is impossible. In his early years, until age eight or ten, the child can develop only highly personalized concepts about what he experiences. Therefore it seems natural to him, since the plants which grow on this earth nourish him as his mother did from her breast, to see the earth as a mother or a female god, or at least as her abode.

Even a young child somehow knows that he was created by his parents; so it makes good sense to him that, like himself, all men and where they live were created by a superhuman figure not very different from his parents—some male or female god. Since his parents watch over the child and provide him with his needs in his home, then naturally he also believes that something like them, only much more powerful, intelligent, and reliable—a guardian angel—will do so out in the world.

A child thus experiences the world order in the image of his parents and of what goes on within the family. The ancient Egyptians, as a child does, saw heaven and the sky as a motherly figure (Nut) who protectively bent over the earth, enveloping it and them serenely.[19] Far from preventing man from later developing a more rational explanation of the world, such a view offers security where and when it is most needed—a security which, when the time is ripe, allows for a truly rational world view. Life on a small planet surrounded by limitless space seems awfully lonely and cold to a child—just the opposite of what he knows life ought to be. This is why the ancients needed to feel sheltered and warmed by an enveloping mother figure. To depreciate protective imagery like this as mere childish projections of an immature mind is to rob the young child of one aspect of the prolonged safety and comfort he needs.

True, the notion of a sheltering sky-mother can be limiting to the mind if clung to for too long. Neither infantile projections nor dependence on imaginary protectors—such as a guardian angel who watches out for one when one is asleep, or during Mother's absence —offers true security; but as long as one cannot provide complete security for oneself, imaginings and projections are far preferable to no security. It is such (partly imagined) security which, when experienced for a sufficient length of time, permits the child to develop that feeling of confidence in life which he needs in order to trust himself—a trust necessary for his learning to solve life's problems through his own growing rational abilities. Eventually the child recognizes that what he has taken as literally true—the earth as a mother —is only a symbol.

A child, for example, who has learned from fairy stories to believe that what at first seemed a repulsive, threatening figure can magically change into a most helpful friend is ready to believe that a strange child whom he meets and fears may also be changed from a menace into a desirable companion. Belief in the "truth" of the fairy tale gives him courage not to withdraw because of the way this stranger appears to him at first. Recalling how the hero of many a fairy tale succeeded in life because he dared to befriend a seemingly unpleasant figure, the child believes he may work the same magic.

I have known many examples where, particularly in late adolescence, years of belief in magic are called upon to compensate for the person's having been deprived of it prematurely in childhood, through stark reality having been forced on him. It is as if these young people feel that now is their last chance to make up for a severe deficiency in their life experience; or that without having had a period of belief in magic, they will be unable to meet the rigors of adult life. Many young people who today suddenly seek escape in drug-induced dreams, apprentice themselves to some guru, believe in astrology, engage in practicing "black magic," or who in some other fashion escape from reality into daydreams about magic experiences which are to change their life for the better, were prematurely pressed to view reality in an adult way. Trying to evade reality in such ways has its deeper cause in early formative experiences which prevented the development of the conviction that life can be mastered in realistic ways.

What seems desirable for the individual is to repeat in his life span the process involved historically in the genesis of scientific thought. For a long time in his history man used emotional projections—such as gods—born of his immature hopes and anxieties to explain man, his society, and the universe; these explanations gave him a feeling of security. Then slowly, by his own social, scientific, and technological progress, man freed himself of the constant fear for his very existence. Feeling more secure in the world, and also within himself, man could now begin to question the validity of the images he had used in the past as explanatory tools. From there man's "childish" projections dissolved and more rational explanations took their place. This process, however, is by no means without vagaries. In intervening periods of stress and scarcity, man seeks for comfort again in the "childish" notion that he and his place of abode are the center of the universe.

Translated in terms of human behavior, the more secure a person feels within the world, the less he will need to hold on to "infantile" projections—mythical explanations or fairy-tale solutions to life's eternal problems—and the more he can afford to seek rational explanations. The more secure a man is within himself, the more he can afford to accept an explanation which says his world is of minor significance in the cosmos. Once man feels truly significant in his human environment, he cares little about the importance of his planet within the universe. On the other hand, the more insecure a man is in himself and his place in the immediate world, the more he withdraws into himself because of fear, or else moves outward to conquer for conquest's sake. This is the opposite of exploring out of a security which frees our curiosity.

For these same reasons a child, as long as he is not sure his immediate human environment will protect him, needs to believe that superior powers, such as a guardian angel, watch over him, and that the world and his place within it are of paramount importance. Here is one connection between a family's ability to provide basic security and the child's readiness to engage in rational investigations as he grows up.

As long as parents fully believed that Biblical stories solved the riddle of our existence and its purpose, it was easy to make a child feel secure. The Bible was felt to contain the answers to all pressing questions: the Bible told man all he needed to know to understand the world, how it came into being, and how to behave in it. In the Western world the Bible also provided prototypes for man's imagination. But rich as the Bible is in stories, not even during the most religious of times were these stories sufficient for meeting all the psychic needs of man.

Part of the reason for this is that while the Old and New Testaments and the histories of the saints provided answers to the crucial questions of how to live the good life, they did not offer solutions for the problems posed by the dark sides of our personalities. The Biblical stories suggest essentially only one solution for the asocial aspects of the unconscious: repression of these (unacceptable) strivings. But children, not having their ids in conscious control, need stories which permit at least fantasy satisfaction of these "bad" tendencies, and specific models for their sublimation.

Explicitly and implicitly, the Bible tells of God's demands on man. While we are told that there is greater rejoicing about a sinner who reformed than about the man who never erred, the message is still that we ought to live the good life, and not, for example, take cruel revenge on those whom we hate. As the story of Cain and Abel shows, there is no sympathy in the Bible for the agonies of sibling rivalry—only a warning that acting upon it has devastating consequences.

But what a child needs most, when beset by jealousy of his sibling, is the permission to feel that what he experiences is justified by the situation he is in. To bear up under the pangs of his envy, the child needs to be encouraged to engage in fantasies of getting even someday; then he will be able to manage at the moment, because of the conviction that the future will set things aright. Most of all, the child wants support for his still very tenuous belief that through growing up, working hard, and maturing he will one day be the victorious one. If his present sufferings will be rewarded in the future, he need not act on his jealousy of the moment, the way Cain did.

Like Biblical stories and myths, fairy tales were the literature which edified everybody—children and adults alike—for nearly all of man's existence. Except that God is central, many Bible stories can be recognized as very similar to fairy tales. In the story of Jonah and the whale, for example, Jonah is trying to run away from his superego's (conscience's) demand that he fight against the wickedness of the people of Nineveh. The ordeal which tests his moral fiber is, as in so many fairy tales, a perilous voyage in which he has to prove himself.

Jonah's trip across the sea lands him in the belly of a great fish. There, in great danger, Jonah discovers his higher morality, his higher self, and is wondrously reborn, now ready to meet the rigorous demands of his superego. But the rebirth alone does not achieve true humanity for him: to be a slave neither to the id and the pleasure principle (avoiding arduous tasks by trying to escape from them) nor to the superego (wishing destruction upon the wicked city) means true freedom and higher selfhood. Jonah attains his full humanity only when he is no longer subservient to either institution of his mind, but relinquishes blind obedience to both id and superego and is able to recognize God's wisdom in judging the people of Nineveh not according to the rigid structures of Jonah's superego, but in terms of their human frailty.

VICARIOUS SATISFACTION
VERSUS CONSCIOUS RECOGNITION

Like all great art, fairy tales both delight and instruct; their special genius is that they do so in terms which speak directly to children. At the age when these stories are most meaningful to the child, his major problem is to bring some order into the inner chaos of his mind so that he can understand himself better—a necessary preliminary for achieving some congruence between his perceptions and the external world.

"True" stories about the "real" world may provide some interesting and often useful information. But the way these stories unfold is as alien to the way the prepubertal child's mind functions as the supernatural events of the fairy tale are to the way the mature intellect comprehends the world.

Strictly realistic stories run counter to the child's inner experiences;

he will listen to them and maybe get something out of them, but he cannot extract much personal meaning from them that transcends obvious content. These stories inform without enriching, as is unfortunately also true of much learning in school. Factual knowledge profits the total personality only when it is turned into "personal knowledge."* Outlawing realistic stories for children would be as foolish as banning fairy tales; there is an important place for each in the life of the child. But a fare of realistic stories only is barren. When realistic stories are combined with ample and psychologically correct exposure to fairy tales, then the child receives information which speaks to both parts of his budding personality—the rational and the emotional.

Fairy tales contain some dreamlike features, but these are akin to what happens in the dreams of adolescents or adults, not of children. Startling and incomprehensible as an adult's dreams may be, all their details make sense when analyzed and permit the dreamer to understand what preoccupies his unconscious mind. By analyzing his dreams, a person can gain a much better understanding of himself through comprehending aspects of his mental life which had escaped his notice, were distorted or denied—not recognized before. Considering the important role such unconscious desires, needs, pressures, and anxieties play in behavior, new insights into oneself from dreams permit a person to arrange his life much more successfully.

Children's dreams are very simple: wishes are fulfilled and anxieties are given tangible form. For example, in a child's dream an animal beats him up, or devours some person. A child's dreams contain unconscious content that remains practically unshaped by his ego; the higher mental functions hardly enter into his dream production. For this reason, children cannot and should not analyze their dreams. A child's ego is still weak and in the process of being built up. Particularly before school age, the child has to struggle continually to prevent the pressures of his desires from overpowering his total personality— a battle against the powers of the unconscious which he loses more often than not.

This struggle, which is never entirely absent from our lives, remains a dubious battle well into adolescence, although as we grow older we

*"The act of knowing includes an appraisal, a personal coefficient which shapes all factual knowledge," writes Michael Polanyi. If the greatest scientist has to rely to a considerable degree on "personal knowledge," it seems obvious that children cannot acquire knowledge truly meaningful to them unless they have first shaped it by introducing their personal coefficients.[20]

also have to contend with the irrational tendencies of the superego. As we mature, all three institutions of the mind—id, ego, and superego—become ever more clearly articulated and separated from each other, each able to interact with the other two without the unconscious overpowering the conscious. The repertoire of the ego for dealing with id and superego becomes more varied, and the mentally healthy individual exercises, in the normal course of events, effective control over their interaction.

In a child, however, whenever his unconscious comes to the fore, it immediately overwhelms his total personality. Far from being strengthened by the experience of his ego recognizing the chaotic content of his unconscious, the child's ego is weakened by such direct contact, because it is overwhelmed. This is why a child has to externalize his inner processes if he is to gain any grasp—not to mention control—of them. The child must somehow distance himself from the content of his unconscious and see it as something external to him, to gain any sort of mastery over it.

In normal play, objects such as dolls and toy animals are used to embody various aspects of the child's personality which are too complex, unacceptable, and contradictory for him to handle. This permits the child's ego to gain some mastery over these elements, which he cannot do when asked or forced by circumstances to recognize these as projections of his own inner processes.

Some unconscious pressures in children can be worked out through play. But many do not lend themselves to it because they are too complex and contradictory, or too dangerous and socially disapproved. For example, the feelings of the Jinny while it was sealed into the jar, as discussed before, are so ambivalent, violent, and potentially destructive that a child could not act these out on his own in play because he could not comprehend these feelings sufficiently to externalize them through play, and also because the consequences might be too dangerous. Here, knowing fairy tales is a great help to the child, as illustrated by the fact that many fairy stories are acted out by children, but only after the children have become familiar with the story, which they never could have invented on their own.

For example, most children are delighted to act out "Cinderella" in dramatic form, but only after the fairy tale has become part of their imaginary world, including especially its happy ending to the situation of intense sibling rivalry. It is impossible for a child to fantasize on his own that he will be rescued, that those who he is convinced despise him and have power over him will come to recognize his superiority. Many a girl is so convinced at moments that her bad (step)mother is the source of all her troubles that, on her own, she is not likely to imagine that it could all suddenly change. But when the idea is presented to her through "Cinderella," she can believe that at any moment a good (fairy) mother may come to the rescue, since the fairy tale tells her in a convincing fashion that this will be the case.

A child can give body to deep desires, such as the oedipal one of wanting to have a baby with mother or father, indirectly by taking care of a toy or real animal as if it were a baby. In doing so, the child is satisfying a deeply felt need by externalizing the wish. Helping the child to become aware of what the doll or animal represents to him, and what he is acting out in his play with it—as would happen in adult psychoanalysis of his dream material—throws the child into deep confusion beyond his years. The reason is that a child does not yet possess a secure sense of identity. Before a masculine or feminine identity is well established, it is easily shaken or destroyed by recognition of complicated, destructive, or oedipal wishes that are contrary to a firm identity.

Through play with a doll or animal, a child can vicariously satisfy a desire for giving birth to and caring for a baby, and a boy can do this as much as a girl. But, unlike a girl, a boy can derive psychological comfort from baby-doll playing only as long as he is not induced to recognize what unconscious desires he is satisfying.

It might be argued that it would be good for boys to recognize consciously this wish to bear children. I hold that a boy's being able to act on his unconscious desire by playing with dolls is good for him, and that it should be accepted positively. Such externalization of unconscious pressures can be valuable, but it becomes dangerous if recognition of the unconscious meaning of the behavior comes to consciousness before sufficient maturity has been achieved to sublimate desires which cannot be satisfied in reality.

Many girls of an older age group are deeply involved with horses; they play with toy horses and spin elaborate fantasies around them. When they get older and have the opportunity, their lives seem to rotate around real horses, which they take excellent care of and seem inseparable from. Psychoanalytic investigation has revealed that over-involvement in and with horses can stand for many different emotional needs which the girl is trying to satisfy. For example, by controlling this powerful animal she can come to feel that she is controlling the male, or the sexually animalistic, within herself. Imagine what it would do to a girl's enjoyment of riding, to her self-respect, if she were made conscious of this desire which she is acting out in riding. She would be devastated—robbed of a harmless and enjoyable sublimation, and reduced in her own eyes to a bad person. At the same time, she would be hard-pressed to find an equally suitable outlet for such inner pressures, and therefore might not be able to master them.

As to fairy tales, one might say that the child who is not exposed to this literature is as badly off as the girl who is anxious to discharge her inner pressures through horseback riding or taking care of horses, but is deprived of her innocent enjoyment. A child who is made aware of what the figures in fairy tales stand for in his own psychology will be robbed of a much-needed outlet, and devastated by having to realize the desires, anxieties, and vengeful feelings that are ravaging him. Like the horse, fairy tales can and do serve children well, can even make an unbearable life seem worth living, as long as the child doesn't know what they mean to him psychologically.

While a fairy tale may contain many dreamlike features, its great advantage over a dream is that the fairy tale has a consistent structure with a definite beginning and a plot that moves toward a satisfying solution which is reached at the end. The fairy tale also has other important advantages when compared to private fantasies. For one, whatever the content of a fairy tale—which may run parallel to a child's private fantasies whether these are oedipal, vengefully sadistic, or belittling of a parent—it can be openly talked about, because the child does not need to keep secret his feelings about what goes on in the fairy tale, or feel guilty about enjoying such thoughts.

The fairy-tale hero has a body which can perform miraculous deeds. By identifying with him, any child can compensate in fantasy and through identification for all the inadequacies, real or imagined, of his own body. He can fantasize that he too, like the hero, can climb into the sky, defeat giants, change his appearance, become the most powerful or most beautiful person—in short, have his body be and do all the child could possibly wish for. After his most grandiose desires have thus been satisfied in fantasy, the child can be more at peace with his body as it is in reality. The fairy tale even projects this acceptance of reality for the child, because while extraordinary transfigurations in the hero's body occur as the story unfolds, he becomes a mere mortal again once the struggle is over. At the fairy story's end we hear no more about the hero's unearthly beauty or strength. This is quite unlike the mythical hero, who retains his superhuman characteristics forever. Once the fairy-tale hero has achieved his true identity at the story's ending (and with it inner security about himself, his body, his life, his position in society), he is happy the way he is, and no longer unusual in any respect.

For the fairy tale to have beneficial externalization effects, the child must remain unaware of the unconscious pressures he is responding to by making fairy-story solutions his own.

The fairy story begins where the child is at this time in his life and where, without the help of the story, he would remain stuck: feeling neglected, rejected, degraded. Then, using thought processes which are his own—contrary to adult rationality as these may be—the story opens glorious vistas which permit the child to overcome momentary feelings of utter hopelessness. In order to believe the story, and to make its optimistic outlook part of his world experience, the child needs to hear it many times. If in addition he acts it out, this makes it that much more "true" and "real."

The child *feels* which of the many fairy tales is true to his inner situation of the moment (which he is unable to deal with on his own), and he also feels where the story provides him with a handle for coming to grips with a difficult problem. But this is seldom an immediate recognition, achieved upon hearing a fairy tale for the first time. For that, some elements of the fairy story are too strange—as they must be in order to speak to deeply hidden emotions.

Only on repeated hearing of a fairy tale, and when given ample time and opportunity to linger over it, is a child able to profit fully from what the story has to offer him in regard to understanding himself and his experience of the world. Only then will the child's free associations to the story yield the tale's most personal meaning to him, and thus help him to cope with problems that oppress him. On the first hearing of a fairy tale, for example, a child cannot cast himself in the role of a figure of the other sex. It takes distance and personal elaboration over time before a girl can identify with Jack in "Jack and the Beanstalk" and a boy with Rapunzel.*

*Here once more fairy tales may be compared with dreams, though this can be done only with great caution and many qualifications, the dream being the most personal expression of the unconscious and the experiences of a particular person, while the fairy tale is the imaginary form that more or less universal human problems have attained as a story has been passed on over generations.

Hardly ever does a dream that goes beyond the most direct wish-fulfilling fantasies permit understanding of its meaning on first recall. Dreams which are the result of complex inner processes need repeated mulling over before comprehension of the dream's latent meaning is arrived at. Frequent and leisurely contemplation of all of the dream's features, rearranging these in a different order from that first recalled; changes in emphasis; and much else is required to find deep meaning in what at first

I have known parents whose child reacted to a fairy story by saying "I like it," and so they moved on to telling another one, thinking that an additional tale would increase the child's enjoyment. But the child's remark, as likely as not, expresses an as yet vague feeling that this story has something important to tell him—something that will get lost if the child is not given repetition of the story and time to grasp it. Redirecting the child's thoughts prematurely to a second story may kill the impact of the first, while doing so at a later time may increase it.

When fairy tales are being read to children in classes, or in libraries during story hour, the children seem fascinated. But often they are given no chance to contemplate the tales or otherwise react; either they are herded immediately to some other activity, or another story of a different kind is told to them, which dilutes or destroys the impression the fairy story had created. Talking with children after such an experience, it appears that the story might as well not have been told, for all the good it has done them. But when the storyteller gives the children ample time to reflect on the story, to immerse themselves in the atmosphere that hearing it creates in them, and when they are encouraged to talk about it, then later conversation reveals that the story offers a great deal emotionally and intellectually, at least to some of the children.

Like the patients of Hindu medicine men who were asked to contemplate a fairy tale to find a way out of the inner darkness which beclouded their minds, the child, too, should be given the opportunity to slowly make a fairy tale his own by bringing his own associations to and into it.

This, incidentally, is the reason why illustrated storybooks, so much preferred by both modern adults and children, do not serve the child's best needs. The illustrations are distracting rather than helpful. Stud-

---

appeared senseless, or quite simple. Only as one goes over the same material repeatedly do features which for some time seemed merely distracting, pointless, impossible, or otherwise nonsensical begin to offer up important clues for grasping what the dream was all about. More often than not, for a dream to yield its deeper meaning, other imaginative material has to be called on to enrich the understanding. Such was the recourse taken by Freud to fairy tales, to elucidate the dreams of the Wolf Man.[21]

In psychoanalysis, free associations are one method to provide additional clues for what one or another detail may signify. In fairy tales, too, the child's associations are needed to have the story gain its full personal importance. Here other fairy tales the child has heard provide additional fantasy material, and can become more meaningful.

ies of illustrated primers demonstrate that the pictures divert from the learning process rather than foster it, because the illustrations direct the child's imagination away from how he, on his own, would experience the story. The illustrated story is robbed of much content of personal meaning which it could bring to the child who applied only his own visual associations to the story, instead of those of the illustrator.[22]

Tolkien, too, thought that "However good in themselves, illustrations do little good to fairy stories. . . . If a story says, 'He climbed a hill and saw a river in the valley below,' the illustrator may catch, or nearly catch, his own vision of such a scene, but every hearer of the words will have his own picture, and it will be made out of all the hills and rivers and dales he has ever seen, but especially out of The Hill, The River, The Valley which were for him the first embodiment of the word."[23] This is why a fairy tale loses much of its personal meaning when its figures and events are given substance not by the child's imagination, but by that of an illustrator. The unique details derived from his own particular life, with which a hearer's mind depicts a story he is told or read, make the story much more of a personal experience. Adults and children alike often prefer the easy way of having somebody else do the hard task of imagining the scene of the story. But if we let an illustrator determine our imagination, it becomes less our own, and the story loses much of its personal significance.

Asking children, for example, what a monster they have heard about in a story looks like, elicits the widest variations of embodiment: huge human-like figures, animal-like ones, others which combine certain human with some animal-like features, etc.—and each of these details has great meaning to the person who in his mind's eye created this particular pictorial realization. On the other hand, seeing the monster as painted by the artist in a particular way, conforming to *his* imagination, which is so much more complete as compared to our own vague and shifting image, robs us of this meaning. The idea of the monster may then leave us entirely cold, having nothing of importance to tell us, or may scare us without evoking any deeper meaning beyond anxiety.

THE IMPORTANCE
OF EXTERNALIZATION

FANTASY FIGURES AND EVENTS

A young child's mind contains a rapidly expanding collection of often ill-assorted and only partially integrated impressions: some correctly seen aspects of reality, but many more elements completely dominated by fantasy. Fantasy fills the huge gaps in a child's understanding which are due to the immaturity of his thinking and his lack of pertinent information. Other distortions are the consequence of inner pressures which lead to misinterpretations of the child's perceptions.

The normal child begins his fantasizing with some more or less correctly observed segment of reality, which may evoke such strong needs or anxieties in him that he gets carried away by them. Things often become so muddled in his mind that he is not able to sort them out at all. But some orderliness is necessary for the child to return to reality not weakened or defeated, but strengthened by this excursion into his fantasies.

Fairy tales, proceeding as the child's mind does, help the child by showing how a higher clarity can and does emerge from all this fantasy. These tales, like the child in his own imagining, usually start out in a quite realistic way: a mother telling her daughter to go all by herself to visit grandmother ("Little Red Riding Hood"); the troubles a poor couple are having feeding their children ("Hansel and Gretel"); a fisherman not catching any fish in his net ("The Fisherman and the Jinny"). That is, the story begins with a real but somewhat problematic situation.

A child presented with perplexing everyday problems and events is stimulated by his schooling to understand the how and why of such situations, and to seek solutions. But since his rationality has as yet poor control over his unconscious, the child's imagination runs away with him under the pressure of his emotions and unsolved conflicts. A child's barely emerging ability to reason is soon overwhelmed by anxieties, hopes, fears, desires, loves, and hates—which become woven into whatever the child began thinking about.

The fairy story, although it may begin with the child's psychological state of mind—such as feelings of rejection when compared to siblings, like Cinderella's—never starts with his physical reality. No child has to sit among the ashes, like Cinderella, or is deliberately deserted in a dense wood, like Hansel and Gretel, because a physical similarity would be too scary to the child, and "hit too close to home for comfort" when giving comfort is one of the purposes of fairy tales.

The child who is familiar with fairy tales understands that these speak to him in the language of symbols and not that of everyday reality. The fairy tale conveys from its inception, throughout its plot, and by its ending that what we are told about are not tangible facts or real persons and places. As for the child himself, real events become important through the symbolic meaning he attaches to them, or which he finds in them.

"Once upon a time," "In a certain country," "A thousand years ago, or longer," "At a time when animals still talked," "Once in an old castle in the midst of a large and dense forest"—such beginnings suggest that what follows does not pertain to the here and now that we know. This deliberate vagueness in the beginnings of fairy tales symbolizes that we are leaving the concrete world of ordinary reality. The old castles, dark caves, locked rooms one is forbidden to enter, impenetrable woods all suggest that something normally hidden will be revealed, while the "long ago" implies that we are going to learn about the most archaic events.

The Brothers Grimm could not have begun their collection of fairy tales with a more telling sentence than the one which introduces their first story, "The Frog King." It starts, "In olden times when wishing still helped, there lived a king whose daughters were all beautiful, but the youngest was so beautiful that the sun itself, which has seen so much, was astonished whenever it shone in her face." This beginning locates the story in a unique fairy-tale time: the archaic period when we all believed that our wishes could, if not move mountains, change our fate; and when in our animistic view of the world, the sun took notice of us and reacted to events. The unearthly beauty of the child, the effectiveness of wishing, and the sun's astonishment signify the absolute uniqueness of this event. Those are the coordinates which place the story not in time or place of external reality, but in a state of mind—that of the young in spirit. Being placed there, the fairy tale can cultivate this spirit better than any other form of literature.

Soon events occur which show that normal logic and causation are suspended, as is true for our unconscious processes, where the most ancient and most unique and startling events occur. The content of the unconscious is both most hidden and most familiar, darkest and most compelling; and it creates the fiercest anxiety as well as the greatest hope. It is not bound by a specific time or location or a logical sequence of events, as defined by our rationality. Without our awareness, the unconscious takes us back to the oldest times of our lives. The strange, most ancient, most distant, and at the same time most familiar locations which a fairy tale speaks about suggest a voyage into the interior of our mind, into the realms of unawareness and the unconscious.

The fairy tale, from its mundane and simple beginning, launches into fantastic events. But however big the detours—unlike the child's untutored mind, or a dream—the process of the story does not get lost. Having taken the child on a trip into a wondrous world, at its end the tale returns the child to reality, in a most reassuring manner. This teaches the child what he needs most to know at this stage of his development: that permitting one's fantasy to take hold of oneself for a while is not detrimental, provided one does not remain permanently caught up in it. At the story's end the hero returns to reality—a happy reality, but one devoid of magic.

As we awake refreshed from our dreams, better able to meet the tasks of reality, so the fairy story ends with the hero returning, or being returned, to the real world, much better able to master life. Recent dream research has shown that a person deprived of dreaming, even though not deprived of sleep, is nevertheless impaired in his ability to manage reality; he becomes emotionally disturbed because of being unable to work out in dreams the unconscious problems that beset him.[24] Maybe someday we will be able to demonstrate the same fact experimentally for fairy tales: that children are much worse off when deprived of what these stories can offer, because the stories help the child work through unconscious pressures in fantasy.

If the dreams of children were as complex as those of normal, intelligent adults, where the latent content is much elaborated, then the child's need for fairy tales would not be so great. On the other hand, if an adult was not exposed as a child to fairy tales, his dreams may be less rich in content and meaning and thus serve him less well in restoring the ability to master life.

The child, so much more insecure than an adult, needs assurance that his need to engage in fantasy, or his inability to stop doing so, is not a deficiency. By telling fairy tales to his child, a parent gives the child an important demonstration that he or she considers the child's inner experiences as embodied in fairy tales worthwhile, legitimate, in some fashion even "real." This gives the child the feeling that since his inner experiences have been accepted by the parent as real and important, he—by implication—is real and important. Such a child will feel later in life like Chesterton, who wrote: "My first and last philosophy, that which I believe in with unbroken certainty, I learnt in the nursery. . . . The things I believed most in then, the things I believe most now, are the things called fairy tales." The philosophy which Chesterton and any child can derive from fairy tales is "that life is not only a pleasure but a kind of eccentric privilege." It is a view of life very different from that which "true-to-reality" stories convey, but one more apt to sustain one undaunted when meeting the hardships of life.

In the chapter of Chesterton's *Orthodoxy* from which these quotations come, titled "The Ethics of Elfland," he stresses the morality inherent in fairy tales: "There is the chivalrous lesson of 'Jack the Giant Killer,' that giants should be killed because they are gigantic. It is a manly mutiny against pride as such. . . . There is the lesson of 'Cinderella,' which is the same as that of the Magnificat—*exaltavit humiles* (He lifted up the humble). There is the great lesson of 'Beauty and the Beast,' that a thing must be loved *before* it is loveable. . . . I am concerned with a certain way of looking at life, which was created in me by fairy tales." When he says that fairy tales are "entirely reasonable things," Chesterton is speaking of them as experiences, as mirrors of inner experience, not of reality; and it is as such that the child understands them.[25]

After the age of approximately five—the age when fairy tales become truly meaningful—no normal child takes these stories as true to external reality. The little girl wishes to imagine she is a princess living in a castle and spins elaborate fantasies that she is, but when her mother calls her to dinner, she knows she is not. And while a grove in a park may be experienced at times as a deep, dark forest full of hidden secrets, the child knows what it really is, just as a little girl knows her doll is not really her baby, much as she calls it that and treats it as such.

Stories which stay closer to reality by starting in a child's living room or backyard, instead of in a poor woodcutter's hut hard by a great forest; and which have people in them very much like the child's parents, not starving woodcutters or kings and queens; but which mix these realistic elements with wish-fulfilling and fantastic devices, are apt to confuse the child as to what is real and what is not. Such stories, failing to be in accord with the child's inner reality, faithful though they may be to external reality, widen the gap between the child's inner and outer experience. They also separate him from his parents, because the child comes to feel that he and they live in different spiritual worlds; as closely as they may dwell in "real" space, emotionally they seem to live temporarily on different continents. It makes for a discontinuity between the generations, painful for both parent and child.

If a child is told only stories "true to reality" (which means false to important parts of his inner reality), then he may conclude that much of his inner reality is unacceptable to his parents. Many a child thus estranges himself from his inner life, and this depletes him. As a consequence he may later, as an adolescent no longer under the emotional sway of his parents, come to hate the rational world and escape entirely into a fantasy world, as if to make up for what was lost in childhood. At an older age, on occasion this could imply a severe break with reality, with all the dangerous consequences for the individual and society. Or, less seriously, the person may continue this encapsulation of his inner self all through his life and never feel fully satisfied in the world because, alienated from the unconscious processes, he cannot use them to enrich his life in reality. Life is then neither "a pleasure" nor "a kind of eccentric privilege." With such separation, whatever happens in reality fails to offer appropriate satisfaction of unconscious needs. The result is that the person always feels life to be incomplete.

When a child is not overwhelmed by his internal mental processes and he is well taken care of in all important respects, then he is able to manage life in his age-appropriate manner. During such times he can solve the problems that arise. But watching young children on a playground, for example, shows how limited these periods are.

Once the child's inner pressures take over—which happens frequently—the only way he can hope to get some hold over these is to externalize them. But the problem is how to do so without letting the externalizations get the better of him. Sorting out the various facets of his outer experience is a very hard job for a child; and unless he gets help, it becomes impossible, once the outer experiences get muddled up with his inner experiences. On his own, the child is not yet able to order and make sense of his internal processes. Fairy tales offer figures onto which the child can externalize what goes on in his mind, in controllable ways. Fairy tales show the child how he can embody his destructive wishes in one figure, gain desired satisfactions from another, identify with a third, have ideal attachments with a fourth, and so on, as his needs of the moment require.

When all the child's wishful thinking gets embodied in a good fairy; all his destructive wishes in an evil witch; all his fears in a voracious wolf; all the demands of his conscience in a wise man encountered on an adventure; all his jealous anger in some animal that pecks out the eyes of his archrivals—then the child can finally begin to sort out his contradictory tendencies. Once this starts, the child will be less and less engulfed by unmanageable chaos.

TRANSFORMATIONS

THE FANTASY OF THE WICKED STEPMOTHER

There is a right time for certain growth experiences, and childhood is the time to learn bridging the immense gap between inner experiences and the real world. Fairy tales may seem senseless, fantastic, scary, and totally unbelievable to the adult who was deprived of fairy-story fantasy in his own childhood, or has repressed these memories. An adult who has not achieved a satisfactory integration of the two worlds of reality and imagination is put off by such tales. But an adult who in his own life is able to integrate rational order with the illogic of his unconscious will be responsive to the manner in which fairy tales help the child with this integration. To the child, and to the adult who, like Socrates, knows that there is still a child in the wisest of us, fairy tales reveal truths about mankind and oneself.

In "Little Red Riding Hood" the kindly grandmother undergoes a sudden replacement by the rapacious wolf which threatens to destroy the child. How silly a transformation when viewed objectively, and how frightening—we might think the transformation unnecessarily scary, contrary to all possible reality. But when viewed in terms of a child's ways of experiencing, is it really any more scary than the sudden transformation of his own kindly grandma into a figure who threatens his very sense of self when she humiliates him for a pants-wetting accident? To the child, Grandma is no longer the same person she was just a moment before; she has become an ogre. How can someone who was so very kind, who brought presents and was more understanding and tolerant and uncritical than even his own mommy, suddenly act in such a radically different fashion?

Unable to see any congruence between the different manifestations, the child truly experiences Grandma as two separate entities—the loving and the threatening. She is indeed Grandma *and* the wolf. By dividing her up, so to speak, the child can preserve his image of the good grandmother. If she changes into a wolf—well, that's certainly scary, but he need not compromise his vision of Grandma's benevolence. And in any case, as the story tells him, the wolf is a passing manifestation—Grandma will return triumphant.

Similarly, although Mother is most often the all-giving protector, she can change into the cruel stepmother if she is so evil as to deny the youngster something he wants.

Far from being a device used only by fairy tales, such a splitting up of one person into two to keep the good image uncontaminated occurs to many children as a solution to a relationship too difficult to manage or comprehend. With this device all contradictions are suddenly solved, as they were for a college student who remembered an incident that occurred when she was not yet five years old.

One day in a supermarket this girl's mother suddenly became very angry with her; and the girl felt utterly devastated that her mother could act this way toward her. On the walk home, her mother continued to scold her angrily, telling her she was no good. The girl became convinced that this vicious person only *looked* like her mother and, although pretending to be her, was actually an evil Martian, a look-alike impostor, who had taken away her mother and assumed her appearance. From then on, the girl assumed on many different occasions that this Martian had abducted the mother and taken her place to torture the child as the real mother would never have done.

This fantasy went on for a couple of years until, when seven, the girl became courageous enough to try to set traps for the Martian. When the Martian had once again taken Mother's place to engage in its nefarious practice of torturing her, the girl would cleverly put some question to the Martian about what had happened between the real mother and herself. To her amazement, the Martian knew all about it, which at first just confirmed the Martian's cunning to the girl. But after two or three such experiments the girl became doubtful; then she asked her mother about events which had taken place between the girl and the Martian. When it became obvious that her mother knew about these events, the fantasy of the Martian collapsed.

During the period when the girl's security had required that

Mother should be all good—never angry or rejecting—the girl had rearranged reality to provide herself with what she needed. When the girl grew older and more secure, her mother's anger or severe criticisms no longer seemed so utterly devastating. Since her own integration had become better established, the girl could dispense with the security-guaranteeing Martian fantasy and rework the double picture of the mother into one by testing the reality of her fantasy.

While all young children sometimes need to split the image of their parent into its benevolent and threatening aspects to feel fully sheltered by the first, most cannot do it as cleverly and consciously as this girl did. Most children cannot find their own solution to the impasse of Mother suddenly changing into "a look-alike impostor." Fairy tales, which contain good fairies who suddenly appear and help the child find happiness despite this "impostor" or "stepmother," permit the child not to be destroyed by this "impostor." Fairy tales indicate that, somewhere hidden, the good fairy godmother watches over the child's fate, ready to assert her power when critically needed. The fairy tale tells the child that "although there are witches, don't ever forget there are also the good fairies, who are much more powerful." The same tales assure that the ferocious giant can always be outwitted by the clever little man—somebody seemingly as powerless as the child feels himself to be. Quite likely it was some story about a child who cleverly outwits an evil spirit which gave this girl the courage to try to expose the Martian.

The universality of such fantasies is suggested by what, in psychoanalysis, is known as the pubertal child's "family romance."[26] These are fantasies or daydreams which the normal youngster partly recognizes as such, but nonetheless also partly believes. They center on the idea that one's parents are not really one's parents, but that one is the child of some exalted personage, and that, due to unfortunate circumstances, one has been reduced to living with these people, who claim to be one's parents. These daydreams take various forms: often only one parent is thought to be a false one—which parallels a frequent situation in fairy tales, where one parent is the real one, the other a step-parent. The child's hopeful expectation is that one day, by chance or design, the real parent will appear and the child will be elevated into his rightful exalted state and live happily ever after.

These fantasies are helpful; they permit the child to feel really angry at the Martian pretender or the "false parent" without guilt. Such fantasies typically begin to appear when guilt feelings are already a part of the child's personality make-up, and when being angry at a parent or, worse, despising him would bring with it unmanageable guilt. So the typical fairy-tale splitting of the mother into a good (usually dead) mother and an evil stepmother serves the child well. It is not only a means of preserving an internal all-good mother when the real mother is not all-good, but it also permits anger at this bad "stepmother" without endangering the goodwill of the true mother, who is viewed as a different person. Thus, the fairy tale suggests how the child may manage the contradictory feelings which would otherwise overwhelm him at this stage of his barely beginning ability to integrate contradictory emotions. The fantasy of the wicked stepmother not only preserves the good mother intact, it also prevents having to feel guilty about one's angry thoughts and wishes about her —a guilt which would seriously interfere with the good relation to Mother.

While the fantasy of the evil stepmother thus preserves the image of the good mother, the fairy tale also helps the child not to be devastated by experiencing his mother as evil. In much the same way that the Martian in the little girl's fantasy disappeared as soon as Mother was once again pleased with her little girl, so a benevolent spirit can counteract in a moment all the bad doings of an evil one. In the fairy-tale rescuer, the good qualities of Mother are as exaggerated as the bad ones were in the witch. But this is how the young child experiences the world: either as entirely blissful or as an unmitigated hell.

When he experiences the emotional need to do so, the child not only splits a parent into two figures, but he may also split himself into two people who, he wishes to believe, have nothing in common with each other. I have known young children who during the day are successfully dry but who wet their bed at night and, waking up, move with disgust to a corner and say with conviction, "Somebody's wet my bed." The child does not do this, as parents may think, to put the blame on somebody else, knowing all the while that it was he who urinated in the bed. The "somebody" who has done it is that part of himself with which he has by now parted company; this aspect of his personality has actually become a stranger to him. To insist that the child recognize that it *was* he who wet the bed is to try to impose prematurely the concept of the integrity of the human personality, and such insistence actually retards its development. In order to develop a secure feeling of his self, the child needs to constrict it for a time to only what is fully approved and desired by himself. After he has thus achieved a self of which he can be unambivalently proud, the child can then slowly begin to accept the idea that it may also contain aspects of a more dubious nature.

As the parent in the fairy tale becomes separated into two figures, representative of the opposite feelings of loving and rejecting, so the child externalizes and projects onto a "somebody" all the bad things which are too scary to be recognized as part of oneself.

The fairy-tale literature does not fail to consider the problematic nature of sometimes seeing Mother as an evil stepmother; in its own way, the fairy tale warns against being swept away too far and too fast by angry feelings. A child easily gives in to his annoyance with a person dear to him, or to his impatience when kept waiting; he tends to harbor angry feelings, and to embark on furious wishes with little thought of the consequences should these come true. Many fairy tales depict the tragic outcome of such rash wishes, engaged in because one desires something too much or is unable to wait until things come about in their good time. Both mental states are typical for the child. Two stories of the Brothers Grimm may illustrate.

In "Hans, My Hedgehog" a man becomes angry when his great desire for having children is frustrated by his wife's inability to have any. Finally he gets carried away enough to exclaim, "I want a child, even if it should be a hedgehog." His wish is granted: his wife begets a child who is a hedgehog on top, while the lower part of his body is that of a boy.*

*The motif that parents who too impatiently desire to have children are punished by giving birth to strange mixtures of human and animal beings is an ancient one, and widely distributed. For example, it is the topic of a Turkish tale in which King Solomon effects the restitution of a child to full humanity. In these stories, if the parents treat the misdeveloped child well and with great patience, he is eventually restored as an attractive human being.

The psychological wisdom of these tales is remarkable: lack of control over emotions on the part of the parent creates a child who is a misfit. In fairy tales and dreams, physical malformation often stands for psychological misdevelopment. In these stories, the upper part of the body including the head is usually animal-like, while the lower part is of normal human form. This indicates that things are wrong with the head—that is, mind—of the child, and not his body. The stories also tell that the damage done to the child through negative feelings can be corrected, through the impact of positive emotions lavished on him, if the parents are sufficiently patient and consistent. The children of angry parents often behave like hedgehogs or porcupines: they seem all spines, so the image of the child that is part hedgehog is most appropriate.

These are also cautionary tales which warn: Do not conceive children in anger; do not receive them with anger and impatience on their arrival. But, like all good fairy

In "The Seven Ravens" a newborn child so preoccupies a father's emotions that he turns his anger against his older children. He sends one of his seven sons to fetch baptismal water for the christening of the infant daughter, an errand on which his six brothers join him. The father, in his anger at being kept waiting, shouts, "I wish all the boys would turn into ravens"—which promptly happens.

If these fairy stories in which angry wishes come true ended there, they would be merely cautionary tales, warning us not to permit ourselves to be carried away by our negative emotions—something the child is unable to avoid. But the fairy tale knows better than to expect the impossible of the child, and to make him anxious about having angry wishes which he cannot help having. While the fairy tale realistically warns that being carried away by anger or impatience leads to trouble, it reassures that the consequences are only temporary ones, and that good will or deeds can undo all the harm done by bad wishing. Hans the Hedgehog helps a king lost in the forest to return safely home. The king promises to give Hans as a reward the first thing he encounters on his return home, which happens to be his only daughter. Despite Hans's appearance, the princess keeps her father's promise and marries Hans the Hedgehog. After the marriage, in the marital bed, Hans at last takes on a fully human form, and eventually he inherits the kingdom.* In "The Seven Ravens" the sister, who was the innocent cause of her brothers being turned into ravens, travels to the end of the world and makes a great sacrifice to undo the spell put on them. The ravens all regain their human form, and happiness is restored.

These stories tell that, despite the bad consequences which evil wishes have, with good will and effort things can be righted again. There are other tales which go much further and tell the child not to fear having such wishes because, although there are momentary consequences, nothing changes permanently; after all the wishing is done, things are exactly as they were before the wishing began. Such stories exist in many variations all over the globe.

In the Western world "The Three Wishes" is probably the best-known wish story. In the simplest form of this motif, a man or a woman is granted some wishes, usually three, by a stranger or an

---

tales, these stories also indicate the right remedies to undo the damage, and the prescription is in line with the best psychological insights of today.

*This ending is typical for stories belonging to the animal-groom cycle, and will be discussed in connection with these stories (pp. 282 ff.).

animal as reward for some good deed. A man is given this favor in "The Three Wishes," but he thinks little of it. On his return home his wife presents him with his daily soup for dinner. " 'Soup again, I wish I had pudding for a change,' says he, and promptly the pudding appears." The wife demands to know how this has happened, and he tells her about his adventure. Furious that he wasted one of his wishes on such a trifle, she exclaims, "I wish the pudding was on your head," a wish which is immediately fulfilled. " 'That's two wishes gone! I wish the pudding was off my head,' says the man. And so the three wishes were gone."[27]

Together, these tales warn the child of the possible undesirable consequences of rash wishing, and assure him at the same time that such wishing has little consequence, particularly if one is sincere in one's desire and efforts to undo the bad results. Maybe even more important is the fact that I cannot recall a single fairy tale in which a child's angry wishes have any consequence; only those of adults do. The implication is that adults are accountable for what they do in their anger or their silliness, but children are not. If children wish in a fairy tale, they desire only good things; and chance or a good spirit fulfills their desires, often beyond their fondest hopes.

It is as if the fairy tale, while admitting how human it is to get angry, expects only adults to have sufficient self-control not to let themselves get carried away, since their outlandishly angry wishes come true— but the tales stress the wonderful consequences for a child if he engages in *positive* wishing or thinking. Desolation does not induce the fairy-tale child to engage in vengeful wishing. The child wishes only for good things, even when he has ample reason to wish that bad things would happen to those who persecute him. Snow White harbors no angry wishes against the evil queen. Cinderella, who has good reason to wish that her stepsisters be punished for their misdeeds, instead wishes them to go to the grand ball.

Left alone for a few hours, a child can feel as cruelly abused as though he had suffered a lifetime of neglect and rejection. Then, suddenly, his existence turns into complete bliss as his mother appears in the doorway, smiling, maybe even bringing him some little present. What could be more magical than that? How could something so simple have the power to alter his life, unless there were magic involved?

Radical transformations in the nature of things are experienced by the child on all sides, although *we* do not share his perceptions. But consider the child's dealings with inanimate objects: some object—a shoelace or a toy—utterly frustrates the child, to the degree that he feels himself a complete fool. Then in a moment, as if by magic, the object becomes obedient and does his bidding; from being the most dejected of humans, he becomes the happiest. Doesn't this prove the magic character of the object? Quite a few fairy tales relate how finding a magic object changes the hero's life; with its help, the fool turns out smarter than his previously preferred siblings. The child who feels himself doomed to be an ugly duckling need not despair; he will grow into a beautiful swan.

A small child can do little on his own, and this is disappointing to him—so much so that he may give up in despair. The fairy story prevents this by giving extraordinary dignity to the smallest achievement, and suggesting that the most wonderful consequences may grow out of it. Finding a jar or bottle (as in the Brothers Grimm's story "The Spirit in the Bottle"), befriending an animal or being befriended by it ("Puss-in-Boots"), sharing a piece of bread with a stranger ("The Golden Goose," another of the Brothers Grimm's stories)—such little everyday events lead to great things. So the fairy tale encourages the child to trust that his small real achievements are important, though he may not realize it at the moment.

The belief in such possibilities needs to be nurtured so that the child can accept his disillusionments without being utterly defeated; and beyond this, it can become a challenge to think with confidence about an existence beyond the parental home. The fairy tale's example provides assurance that the child will receive help in his endeavors in the outside world, and that eventual success will reward his sustained efforts. At the same time, the fairy tale stresses that these events happened once upon a time, in a far-distant land, and makes clear that it offers food for hope, not realistic accounts of what the world is like here and now.

The child intuitively comprehends that although these stories are *unreal,* they are not *untrue;* that while what these stories tell about does not happen in fact, it must happen as inner experience and personal development; that fairy tales depict in imaginary and symbolic form the essential steps in growing up and achieving an independent existence.

While fairy tales invariably point the way to a better future, they concentrate on the process of change, rather than describing the exact details of the bliss eventually to be gained. The stories start where the child is at the time, and suggest where he has to go—with emphasis on the process itself. Fairy tales can even show the child the way through that thorniest of thickets, the oedipal period.

BRINGING ORDER
INTO CHAOS

Before and well into the oedipal period (roughly ages three to six or
seven), the child's experience of the world is chaotic, but only as seen
from an adult point of view, because chaos implies an awareness of
this state of affairs. If this "chaotic" fashion of experiencing the world
is all one knows, then it is accepted as the way the world is.

In the language of the Bible, which expresses the deepest feelings
and insights of man, in the beginning the world was "without form."
The way to overcome chaos is also told in the Bible: "God divided the
light from darkness." During and because of the oedipal struggles, the
outside world comes to hold more meaning for the child, and he
begins to try to make sense of it. He no longer takes for granted that
the confused way he sees the world is the only possible and appropriate one. The manner in which the child can bring some order into his
world view is by dividing everything into opposites.

In the later oedipal and post-oedipal ages, this splitting extends to
the child himself. The child, like all of us, is at any moment in a welter
of contradictory feelings. But while adults have learned to integrate
these, the child is overwhelmed by these ambivalences within himself. He experiences the mixture of love and hate, desire and fear
within himself as an incomprehensible chaos. He cannot manage feeling at one and the same moment both good and obedient, yet bad and
rebellious, although he is. Since he cannot comprehend intermediate
stages of degree and intensity, things are either all light or all darkness. One is either all courage or all fear; the happiest or the most
miserable; the most beautiful or the ugliest; the smartest or the dumb-
est; one either loves or hates, never anything in between.

This is also how the fairy tale depicts the world: figures are ferocity
incarnate or unselfish benevolence. An animal is either all-devouring
or all-helpful. Every figure is essentially one-dimensional, enabling
the child to comprehend its actions and reactions easily. Through
simple and direct images the fairy story helps the child sort out his
complex and ambivalent feelings, so that these begin to fall each one
into a separate place, rather than being all one big muddle.

As he listens to the fairy tale, the child gets ideas about how he may create order out of the chaos which is his inner life. The fairy tale suggests not only isolating and separating the disparate and confusing aspects of the child's experience into opposites, but projecting these onto different figures. Even Freud found no better way to help make sense out of the incredible mixture of contradictions which coexist in our mind and inner life than by creating symbols for isolated aspects of the personality. He named these id, ego, and superego. If we, as adults, must take recourse to the creation of separate entities to bring some sensible order into the chaos of our inner experiences, how much greater is the child's need for this! Today adults use such concepts as id, ego, superego, and ego-ideal to separate our internal experiences and get a better grasp on what they are all about. Unfortunately, in doing so we have lost something which is inherent in the fairy tale: the realization that these externalizations are fictions, useful only for sorting out and comprehending mental processes.*

When the hero of a fairy tale is the youngest child, or is specifically called "the dummy" or "Simpleton" at the start of the story, this is the fairy tale's rendering of the original debilitated state of the ego as it begins its struggle to cope with the inner world of drives, and with the difficult problems which the outer world presents.

The id, not unlike how psychoanalysis views it, is frequently depicted in the form of some animal, standing for our animal nature. Fairy-tale animals come in two forms: dangerous and destructive animals, such as the wolf in "Little Red Riding Hood," or the dragon that

---

*Giving the inner processes separate names—id, ego, superego—made them entities, each with its own propensities. When we consider the emotional connotations these abstract terms of psychoanalysis have for most people using them, then we begin to see that these abstractions are not all that different from the personifications of the fairy tale. When we speak of the asocial and unreasonable id pushing the weak ego around, or the ego doing the superego's bidding, these scientific similes are not much different from the allegories of the fairy tale. In the latter, the poor and weak child is confronted by the powerful witch that knows only its own desires and acts on them, without regard to any consequences. When the meek tailor in the Brothers Grimm's "The Valiant Little Tailor" manages to subdue two huge giants by making them fight each other, is he not acting as the weak ego does when it plays id against superego and, by neutralizing their opposite energies, gains rational control over these irrational forces?

Many errors in understanding how our minds work could be avoided if modern man would at all times remain aware that these abstract concepts are nothing but convenient handles for manipulating ideas which, without such externalization, would be too difficult to comprehend. There is in actuality, of course, no separation between them, just as there is no real separation between mind and body.

devastates an entire country unless each year a virgin is sacrificed to it, in "The Two Brothers," a Brothers Grimm story; and wise and helpful animals which guide and rescue the hero—as in the same story, "The Two Brothers," where a group of helpful animals revives the dead hero and gains him his just reward of the princess and his kingdom. Both dangerous and helpful animals stand for our animal nature, our instinctual drives. The dangerous ones symbolize the untamed id, not yet subjected to ego and superego control, in all its dangerous energy. The helpful animals represent our natural energy —again the id—but now made to serve the best interests of the total personality. There are also some animals, usually white birds such as doves, which symbolize the superego.

"THE QUEEN BEE"

ACHIEVING INTEGRATION

No single fairy tale does justice to the richness of all the images which give external body to the most complex inner processes, but a little-known story by the Brothers Grimm called "The Queen Bee" may illustrate the symbolic struggle of personality integration against chaotic disintegration. A bee is a particularly apt image for the two opposite aspects of our nature, since the child knows that the bee produces sweet honey but can also sting painfully. He knows, too, that the bee works hard to achieve its positive propensities, collecting the pollen out of which it produces the honey.

In "The Queen Bee" the two older sons of a king go out to seek adventure and live such wild, dissolute lives that they never return home. In short, they live an id-dominated existence, without any regard for the requirements of reality or the justified demands and criticisms of the superego. The third and youngest son, called Simpleton, sets out to find them, and through persistence succeeds. But they mock him for thinking that he in his simplicity could get through life better than they, who are supposedly so much more clever. On the surface the two brothers are right: as the story unfolds, Simpleton would be just as incapable of mastering life, represented by the difficult tasks they are all asked to perform, as they are—except that he proves able to call for help on his inner resources, represented by the helpful animals.

As the three brothers travel through the world, they come to an anthill. The two older brothers want to destroy it just to enjoy the ants' terror. Simpleton does not permit this; he says: "Leave the animals in peace. I will not allow you to disturb them." Next they come to a lake where ducks are swimming. The older brothers, considering nothing but their pleasure and oral cravings, want to catch some ducks and roast them. Simpleton prevents this also. They proceed onward, coming to a bees' nest, and the two brothers now want to set fire to the tree holding the nest, to get at the honey. Simpleton again interferes, insisting that the animals must be neither disturbed nor killed.

The three brothers finally arrive at a castle where everything has been turned to stone or is in a deathlike sleep, with the exception of a little gray man who lets them in, feeds them, and beds them down for the night. The next morning the little man presents the oldest brother with three tasks, each of which must be accomplished within a day, to undo the spell cast on the castle and its inhabitants. The first task is to gather a thousand pearls which are spread and hidden in the moss of the forest. But the brother is warned that if he fails in this task, he will be turned to stone. The oldest son tries and fails, and the same thing happens to the second brother.

When Simpleton's turn comes, he finds he also is not up to this task. Feeling defeated, he sits down and cries. At this point the five thousand ants which he had saved come to his help and gather the pearls for him. The second task is to fetch the key to the king's daughter's bedchamber out of a lake. This time the ducks Simpleton had protected come, dive into the lake, and give him the key. The final task is to select from among three sleeping princesses who look exactly alike the youngest and most lovable. The queen of the beehive Simpleton saved now comes to his help, and she settles on the lips of the princess Simpleton must choose. With the three tasks fulfilled, the spell is broken and the enchantment at its end. All who have been asleep or turned to stone—including Simpleton's two brothers—come to life. Simpleton marries the youngest princess and eventually inherits the kingdom.

The two brothers who were unresponsive to the requirements of personality integration failed to meet the tasks of reality. Insensitive to anything but the proddings of the id, they were turned into stone. As in many other fairy stories, this does not symbolize death; rather it stands for a lack of true humanity, an inability to respond to higher values, so that the person, being dead to what life is all about in the best sense, might as well be made of stone. Simpleton (standing for the ego), despite his obvious virtues, and although he obeys the commands of his superego which tells him it is wrong to disturb wantonly or kill, is by himself also unequal to the demands of reality (symbolized by the three tasks he has to perform), as his brothers were. Only when animal nature has been befriended, recognized as important, and brought into accord with ego and superego does it lend its power to the total personality. After we have thus achieved an integrated personality, we can accomplish what seem like miracles.

Far from suggesting that we subjugate animal nature to our ego or superego, the fairy tale shows that each element must be given its due; had Simpleton not followed his inner goodness (read superego) and protected the animals, these id representations would never have come to his aid. The three animals, incidentally, represent different elements: the ants stand for earth; the ducks, for the water in which they swim; and the bees, the air in which they fly. Again, only the cooperation of all three elements, or aspects of our nature, permits success. Only after Simpleton has achieved his full integration, symbolically expressed by his having mastered the three tasks, does he become master of his fate, which in fairy-tale fashion is expressed by his becoming king.

"BROTHER AND SISTER"

UNIFYING OUR DUAL NATURE

In this Brothers Grimm's story, like many other fairy tales which feature the adventures of two siblings, the protagonists represent the disparate natures of id, ego, and superego; and the main message is that these must be integrated for human happiness. This type of fairy tale presents the necessity of integrating the personality in a different way than "The Queen Bee"—here the nefarious doings of an "evil spirit" turn one sibling into an animal, while the other remains human. It is hard to conceive of a more vivid, succinct, and immediately convincing image of our contradictory propensities. Even the earliest philosophers viewed man as having both an animal and a human nature.

During much of our life, when we have not succeeded in achieving or maintaining inner integration, these two aspects of our psyche war against each other. When we are young, whatever we feel at the moment fills our entire existence. Becoming aware that he feels two ways about something at the same time—for example, when the child wants to grab the cookie, but also wants to obey Mother's order not to—confuses the child. Understanding this duality requires a cognizance of inner processes which is greatly facilitated by fairy tales illustrating our dual nature.

Such fairy tales begin with an original lack of differentiation between the two siblings: they live together and feel alike; in short, they are inseparable. But then, at a certain moment in growing up, one of them begins an animal existence, and the other does not. At the end of the tale the animal is changed back into his human form; the two are reunited, never to be separated again. This is the fairy tale's symbolic way of rendering the essentials of human personality development: the child's personality is at first undifferentiated; then id, ego, and superego develop out of the undifferentiated stage. In a process of maturation these must be integrated, despite opposite pulls.

In the Brothers Grimm's story "Brother and Sister," "Little brother took his little sister by the hand and said . . . 'Come, we will go forth together out into the wide world' " to escape from a home which had become a depriving one. "They walked the whole day over meadows, fields and rocky expanses; and when it rained, little sister said: 'Heaven and our hearts are weeping together.' "

Here, as in many fairy tales, being pushed out of the home stands for having to become oneself. Self-realization requires leaving the orbit of the home, an excruciatingly painful experience fraught with many psychological dangers. This developmental process is inescapable; the pain of it is symbolized by the children's unhappiness about being forced to leave home. The psychological risks in the process, as always in fairy stories, are represented by the dangers the hero encounters on his travels. In this story the brother represents the endangered aspect of an essentially inseparable unity, and the sister, as symbol of motherly care once one has become alienated from home, is the rescuer.

The fairy tale leaves no doubt in the child's mind that the pain must be endured and the risky chances taken, since one must achieve one's personal identity; and, despite all anxieties, there is no question about the happy ending. While not every child can or will inherit a kingdom, the child who understands and makes his own the message of the fairy tale will find the true home of his inner self; he will become master over its vast realm by knowing his mind, so it will serve him well.

To continue with the story of "Brother and Sister": The next day on their wanderings brother and sister come to a spring from which brother wants to drink; but sister, who is not carried away by her id (instinctual pressures), understands that the water is murmuring: "Who drinks of me becomes a tiger." Because of her entreaties, her brother abstains from drinking despite the promptings of his thirst.

The sister, representing the higher mental functions (the ego and superego), warns her brother, who—id-dominated—is ready to permit himself to be carried away by his wish for immediate gratification (of his thirst), no matter what the cost of doing so. But should the brother give in to the pressure of the id, he would become asocial, as violent as a tiger.

They come to another spring, which warns that it has the power to change the drinker into a wolf. Again the sister, representing ego and superego, recognizes the danger of seeking immediate satisfaction, and persuades the brother to resist his thirst. Finally they come to a third spring, which murmurs that its punishment for giving in to id desires is a change into a deer, a much tamer animal. So much does delay—a partial obedience to the restraining aspects of our mental apparatus—achieve. But as the pressure of the id (brother's thirst) increases, it overpowers the restraints of ego and superego: the sister's admonitions lose the power to control, and as brother drinks from the spring, he turns into a fawn.*[28]

Sister promises that she will never leave her fawn-brother. She symbolizes ego control, since, despite her thirst, she was able to abstain from drinking. She unties her golden garter and fastens it around the fawn's neck, and plucks some rushes and weaves these into a soft leash which she fastens to the little animal. Only a very positive personal tie—the golden garter—can make us forgo giving in to our asocial desires and lead us on to a higher humanity.

Then sister and fawn move on. As they proceed through the forest, they come to a deserted little house in the woods—which appears in so many fairy tales—and find shelter there. They make it their abode. Out of leaves and moss the sister makes a bed for the fawn; each

*A comparison of "Brother and Sister" with "The Fisherman and the Jinny" illustrates that only through hearing and assimilating many fairy stories does the richness of this literature become fully available to the child. The Jinny, carried away by id pressure, intends to destroy his rescuer; the consequence is that the Jinny is returned to permanent incarceration in the jar. "Brother and Sister," by contrast, tells how beneficial it is to be able to control id pressures. Even when this ability is by no means perfectly developed—which it cannot be in a child—even a limited degree of id control achieves a high measure of humanization, as the reduction of animal ferocity from tiger to wolf to deer symbolizes.

morning she gathers roots and berries for herself, and for the fawn, tender grass: the ego provides what the person needs. All goes well, as long as the id does what the ego bids it do. "If brother just would have had his human form, it would have been a marvelous life."

But until we have achieved full personality integration, our id (our instinctual pressures, our animal nature) lives in uneasy peace with our ego (our rationality). The fairy tale tells how when the animal instincts are strongly aroused, rational controls lose the power to restrain. After the sister and fawn-brother have lived happily for some time in the wilderness, the king of the country arranges for a big hunt. When the fawn hears the blowing of horns, the barking of the hounds, and the merry shouting of the hunters, he says to his sister, "Let me out to join the hunt; I can't stand it any longer," and begs so long that at last she consents.

The first day of the hunt all goes well, and at nightfall the deer-brother returns to his sister and the safety of their little hut. The next morning he hears again the tempting noises of the hunt and becomes restless, demanding to be let out. Toward the end of the day he is slightly wounded in the leg and manages to limp home, but this time the deer, with his golden collar, is observed by one of the hunters, who reports it to the king. The king recognizes the meaning of the garter, and he orders that on the next day the deer is to be pursued and caught, but not to be hurt.

At home, sister takes care of brother's wound. The following day, despite her tears and entreaties, the deer forces her to let him out again. In the evening not only the fawn but the king too comes to the hut. Captivated by the girl's beauty, the king asks her to marry him; she agrees, provided the fawn will live with them.

For a long time they all live happily together. But, as so often in fairy tales, three repetitions of the same ordeal—the three days the deer was being hunted—are not sufficient for the final resolution. While brother has undergone his ordeal which could become his initiation to a higher form of existence, the sister has not.

All goes well until one day, when the king is out hunting,* the queen gives birth to a boy.

The king's absence when his wife gives birth indicates that this is

---

*In terms of the fairy story, hunting is not to be understood as an unnecessary killing of animals—rather it symbolizes a life close to and in accordance with nature; an existence in line with our more primitive being. In many fairy stories hunters are kind-hearted, helpful persons, as in "Little Red Riding Hood." Nevertheless, the king's having gone away to hunt suggests his having given in to his more primitive tendencies.

another transition—the greatest miracle of life—in which others, even the husband, can be of only limited help. Childbirth represents an inner transformation which changes the girl-child into mother. Like all important transformations, it is fraught with great dangers. Today these are mainly psychological; in times past, woman's very life was in jeopardy, because so many died during or in consequence of childbirth. These dangers are given body in this story by a witch stepmother, who, after the child has been born, insinuates herself into the queen's life by assuming the form of her lady-in-waiting. She entices the queen, who is sick from childbirth, to take a bath—where she causes the queen to suffocate. The witch then has her own ugly daughter take the queen's place in the royal bed.

At midnight the queen reappears in the nursery to take her child into her arms and nurse him; nor does she forget to take care of the roebuck. This is observed by the nursemaid, who doesn't tell anybody for a while. After some time has passed, the queen begins to talk during her midnight visits with her child, and says,

"How is my child? How is my deer?
Twice shall I come, then nevermore."

The nursemaid tells this to the king, who sits up the following night to watch the same thing happen, with the difference that the queen says that she will come only once more. The third night, when the queen says that she'll never come again, the king no longer restrains himself and calls her his beloved wife, at which she comes back to life.

As there were three repetitions of the brother trying to drink from a brook, and of the deer running out to join the hunt, so there were three visits by the dead queen to her child during which she spoke the verses. But the queen's being restored to life and reunited with her king still leaves her brother in his animal form. Only after justice has been meted out and the witch is burned to ashes does the fawn regain his human form, and "sister and brother lived happily together until their end."

No final word is said about the queen's living with the king or her child, because the two are of little importance. The real issue of "Brother and Sister" is that the animalistic tendencies in man, as represented by the deer, and the asocial ones, symbolized by the witch, are done away with; and this permits the human qualities to blossom. The discrepancy in human nature indicated by the sister's and fawn-brother's existence is resolved through human integration as brother and sister are reunited in their human form.

In the story's ending, two strands of thought are combined: integration of the disparate aspects of our personality can be gained only after the asocial, destructive, and unjust have been done away with; and this cannot be achieved until we have reached full maturity, as symbolized by sister's giving birth to a child and developing mothering attitudes. The story also suggests the two great upheavals in life: leaving the parental home, and creating one's own family. These are the two periods of life when we are most vulnerable to disintegration, because an old way of life has to be given up and a new one achieved. In the first of these two turning points, brother gets temporarily swept away; in the second, the sister.

While no inner evolution is spelled out, its nature is implied: what redeems us as human beings and restores us to our humanity is solicitude for those whom we love. The queen, on her nocturnal visits, does not try to satisfy any of her own desires, but worries about others who depend on her: her child and her deer. This shows that she has successfully made the transition from wife to mother, and thus she is reborn to a higher stage of existence. The contrast between the brother's giving in to the proddings of his instinctual desires and the sister's ego- and superego-motivated concern for her obligations to others clearly indicates what the battle for integration and victory in it consist of.

"SINDBAD THE SEAMAN AND SINDBAD THE PORTER"

FANCY VERSUS REALITY

There are many fairy tales in which the disparate aspects of one personality are projected onto different figures, such as one of the stories of *Thousand and One Nights,* "Sindbad the Seaman and Sindbad the Porter."[29] Often called simply "Sindbad the Sailor" and occasionally "Sindbad's Marvelous Travels," this story shows how little those who deprive a tale of its true title understand what is essential to the story. The altered names stress the story's fantastic content, to the detriment of its psychological meaning. The true title suggests immediately that the story is about the opposite aspects of one and the same person: that which pushes him to escape into a faraway world of adventure and fantasy, and the other part which keeps him bound to common practicality—his id and his ego, the manifestation of the reality principle and the pleasure principle.

As the story starts, Sindbad, a poor porter, is resting in front of a beautiful home. Contemplating his situation, he says: "The owner of this place abideth in all joyance of life and delighteth himself with pleasant scents and delicious meats and exquisite wines . . . whilst others suffer the extreme of travail . . . as I do." He thus juxtaposes an existence based on pleasurable satisfactions with one based on necessity. To make sure we understand that these remarks pertain to two aspects of one and the same person, Sindbad remarks about himself and the as yet unknown owner of the palace: "Thine origin is mine and my provenance is thine."

After we have been made to understand that these two are the same person in different forms, the porter is invited into the palace, where on seven consecutive days its owner tells of his seven fabulous voyages. In these travels he meets with outrageous perils, from which he is miraculously rescued to return home with great fortunes. During these accounts, to further emphasize the identity of the poor porter and the fabulously rich voyager, the latter says, "Know, O Porter, that thy name is even as mine" and "thou art become my brother." The force which drives him to seek such adventures the voyager calls "the old bad man within me" and "the carnal man . . . [whose] heart is naturally prone to evil"—apt images of a person who gives in to the proddings of his id.

Why does this fairy tale consist of seven parts, and why do the two protagonists separate each day only to reunite on the next? Seven is the number of days in a week; in fairy tales the number seven often stands for every day of the week and is also a symbol of each day of our life. Thus it seems the story tells that as long as we live there are two different aspects to our existence, as the two Sindbads are both the same and different, one having a hard life in reality, the other having a life of fantastic adventures. Another way to interpret this is to view these opposite existences as the day and night views of life— as waking and dreaming, as reality and fantasy, or as the conscious and the unconscious realms of our being. Seen this way, the story tells mainly how different life is when viewed from the two different perspectives of the ego and the id.

The story begins by telling how Sindbad the Porter, who was "carrying a heavy load, became exceedingly weary, the heat and the weight alike oppressing him." Saddened by the hardships of his existence, he speculates on what a rich man's life may be like. Sindbad the Seaman's stories may be viewed as fantasies in which the poor porter engages to escape his burdensome life. The ego, exhausted by its tasks, then permits itself to be overwhelmed by the id. The id, in contrast to the reality-oriented ego, is the seat of our wildest wishes, wishes that can lead to satisfaction or to extreme danger. This is given body in the seven stories of Sindbad the Seaman's voyages. Carried away by what he recognizes as "the bad man within me," Sindbad the Seaman desires fantastic adventures, and encounters horrible dangers which are akin to nightmares: giants who roast human beings on spits before eating them; evil creatures that ride Sindbad as if he were a horse; serpents which threaten to swallow him alive; huge birds that carry him through the sky. Eventually the wish-fulfilling fantasies win out over the anxious ones, as he is rescued and returns home with great riches to a life of leisure and satisfaction. But each day the requirements of reality must also be met. The id having held sway for a time, the ego reasserts itself and Sindbad the Porter returns to his everyday life of hard labor.

The fairy tale helps us to understand ourselves better, as in the story the two sides of our ambivalences are isolated and projected each onto a different figure. We can visualize these ambivalences much better when the instinctual id pressures are projected onto the intrepid, immensely rich voyager who survives when all others are destroyed, and brings home unheard-of treasure to boot, while the opposite, reality-oriented ego tendencies are embodied in the hard-working, poor porter. What Sindbad the Porter (representing our ego) has too little of—imagination, ability to see beyond the immediate surroundings—Sindbad the Seaman has too much of—since he says that he cannot be satisfied with a normal life "of ease and comfort and repose."

When the fairy story indicates that these two very different persons are actually "brothers under the skin," it guides the child toward the preconscious realization that these two figures are really two parts of one and the same person; that the id is as much an integral part of our personality as the ego. One of the great merits of this tale is that Sindbad the Seaman and Sindbad the Porter are equally appealing figures; neither of the two sides of our nature is denied its attractiveness, importance, validity.

Unless to some measure a separation of our complex inner tendencies has been accomplished in our mind, we have no comprehension of the sources of our confusion about ourselves, about how we are torn between opposite feelings, and our need to integrate these. Such integration requires the realization that there are discordant aspects to our personality, and what these are. "Sindbad the Seaman and Sindbad the Porter" suggests both the isolation of the discordant aspects of our psyche, and that these belong with each other and must be integrated—the two Sindbads part company each day, but come together again after each separation.

When viewed in isolation, a relative weakness of this fairy tale is that at its end it fails to express symbolically the need for the integration of the disparate aspects of our personality which have been projected onto the two Sindbads. If this were a fairy tale of the Western world, it would end with the two living happily together ever after. As it is, the listener feels somewhat let down by the story's end, as he wonders why these two brothers continue to separate and come together anew each day. It would seem on the surface to make much better sense if they settled down to live together permanently in complete harmony, an ending which would symbolically express the hero's successful achievement of psychic integration.

But if that were the story's end, there would be little reason to continue with the telling of fairy tales the next night. "Sindbad the Seaman and Sindbad the Porter" is part of *The Arabian Nights' Entertainments.** According to the arrangement of the *Thousand and One Nights,* Sindbad the Seaman's seven voyages were actually told over thirty nights.

THE FRAME STORY OF
THOUSAND AND ONE NIGHTS

Since the stories of the two Sindbads are part of such a long cycle of fairy tales, the final resolution—or integration—occurs only at the very end of *The Arabian Nights' Entertainments.* Therefore we must

*The collection of fairy tales which became known as *Thousand and One Nights* or, in Burton's translation, as *The Arabian Nights' Entertainments,* is of Indian and Persian origin and can be traced as early as the tenth century. The number 1001 is not to be taken literally. On the contrary, "thousand" in Arabic means "innumerable," so 1001 signifies an infinite number. Later compilers and translators took this number literally and arrived at a collection which contained this number of stories by subdividing and adding fairy tales.[30]

now consider the frame story which introduces and ends the entire cycle.[31] King Shahryar is deeply disillusioned with women and a viciously angry man because he has found out that not only has his wife betrayed him with his black slaves, but that the same thing had happened to his brother, King Shahzeman; and further, that even a most powerful and cunning Jinny is continually betrayed by a woman he believes to be most carefully locked up.

King Shahryar has had his eyes opened to his wife's betrayal by his brother, King Shahzeman. About the latter we are told: "He could not forget the perfidy of his wife and grief grew on him more and more and his color changed and his body became weak." When questioned by King Shahryar about the reasons for his decline, King Shahzeman answers: "O my brother, I have an internal wound." Since his brother seems to be a double for King Shahryar, we can assume that he also suffers terribly from an internal wound: the belief that nobody could truly love him.

King Shahryar, having lost all trust in mankind, decides that henceforth he will give no woman a chance to betray him ever again, and that he will live a life of lust only. From then on, he sleeps each night with a virgin, who is killed the following morning. Finally, no nubile virgin is left in his kingdom but Scheherazade, the daughter of the king's vizier. The vizier has no intention of sacrificing his daughter, but she insists that she wishes to become "the means of deliverance." She accomplishes this by telling each night for a thousand nights a story which so enthralls the king that he does not have her killed because he wishes to hear the story's continuation on the following night.

Delivery from death through the telling of fairy tales is a motif which starts the cycle; it also reappears throughout the cycle, and ends it. For example, in the very first of the 1001 tales, "The Story of the Three Sheiks," a Jinny threatens to destroy a merchant but is so taken by the merchant's story that he spares the merchant. At the cycle's end, the king declares his trust in and love for Scheherazade; he is cured forever of his hatred for women by Scheherazade's love, and they live happily together for the rest of their lives, or so we are given to understand.

According to the frame story, two protagonists, one male and one female, meet in the great crises of their lives: the king disgusted with life and full of hatred of women; Scheherazade fearing for her life, but determined to achieve his and her deliverance. She attains her goal through the telling of many fairy tales; no single story can accomplish it, for our psychological problems are much too complex and difficult of solution. Only a wide variety of fairy tales could provide the impetus for such catharsis. It takes nearly three years of continued telling of fairy tales to free the king of his deep depression, to achieve his cure. It requires his attentive listening to fairy tales for a thousand nights to reintegrate his completely disintegrated personality. (Here it should be recalled that in Hindu medicine—and the *Thousand and One Nights* cycle is of Indian-Persian origin—the mentally deranged person is told a fairy story, contemplation of which will help him overcome his emotional disturbance.)

Fairy tales have meaning on many different levels. On another level of meaning, the two protagonists in this story stand for the warring tendencies within us which, if we fail to integrate them, will surely destroy us. The king symbolizes a person completely dominated by his id because his ego, due to severe disappointments in life, has lost its strength to keep his id in bounds. After all, the task of the ego is to protect us against devastating deprivation, which in the story is symbolized by the king's being sexually betrayed; if the ego fails to do so, it loses its power to guide our lives.

The other figure of the frame story, Scheherazade, represents the ego, as is clearly suggested by our being told that "she had collected a thousand books of chronicles of past peoples and bygone poets. Moreover, she had read books of science and medicine; her memory was stored with verses and stories and folklore and the sayings of kings and sages, and she was wise, witty, prudent and well-bred"—an exhaustive enumeration of ego attributes. Thus, uncontrolled id (the king) in a long-drawn-out process becomes finally civilized through the impact of an ego incarnate. But it is an ego very much dominated by the superego, so much so that Scheherazade is determined to risk her life. She says: "Either I will be the means of the deliverance of the daughters of the Muslims from slaughter or I will die and perish as others have perished." Her father tries to dissuade her and admonishes her: "Do not thus adventure thy life!" But nothing can deter her from her purpose, as she insists: "It must be so."

In Scheherazade we thus see a superego-dominated ego which has become so cut off from selfish id that it is ready to risk the person's very existence to obey a moral obligation; in the king, an id which has cut loose from ego and superego. Having such a strong ego, Scheherazade enters her moral mission with a plan: she will arrange it so that she can tell the king a story of such an intriguing nature that he will want to hear the rest of it, and for that reason will spare her life. And indeed when the morning dawns and she interrupts her story, the king says to himself: "I will not kill her till I hear the rest of the story!"

But her entrancing stories, the continuation of which the king wishes to hear, postpone her death only from day to day. For the "deliverance" Scheherazade has made her goal, more is needed.

Only a person whose ego has learned to draw on the positive energies of the id for its constructive purposes can then set that ego to control and civilize the murderous propensities of the id. Only when Scheherazade's love for the king further inspires her storytelling— that is, when superego (the wish to deliver "the daughters of the Muslims from slaughter") and id (her love for the king, whom she now also wishes to deliver from his hatred and depression) both endow the ego—has she become a fully integrated person. Such a person, the frame story tells, is able to deliver the world from evil as she gains happiness for herself and for the dark other, who believed that none was available to him. As she declares her love for the king, he declares his for her. What greater testimony can we have to the power of all fairy tales to change our personality than the ending of this one tale, the frame story of *Thousand and One Nights:* murderous hatred has been changed into enduring love.

One more element of the frame story of *Thousand and One Nights* is worth mentioning. Scheherazade from the very beginning expresses the hope that telling the fairy tales may help her to "turn the king from his custom," but for this she needs the help of her little sister Dunayazad, whom she instructs what to do: "When I go up to the Sultan, I will send after thee, and when thou comest to me and seest that the king has done his will of me, do thou say to me, 'O my sister, an thou be not asleep, tell us some of thy delightful stories, to pass away the watches of this our night.' " Thus, in a fashion, Scheherazade and the king are as husband and wife, and Dunayazad is like their child. It is her spoken wish to hear fairy tales which forms the first bond between the king and Scheherazade. At the cycle's end Dunayazad is replaced by a little boy, the king's and Scheherazade's son, whom she brings to the king as she declares her love for him. The integration of the king's personality is sealed by his having become the father of a family.

But before we can achieve mature integration of our personality such as that projected in the figure of the king at the end of *Thousand and One Nights,* we have to struggle through many developmental crises, two of which, closely connected to each other, are among the most difficult to master.

The first of them centers on the question of personality integration: Who am I really? Given the contradictory tendencies residing within me, which of them should I respond to? The fairy-tale answer is the same one which psychoanalysis offers: To avoid being tossed about and, in extreme cases, torn apart by our ambivalences requires that we integrate them. Only in this way can we achieve a unified personality able to meet successfully, with inner security, the difficulties of living. Inner integration is not something that is achieved once and for all; it is a task that confronts us all our lives, although in different forms and degrees. Fairy tales do not present such integration as a lifelong endeavor; this would be too discouraging to the child, who finds it difficult to achieve even temporary integration of his ambivalences. Instead, each tale projects at its "happy" ending the integration of some inner conflict. Since there are innumerable fairy tales, each having some different form of a basic conflict for its topic, in their combination these stories demonstrate that in life we encounter many conflicts which we must master, each at its time.

The second very difficult developmental crisis is the oedipal conflict. It is a series of painful and confusing experiences through which the child becomes truly himself if he succeeds in separating himself from his parents. To do so, he must free himself from the power his parents have over him and—much more difficult—from the power he has given them out of his anxiety and dependency needs, and from his wish that they should forever belong only to him, as he feels he has belonged to them.

Most of the fairy stories discussed in the first part of this book project the need for inner integration, while those in Part Two deal also with oedipal problems. In considering them we shall have moved from the most famous fairy-tale cycle of the Eastern world to the germinal tragedy of Western drama and—according to Freud—of life for all of us.

TALES OF
TWO BROTHERS

Unlike "Brother and Sister," in other fairy tales in which two protagonists—usually brothers—stand for seemingly incompatible aspects of the human personality, the two usually separate after an original period of having been united, and then have different fates. In these fairy tales—which, though little noticed today, are among the oldest and most widely disseminated ones—the stay-at-home brother and the adventurous one remain in touch through magic. When the adventurous brother perishes because he has permitted himself to live in accordance with his desires or to disregard dangers, his brother sets out to rescue him, succeeds, and forever after the two live happily reunited. The details vary; sometimes—though rarely—instead of two brothers, there are two sisters, or a brother and a sister. What all these stories have in common are features which suggest the identity of the two heroes, one of whom is cautious and reasonable, but ready to risk his life to rescue the other brother, who foolishly exposes himself to terrible perils; and also some magic object, a life token, which usually disintegrates as soon as one dies, serving as the sign for the other to set out on the rescue.

The motif of the two brothers is central to the oldest fairy tale, which was found in an Egyptian papyrus of 1250 B.C.[32] In over three thousand years since then it has taken on many forms. One study enumerates 770 different versions, but probably there are many more.[33] In some versions one meaning becomes more prominent, in others, another. The full flavor of a fairy story can best be gained by not only retelling it or by hearing it many times—then some detail at first overlooked becomes ever more meaningful, or is seen in a new light—but also through becoming acquainted with the same motif in several variations.

In all variations of this tale, the two figures symbolize opposite aspects of our nature, impelling us to act in contrary ways. In "Brother and Sister," the choices are whether to follow the proddings of our animal nature or to restrain the expression of our physical desires for the sake of our humanity. The figures thus give concrete embodiment to an internal dialogue that we engage in when we consider what course to take.

The stories on the "Two Brothers" theme add to this internal dialogue between id, ego, and superego another dichotomy: the striving for independence and self-assertion, and the opposite tendency to remain safely home, tied to the parents. From the earliest version on, the stories stress that both desires reside in each of us, and that we cannot survive deprived of either: the wish to stay tied to the past, and the urge to reach out to a new future. Through the unfolding of events, the story most often teaches that entirely cutting oneself off from one's past leads to disaster, but that to exist only beholden to the past is stunting; while it is safe, it provides no life of one's own. Only the thorough integration of these contrary tendencies permits a successful existence.

While in most fairy tales on the "Two Brothers" theme the brother who leaves home runs into trouble and is rescued by the brother who stayed home, some others, including the oldest Egyptian version, stress the opposite: the undoing of the brother who remained home. If we do not spread our wings and leave the nest, these stories seem to teach, we fail to do so out of an oedipal attachment, which then destroys us. This ancient Egyptian story seems to have developed out and away from the central motif of the destructive nature of oedipal attachments and of sibling rivalry—that is, the need to separate oneself from one's childhood home and create an independent existence. A happy resolution requires that the brothers free themselves of oedipal and sibling jealousy and support each other.

In the Egyptian tale the younger and unmarried brother rejects the efforts of his brother's wife to seduce him. Fearing that he might tell on her, she vilifies him, pretending to her husband that his brother tried to seduce her.* In his jealous anger, the married brother tries to kill his younger sibling. Only through the intervention of gods is the younger brother's reputation saved and the truth made known, but by then the younger brother has sought safety in flight. He dies, a fact that becomes known to his older brother when his drinks turn bad; he goes to the rescue of his younger brother and manages to revive him.

This ancient Egyptian tale contains the element of a person accused of what the accuser himself wants to do: the wife accuses the younger brother, whom she tried to seduce, of seducing her. Thus, the plot describes the projection of an unacceptable tendency in oneself onto another person; this suggests that such projections are as ancient as man. Since the story is told from the brothers' side, it's also possible that the younger brother projected his desires onto his older brother's wife, accusing her of what he wanted to but dared not do.

In the story the married brother is master of an extended household in which his younger brother lives. The master's wife is, in a sense, "mother" to all the young people in this family, including the younger brother. So we can interpret the story as telling either about a mother figure who gives in to her oedipal desires for a young man who stands in the role of a son, or of a son accusing a mother figure of his own oedipal desires for her.

Be this as it may, the story clearly suggests that for the younger son's benefit and for protection against oedipal problems—irrespective of

*The Biblical story of Joseph and Potiphar's wife, which is placed in an Egyptian setting, probably goes back to this part of the ancient tale.

whether these are the son's or the parent's—at this time of life the young person does well to leave home.

In this ancient rendering of the "Two Brothers" theme, the tale barely touches on the need for inner transformation to bring about the happy solution, in the form of the persecuting brother's deep regret when he learns that his wife has unfairly accused his younger sibling, whom he had set out to destroy. In this form the tale is essentially a cautionary one, warning that we must free ourselves of our oedipal attachments, and teaching that we can do so most successfully by establishing an independent existence away from our parental home. Sibling rivalry is also shown as a strong motif in this tale, as the first impulse of the older brother is to kill his sibling out of jealousy. His better nature battles against his lower impulses and eventually wins.

In the stories of the "Two Brothers" type, the heroes are depicted as being in what we would call the adolescent age—that period in life when the relative emotional tranquility of the prepubertal child is replaced by adolescent stress and turmoil, brought about by new psychological developments. Hearing such a story, the child comprehends (at least subconsciously) that although what he is told about are adolescent conflicts, the problems are typical of our predicament whenever we are confronted with having to move from one developmental stage to the next. This conflict is as characteristic of the oedipal child as it is of the adolescent. It occurs whenever we have to decide whether to move from a less to a more differentiated state of mind and personality, which requires loosening old ties before we have yet formed new ones.

In more modern versions, such as the Brothers Grimm's tale "The Two Brothers," they are at first undifferentiated. "The two brothers went together into the forest, took counsel with each other, and came to an agreement. And as they sat down in the evening to eat, they said to their foster father: 'We won't touch the food and won't take a bite until you grant us one request.' " Their demand is that " 'We must try ourselves in the world, so permit us to go forth and journey.' " The forest, where they go to decide that they want to have a life of their own, symbolizes the place in which inner darkness is confronted and worked through; where uncertainty is resolved about who one is; and where one begins to understand who one wants to be.

In most stories of two brothers, one, like Sindbad the Sailor, rushes out into the world and courts dangers, while the other, like Sindbad the Porter, simply remains home. In many European fairy tales the brother who leaves soon finds himself in a deep, dark forest, where he feels lost, having given up the organization of his life which the parental home provided, and not yet having built up the inner structures which we develop only under the impact of life experiences we have to master more or less on our own. Since ancient times the near-impenetrable forest in which we get lost has symbolized the dark, hidden, near-impenetrable world of our unconscious. If we have lost the framework which gave structure to our past life and must now find our own way to become ourselves, and have entered this wilderness with an as yet undeveloped personality, when we succeed in finding our way out we shall emerge with a much more highly developed humanity.*

In this dark forest the fairy-tale hero often encounters the creation of our wishes and anxieties—the witch—as does one of the brothers in the Brothers Grimm's tale "The Two Brothers." Who would not like to have the power of the witch—or a fairy, or a sorcerer—and use it to satisfy all his desires, to give him all the good things he wishes for himself, and to punish his enemies? And who does not fear such powers if some other possesses them and might use them against him? The witch—more than the other creations of our imagination which we have invested with magic powers, the fairy and the sorcerer—in her opposite aspects is a reincarnation of the all-good mother of infancy and the all-bad mother of the oedipal crisis. But she is no longer seen halfway realistically, as a mother who is lovingly all-giving and an opposite stepmother who is rejectingly demanding, but entirely unrealistically, as either superhumanly rewarding or inhumanly destructive.

These two aspects of the witch are clearly delineated in fairy tales where the hero, lost in the forest, encounters an irresistibly attractive witch who, at first, satisfies all his desires during their relation. This is the all-giving mother of our infancy, whom we all hope to encounter again in our life. Preconsciously or unconsciously, it is this hope of finding her somewhere which gives us the strength to leave home. Thus, in fairy-story manner, we are given to understand that false hopes often lure us on, when we fool ourselves that all we are seeking is an independent existence.

After the witch has fulfilled all the desires of the hero who went out into the world, at some point—usually when he refuses to do her

*It is this ancient image Dante evokes at the beginning of The Divine Comedy: "In the middle of the journey of our life I found myself in a dark wood where the straight way was lost." There he also finds a "magic" helper, Virgil, who offers guidance on this most famous peregrination, which first leads Dante through hell, then purgatory, until heaven is reached at the journey's end.

bidding—she turns against him and changes him into an animal, or into stone. That is, she deprives him of all humanity. In these stories the witch resembles the way in which the pre-oedipal mother appears to the child: all-giving, all-satisfying, as long as he does not insist on doing things his way and remains symbiotically tied to her. But as the child begins to assert himself more and do more on his own, the "No's" naturally increase. The child who has put all his trust in this woman, has tied his fate to her—or felt that it is tied to her—now experiences deepest disenchantment; what has given him bread has turned to stone, or so it seems.

Whatever the details, in the stories of the "Two Brothers" type there comes the moment when the brothers differentiate from each other, as every child has to move out of the undifferentiated stage. What happens then symbolizes as much the inner conflict within us —represented by the different actions of the two brothers—as the necessity to give up one form of existence to achieve a higher one. Whatever the age of a person, when he is confronted with the problem of whether to break away from his parents—which we all do to different degrees at various times in our lives—there is always a wish to have an existence entirely free of them and what they stand for in our psyche, along with the opposite desire to remain bound closely to them. This is acutely so during the period that immediately precedes school age, and also during the other one which ends it. The first of the two separates infancy from childhood; the second, childhood from early adulthood.

The Brothers Grimm's "The Two Brothers" begins by impressing the hearer with the idea that tragedy occurs if the two brothers—i.e., the two divergent aspects of our personality—do not become integrated. It starts, "Once upon a time there were two brothers, a rich one and a poor one. The rich one was a goldsmith, and his heart was evil; the poor one sustained himself by making brooms, and he was good and honest. The poor man had two children who were twins and looked so alike as one drop of water is to another."

The good brother finds a golden bird, and in a roundabout way his twin children, through eating the heart and liver of the bird, acquire the ability to find each morning a piece of gold under their pillows. The evil brother, eaten up by envy, persuades the father of the twins that this is the doing of the devil, and that for his salvation he must rid himself of the boys. Confounded by his evil brother, the father casts the children out; a hunter chances upon them and adopts them as his foster children. After the children have grown, they retire into the forest and decide there that they must go out into the world. Their foster father agrees that they ought to do so, and on parting gives them a knife, which is the magic object of this story.

As was mentioned at the beginning of the discussion of the "Two Brothers" motif, one typical feature of these stories is that some magic life token, which symbolizes the identity of the two, indicates to one when the other is in serious danger, and this sets the rescue going. If, as suggested above, the two brothers stand for inner psychic processes which must all be functioning together for us to exist, then the dying or rotting of the magic object—that is, its disintegration—suggests the disintegration of our personality if not all of its aspects are cooperating. In "The Two Brothers" the magic object is "a bright and shiny knife" which their foster father gives them on parting, telling them, "If you separate some day, drive the knife into a tree at the crossroad; if one returns, he can see from it how things stand with the absent one, because the side of the knife in the direction of which he left rusts if he dies; as long as he is alive it remains shiny."

The twin brothers part (after having stuck the knife in a tree) and lead different lives. After many adventures, one is turned into stone by a witch. The other happens upon the knife and finds his brother's side of it rusty; realizing that his brother has died, he goes to rescue him and succeeds. After the brothers are united—which is a symbol of having achieved integration of the discordant tendencies within us —they live happily ever after.

By juxtaposing what happens between the good and the evil brother and the twin sons of the first, the story implies that if the contradictory aspects of the personality remain separated from each other, nothing but misery is the consequence: even the good brother is defeated by life. He loses his sons because he fails to comprehend the evil propensities of our nature—represented by his brother—and hence is helpless to free himself of its consequences. The twin brothers, by contrast, after having lived very different lives, come to each other's rescue, which symbolizes achieving inner integration, and hence can have a "happy" life.*

*The identity of the twins is repeatedly emphasized, although in symbolic ways. For example, they encounter a hare, a fox, a wolf, a bear, and finally a lion. They spare the lives of these animals, and, in gratitude, each gives them two young ones of its breed. When they separate, each takes with him one of these two sets of animals, which remain their faithful companions. The animals work together and, through doing so repeatedly, help their masters escape great dangers. This shows once more in fairy-tale fashion that successful living requires the working together, the integration of the quite different aspects of our personality—here symbolized by the differences between hare, fox, wolf, bear, and lion.

"THE THREE LANGUAGES"

BUILDING INTEGRATION

If we want to understand our true selves, we must become familiar with the inner workings of our mind. If we want to function well, we have to integrate the discordant tendencies which are inherent in our being. Isolating these tendencies and projecting them into separate figures, as illustrated by "Brother and Sister" and "The Two Brothers," is one way fairy tales help us visualize and thus better grasp what goes on within us.

Another fairy-tale approach to showing the desirability of this integration is symbolized by a hero who encounters these various tendencies one at a time and builds them into his personality until all coalesce within him, as is necessary for gaining full independence and humanity. The Brothers Grimm's "The Three Languages" is a fairy story of this type. It has a history reaching quite far back, and versions were found in many European and some Asian countries. Despite its antiquity, this timeless fairy tale reads as if it could have been written for the adolescent of today about his conflicts with his parents, or about parents' inability to understand what moves their adolescent children.

The story begins: "In Switzerland there once lived an old count who had only one son, but he was stupid and couldn't learn anything. So the father said, 'Listen, my son, I can't get anything into your head, as hard as I try. You've got to get away from here. I'll turn you over to a famous master; he shall have a try with you.' "[34] The son studied with this master for a year. When he returned, the father was disgusted to hear that all he had learned was "what the dogs bark." Sent out for another year of study with a different master, the son returned to tell that he had learned "what the birds speak." Furious that his son had again wasted his time, the father threatened, "I'll send you to a third master, but if again you learn nothing, I shall no longer be your father." When the year was over, the son's reply to the question of what he had learned was "what the frogs croak." In great rage, the father cast his son out, ordering his servants to take the son into the forest and do away with him. But the servants had pity on the son, and simply left him in the forest.

Many fairy-tale plots begin with children being cast out, an event which occurs in two basic forms: prepubertal children who are forced to leave on their own ("Brother and Sister") or are deserted in a place from which they cannot find their way back ("Hansel and Gretel"); and pubertal or adolescent youngsters who are handed over to servants ordered to kill them, but are spared because the servants take pity and only pretend to have murdered the child ("The Three Languages," "Snow White"). In the first form the child's fear of desertion is given expression; in the second, his anxiety about retaliation.

Being "cast out" can unconsciously be experienced either as the child wishing to be rid of the parent, or as his belief that the parent wants to be rid of him. The child's being sent out into the world, or deserted in a forest, symbolizes both the parent's wish that the child become independent and the child's desire for, or anxiety about, independence.

The young child in such tales is simply deserted—like Hansel and Gretel—for the anxiety of the prepubertal age is "If I am not a good, obedient child, if I give trouble to my parents, they will no longer take good care of me; they might even desert me." The pubertal child, more confident that he might be able to take care of himself, feels less anxious about desertion and thus has more courage to stand up to his parent. In the stories where the child is handed over to a servant to be killed, he has threatened the parent's dominance or self-respect, as Snow White does by being more beautiful than the queen. In "The Three Languages" the count's parental authority is put into question by the son's so obviously not learning what the father thinks he should.

Because the parent does not murder his child but entrusts the evil deed to a servant, and because the servant releases the child, this suggests that on one level the conflict is not with adults in general, but only with the parents. The other adults are as helpful as they dare to be, without coming directly into conflict with the authority of the parent. On another level this indicates that, despite the adolescent's anxiety about the parent holding power over his life, this is not so—because, as outraged as the parent is, he does not vent his anger directly on the child, but has to use an intermediary such as the servant. Since the parent's plan is not carried out, this shows the inherent impotence of the parent's position when he tries to misuse his authority.

Maybe if more of our adolescents had been brought up on fairy tales, they would (unconsciously) remain aware of the fact that their conflict is not with the adult world, or society, but really only with their parents. Further, threatening as the parent may seem at some time, it is always the child who wins out in the long run, and it is the parent who is defeated, as the ending of all these tales makes amply clear. The child not only survives the parents but surpasses them. This conviction, when built into the unconscious, permits the adolescent to feel secure despite all the developmental difficulties from which he suffers, because he feels confident about his future victory.

Of course, if more adults had been exposed to the messages of fairy tales as children and profited from them, they might as adults have retained some dim recognition of how foolish any parent is who believes he knows what his child ought to be interested in studying, and who feels threatened if the adolescent goes against his will in this respect. A particularly ironic twist of "The Three Languages" is that it is the father himself who sends his son away to study and selects the masters, only to be outraged by what they teach his son. This shows that the modern parent who sends his child to college and then is furious about what he learns there, or about how it changes his child, is by no means a new arrival on the scene of history.

The child both wishes and fears that his parents will be unwilling to accept his striving for independence and will take revenge. He wishes this because it would demonstrate that the parent cannot let go, which proves the child's importance. To become a man or a woman really means to stop being a child, an idea which does not occur to the prepubertal child, but which the adolescent realizes. If a child wishes to see his parent stop having parental power over him, in his unconscious the child also feels he has destroyed the parent (since the child wants to remove parental powers) or is about to do so. How natural for him to think that the parent wishes to seek retaliation.

In "The Three Languages" a son repeatedly goes against his father's will, and asserts himself in doing so; and at the same time he defeats his father's paternal powers through his actions. For this, he fears his father will have him destroyed.

So the hero of "The Three Languages" goes off into the world. On his wanderings he comes first to a land in deep trouble because the furious bark of wild dogs permits nobody to rest; and, worse, at certain hours a man must be handed over to the dogs to be devoured. Since the hero can understand the dogs' language, the dogs talk to him, tell him why they are so ferocious, and what must be done to pacify them. When this is done, they leave the country in peace, and the hero stays there awhile.

After some years the hero, who has grown older, decides to travel to Rome. On his way, croaking frogs reveal his future to him, and this gives him much to think about. Arriving in Rome, he finds that the Pope has just died and the cardinals cannot make up their minds whom to elect as the new Pope. Just as the cardinals decide that some miraculous token should designate the future Pope, two snow-white doves settle on the hero's shoulders. Asked whether he would be Pope, the hero does not know if he is worthy; but the doves counsel him to accept. Thus, he is consecrated, as the frogs had prophesied. When the hero has to sing Mass and does not know the words, the doves, which continually sit upon his shoulders, tell him all the words in his ears.

This is the story of an adolescent whose needs are not understood by his father, who thinks his son is stupid. The son will not develop himself as the father thinks he should, but stubbornly insists on learning instead what *he* thinks is of real value. To achieve his complete self-realization, the young man first has to become acquainted with his inner being, a process no father can prescribe even if he realizes the value of it, as the youth's father does not.

The son of this story is youth in search of itself. The three different masters in faraway places to whom the son goes to learn about the world and himself are the up-to-now-unknown aspects of the world and himself which he needs to explore, something he could not do as long as he was tied too closely to his home.

Why did the hero first learn to understand the language of dogs, then that of birds, and finally of frogs? Here we encounter another aspect of the importance of the number three. Water, earth, and air are the three elements in which our life unfolds. Man is a land animal, and so are dogs. Dogs are the animals living in closest proximity to man. They are the animals which to the child seem most like man, but they also represent instinctual freedom—freedom to bite, to excrete in an uncontrolled way, and to indulge sexual needs without restraint —and at the same time they stand for higher values such as loyalty and friendship. Dogs can be tamed to control their aggressive biting and trained to control their excretions. So it seems natural that learning dog language comes first and easiest. It would seem that dogs represent the ego of man—that aspect of his personality closest to the surface of the mind, since it has as its function the regulation of man's relation to others and to the world around him. Dogs have since prehistory served somewhat this function, aiding man in fending off enemies as well as showing him new ways of relating to savage and other beasts.

Birds which can fly high into the sky symbolize a very different freedom—that of the soul to soar, to rise seemingly free from what binds us to our earthly existence, so appropriately represented by the dogs and frogs. Birds stand in this story for the superego, with its investment in high goals and ideals, its soaring flights of fancy and imagined perfections.

If birds stand for the superego, and dogs for the ego, so frogs symbolize the most ancient part of man's self, the id. It might seem a remote connection to think that the frogs stand for the evolutionary process in which land animals, including man, in ancient times moved from the watery element onto dry land. But even today we all begin our life surrounded by a watery element, which we leave only as we are born. Frogs live first in water in tadpole form, which they shed and change as they move to living in both elements. Frogs are a form of life developed earlier in the evolution of animal life than either dogs or birds, while the id is that part of the personality which exists before ego and superego.

Thus, while on the deepest level frogs may symbolize our earliest existence, on a more accessible level they represent our ability to move from a lower to a higher stage of living. If we want to be fanciful, we could say that learning the language of the dogs and the birds is the precondition for gaining the most important ability: to develop oneself from a lower into a higher state of existence. The frogs may symbolize both the lowest, most primitive, and earliest state of our being, and the development away from it. This can be seen as similar to the development from archaic drives seeking the most elemental satisfactions, to a mature ego able to use the vast resources of our planet for its satisfactions.

This story also implies that simply learning to understand all aspects of the world and our existence in it (earth, air, water) and of our inner life (id, ego, superego) does little for us. We profit from such understanding in meaningful ways only as we apply it to our dealings with the world. To know the language of dogs is not enough; we must also be able to deal with that which the dogs represent. The ferocious dogs, whose language the hero has to learn before any higher humanity becomes possible, symbolize the violent, aggressive, and destructive drives in man. If we remain alienated from these drives, then they can destroy us as the dogs devour some men.

The dogs are closely linked to anal possessiveness because they watch over a great treasure, which explains their ferociousness. Once these violent pressures are understood, once one has become conversant with them (as symbolized by having learned the language of the dogs), the hero can tame them, which brings immediate benefit: the treasure the dogs so savagely protected becomes available. If the unconscious is befriended and given its due—the hero brings food to the dogs—then that which was so fiercely kept hidden, the repressed, becomes accessible and, from being detrimental, turns beneficial.

Learning the language of the birds follows naturally from having learned that of the dogs. The birds symbolize the higher aspirations of the superego and ego ideal. Then after the fierceness of the id and the possessiveness of anality have been overcome, and his superego has been established (learning the language of the birds), the hero is ready to cope with the ancient and primitive amphibian. This also suggests the hero's mastering sex, which in fairy-tale language is suggested by his mastering the language of frogs. (Why frogs, toads, etc., represent sex in fairy tales is discussed later in considering "The Frog King.") It also makes sense that the frogs, which in their own life cycle move from a lower to a higher form, tell the hero of his impending transformation to a higher existence, his becoming Pope.

White doves—which in religious symbolism stand for the Holy Ghost—inspire and enable the hero to achieve the most exalted position on earth; he gains it because he has learned to listen to the doves and do as they bid him. The hero has successfully gained personality integration, having learned to understand and master his id (the ferocious dogs), listen to his superego (the birds) without being completely in its power, and also pay attention to what valuable information the frogs (sex) have to give him.

I know of no other fairy tale in which the process of an adolescent reaching his fullest self-actualization within himself and also in the world is described so concisely. Having achieved this integration, the hero is the right person for the highest office on earth.

"THE THREE FEATHERS"

THE YOUNGEST CHILD AS SIMPLETON

The number three in fairy tales often seems to refer to what in psychoanalysis is viewed as the three aspects of the mind: id, ego, and superego. This may in part be corroborated by another of the Brothers Grimm's stories, "The Three Feathers."

In this fairy tale it is not so much the tripartite division of the human mind which is symbolized, as the necessity of familiarizing ourselves with the unconscious, learning to appreciate its powers and use its resources. The hero of "The Three Feathers," though considered stupid, is victorious because he does this, while his competitors who rely on "cleverness" and remain fixated to the surface of things turn out to have been the stupid ones. Their derision of the "simple" brother, the one who remains close to his natural basis, followed by his victory over them, suggests that a consciousness which has separated itself from its unconscious sources leads us astray.

The fairy-tale motif of the child abused and rejected by older siblings is well known all through history, especially in the form of "Cinderella." But the stories centering on a stupid child, of which "The Three Languages" and "The Three Feathers" are examples, tell a different tale. The unhappiness of the "dumb" child whom the rest of the family holds in low esteem is not mentioned. His being considered stupid is stated as a fact of life which does not seem to concern him much. Sometimes one gets the feeling that the "simpleton" does not mind this condition, since others thus expect nothing of him. Such stories begin to unfold when the simpleton's uneventful life is interrupted by some demand—such as the count sending his son out to become educated. The innumerable fairy tales in which the hero is at first depicted as a simpleton require some explanation of our tendency to identify with him long before he turns out to be superior to those who think little of him.

A small child, bright though he may be, feels himself stupid and inadequate when confronted with the complexity of the world which surrounds him. Everybody else seems to know so much more than he, and to be so much more capable. This is why many fairy tales begin with the hero being depreciated and considered stupid. These are the child's feelings about himself, which are projected not so much onto the world at large as onto his parents and older siblings.

Even when in some fairy stories, like "Cinderella," we are told that the child had lived in bliss before misfortune befell her, this is never described as a time when the child was competent. The child was happy because nothing had been expected of her; everything was provided for her. A young child's inadequacy, which makes him fear that he is stupid, is not his fault—and so the fairy tale which never explains why the child is considered stupid is psychologically correct.

As far as a child's consciousness is concerned, nothing happened during his first years, because in the normal course of events the child remembers no inner conflicts before parents begin making specific demands which run counter to the child's desires. It is in part because of these demands that the child experiences conflicts with the world, and internalization of these demands contributes to the establishment of the superego, and awareness of inner conflicts. Hence these first few years are remembered as conflict-free and blissful, but empty. This is represented in the fairy tale by nothing having happened in the child's life until he awakens to the conflicts between him and his parents, and also to those within himself. Being "dumb" suggests an undifferentiated stage of existence which precedes the struggles between id, ego, and superego of the complex personality.

On the simplest and most direct level, fairy tales in which the hero is the youngest and most inept offer the child the consolation and hope for the future he needs most. Though the child thinks little of himself—a view he projects onto others' views of him—and fears he will never amount to anything, the story shows that he is already started on the process of realizing his potentials. As the son learns the language of dogs and later of birds and frogs in "The Three Languages," the father sees in this only a clear indication of his son's stupidity, but actually the son has made very important steps toward selfhood. The outcome of these stories tells the child that he who has been considered by himself or by others as least able will nonetheless surpass all.

Such a message can best carry conviction through repeated telling of the story. When first told a story with a "dumb" hero, a child may not be able to afford to identify with him, much as he feels himself to be stupid. That would be too threatening, too contrary to his self-love. Only when the child feels completely assured of the hero's proven superiority through repeated hearings can he afford to identify with the hero from the beginning. And only on the basis of such identification can the story provide encouragement to the child that his depreciated view of himself is erroneous. Before such identification occurs, the story means little to the child as a person. But as the child comes to identify with the stupid or degraded hero of the fairy tale, who he knows will eventually show his superiority, the child himself is also started on the process of realizing his potential.

Hans Christian Andersen's "The Ugly Duckling" is the story of a bird which is thought little of as a fledgling but which in the end proves its superiority to all those which had scoffed and mocked it. The story even contains the element of the hero being the youngest and the last-born, since all the other ducklings pecked their way out of their eggs and into the world sooner. As is true of most Andersen stories, charming as it is, this is much more a story for adults. Children enjoy it too, of course, but this story is not helpful to the child; even though he enjoys it, it misdirects his fantasy. The child who feels misunderstood and not appreciated may wish to be of a different breed, but he knows he is not. His chance for success in life is *not* to grow into a being of a different nature as the duckling grows into a swan, but to acquire better qualities and to do better than others expect, being of the same nature as his parents and siblings. In true fairy tales we find that, however many transformations the hero undergoes, including being turned into an animal or even a stone, in the end he is always a human being, as he started out.

To encourage a child to believe he is of a different breed, much as he may like the thought, can lead him in the opposite direction from what fairy tales suggest: that he must do something to achieve his superiority. No need to accomplish anything is expressed in "The Ugly Duckling." Things are simply fated and unfold accordingly, whether or not the hero takes some action, while in the fairy story it is the hero's doing which changes his life.

That one's fate is inexorable—a depressive world-view—is as clear in "The Ugly Duckling" with its favorable outcome as in the sad ending of Andersen's "The Little Match Girl," a deeply moving story, but hardly one suitable for identification. The child in his misery may indeed identify with this heroine, but if so, this leads only to utter pessimism and defeatism. "The Little Match Girl" is a moralistic tale about the cruelty of the world; it arouses compassion for the downtrodden. But what the child who feels downtrodden needs is not compassion for others who are in the same predicament, but rather the conviction that he can escape this fate.

When the hero of a fairy tale is not an only child but one of several, and when he is the least adequate or most abused to begin with (though in the end he far surpasses those who initially were superior to him), he is nearly always the third child. This does not necessarily represent the sibling rivalry of the youngest child; then any number would do—jealousy is as acute in an older child. But since every child at times views himself as being low man in the family, in the fairy tale this is suggested by his being either the youngest or the least thought of, or both. But why is he so often the third?

To understand the reason, we have to consider still one more meaning of the number three in fairy tales. Cinderella is abused by her two stepsisters, who make her assume not just the lowest position, but the third in rank; the same is true for the hero of "The Three Feathers," and of innumerable other fairy stories in which the hero starts out as the low man on the totem pole. Another characteristic of these stories is that the other two siblings are hardly differentiated from each other; they act and look the same.

Both in the unconscious and in the conscious, numbers stand for people: family situations and relations. We are quite consciously aware that "one" stands for ourselves in relation to the world, as the popular reference to "Number One" bears out. "Two" signifies a twosome, a couple, as in a love or marital relation. "Two against one" stands for being unfairly, even hopelessly outclassed in a competition. In the unconscious and in dreams, "one" can stand either for oneself, as it does in our conscious mind, or—particularly with children—for the dominant parent. For adults, "one" also refers to the person who holds power over us, such as the boss. In the child's mind, "two" stands usually for the two parents, and "three" for the child himself in relation to his parents, but not to his siblings. That is why, whatever the child's position within the sibship, the number three refers to himself. When in a fairy story a child is the third one, the hearer easily identifies with him because within the most basic family constellation the child is third down, irrespective of whether he is the oldest, middle, or youngest among his siblings.

Surpassing the two stands in the unconscious for doing better than the two parents. In respect to his parents the child feels abused, insignificant, neglected; to excel them means coming into his own, much more than triumphing over a sibling would. But since it is difficult for the child to admit to himself how great this desire to surpass his parents is, in the fairy tale it is camouflaged as outdoing the two siblings who think so little of him.

Only in comparison to the parents does it make sense that "the third," meaning the child, is at the beginning so incompetent or lazy, a simpleton; and only in regard to them does he catch up so magnificently as he grows up. The child can do so only if he is helped, taught, and promoted by an older person; as the child may reach or surpass the parents' level through the help of an adult teacher. In "The Three Languages" the three masters in foreign cities make this possible; in "The Three Feathers" it is an old toad, very much akin to a grandmother, who helps the youngest son.

"The Three Feathers" begins: "Once upon a time there was a king who had three sons. Two of them were clever and bright, but the third didn't say much, was simple, and was only called the dummy. As the king grew old and weak and thought of his end, he did not know which of his sons should inherit the kingdom. So he spoke to them, 'Go out and who brings me the finest carpet, he shall be king after my death.' So that there should be no fight among them, he took them outside his castle, blew three feathers into the air and said, 'As these fly, there you go.' One feather flew east, the other west, and the third straight ahead, but not far; it soon fell to the earth. Now one brother went right, the other left, and they laughed at the dummy who had to stay where the feather had fallen down. The dummy sat down and was sad. Then he noticed that beside the feather was a trap door. He lifted it, found a stair and stepped down. . . ."

Blowing a feather into the air and following it, if one is undecided in which direction to go, is an old German custom. Many other versions of this story, such as Greek, Slavic, Finnish, and Indian variations, tell of three arrows being shot into the air to determine the direction in which the brothers ought to go.[35]

Today it does not make much sense that the king should decide his succession on the basis of which of his sons brought home the finest carpet, but in times past, "carpet" was also the name given to most intricate weavings; and the fates wove the web which decided man's fate. Thus, in a way, what the king said was that the fates should decide.

Going down into the darkness of the earth is a descent into the netherworld. Dummy undertakes this voyage into the interior, while his two brothers roam around on the surface. It does not seem far-fetched to view this as a tale of Dummy embarking on exploring his unconscious mind. This possibility was suggested at the very beginning of the story, which opposes the brothers' cleverness with Dummy's simplicity and his not talking much. The unconscious speaks to us in images rather than words, and it is simple when compared with the productions of the intellect. And—as is Dummy—it is viewed as the lowliest aspect of our mind when compared with ego and superego, but when well used it is the part of our personality from which we can gain our greatest strength.

When Dummy walks down the stairs, he comes to another door, which opens itself. He enters a room where a big, fat toad sits, surrounded by little toads. The big toad asks him what he wants. In reply, Dummy requests the most beautiful carpet, which is given to him. In other versions it is some other animal which provides Dummy with what he needs, but it is always an animal, suggesting that what enables Dummy to win out is his reliance on his animal nature, the simple and primitive forces within us. The toad is experienced as an uncouth animal, something from which we do not normally expect refined products. But this earthy nature, when well used for higher purposes, proves itself far superior to the superficial brightness of the brothers, who take the easy way by remaining on the surface of things.

As usual in stories of this type, the other brothers are not at all differentiated. They act so alike that one may wonder why more than one is needed to make the tale's point. It would seem that their being undifferentiated is essential because it symbolizes the fact that their personalities are undifferentiated. To impress the hearer with this, more than one brother is needed. The brothers function only on the basis of a much-depleted ego, since it is cut off from the potential source of its strength and richness, the id. But they also have no superego; they have no sense of the higher things, and are satisfied with taking the easy way. The story tells, "But the two others had taken their younger brother for so silly that they thought he would find and come up with nothing. 'Why should we take great pains with the search?' they said, and took the coarse rags off the first shepherds' wives and carried these home to the king."

When the youngest brother at the same time returns with his beautiful carpet, the king is astonished and says that, by right, the kingdom should go to Dummy. The others argue against it, and ask for another test. This time the winner shall return with the finest ring. Once more the three feathers are blown and fly in exactly the same directions. Dummy receives a beautiful ring from the toad and wins, since "the two oldest laughed at Dummy for trying to find a golden ring, took no pains, but knocked the nails out of an old carriage ring and brought it to the king."

The two older brothers plague the king till he agrees to a third test; this time, whoever brings back the most beautiful woman shall win. The previous course of events is repeated. But this third time there is a difference as far as Dummy is concerned. He descends as before to the fat toad, and tells her that he is supposed to bring home the most beautiful woman. Now the big toad does not just hand over to him what he requests, as had happened before. Instead the big toad gives him a hollowed-out yellow turnip to which six mice are harnessed. Dummy sadly asks what he should do with it, to which the big toad replies, "Just put one of my little toads into it." He picks one out of the circle of little toads and puts it in the yellow turnip. As soon as the toad sits in the turnip, she becomes a wonderfully beautiful maiden, the turnip turns into a carriage, and the mice become horses.

Dummy embraces her and takes them all to the king. "His brothers came too. They had given themselves no trouble but had taken along the first peasant women they had met. When the king saw them, he said, 'To the youngest belongs the kingdom after my death.'"

The two other brothers object once more and suggest that each of the women the three brothers have brought home should jump through a large ring which hangs in the hall because they believe the dainty girl Dummy has brought home would not be able to do so. The peasant women the two have brought are clumsy and break their bones, but the beautiful girl Dummy has gained from the toad jumps easily through the ring. At this, all opposition has to cease. Dummy "received the crown and ruled a long time and with great wisdom."

Since the two brothers who roamed on the surface found only coarse things despite all their supposed cleverness, this suggests the limitations of an intellect that is not founded on, and supported by, the powers of the unconscious, both id and superego.

The extraordinary frequency with which the number three appears in fairy tales has been discussed before, as has its possible meaning. In this story it is emphasized even more than in some others. There are three feathers, three brothers, three tests—with a variant fourth one added on. I have already suggested what some of the meanings of the beautiful carpet may be. The story tells that the carpet Dummy brought back was "so beautiful and so fine, as none could be woven on earth" and "the ring sparkled with jewels and was so beautiful that no goldsmith on earth could have fashioned it." Thus, what Dummy receives are no ordinary objects, but works of great art.

Relying once more on insights of psychoanalysis, we may say that the unconscious is the source of art, the mainspring from which it originates; that the superego's ideas fashion it; and that it is the ego forces which execute the unconscious and conscious ideas that enter into the creation of a work of art. Thus, in some ways these art objects signify the integration of the personality. The coarseness of what the two clever brothers bring home emphasizes, by comparison, the artistry of the objects Dummy presents in his efforts to meet the tasks.

No child who thinks about the story can help wondering why the brothers, who at the end of the first test saw that Dummy should not be underestimated, made no greater efforts the second and third times. But the child soon realizes that while these brothers were clever, they were unable to learn from experience. Cut off from their unconscious, they could not grow, could not appreciate the finer things in life, could not differentiate between qualities. Their choices were as undifferentiated as they were. The fact that they were clever and yet did no better the next time symbolizes that they will remain on the surface, where nothing of great value can be found.

Twice the big fat toad hands Dummy what he needs. Going down into the unconscious and coming up with what one unearthed there is much better than remaining on the surface, as the brothers did, but it is not enough. That is why more than one test is needed. Becoming familiar with the unconscious, the dark powers within us which dwell below the surface, is necessary but not sufficient. Acting on these insights must be added; we must refine and sublimate the content of the unconscious. That is why, the third and last time, Dummy himself has to choose one of the little toads. Under his hands the turnip turns into a carriage, the mice into horses. And, as in many other fairy tales, when the hero embraces—that is, loves—the toad, it turns into a beautiful girl. It is, in the final analysis, love which transforms even ugly things into something beautiful. It is ourselves alone who can turn the primordial, uncouth, and most ordinary content of our unconscious—turnips, mice, toads—into the most refined products of our mind.

Finally, the tale suggests that merely repeating the same things with variations is not enough. That is why, after the three similar tests in which the three feathers fly in different directions—representing the role chance plays in our lives—a new and different achievement not relying on chance is needed. Jumping through the ring depends on talent—on what one can do oneself, as different from what one may find through search. Just developing one's personality in all its richness, or just making the vital sources of the unconscious available to the ego, is not sufficient; one must also be able to use one's ability skillfully, gracefully, and with purpose. The beautiful girl who does so well in jumping through the ring is but another aspect of Dummy, as the coarse and clumsy women are other aspects of the brothers. This is suggested by the fact that nothing else is said about her. Dummy does not marry her; at least, we are not told so. The very last words of the fairy tale contrast the wisdom with which Dummy reigns with the cleverness of the two brothers which began the story. Cleverness may be a gift of nature; it is intellect independent of character. Wisdom is the consequence of inner depth, of meaningful experiences which have enriched one's life: a reflection of a rich and well-integrated personality.

The first steps toward achieving this well-integrated personality are made as the child begins to struggle with his deep and ambivalent attachments to his parents—that is, his oedipal conflicts. In regard to these, too, fairy tales help the child to comprehend better the nature of his predicaments and offer ideas which give him courage to struggle with his difficulties and strengthen hopes for their successful resolution.

OEDIPAL CONFLICTS
AND RESOLUTIONS

THE KNIGHT IN SHINING ARMOR
AND THE DAMSEL IN DISTRESS

In the throes of oedipal conflict, a young boy resents his father for standing in his way of receiving Mother's exclusive attention. The boy wants Mother to admire *him* as the greatest hero of all; that means that somehow he must get Father out of the way. This idea, however, creates anxiety in the child, because without Father to protect and take care of them, what would happen to the family? And what if Father were to find out that the little boy wanted him out of the way . . . might he not take a most terrible revenge?

One can tell a small boy many times that someday he will grow up, marry, and be like his father—without avail. Such realistic advice provides no relief from the pressures the child feels right now. But the fairy tale tells the child how he can live with his conflicts: it suggests fantasies he could never invent for himself.

The fairy tale, for example, offers the story of the unnoticed little boy who goes out into the world and makes a great success of life. Details may differ, but the basic plot is always the same: the unlikely hero proves himself through slaying dragons, solving riddles, and living by his wits and goodness until eventually he frees the beautiful princess, marries her, and lives happily ever after.

No little boy has ever failed to see himself in this starring role. The story implies: it's not Father whose jealousy prevents you from having Mother all to yourself, it's an evil dragon—what you really have in mind is to slay an evil dragon. Further, the story gives veracity to the boy's feeling that the most desirable female is kept in captivity by an evil figure, while implying that it is not Mother the child wants for himself, but a marvelous and wonderful woman he hasn't met yet, but certainly will. The story tells more of what the boy wants to hear and believe: that it is not of her own free will that this wonderful female (i.e., Mother) abides with this bad male figure. On the contrary, if only she could, she would much prefer to be with a young hero (like the child). The dragon slayer always has to be young, like the child, and innocent. The innocence of the hero with whom the child identifies proves by proxy the child's innocence, so that, far from having to feel guilty about these fantasies, the child can feel himself to be the proud hero.

It is characteristic of such stories that once the dragon is slain—or whatever deed that frees the beautiful princess from her captivity is accomplished—and the hero is united with his beloved, we are given no details about their later life, beyond being told that they lived "happily ever after." If their children are mentioned, it's usually a later interpolation by someone who thought the story would become more enjoyable or realistic if such information were offered. But introducing children into the story's ending shows little comprehension of a small boy's imaginings about a blissful existence. A child cannot and does not want to imagine what is actually involved in being a husband and father. This would imply, for example, that he would have to leave Mother for most of the day to work—while the oedipal fantasy is a situation where the boy and Mother will never be separated for a moment. The little boy certainly doesn't want Mother to be busy with housekeeping, or taking care of other children. He doesn't want to have sex with her either, because that is still an area full of conflict for him, if he has much awareness of it at all. As in most fairy tales, the little boy's ideal is just he and his princess (Mother), all their needs and wishes taken care of, living by themselves and for each other forever.

The oedipal problems of a girl are different from those of a boy, and so the fairy stories which help her to cope with her oedipal situation are of a different character. What blocks the oedipal girl's uninterrupted blissful existence with Father is an older, ill-intentioned female (i.e., Mother). But since the little girl also wants very much to continue enjoying Mother's loving care, there is also a benevolent female in the past or background of the fairy tale, whose happy memory is kept intact, although she has become inoperative. A little girl wishes to see herself as a young and beautiful maiden—a princess or the like—who is kept captive by the selfish, evil female figure and hence unavailable to the male lover. The captive princess' real father is depicted as benevolent, but helpless to come to the rescue of his lovely girl. In "Rapunzel" it is a vow that stymies him. In "Cinderella" and "Snow White" he seems unable to hold his own against the all-powerful stepmother.

The oedipal boy, who feels threatened by his father because of the wish to replace him in Mother's attention, casts Father in the role of the threatening monster. This also seems to prove to the boy how dangerous a rival to the father he is, because otherwise why would this father figure be so threatening? Since the desirable female is held captive by the old dragon, the little boy can believe that only brute force prevents this lovely girl (Mother) from joining him, the much-preferred young hero. In fairy stories which help the oedipal girl to understand her feelings and find vicarious satisfaction, it is the (step)-mother's or the enchantress' intense jealousy which keeps the lover from finding the princess. This jealousy proves that the older woman knows the young girl is preferable, more lovable, and more deserving of being loved.

While the oedipal boy does not want any children to interfere with Mother's complete involvement in him, matters are different for the oedipal girl. She does want to give her father the love-gift of being mother to his children. Whether this is an expression of her need to compete with Mother in this respect, or a dim anticipation of her motherhood to come, is difficult to determine. This desire to give Father a child doesn't mean having sexual relations with him—the little girl, like the little boy, doesn't think in such concrete terms. The little girl knows that children are what bind the male even more strongly to the female. That is why in fairy stories dealing in symbolic form with the oedipal wishes, problems, and hardships of a girl, children *are* occasionally mentioned as part of the happy ending.

In the Brothers Grimm's version of "Rapunzel" we are told that the prince in his wanderings "at length came to the desert where Rapunzel, with the twins to which she had given birth, a boy and a girl, lived in wretchedness," though no children had been mentioned before. When she embraces the prince, two of Rapunzel's tears wet his eyes (which had been pierced and blinded) and cure his blindness; and "he led her to his kingdom where he was joyfully received, and where they lived happily for a long time." Once they are united, no more is said about the children. They are only a symbol in the story of the bond between Rapunzel and the prince during their separation. Since we are not told of the two having been married, and there is no other suggestion of any form of sexual relation, this mention of children in fairy tales supports the idea that children can be gotten without sex, just as a result of love.

In the usual course of family life, the father is often out of the home, while the mother, having given birth to the child and nursed him, continues to be heavily involved in all child care. As a result, a boy can easily pretend that Father is not all that important in his life. (A girl cannot as readily imagine dispensing with Mother's care, however.) That is why replacement of an original "good" father by a bad stepfather is as rare in fairy tales as the evil stepmother is frequent. Since fathers have typically given much less attention to the child, it is not such a radical disappointment when this father begins to stand in the child's way, or to make demands of him. So the father who blocks the boy's oedipal desires is not seen as an evil figure within the home, or split into two figures, one good and one bad, as the mother often is. Instead, the oedipal boy projects his frustrations and anxieties onto a giant, monster, or dragon.

In a girl's oedipal fantasy, the mother is split into two figures: the pre-oedipal wonderful good mother and the oedipal evil stepmother. (Sometimes there are bad stepmothers in fairy stories with boys, such as in "Hansel and Gretel," but such tales deal with problems other than oedipal ones.) The good mother, so the fantasy goes, would never have been jealous of her daughter or have prevented the prince (father) and the girl from living happily together. So for the oedipal girl, belief and trust in the goodness of the pre-oedipal mother, and deep loyalty to her, tend to reduce the guilt about what the girl wishes would happen to the (step)mother who stands in her way.

Thus, both oedipal girls and boys, thanks to the fairy tale, can have the best of two worlds: they can fully enjoy oedipal satisfactions in fantasy and keep good relations to both parents in reality.

For the oedipal boy, if Mother disappoints him, there is the fairy princess in the back of his mind—that wonderful woman of the future who will compensate for all his present hardships, and the thought of whom makes it much easier to bear up under them. If Father is less attentive to his little girl than *she* desires, she can endure such adversity because a prince will arrive who will prefer her to all competitors. Since everything takes place in never-never-land, the child need not feel guilty or anxious about casting Father in the role of a dragon or evil giant, or Mother in the role of a miserable stepmother or witch. The little girl can love her real father all the better because her resentment over his failure to prefer her to her mother is explained by his unfortunate ineffectuality (as with fathers in fairy tales), for which nobody can blame him since it is due to superior powers; besides, it will not prevent her from getting her prince. A girl can love her mother more because she puts out all her anger at the mother-competitor, who gets what she deserves—as Snow White's stepmother is forced to put on "red-hot shoes, and dance until she dropped dead." And Snow White—and with her the little girl—need not feel guilty because her love of her true mother (who preceded the stepmother) has never stopped. The boy can love his real father even better after having gotten out all his anger at him through a fantasy of destroying the dragon or the bad giant.

Such fairy-tale fantasies—which most children would have a hard time inventing so completely and satisfactorily on their own—can help a child a great deal to overcome his oedipal anguish.

The fairy story has other unequaled values in helping the child with oedipal conflicts. Mothers cannot accept their little boys' wishes to do away with Daddy and marry Mommy; but a mother can participate with pleasure in her son's imagining himself as the dragon slayer who gains possession of the beautiful princess. Also, a mother can fully encourage her daughter's fantasies about the handsome prince who will join her, thus helping her to believe in a happy solution despite her present disappointment. Thus, far from losing Mother because of the oedipal attachment to Father, the daughter realizes that Mother not only approves of such wishes in disguise, but even hopes for their realization. Through fairy tales the parent can join the child in all voyages of fancy, while still retaining the all-important function of fulfilling the parental tasks in reality.

Thus a child can have the best of both worlds, which is what he needs to grow up into a secure adult. In fantasy a girl can win out over the (step)mother whose efforts to prevent her happiness with the prince fail; a boy can slay the monster and gain what he wishes in a far-distant land. At the same time, both girls and boys can retain at home the real father as protector and the real mother who dispenses all the care and satisfactions a child needs. Since it is clear all along that slaying the dragon and marrying the enslaved princess, or being discovered by the fairy prince and punishing the wicked witch, occur in faraway times and countries, the normal child never mixes them up with reality.

Oedipal-conflict stories are typical of a large class of fairy tales that extend the child's interests outside the immediate family. To make his first steps toward becoming a mature individual, the child must begin to look to the larger world. If the child does not receive support from his parents in his real and imaginary investigation of the world outside his home, it is at the risk of impoverishing the development of his personality.

It is not wise to urge a child in so many words to begin to enlarge his horizons, or to inform him specifically how far to go in his explorations of the world, or how to sort out feelings about his parents. If a parent verbally encourages a child to "mature," to move out psychologically or geographically, the child interprets this as meaning "they want to get rid of me." The result is the direct opposite of what is intended. For the child then feels unwanted and unimportant, and such feelings are most detrimental to the development of his ability to cope with this wider world.

The child's learning task is precisely that of making decisions about moving out on his own, in his own good time, and into the areas of living he himself selects. The fairy tale helps in this process because it only beckons; it never suggests, demands, or tells. In the fairy tale all is said implicitly and in symbolic form: what the tasks for one's age might be; how one might deal with one's ambivalent feelings about one's parents; how this welter of emotions can be mastered. It also warns the child of some of the pitfalls he can expect and perhaps avoid, always promising a favorable outcome.

FEAR OF FANTASY

WHY WERE FAIRY TALES OUTLAWED?

Why do many intelligent, well-meaning, modern, middle-class parents, so concerned about the happy development of their children, discount the value of fairy tales and deprive their children of what these stories have to offer? Even our Victorian ancestors, despite their emphasis on moral discipline and their stodgy way of life, not only permitted but encouraged their children to enjoy the fantasy and excitement of fairy tales. It would be simple to blame such a prohibition of fairy tales on a narrow-minded, uninformed rationalism, but this is not the case.

Some people claim that fairy tales do not render "truthful" pictures of life as it is, and are therefore unhealthy. That "truth" in the life of a child might be different from that of adults does not occur to these people. They do not realize that fairy tales do not try to describe the external world and "reality." Nor do they recognize that no sane child ever believes that these tales describe the world realistically.

Some parents fear that by telling their children about the fantastic events found in fairy tales, they are "lying" to them. Their concern is fed by the child's asking, "Is it true?" Many fairy tales offer an answer even before the question can be asked—namely, at the very beginning of the story. For example, "Ali Baba and the Forty Thieves" starts: "In days of yore and times and tides long gone. . . ." The Brothers Grimm's story "The Frog King, or Iron Henry" opens: "In olden times when wishing still helped one. . . ." Such beginnings make it amply clear that the stories take place on a very different level from everyday "reality." Some fairy tales do begin quite realistically: "There once was a man and a woman who had long in vain wished for a child." But the child who is familiar with fairy stories always extends the times of yore in his mind to mean the same as "In fantasy land . . ." This exemplifies why telling just one and the same story to the neglect of others weakens the value fairy tales have for children, and raises problems which are answered by familiarity with a number of tales.

The "truth" of fairy stories is the truth of our imagination, not that of normal causality. Tolkien, addressing himself to the question of "Is it true?" remarks that "It is not one to be rashly or idly answered." He adds that of much more real concern to the child is the question: " 'Was he good? Was he wicked?' That is, [the child] is more concerned to get the Right side and the Wrong side clear."

Before a child can come to grips with reality, he must have some frame of reference to evaluate it. When he asks whether a story is true, he wants to know whether the story contributes something of importance to his understanding, and whether it has something significant to tell him in regard to *his* greatest concerns.

To quote Tolkien once more: "Often enough what children mean when they ask: 'Is it true?' [is] 'I like this, but is it contemporary? Am I safe in my bed?' The answer: 'There is certainly no dragon in England today' is all that they want to hear." "Fairy stories," he continues, are "plainly not primarily concerned with possibility, but with desirability." This the child clearly recognizes, since nothing is more "true" to him than what he desires.

Speaking of his childhood, Tolkien recalls: "I had no desire to have either dreams or adventures like *Alice*, and the account of them merely amused me. I had little desire to look for buried treasure or fight pirates, and *Treasure Island* left me cool. But the land of Merlin and Arthur was better than these, and best of all the nameless North of Sigurd of the Voelsungs, and the prince of all dragons. Such lands were preeminently desirable. I never imagined that the dragon was of the same order as the horse. The dragon had the trademark *Of Faerie* written plainly upon him. In whatever world he had his being it was of Other-world. . . . I desired dragons with a profound desire. Of course, I in my timid body did not wish to have them in the neighborhood, intruding in my relatively safe world."[36]

In reply to the question whether the fairy story tells the truth, the answer should address itself not to the issue of truth in factual terms, but to the child's concern of the moment, be this his fear that he is apt to be bewitched, or his feelings of oedipal rivalry. For the rest, an explanation that these stories do not take place in the here and now, but in a faraway never-never-land is nearly always sufficient. A parent who from his own childhood experience is convinced of the value of fairy tales will have no difficulty in answering his child's questions; but an adult who thinks these tales are only a bunch of lies had better not try telling them; he won't be able to relate them in a way which would enrich the child's life.

Some parents fear that their children may get carried away by their fantasies; that when exposed to fairy tales, they will come to believe in magic. But every child believes in magic, and he stops doing so when he grows up (with the exception of those who have been too disappointed in reality to be able to trust its rewards). I have known disturbed children who had never been told fairy stories but who invested an electric fan or motor with as much magic and destructive power as any fairy story ever ascribed to its most powerful and nefarious figure.[37]

Other parents fear that a child's mind may become so overfed by fairy-tale fantasies as to neglect learning to cope with reality. Actually, the opposite is true. Complex as we all are—conflicted, ambivalent, full of contradictions—the human personality is indivisible. Whatever an experience may be, it always affects all the aspects of the personality at the same time. And the total personality, in order to be able to deal with the tasks of living, needs to be backed up by a rich fantasy combined with a firm consciousness and a clear grasp of reality.

Faulty development sets in when one component of the personality —id, ego, or superego; conscious or unconscious—overpowers any of the others and depletes the total personality of its particular resources. Because some people withdraw from the world and spend most of their days in the realm of their imaginings, it has been mistakenly suggested that an over-rich fantasy life interferes with our coping successfully with reality. But the opposite is true: those who live completely in their fantasies are beset by compulsive ruminations which rotate eternally around some narrow, stereotypical topics. Far from having a rich fantasy life, such people are locked in, and they cannot break out of one anxious or wish-fulfilling daydream. But free-floating fantasy, which contains in imaginary form a wide variety of issues also encountered in reality, provides the ego with an abundance of material to work with. This rich and variegated fantasy life is provided to the child by fairy stories, which can help prevent his imagination from getting stuck within the narrow confines of a few anxious or wish-fulfilling daydreams circling around a few narrow preoccupations.

Freud said that thought is an exploration of possibilities which avoids all the dangers inherent in actual experimentation. Thought requires a small expenditure of energy, so we have energy available for action after we have reached decisions through speculating about the chances for success and the best way to achieve it. This is true for adults; for example, the scientist "plays with ideas" before he starts to explore them more systematically. But the young child's thoughts do not proceed in an orderly way, as an adult's do—the child's fantasies are his thoughts. When a child tries to understand himself and others, or figure out what the specific consequences of some action might be, he spins fantasies around these issues. It is his way of "playing with ideas." To offer a child rational thought as his major instrument for sorting out his feelings and understanding the world will only confuse and restrict him.

This is true even when the child seems to ask for factual information. Piaget describes how a girl not yet four years old asked him about an elephant's wings. He answered that elephants don't fly. To which the girl insisted, "Yes, they do; I've seen them." His reply was that she must be joking.[38] This example shows the limits of a child's fantasies. The little girl was obviously struggling with some problem, and factual explanations were no help at all, because they did not address themselves to that problem.

If Piaget had engaged in conversation about where the elephant needed to fly to in such a hurry, or what dangers he was trying to escape from, then the issues which the child was grappling with might have emerged, because Piaget would have shown his willingness to accept her method of exploring the problem. But Piaget was trying to understand how this child's mind worked on the basis of his rational frame of reference, while the girl was trying to understand the world on the basis of her understanding: through fantasy elaboration of reality as *she* saw it.

This is the tragedy of so much "child psychology": its findings are correct and important, but do not benefit the child. Psychological discoveries aid the adult in comprehending the child from within an adult's frame of reference. But such adult understanding of the machinations of a child's mind often increases the gap between them—the two seem to look at the same phenomenon from such different points of view that each sees something quite different. If the adult insists that the way he sees things is correct—as it may well be, seen objectively and with adult knowledge—this gives the child a hopeless feeling that there is no use in trying to arrive at a common understanding. Knowing who holds the power, the child, to avoid trouble and have his peace, says that he agrees with the adult, and is then forced to go it alone.

Fairy tales underwent severe criticism when the new discoveries of psychoanalysis and child psychology revealed just how violent, anxious, destructive, and even sadistic a child's imagination is. A young child, for example, not only loves his parents with an incredible intensity of feeling, but at times also hates them. With this knowledge, it should have been easy to recognize that fairy tales speak to the inner mental life of the child. But, instead, doubters claimed that these stories create or at least greatly encourage these upsetting feelings.

Those who outlawed traditional folk fairy tales decided that if there were monsters in a story told to children, these must all be friendly —but they missed the monster a child knows best and is most concerned with: the monster he feels or fears himself to be, and which also sometimes persecutes him. By keeping this monster within the child unspoken of, hidden in his unconscious, adults prevent the child from spinning fantasies around it in the image of the fairy tales he knows. Without such fantasies, the child fails to get to know his monster better, nor is he given suggestions as to how he may gain mastery over it. As a result, the child remains helpless with his worst anxieties —much more so than if he had been told fairy tales which give these anxieties form and body and also show ways to overcome these monsters. If our fear of being devoured takes the tangible form of a witch, it can be gotten rid of by burning her in the oven! But these considerations did not occur to those who outlawed fairy tales.

It is a strangely limited, one-sided picture of adults and life which children are expected to accept as the only correct one. Starving the imagination of the child was expected to extinguish the giants and ogres of the fairy tale—that is, the dark monsters residing in the unconscious—so that these would not obstruct the development of the child's rational mind. The rational ego was expected to reign supreme from babyhood on! This was not to be achieved by the ego's conquering the dark forces of the id, but by preventing the child from paying attention to his unconscious or hearing stories which would speak to it. In short, the child would supposedly repress his unpleasant fantasies and have only pleasant ones.*

Such id-repressing theories do not work, however. What may happen when a child is forced to repress the content of his unconscious may be illustrated by an extreme example. After long therapeutic work, a boy who at the end of his latency period had suddenly become mute explained the origin of his mutism. He said: "My mother washed out my mouth with soap because of all the bad words I used, and these had been pretty bad, I admit. What she did not know was that by washing out all the bad words, she also washed out all the good ones." In therapy all these bad words were freed, and with this, the good ones also reappeared. Many other things had gone wrong in this boy's early life; washing his mouth with soap was not the main cause of his mutism, though it was a contributing one.

The unconscious is the source of raw materials and the basis upon which the ego erects the edifice of our personality. In this simile our fantasies are the natural resources which provide and shape this raw material, making it useful for the ego's personality-building tasks. If we are deprived of this natural resource, our life remains limited; without fantasies to give us hope, we do not have the strength to meet the adversities of life. Childhood is the time when these fantasies need to be nurtured.

We do encourage our children's fantasies; we tell them to paint what they want, or to invent stories. But unfed by our common fantasy heritage, the folk fairy tale, the child cannot invent stories on his own which help him cope with life's problems. All the stories he can invent

*It is as if Freud's dictum on the essence of development toward higher humanity consisting of "where there was id, there should be ego" were perverted into its opposite: "where there was id, there should be none of it." But Freud clearly implied that only the id can provide the ego with the energy necessary to mold unconscious tendencies and use them constructively. Although more recent psychoanalytic theory posits that the ego is also invested from birth with its own energy, an ego which cannot draw on the much larger sources of id energies in addition will be a weak one. Further, an ego which is forced to expend its limited amount of energy on keeping the id's energy repressed is doubly depleted.

are just expressions of his own wishes and anxieties. Relying on his own resources, all the child can imagine are elaborations of where he presently is, since he cannot know where he needs to go, nor how to go about getting there. This is where the fairy tale provides what the child needs most: it begins exactly where the child is emotionally, shows him where he has to go, and how to do it. But the fairy tale does this by implication, in the form of fantasy material which the child can draw on as seems best to him, and by means of images which make it easy for him to comprehend what is essential for him to understand.

The rationalizations for continuing to forbid fairy tales despite what psychoanalysis revealed about the unconscious, particularly that of children, took many forms. When it could no longer be denied that the child is beset by deep conflicts, anxieties, violent desires, and helplessly tossed about by all kinds of irrational processes, it was concluded that because the child is already afraid of so many things, anything else that looked fearsome should be kept from him. A particular story may indeed make some children anxious, but once they become better acquainted with fairy stories, the fearsome aspects seem to disappear, while the reassuring features become ever more dominant. *The original displeasure of anxiety then turns into the great pleasure of anxiety successfully faced and mastered.*

Parents who wish to deny that their child has murderous wishes and wants to tear things and even people into pieces believe that their child must be prevented from engaging in such thoughts (as if this were possible). By denying access to stories which implicitly tell the child that others have the same fantasies, he is left to feel that he is the only one who imagines such things. This makes his fantasies really scary. On the other hand, learning that others have the same or similar fantasies makes us feel that we are a part of humanity, and allays our fear that having such destructive ideas has put us beyond the common pale.

A strange contradiction is that well-educated parents outlawed fairy tales for their children at just about the time when the findings of psychoanalysis made them aware that, far from being innocent, the mind of the young child is filled with anxious, angry, destructive imaginings.* It is also quite remarkable that these parents, so worried

---

*Fairy stories stimulate the child's fantasies—as do many other experiences. Since parental objection to fairy stories is often based on the violent or scary events which occur in these tales, an experimental study of fifth-graders may be mentioned which demonstrates that when a child who has a rich fantasy life—something which fairy tales stimulate—is exposed to aggressive fantasy material as it occurs in fairy stories

about not increasing their child's anxieties, remained oblivious to all the reassuring messages in fairy tales.

The answer to the puzzle may be found in the fact that psychoanalysis also revealed the child's ambivalent feelings about his parents. It is perturbing to parents to realize that the child's mind is filled not only by deep love, but also by strong hatred of his parents. Wishing to be loved by their child, parents shrink from exposing him to tales which might encourage him to think of parents as bad or rejecting.

Parents wish to believe that if a child sees them as stepmothers, witches, or giants, this has nothing to do with them and how they at moments appear to the child, but is only the result of tales he has heard. These parents hope that if their child is prevented from learning about such figures, he will not see his own parents in this image. In a complete reversal of which they remain largely unaware, such parents fool themselves into believing that if they are seen in such form by the child it is due to the stories he has heard, while actually the opposite is true: fairy tales are loved by the child not because the imagery he finds in them conforms to what goes on within him, but because—despite all the angry, anxious thoughts in his mind to which the fairy tale gives body and specific content—these stories always result in a happy outcome, which the child cannot imagine on his own.

TRANSCENDING INFANCY
WITH THE HELP OF FANTASY

If one believed in a grand design to human life, one could admire the wisdom by which it is arranged that a wide variety of psychological events coincide just at the right time, reinforcing each other so that

---

(in the experiment a film with aggressive content), he responds to this experience with a marked *decrease* in aggressive behavior. When not stimulated to engage in aggressive fantasies, no reduction in aggressive behavior could be observed (Ephraim Biblow, "Imaginative Play and the Control of Aggressive Behavior," in Jerome L. Singer, *The Child's World of Make-Believe* [New York: Academic Press, 1973]).

Since fairy tales strongly stimulate a child's fantasy life, the two concluding sentences of this study may be quoted: "The low-fantasy child, as observed during play, presented himself as more motorically oriented, revealing much action and little thought in play activities. The high-fantasy child in contrast was more highly structured and creative and tended to be verbally rather than physically aggressive."

the impact on the young human propels him out of infancy into childhood. Just when the child begins to be tempted by the beckoning of the wider world to move beyond the narrow circle encompassing him and his parents, his oedipal disappointments induce him to detach himself a bit from his parents, who up to this time were the sole source of his physical and psychological sustenance.

As this happens, the child becomes able to gain some emotional satisfaction from persons who are not part of his immediate family, which compensates to a small degree for his disillusionment with his parents. One could view it as part of this same design that as the child becomes deeply and painfully disenchanted with his parents because they fail to live up to his infantile expectations, he becomes physically and mentally able to provide for some of his wants himself. All of these and many other important developments take place at the same time or in short succession; they are interrelated, each one a function of all the others.

Because of the child's growing ability to cope, he can have more contact with others, and with wider aspects of the world. Because he is able to do more, his parents feel the time has come to expect more of the child, and they become less ready to do for him. This change in their relations is an enormous disappointment of the child's hope that he would always receive endlessly; it is the most severe disillusionment of his young life, made infinitely worse because it is inflicted by those who he believes owe him unlimited care. But this event is also a function of the child's having more significant contact with the outside world, of his receiving at least some emotional supplies from it, and his growing ability to satisfy some of his own needs to some small degree. Because of his new experiences with the outside world, the child can afford to become aware of the "limitations" of his parents—that is, their shortcomings as seen from the standpoint of his unrealistic expectations of them. In consequence, the child becomes so disgusted with his parents that he ventures to seek satisfaction elsewhere.

When this comes about, so overwhelming are the new challenges presented to the child by his enlarging experiences, and so very small are his ability to achieve these new things and his chance to solve the problems which his steps toward independence arouse, that he needs fantasy satisfactions in order not to give up in despair. Considerable as the child's real achievements are, they seem to vanish into insignificance when compared to his failures, if only because he has no comprehension of what is actually possible. This disillusionment may lead to such severe disappointment in himself that the child may give up all effort and completely withdraw into himself, away from the world, unless fantasy comes to his rescue.

If any one of these various steps the child is taking in growing up could be viewed in isolation, it might be said that the ability to spin fantasies beyond the present is the new achievement which makes all others possible—because it makes bearable the frustrations experienced in reality. If only we could recall how we felt when we were small, or could imagine how utterly defeated a young child feels when his play companions or older siblings temporarily reject him or can obviously do things better than he can, or when adults—worst of all, his parents—seem to make fun of him or belittle him, then we would know why the child often feels like an outcast: a "simpleton." Only exaggerated hopes and fantasies of future achievements can balance the scales so that the child can go on living and striving.

How enormous the frustration, disappointment, and despair of the child are at moments of utter, unrelieved defeat can be seen from his temper tantrums, which are the visible expression of the conviction that he can do nothing to improve the "unbearable" conditions of his life. As soon as a child is able to imagine (that is, to fantasize) a favorable solution to his present predicament, temper tantrums disappear —because with hope for the future established, the present difficulty is no longer insufferable. Random physical discharge through kicking and screaming is then replaced by thought or activity designed to reach a desired goal, either now or at some future date. Thus the problems a child encounters and cannot solve at the moment become manageable, because disappointment in the present is mitigated by visions of future victories.

If a child is for some reason unable to imagine his future optimistically, arrest of development sets in. The extreme example of this can be found in the behavior of the child suffering from infantile autism. He does nothing or intermittently breaks out into severe temper tantrums, but in either case insists that nothing must be altered in his environment and the conditions of his life. All this is the consequence of his complete inability to imagine any change for the better. When one such child after prolonged therapy finally emerged from her total autistic withdrawal and reflected on what characterizes good parents, she said: "They hope for you." The implication was that her parents had been bad parents because they had failed both to feel hope for her and to give her hope for herself and her future life in this world.

We know that the more deeply unhappy and despairing we are, the more we need to be able to engage in optimistic fantasies. But these are not available to us at such periods. Then, more than at any other time, we need others to uplift us with their hope for us and our future. No fairy tale all by itself will do this for the child; as the autistic girl reminded us, first we need our parents to instill hope in us. On this firm and real basis—the positive ways in which our parents view us and our future—we can then build castles in the air, half aware that these are just that, but gaining deep reassurance from it nonetheless. While the fantasy is *unreal*, the good feelings it gives us about ourselves and our future *are real*, and these real good feelings are what we need to sustain us.

Every parent responsive to his child's feeling down and out tells his child that things will take a turn for the better. But the child's despair is all-encompassing—because he does not know gradations, he feels either in darkest hell or gloriously happy—and therefore nothing but the most perfect everlasting bliss can combat his fear of total devastation at the moment. No reasonable parent can promise his child that perfect bliss is available to him in reality. But by telling his child fairy tales, the parent can encourage him to borrow for his private use fantastic hopes for the future, without misleading him by suggesting that there is reality to such imaginings.*

*Telling a child the story of "Cinderella" and letting him fantasize himself into Cinderella's role and use the story to imagine what his own delivery will be like is a very different matter from letting him act out the fantasy in all seriousness. The first is encouraging hope; the latter is creating delusions.

A father, rather than telling his little girl fairy tales, decided—out of his own emotional needs and as an escape through fantasy from his marital difficulties—that he would do better than fairy tales. Night after night he spun out for his daughter a Cinderella fantasy in which he was the prince who recognized that despite her rags and ashes she was the most wonderful girl in the world, and therefore she would henceforth—thanks to him—live the life of a fairy princess. The father did not tell this as a fairy tale, but as if it were something that was happening between the two of them in reality, and a valid promise of things to come. He did not understand that in depicting to his daughter her real-life conditions as those of Cinderella, he made her mother—his wife—out to be a malicious betrayer of her own daughter. Since it was not a fairy prince in never-never-land but he himself who chose Cinderella as his beloved, these nightly tales kept the girl fixated in the oedipal situation with her father.

This father certainly "hoped" for his daughter, but in a drastically unrealistic fashion. The result was that, as the child grew older, she got so much gratification from her nightly embarkation with her father on these fantasies that she did not want reality to interfere and refused to come to terms with it. For this and other, related

Feeling acutely the dissatisfactions which come with being dominated by adults, and dispossessed of the small child's kingdom where
no demands were made on him and it seemed all his wishes were
satisfied by his parents, no child can help wishing for a kingdom of his
or her own. Realistic statements about what the child may achieve as
he grows cannot satisfy or even compare with such extravagant
desires.

What is this kingdom which many fairy-tale heroes gain at the
story's end? Its main characteristic is that we are never told anything
about it, not even what the king or queen does. There is no purpose
to being the king or queen of this kingdom other than being a ruler
rather than being ruled. To have become a king or queen at the
conclusion of the story symbolizes a state of true *independence*, in
which the hero feels as secure, satisfied, and happy as the infant felt
in his most *dependent* state, when he was truly well taken care of in
the kingdom of his cradle.

The fairy tale begins with the hero at the mercy of those who think
little of him and his abilities, who mistreat him and even threaten his
life, as the wicked queen does in "Snow White." As the story unfolds,
the hero is often forced to depend on friendly helpers: creatures of the
underworld like the dwarfs in "Snow White," or magic animals like
the birds in "Cinderella." At the tale's end the hero has mastered all
trials and despite them remained true to himself, or in successfully
undergoing them has achieved his true selfhood. He has become an
autocrat in the best sense of the word—a self-ruler, a truly autono-
mous person, not a person who rules over others. In fairy tales, unlike
myths, victory is not over others but only over oneself and over vil-

---

reasons she did not function age-appropriately. She was examined psychiatrically, and
the diagnosis was that she had lost contact with reality. Actually she had not "lost"
contact with reality, but had failed to establish it, in order to protect her imaginary
world. She did not want to have any truck with the everyday world, since her father's
behavior indicated to her that he did not wish her to, and that she did not need it.
She lived all day in her fantasies and became schizophrenic.

Her story highlights the difference between fantasy playing in a never-never-land
and falsely based predictions of what is about to happen in everyday reality. The
promises of fairy tales are one thing; our hopes for our children are another, and these
must remain rooted in reality. We ought to know that the frustrations children
experience, the difficulties they have to master, are not more than what we all
encounter under normal circumstances. But because in the child's mind these difficulties are the greatest imaginable, he needs the encouragement of fantasies in which
the hero, with whom he can identify, successfully finds his way out of incredibly
difficult situations.

lainy (mainly one's own, which is projected as the hero's antagonist). If we are told anything about the rule of these kings and queens, it is that they ruled wisely and peacefully, and that they lived happily. This is what maturity ought to consist of: that one rules oneself wisely, and as a consequence lives happily.

The child understands this very well. No child believes that one day he will become ruler over a kingdom other than the realm of his own life. The fairy story assures him that someday this kingdom can be his, but not without struggle. How the child specifically imagines the "kingdom" depends on his age and state of development, but he never takes it literally. To the younger child, it may simply mean that then nobody will order him around, and that all his wishes will be fulfilled. To the older child, it will also include the obligation to rule—that is, to live and act wisely. But at any age a child interprets becoming king or queen as having gained mature adulthood.

Since maturity requires a positive solution to the child's oedipal conflicts, let us consider how the hero gains this kingdom in the fairy tale. In the Greek myth, Oedipus became king by slaying his father and marrying his mother after solving the riddle of the Sphinx, which then killed itself. Solving this riddle required understanding of what the three stages of human development consist of. To a child the greatest riddle is what sex consists of; that is the secret of adults which he wishes to discover. Since solving the riddle of the Sphinx enabled Oedipus to come into his kingdom by marrying his mother, we may assume that this riddle had something to do with sexual knowledge, at least on an unconscious level.

In many fairy tales, too, solving "the riddle" leads to marriage and gaining the kingdom. For example, in the Brothers Grimm's story "The Clever Little Tailor," only the hero is able to correctly guess the two colors of the princess' hair, and therefore he wins the princess. Similarly, the story of Princess Turandot tells that she can be won only by the man who correctly guesses the answers to her three riddles. Solving the riddle posed by a particular woman stands for the riddle of woman in general, and since marriage usually follows the right solution, it does not seem farfetched that the riddle to be solved is a sexual one: whoever understands the secret which the other sex presents has gained his maturity. But while in the myth of Oedipus the figure whose riddle has been correctly answered destroys itself and marital tragedy follows, in fairy tales the discovery of the secret leads to the happiness of both the person who solved the riddle and the one who posed it.

Oedipus marries a woman who is his mother, so obviously she is much older than he. The fairy-tale hero, whether male or female, marries a partner of about the same age. That is, whatever oedipal attachment the fairy-tale hero may have had to his parent, he has successfully transferred it to a most suitable non-oedipal partner. Again and again in fairy tales an unsatisfactory relation to a parent—such as an oedipal relation invariably is—is replaced, like Cinderella's link to a weak and ineffective father, by a happy relation to the rescuing marital partner.

The parent in such fairy tales, far from resenting the child's transcending his oedipal attachment to him, is delighted that he has and often is instrumental in arranging it. For example, in "Hans, My Hedgehog" and in "Beauty and the Beast" the father (willingly or unwillingly) causes his daughter to marry; relinquishing his oedipal attachment to his daughter and inducing her to give up hers to him lead to a happy solution for both.

Never in a fairy tale does a son take his father's kingdom away from him. If a father gives it up, it is always because of old age. Even then the son has to earn it, by finding the most desirable woman for himself, as in "The Three Feathers." This story makes it quite clear that gaining the kingdom is tantamount to having reached moral and sexual maturity. First one task is demanded of the hero which he must perform to inherit the kingdom. When the hero succeeds, this turns out to be not sufficient. The same thing happens the second time. The third task is to find and bring home the right bride; when the hero manages to do this, the kingdom is finally his. Thus, far from projecting the son's being jealous of his father, or the father's resenting his son's sexual endeavors, the fairy story tells the opposite: when the child has reached the right age and maturity, the parent wants him to come into his own sexually also; in fact, he will accept his son as a worthy successor only after he has done so.

In many fairy stories a king gives his daughter in marriage to the hero and either shares his kingdom with him or installs him as the eventual successor. This is, of course, a wishful fantasy of the child. But since the story assures him that this is indeed what is going to happen, and since in the unconscious the "king" stands for one's own father, the fairy tale promises the highest possible reward—a happy life and the kingdom—to the son who through his struggles has found the right solution to his oedipal conflicts: to transfer his love for his mother to a suitable partner of his own age; and to recognize that the father (far from being a threatening competitor) is really a benevolent protector who approves of his son's finding adult fulfillment.

Gaining his kingdom through being united in love and marriage with the most appropriate and desirable partner—a union which the parents thoroughly approve and which leads to happiness for everybody but the villains—symbolizes the perfect resolution of oedipal difficulties, as well as the gaining of true independence and complete personality integration. Is it really all that unrealistic to speak of such high achievement as coming into one's own kingdom?

This may also suggest why the achievements of the heroes in "realistic" children's stories often seem ordinary and trite by comparison. These stories also offer assurance to the child that he will solve important problems he encounters in his "real" life—as adults define these problems. In doing so, the stories have definite but limited merits. But what problems could be more difficult to grasp, and more "real" to the child, than his oedipal conflicts; integration of his personality; and gaining maturity, which includes sexual maturity—what it consists of, and how to gain it? Since detailing what these matters entail would overwhelm and confuse the child, the fairy tale uses universal symbols that permit the child to choose, select, neglect, and interpret the tale in ways congruent with his state of intellectual and psychological development. Whatever this state of development may be, the fairy tale intimates how the child may transcend it, and what may be involved in reaching the next stage on his progress toward mature integration.

A comparison of two well-known children's stories with a fairy tale may illustrate the relative shortcomings of the modern realistic children's story.

There are many modern children's stories, such as *The Little Engine That Could*, which encourage the child to believe that if he tries hard enough and does not give up, he will finally succeed.[39] A young adult recalled how impressed she had been when her mother read her this story. She became convinced that one's attitude indeed affected one's achievements; that if she would now approach a task with the conviction that she could conquer it, she would succeed. A few days later this child encountered in first grade a challenging situation: she was trying to make a house out of paper, gluing various sheets together. But her house continually collapsed. Frustrated, she began to doubt seriously that her idea of building such a paper house could be realized. But then the story of *The Little Engine That Could* came to her mind; twenty years later she recalled how at this moment she began to sing to herself the magic formula "I think I can, I think I can, I think I can. . . ." So she continued to work on her paper house, and it continued to collapse. The project ended in complete defeat, with this little girl convinced that she had failed where anybody else could have succeeded as the Little Engine had.

Since *The Little Engine That Could* is a story set in the present, using such common props as engines that pull trains, this girl had tried to apply its lesson directly in her daily life, without any fantasy elaboration, and had experienced a defeat which still rankled twenty years later.

Very different was the impact of *The Swiss Family Robinson* on another child. The story tells how a shipwrecked family manages to live an adventurous, idyllic, constructive, and pleasurable life—a life very different from what this child's existence was like. Her father had to be away from home a great deal, and her mother was mentally ill and spent protracted periods in institutions. So the girl was shuttled from her home to an aunt, then to a grandmother, and back home again as the need arose. During these years the girl read over and over again the story of this happy family who lived on a desert island, which prevented any member from ever being away from the rest of the family. Many years later she recalled what a warm, cozy feeling she had when, propped up by a few large pillows, she forgot all about her present predicament as she read this story. As soon as she had finished it, she started to read it all over again. The happy hours she spent with the Family Robinson in that fantasy land kept her from being defeated by the difficulties which reality presented to her. She was able to counteract the impact of harsh reality by imaginary gratifications. But since the story was not a fairy tale, it did not hold out any promise that her life would take a turn for the better—a hope which would have made life much more bearable for her.

Another graduate student recalled that as a child "I thrived on fairy tales, traditional ones as well as ones of my own creation. But 'Rapunzel' dominated my thoughts." When this woman was still a little girl, her mother had died in a car accident. The girl's father, deeply upset by what had happened to his wife (he had been driving the car), withdrew entirely into himself, and handed the care of his daughter over to a nurse, who was little interested in the girl. When the girl was seven, her father remarried, and, as she recalled it, it was around that time that "Rapunzel" became so important to her. Her stepmother was clearly the witch of the story, and she was the girl locked away in the tower. The girl recalled that she felt akin to Rapunzel, since the "witch had forcibly" obtained her, as her stepmother had forcibly worked her way into the girl's life. The girl felt imprisoned in her new home, as the nurse who had cared little had given her complete freedom to do as she wanted. She felt as victimized as Rapunzel, who, in her tower, had so little control over her life. Rapunzel's long hair was the key to the story for her. The girl wanted her hair to grow long, but her stepmother cut it short; long hair in itself became the symbol of freedom and happiness to her. As an adult, she realized that the prince for whose coming she had pined was her father. The story convinced her that he would come someday and rescue her, and this conviction sustained her. If life became too difficult, all she needed to do was to imagine herself as Rapunzel, her hair grown long, and the prince loving and rescuing her. And she gave "Rapunzel" a happy ending. In the story the prince was blinded for a time—this meant to her that her father had become blinded, by the "witch" with whom he lived, to how preferable his daughter was—but eventually her hair which the stepmother had cut grew long again, and the prince came to live with her happily forever after.

A comparison of "Rapunzel" with *The Swiss Family Robinson* suggests why fairy tales can offer more to the child than even such a very nice children's story. In *The Swiss Family Robinson* there is no witch whom the child can discharge her anger against in fantasy, and on whom she can blame the father's lack of interest. *The Swiss Family Robinson* offers escape fantasies, and it did help the girl who read it over and over again to forget temporarily how difficult life was for her. But it offered no specific hope for the future. "Rapunzel," on the other hand, offered the girl a chance to see the witch of the story as being so evil that, by comparison, even the "witch" stepmother at home was not all that bad. "Rapunzel" also promised the girl that her rescue would be effected by her own body, when her hair grew long. Most important of all, it promised that the "prince" was only temporarily blinded; that he would regain his sight and rescue his princess. This fantasy continued to sustain the girl, though to a less intense degree, until she fell in love and got married, when she no longer needed it.

We can understand why at first glance the stepmother, if she had known the meaning of "Rapunzel" to her stepdaughter, would have felt that fairy tales are bad for children. What she would not have known was that unless the stepdaughter could find that fantasy satisfaction through "Rapunzel," she would have tried to break up her father's marriage; and without the hope for the future which the story gave her, she might have gone badly astray in life.

It has been argued that when a story raises unrealistic hopes, the child will necessarily experience disappointment and suffer the more because of it. But to suggest to the child reasonable—that is, limited and provisional—hopes for what the future has in store is no palliative for the child's immense anxieties about what will happen to him and his aspirations. His unrealistic fears require unrealistic hopes. By comparison with the child's wishes, realistic and limited promises are experienced as deep disappointment, not as consolation. But they are all that a relatively realistic story can offer.

The fairy tale's extravagant promise of a happy ending would also lead to disenchantment with the child's real life if it were part of a realistic story, or projected as something that will happen where the real child lives. But the fairy story's happy ending occurs in fairyland, a country that we can visit only in our minds.

The fairy tale offers the child hope that someday the kingdom will be his. Since the child cannot settle for less, but does not believe that he can achieve this kingdom on his own, the fairy tale tells him that magic forces will come to his aid. This rekindles hope, which without such fantasy would be extinguished by harsh reality. Since the fairy tale promises the type of triumph the child wishes for, it is psychologically convincing as no "realistic" tale can be. And because it pledges that the kingdom will be his, the child is willing to believe the rest of what the fairy story teaches: that one must leave home to find one's kingdom; that it cannot be gained immediately; that risks must be taken, trials submitted to; that it cannot be done all by oneself, but that one needs helpers; and that to secure their aid, one must meet some of their demands. Just because the ultimate promise coincides with the child's wishes for revenge and a glorious existence, the fairy tale enriches the child's fantasy beyond compare.

The trouble with some of what is considered "good children's literature" is that many of these stories peg the child's imagination to the level he has already reached on his own. Children like such a story, but benefit little from it beyond momentary pleasure. From such stories the child gains neither comfort nor consolation in regard to his pressing problems; he only escapes them for the moment.

For example, there are "realistic" stories in which the child takes his revenge on a parent. When the child moves out of the oedipal stage and is no longer utterly dependent on the parent is when his desire for revenge is most acute. Revenge fantasies are something every child entertains at this time in his life, but in his more lucid moments he recognizes them as extremely unfair, since he knows that the parent provides him with all he needs to survive, and works hard to do so. Ideas of revenge always create guilt, and anxiety about retribution. A story which encourages this fantasy of actually taking revenge increases both, and all the child can do on his own is to repress such ideas. Often the result of such repression is that a dozen years later the adolescent acts out in reality these childish revenge fantasies.

There is no need for the child to repress such fantasies; on the contrary, he can enjoy them to the fullest, if he is subtly guided to direct them to a target which is close enough to the true parent but clearly not his parent. What more suitable object of vengeful thoughts than the person who has usurped the parent's place: the fairy-story step-parent? If one vents vicious fantasies of revenge against such an evil usurper, there is no reason to feel guilty or need to fear retaliation, because that figure clearly deserves it. If it is objected that thoughts of revenge are immoral and the child should not have any such thoughts, it should be stressed that the idea that one should not have certain fantasies has never stopped people from having them, but only banished them into the unconscious, where the resulting havoc to the mental life is much greater. Thus, the fairy story permits the child to have the best of both worlds: he can fully engage in and enjoy revenge fantasies about the step-parent of the story, without any guilt or fear in respect to the true parent.

Milne's poem in which James James Morrison Morrison warns his mother not to go to the end of the town without him because she might never find her way back but disappear forever, which in the poem then actually happens, is a delightfully funny story—to adults.[40] To the child, it gives body to his worst nightmarish anxiety about desertion. What seems funny to the adult is that here the roles of guardian and guarded are reversed. Much as the child may wish that this were so, he cannot entertain the idea when permanent loss of the parent is projected as the outcome. What the child takes pleasure in, on hearing this poem, is the warning to parents never to go without him. He does enjoy that, but then he has to repress the much deeper and greater anxiety that he will be permanently deserted, which is what the poem suggests will happen.

There are quite a few similar modern stories in which the child is more able and more intelligent than the parent, not in never-never-land, as in the fairy tale, but in everyday reality. The child enjoys such a story because it is in line with what he would like to believe; but the ultimate consequences are distrust of the parent on whom he still has to rely, and disappointment—because, contrary to what the story makes him believe, parents remain superior for quite some time.

No traditional fairy tale would rob the child of the needed security he gets from the knowledge that the parent knows better, with one crucial exception: when the parent turns out to have been in error about the child's abilities. The parent in many fairy tales thinks little of one of his children—often called simpleton—who, as the story proceeds, proves the parent wrong in this evaluation of him. Here again the fairy tale is true psychologically. Almost every child is convinced that his parents know better about nearly everything, with one exception: they do not think well enough of him. To encourage this thought is beneficial because it suggests to the child that he should develop his abilities—not to do better than the parent, but to correct the parent's low opinion of the child.

In respect to excelling the parent, the fairy story frequently uses the device of splitting him into two figures: the parent who thinks little of the child, and another figure—a wise old man, or an animal the youngster encounters, who gives him sound advice on how to win out, not over the parent, which would be too scary, but over a preferred sibling. Sometimes this other figure aids the hero in achieving a nearly impossible task, which shows the parent that his low opinion of his child was wrong. The parent is thus split into his doubting and supporting aspects, with the latter winning out.

The fairy-tale rendering of the problem of the competition of the generations, of the child's wish to surpass his parent, is that when a parent feels that the time has become ripe for it, he sends his child (or children) out into the world to prove himself, and thus demonstrate his ability and worthiness to take over from the parent, to replace him. The extraordinary feats which the child performs on his errands, while objectively beyond belief, are not any more fantastic to the child than the idea that he possibly could be superior to his parent and hence replace him.

Tales of this type (which, in different forms, can be found all over the world) begin quite realistically with a father who is getting old and has to decide which of his children is worthy of inheriting his wealth, or of otherwise replacing him. On being presented with the task he has to perform, the story hero feels exactly as the child does: it seems impossible to carry out. Despite this conviction, the fairy tale shows that the task can be mastered, but only through the help of superhuman powers or some other intermediary. And indeed only a most extraordinary achievement can give a child the feeling that he is superior to his parent; to believe in it without such proof would be empty megalomania.

"THE GOOSE GIRL"

ACHIEVING AUTONOMY

Gaining autonomy from one's parents is the topic of a once famous but now less well known Brothers Grimm story, "The Goose Girl." In variations, this story can be found in nearly all European countries, as well as on other continents. In the Brothers Grimm's version, the tale begins: "There once lived an old queen whose husband had died many years ago, and she had a beautiful daughter. . . . When the time came for her to be married and the child had to travel into the alien country," the mother gave her precious jewelry and treasures. A chambermaid was assigned to accompany her. Each woman was given a horse to ride on, but the princess' horse could talk, and was named Falada.[41] "When the hour of parting had arrived, the old mother went into her bedchamber, took a small knife and cut her fingers until she bled; then she let three drops of blood fall onto a white handkerchief, gave it to her daughter and said, 'Preserve this carefully, dear child, it will be of great service to you on your trip.' " After the two had been traveling for an hour, the princess got thirsty and asked the maid to fetch her some water from a stream in her golden cup. The maid refused, and seized the princess' cup, telling her to get down and drink from the river; that she would no longer be her servant.

Later on, the same thing happened again, but this time as the princess bent over to drink, she dropped and lost the handkerchief with the three drops of blood; with this loss she became weak and powerless. The maid took advantage of this and forced the princess to change horses and dresses, making her swear to tell no person at the royal court of this exchange. On arrival, the maid was taken for the princess-bride. Asked about her companion, she told the old king that he should give her some work to do, and the princess was assigned to help a boy tend geese. Soon afterward the false bride asked the young king, her betrothed, the favor of having Falada's head chopped off, because she feared the horse would reveal her evil deed. This was done, but the horse's head, thanks to the pleading of the real princess, was nailed over a dark gateway through which the princess had to pass each day when she went out to tend the geese.

Each morning as the princess and the boy with whom she was herding geese passed through the gate, she greeted Falada's head with great sorrow, to which it replied:

> "If this your mother knew,
> Her heart would break in two."

Out in the pasture, the princess let her hair down. Since it was like pure gold, it tempted the boy to try to pluck some out, which the princess prevented by summoning a wind which blew away the boy's hat so that he had to run after it. The same events were repeated on two consecutive days, which so greatly annoyed the boy that he complained to the old king. On the next day the old king hid at the gate and observed it all. In the evening, on the goose girl's return to the castle, he inquired what these things meant. She told him that she was bound by a vow not to tell any human being. She resisted his pressure to reveal her story, but finally followed his suggestion to tell it to the hearth. The old king hid behind the hearth so that he could learn the goose girl's story.

After this, the true princess was given royal garments, and everybody was invited to a great feast, at which the true bride sat on one side of the young king, the pretender on the other. At the end of the meal the old king asked the pretender what would be the right punishment for a person who had acted in a certain way—and he described to her the way she had in fact behaved. The pretender, not knowing she was found out, answered: " 'She deserves nothing better than to be stripped naked and to be put into a barrel studded inside with pointed nails; and two white horses should drag it up street and down until she is dead.' 'It's you,' said the old king, 'and you have found your own sentence, and thus shall it happen to you.' And when the sentence was carried out, the young king married his right bride, and both ruled their kingdom in peace and sanctity."

At the very beginning of this tale, the problem of the succession of generations is projected as the old queen sends her daughter to be betrothed to a faraway prince—that is, to establish a life of her own, independent of her parents. Despite great hardship, the princess keeps her promise not to reveal to any human being what has happened to her; thus she proves her moral virtue, which finally brings about retribution and a happy ending. Here the dangers which the heroine must master are inner ones: not to give in to the temptation to reveal the secret. But the main theme of this tale is the usurpation of the hero's place by a pretender.

The reason this story and motif are widely found among all cultures is their oedipal meaning. While the main figure is usually female, the story also appears with a male hero—as in the best-known English version of the story, "Roswal and Lillian," in which a boy is sent to the court of another king to be educated, which makes it even clearer that the theme concerns the process of growing up, maturing, and coming into one's own.[42] As in "The Goose Girl," on the boy's trip his attendant forces him to change places with him. Arriving at the foreign court, the usurper is taken for the prince, who, though degraded to the role of a servant, nevertheless wins the heart of the princess. Through the help of benevolent figures, the usurper is unmasked and in the end severely punished, while the prince is restored to his rightful place. Since the pretender in this tale also tried to replace the hero in his marriage, the plot is essentially the same, with only the sex of the hero changed, which suggests that it is not important. This is because the story deals with an oedipal problem which occurs in the lives of girls and boys alike.

"The Goose Girl" gives symbolic body to two opposite facets of oedipal development. In the earlier stage a child believes that the parent of his own sex is a pretender who has wrongfully assumed the child's place in the affections of the parent of the other sex, who would really much prefer having him as a marital partner. The child suspects that the parent of the same sex, through his cunning (he was around before the child arrived), has cheated him out of what ought to be his birthright, and hopes that through some higher intervention things will be righted and he will become the partner of the parent of the other sex.

This fairy tale also guides the child out of the early oedipal stage to the next higher one, when wishful thinking is replaced by a somewhat more correct view of the child's true situation during the oedipal phase. As he grows in understanding and maturity, the child begins to comprehend that his thought that the parent of the same sex is arrogating the place which should be his does not accord with reality. He begins to realize that it is *he* who wishes to be the usurper, and *he* who desires to take the place of the parent of the same sex. "The Goose Girl" warns that one must give up such ideas because of the terrible retribution which is meted out to those who, for a time, succeed in replacing the rightful marital partner. The story shows it is better to accept one's place as a child than to try to take that of a parent, much as one may desire to do so.

Some might wonder whether it makes any difference to children that this motif appears mainly in story versions having a heroine. But irrespective of the child's sex, this story strongly impresses any child because on a preconscious level the child comprehends that the tale deals with oedipal problems which are very much his own. In one of his most famous poems, "Germany, a Winter Fairy Tale" *("Deutschland, ein Wintermärchen")*, Heinrich Heine tells what a deep impression "The Goose Girl" made on him. He writes:

> How my heart used to beat when the old nurse told how
> The king's daughter, in days now olden,
> Sat alone on the desert heath
> While glistened her tresses so golden.
>
> Her business was to tend the geese
> As a goose girl, and when at nightfall
> She drove the geese home again through the gate
> Her tears would in piteous plight fall. . . .[43]

"The Goose Girl" also contains the important lesson that the parent, even if she is as powerful as a queen, is helpless to assure her child's development to maturity. To become himself, the child must face the trials of his life on his own; he cannot depend on the parent to rescue him from the consequences of his own weakness. Since all the treasure and jewels given the princess by her mother are of no help to her, this suggests that what a parent can give his child by way of earthly goods is of little aid if the child does not know how to use it well. As her last gift, and the most important one, the queen gives her daughter the handkerchief with the three drops of her own blood. But the princess loses even that through carelessness.

The three drops of blood as a symbol of achieving sexual maturity will be discussed more fully later in connection with "Snow White" and "The Sleeping Beauty." Since the princess leaves to get married and thus is to change from a maiden to a woman and wife, and her mother stresses the importance of the gift of the handkerchief with the blood even over the talking horse, it does not seem farfetched to think that these drops of blood spilled onto a piece of white linen symbolize sexual maturity, a special bond forged by a mother who is preparing her daughter to become sexually active.*

*How important an element these three drops of blood are in this fairy tale can be seen from the fact that one German version of the story, found in Lorraine, is titled "The Cloth with the Three Drops of Blood." In a French story the gift with the magic power is a golden apple, reminiscent of the apple given to Eve in paradise, which signifies sexual knowledge.[44]

Therefore, when the princess loses the fateful token which, if she had held on to it, would have protected her against the nefarious doings of the usurper, this suggests that deep down she was not yet mature enough to become a woman. One might think that her negligently losing the handkerchief was a "Freudian" slip, by means of which she avoided what she did not wish to be reminded of: the impending loss of her maidenhood. As a goose girl, her role reverted to being a young unmarried girl, an immaturity further emphasized by her having to join a little boy in herding the geese. But the story tells that hanging on to one's immaturity when it is time to become mature brings about tragedy for oneself and those closest to one, such as the faithful horse Falada.

The verses Falada speaks three times—each time in response to the goose girl's lament on encountering its head: "Oh, Falada, thou who hangest there"—do not so much bemoan the girl's fate as express the helpless grief of her mother. Falada's implied admonition is that not only for her own sake, but also for her mother's, the princess should stop accepting passively whatever happens to her. It is also a subtle accusation that, had the princess not acted so immaturely in dropping and losing the handkerchief and in letting herself be pushed around by her maid, Falada would not have been killed. All the bad things that happen are the girl's own fault because she fails to assert herself. Not even the talking horse can help her out of her predicament.

The story emphasizes the difficulties one encounters on life's voyage: coming into sexual maturity, gaining independence and self-realization. Dangers must be overcome, ordeals endured, decisions made; but the story tells that if one remains true to oneself and one's values, then, despite how desperate things may look for a while, there will be a happy ending. And, of course, in line with the resolution of the oedipal situation, the story stresses that to usurp another person's place because one desires it so much will be the usurper's destruction. The only way to come into one's own is through one's own doing.

One could compare once more the depth of this short fairy tale—it is barely five printed pages long—with a modern story mentioned before that has found very wide acceptance, *The Little Engine That Could,* which also encourages the child to believe that if he tries hard enough, he will finally succeed. This modern story and others like it do give the child hope and thus serve a good but very limited purpose. But the child's deeper unconscious desires and anxieties remain untouched by them, and in the last analysis it is these unconscious elements that stand in the way of the child's trusting himself in life. Such stories neither directly nor indirectly reveal to the child his deeper anxieties, nor offer relief at the level of these pressing feelings. Contrary to *The Little Engine*'s message, success does not, by itself, do away with inner difficulties. Otherwise there would not be so many adults who keep trying, who do not give up, and who finally succeed in achieving externals, but whose inner difficulties remain unrelieved by their "success."

The child is not simply afraid of failure as such, though it is part of his anxiety. But this is what the authors of such stories seem to think, maybe because this is what adults' fears center on: i.e., the disadvantages failure realistically brings about. The child's anxiety over failure centers on the idea that if he should fail, he will be rejected, deserted, and utterly destroyed. Thus, only a story in which some ogre or other evil figure threatens the hero with destruction if he should fail to show himself strong enough to stand up to the usurper is correct according to the child's psychological view of the consequences of his failure.

Final success is experienced as meaningless by the child if his underlying unconscious anxieties are not also resolved. In the fairy tale, this is symbolized by the destruction of the evildoer. Without that, the hero's finally achieving his rightful place would not be complete, because if evil continued to exist, it would remain a permanent threat.

Adults often think that the cruel punishment of an evil person in fairy tales upsets and scares children unnecessarily. Quite the opposite is true: such retribution reassures the child that the punishment fits the crime. The child often feels unjustly treated by adults and the world in general, and it seems that nothing is done about it. On the basis of such experiences alone, he wants those who cheat and degrade him—as the imposter maid cheats the princess in this story—most severely punished. If they are not, the child thinks that nobody is serious about protecting him; but the more severely those bad ones are dealt with, the more secure the child feels.

Here it is important to note that the usurper pronounces her own sentence. As the maid chose to take the place of the princess, so now she chooses the manner of her own destruction; both are the consequence of her viciousness which makes her invent such a cruel punishment—thus, it is not inflicted on her from the outside. The message is that evil intentions are the evil person's own undoing. In choosing two white horses as executioners, the usurper reveals her unconscious guilt about having done away with Falada—since it was the horse on which a bride rode to her wedding, one assumes that Falada was white, the color standing for purity, so it seems fitting that white horses avenge Falada. The child appreciates this all on a preconscious level.

It was mentioned before that success in meeting external tasks is not sufficient to quiet inner anxieties. Therefore, a child needs to receive suggestions as to what else besides persevering is needed. It may seem on the surface that the Goose Girl does nothing to change her fate and is restored only thanks to the interference of benevolent powers or of chance, which sets the king's discovery and her rescue going. But what may seem like nothing or very little to an adult is understood as a considerable achievement by a child, who also can do very little to change his fate at any moment. The fairy tale suggests that it is less impressive deeds which count, but an inner development must take place for the hero to gain true autonomy. Independence and transcending childhood require personality development, not becoming better at a particular task, or doing battle with external difficulties.

I have already discussed how "The Goose Girl" projects the two aspects of the oedipal situation: feeling that a usurper has taken one's rightful place, and the later recognition that the child wishes to usurp a position that in reality belongs to his parent. The story also highlights the dangers of a childish dependence clung to for too long a time. The heroine at first transfers her dependence from her parent to her attendant, and does as she is told, without using her own judgment. As a child does not wish to give up dependence, so does the Goose Girl fail to respond to the change in her situation; this, the story tells, is her undoing. Holding on to dependence will not gain her higher humanity. If she goes out into the world—as symbolized by the princess's leaving home to gain her kingdom somewhere else—she must become independent. This is the lesson the Goose Girl learns while tending geese.

The boy who is her partner in herding the geese tries to rule her, as the maid had done on the trip to her new home. Motivated only by his own desires, he disregards the princess' autonomy. On the trip away from her childhood home, she let the maid get away with taking her golden drinking cup. Now as the princess sits down in the pasture and combs her hair (the tresses that "glistened . . . so golden" in Heine's poem), the boy wants to get hold of her hair, to usurp, so to say, part of her body. This she does not permit; now she knows how to ward him off. Where she was too fearful of the maid's anger to resist her, now she knows better than to permit herself to be pushed around by the boy's anger at her for not giving in to his desires. The stress in the story that both the cup and the girl's hair are golden alerts the listener to the importance of the girl's *different* reactions to similar situations.

It is his anger at the Goose Girl's refusal to do his bidding which leads the boy to complain to the king about her, and thus brings about the denouement. It is the heroine's assertion of herself when degraded by the boy which is the turning point in her life. She, who dared no opposition when the maid had degraded her, has learned what autonomy requires. This is confirmed by her *not* going against her sworn statement, unlawfully though it had been extracted from her. She realizes that she should not have permitted herself to make this promise, but once it is made, she must keep it. But this does not preclude her telling the secret to an object, as a child will feel free to pour out his grief to some toy. The hearth, which stands for the sanctity of the home, is an apt object to confess her sad fate to. In the Brothers Grimm's story the hearth has become an oven or stove, which, as the place where food is prepared, also stands for basic security. But the essential is that by asserting her dignity and the inviolability of her body—the girl's refusal to let the boy pull off some of her hair against her will—the happy solution came about. The evildoer could think only of trying to be—or appear to be—somebody she was not. The Goose Girl learned that it is much harder to be truly oneself, but that this alone will gain her true autonomy and change her fate.

FANTASY, RECOVERY, ESCAPE, AND CONSOLATION

The shortcomings of modern fairy stories highlight the elements which are most enduring in traditional fairy tales. Tolkien describes the facets which are necessary in a good fairy tale as fantasy, recovery, escape, and consolation—recovery from deep despair, escape from some great danger, but, most of all, consolation. Speaking of the happy ending, Tolkien stresses that all complete fairy stories must have it. It is "a sudden joyous 'turn.'" . . . However fantastic or terrible the adventure, it can give to child or man that hears it, when the 'turn' comes, a catch of breath, a beat and lifting of the heart, near to tears."[45]

How understandable, then, that when children are asked to name their favorite fairy tales, hardly any modern tales are among their choices.[46] Many of these new tales have sad endings, which fail to provide the escape and consolation which the fearsome events in the fairy tale make necessary, to strengthen the child for meeting the vagaries of his life. Without such encouraging conclusions, the child, after listening to the story, would feel that there is indeed no hope of extricating himself from the despairs of his life.

In the traditional fairy tale, the hero is rewarded and the evil person meets his well-deserved fate, thus satisfying the child's deep need for justice to prevail. How else can a child hope that justice will be done to him, who so often feels unfairly treated? And how else can he convince himself that he must act correctly, when he is so sorely tempted to give in to the asocial proddings of his desires? Chesterton once remarked that some children with whom he saw Maeterlinck's play *The Blue Bird* were dissatisfied "because it did not end with a Day of Judgment, and it was not revealed to the hero and the heroine that the Dog had been faithful and the Cat faithless. For children are innocent and love justice, while most of us are wicked and naturally prefer mercy."[47]

One may rightly question Chesterton's belief in the innocence of children, but he is absolutely correct in observing that the appreciation of mercy for the unjust, while characteristic of a mature mind, baffles the child. Furthermore, consolation not only requires, but is the direct result of, justice (or, in the case of adult listeners, mercy) being done.

It seems particularly appropriate to a child that exactly what the evildoer wishes to inflict on the hero should be the bad person's fate —as the witch in "Hansel and Gretel" who wants to cook children in the oven is pushed into it and burned to death, or the usurper in "The Goose Girl" who names and suffers her own punishment. Consolation requires that the right order of the world is restored; this means punishment of the evildoer, tantamount to the elimination of evil from the hero's world—and then nothing stands any longer in the way of the hero's living happily ever after.

Maybe it would be appropriate to add one more element to the four Tolkien enumerates. I believe that an element of threat is crucial to the fairy tale—a threat to the hero's physical existence or to his moral existence, as the Goose Girl's degradation is experienced as a moral predicament by the child. If one contemplates it, it is startling how the fairy-tale hero accepts without question that he is thus threatened

—it just happens. The angry fairy utters a curse in "The Sleeping Beauty," and nothing can prevent it from coming to pass, at least in its reduced form. Snow White does not wonder why the queen pursues her with such deadly jealousy, nor do the dwarfs, although they warn Snow White to avoid the queen. No question is raised as to why the enchantress in Rapunzel wants to take her away from her parents —it just happens to poor Rapunzel. The rare exceptions concern a stepmother's wanting to promote her own children at the expense of the heroine, as in "Cinderella"—but even then we are not told why Cinderella's father permits it.

In any case, as soon as the story begins, the hero is projected into severe dangers. And this is how the child sees life, even when in actuality his own life proceeds in very favorable circumstances, as far as externals are concerned. To the child it seems that his life is a sequence of periods of smooth living which are suddenly and incomprehensibly interrupted as he is projected into immense danger. He has felt secure, with hardly a worry in the world, but in an instant everything changes, and the friendly world turns into a nightmare of dangers. This happens when a loving parent suddenly makes what seem like utterly unreasonable demands and terrifying threats. A child is convinced that there is no reasonable cause for these things; they just occur; it is his inexorable fate that it should happen. Then the child either gives in to his despair (and some fairy-tale heroes do exactly that—sit there crying until a magic helper arrives and shows the way to proceed and combat the threat) or else he attempts to run away from it all, trying to escape a horrid fate as Snow White did: "The poor child was desperately alone in the vast forest and was so terrified . . . that she did not know how to help herself. So she began to run and run over pointed stones and through the thorns."

There is no greater threat in life than that we will be deserted, left all alone. Psychoanalysis has named this—man's greatest fear—separation anxiety; and the younger we are, the more excruciating is our anxiety when we feel deserted, for the young child actually perishes when not adequately protected and taken care of. Therefore, the ultimate consolation is that we shall never be deserted. There is a cycle of Turkish fairy tales in which the heroes again and again find themselves in the most impossible situations, but succeed in evading or overcoming the danger as soon as they have gained a friend. For example, in one famous fairy tale the hero, Iskender, arouses the enmity of his mother, who forces his father to put Iskender into a casket and set him adrift on the ocean. Iskender's helper is a green bird, which rescues him from this and innumerable later dangers, each more threatening than the preceding one. The bird assures Iskender each time with the words "Know, that you are never deserted."[48] This, then, is the ultimate consolation, the one that is implied in the common fairy-tale ending, "And they lived happily ever after."

The happiness and fulfillment which are the ultimate consolation of the fairy tale have meaning on two levels. The permanent union of, for example, a prince and a princess symbolizes the integration of the disparate aspects of the personality—psychoanalytically speaking, the id, ego, and superego—and of achieving a harmony of the theretofore discordant tendencies of the male and the female principles, as discussed in connection with the ending of "Cinderella."

Ethically speaking, that union symbolizes, through the punishment and elimination of evil, moral unity on the highest plane—and, at the same time, that separation anxiety is forever transcended when the ideal partner has been found with whom the most satisfying personal relation is established. Depending on the fairy tale and what psychological problem area or developmental level it is mainly addressing, this takes quite different external forms, although the intrinsic meaning is always the same.

For example, in "Brother and Sister," during most of the story the two do not part; they represent the animal and spiritual sides of our personality, which become separated but must be integrated for human happiness. But the main threat occurs after the sister has married her king and is replaced by a usurper after she gives birth to a child. Sister still returns nightly, to take care of her child and her fawn-brother. Her recovery is described as follows: "The king . . . sprang towards her and said, 'You can't be anybody but my dear wife.' At that she answered, 'Yes, I am your dear wife,' and in the same moment she was restored to life by the grace of God, was fresh, rosy and of good health." The ultimate consolation has to wait until evil is done away with: "The witch was cast into the fire and had to burn miserably till she was dead. And as she was burnt to ashes the little deer was returned to his human form, but little sister and little brother lived happily united until their end." Thus the "happy ending," the final consolation, consists of both the integration of the personality and the establishment of a permanent relation.

On the surface, things are different in "Hansel and Gretel." These children achieve their higher humanity as soon as the witch is burned to death, and this is symbolized by the treasures they gain. But since the two are definitely not of marriageable age, the establishment of human relations which will forever ban separation anxiety is symbolized not by their getting married, but by their happy return home to their father, where—with the death of the other evil figure, the mother—now "All worries had ended, and they lived together in pure joyfulness."

Compared to what these just and consoling endings tell about the hero's development, the hero's suffering in many modern fairy tales, while deeply moving, seems much less purposeful because it does not lead to the ultimate form of human existence. (Naïve as it may seem, the prince and princess getting married and inheriting the kingdom, ruling it in peace and happiness, symbolizes to the child the highest possible form of existence because this is all he desires for himself: to run his kingdom—his own life—successfully, peacefully, and to be happily united with the most desirable partner who will never leave him.)

Failure to experience recovery and consolation is true enough in reality, but this hardly encourages the child to meet life with steadfastness which will permit him to accept that going through severe trials can lead to existing on a higher plane. Consolation is the greatest service the fairy tale can offer a child: the confidence that, despite all tribulations he has to suffer (such as the threat of desertion by parents in "Hansel and Gretel"; jealousy on the part of parents in "Snow White" and of siblings in "Cinderella"; the devouring anger of the giant in "Jack and the Beanstalk"; the nastiness of evil powers in "The Sleeping Beauty"), not only will he succeed, but the evil forces will be done away with and never again threaten his peace of mind.

Prettified or bowdlerized fairy tales are rightly rejected by any child who has heard them in their original form. It does not seem fitting to the child that Cinderella's evil sisters should go scot-free, or even be elevated by Cinderella. Such magnanimity does not impress the child favorably, nor will he learn it from a parent who bowdlerizes the story so the just and the wicked are both rewarded. The child knows better what he needs to be told. When a seven-year-old was read the story of "Snow White," an adult, anxious not to disturb the child's mind, ended the story with Snow White's wedding. The child, who knew the story, promptly demanded: "What about the red-hot shoes that killed the wicked queen?" The child feels that all's well with the world, and that he can be secure in it, only if the wicked are punished in the end.

This does not mean that the fairy tale fails to take into account the

vast difference between evil as such and the unfortunate consequences of selfish behavior. "Rapunzel" illustrates this point. Despite
the fact that eventually the sorceress forces Rapunzel to live in a
desert "in great grief and misery," the sorceress is not punished for
it. The reason becomes clear from the events of the story. Rapunzel
is named after the German word for rampion (a European vegetable
used in salads), and her name is the clue for understanding what
happens. Rapunzel's mother, while pregnant with Rapunzel, was beset by a huge desire for the rampion which grew in the walled-in
garden of the sorceress. She persuaded her husband to enter the
forbidden garden and get her some rampion. The second time he did
so, he was caught by the sorceress, who threatened to punish him for
his thievery. He pleaded his case: his pregnant wife's uncontrollable
desire for rampion. The sorceress, moved by his plea, permitted him
to take as much of her rampion as he wished, provided "you give me
the child your wife will give birth to. The child will fare well, and I
shall take care of it like a mother." The father agreed to those conditions. Thus the sorceress gains the care of Rapunzel because her parents had, first, transgressed into her forbidden domain and, second,
agreed to hand Rapunzel over. So the sorceress wanted Rapunzel
more than her parents did, or so it seems.

All goes well until Rapunzel is twelve years old—that is, as one must
guess from the story, she reaches the age of sexual maturity. With this,
there is danger that she may leave her adoptive mother. True, it is
selfish of the sorceress to try to hold on to Rapunzel no matter what,
by secluding her in an inaccessible chamber in a tower. While it is
wrong to deprive Rapunzel of the liberty to move about, the sorceress' desperate wish not to let go of Rapunzel does not seem a serious
crime in the eyes of a child, who wants desperately to be held on to
by his parents.

The sorceress visits Rapunzel in her tower by climbing up by her
tresses—the same tresses which permit Rapunzel to establish a relation to the prince. Thus the transfer from a relationship established
to a parent to that of a lover is symbolized. Rapunzel must know how
terribly important she is to her sorceress substitute-mother, because
in this story occurs one of the rare "Freudian" slips to be found in fairy
tales: Rapunzel, obviously guilty about her clandestine meetings with
the prince, spills her secret as she asks the unwary sorceress, "How
come you are so much heavier to pull up than the young son of the
king?"

Even a child knows that nothing causes greater fury than love betrayed, and Rapunzel, even while thinking about her prince, knew that the sorceress loved her. Although selfish love is wrong and always loses out, as does the sorceress', again the child can understand that if one loves somebody exclusively, one does not want some other person to enjoy that love and deprive one. To love so selfishly and foolishly is wrong, but not evil. The sorceress does not destroy the prince; all she does is gloat when he becomes deprived of Rapunzel as *she* is. The prince's tragedy is the result of his own doing: in his despair that Rapunzel is gone, he jumps down from the tower, falling into thorns which pierce his eyes. Having acted foolishly and selfishly, the sorceress loses out—but since she acted from too much love for Rapunzel and not out of wickedness, no harm befalls her.

I mentioned before how consoling it is to the child to be told, in symbolic fashion, that in his own body he possesses the means to gain what he wishes—as the prince reaches Rapunzel on her tresses. The happy ending in Rapunzel is again brought about by Rapunzel's body: her tears heal her lover's eyes, and with this they regain their kingdom.

"Rapunzel" illustrates fantasy, escape, recovery, and consolation, although innumerable other folk fairy tales could serve equally well. The story unfolds as one deed is balanced by another, following each other with geometrical ethical rigor: rampion (Rapunzel) stolen leads to rampion returned from where it was originally taken. The selfishness of the mother, which forces her husband to take the rampion illegally, is balanced by the selfishness of the sorceress, who wishes to keep Rapunzel to herself. The fantastic element is that which provides the final consolation: the power of the body is imaginatively exaggerated by the overlong tresses, on which one can climb up a tower, and by the tears, which can restore sight. But what more reliable source of recovery do we have than our own body?

Both Rapunzel and the prince act immaturely: he spies on the sorceress and sneaks up the tower behind her back, instead of openly approaching her with his love for Rapunzel. And Rapunzel also cheats by not telling what she did, short of her revealing slip. This is why Rapunzel's removal from the tower and her domination by the sorceress do not immediately bring about the happy ending. Both Rapunzel and the prince have to undergo a period of trial and tribulation, of inner growth through misfortune—as is true for the heroes of many fairy tales.

The child is unaware of his inner processes, which is why these are externalized in the fairy tale and symbolically represented by actions standing for inner and outer struggles. But deep concentration is also required for personal growth. This is typically symbolized in fairy tales by years devoid of overt events, suggesting inner, silent developments. Thus, the physical escape of the child from his parents' domination is followed by a lengthy period of recovery, of gaining maturity.

In the story, after Rapunzel's banishment into the desert, the time comes when she is no longer taken care of by her substitute mother, nor the prince by his parents. Both of them now have to learn to take care of themselves, even in the most adverse circumstances. Their relative immaturity is suggested by their having given up hope—not trusting the future really means not trusting oneself. That is why neither the prince nor Rapunzel is able to search with determination for the other. He, we are told, "wandered blindly through the forest, ate nothing but roots and berries, and did nothing but moan and cry because he had lost his beloved." Nor are we told that Rapunzel did much of a positive nature; she too lived in misery and moaned and decried her fate. We must assume, nevertheless, that it was for both a period of growing, of finding themselves, an era of recovery. At its end they are ready not only to rescue each other, but to make a good life, one for the other.

ON THE TELLING
OF FAIRY STORIES

To attain to the full its consoling propensities, its symbolic meanings, and, most of all, its interpersonal meanings, a fairy tale should be told rather than read. If it is read, it ought to be read with emotional involvement in the story and in the child, with empathy for what the story may mean to him. Telling is preferable to reading because it permits greater flexibility.

It was mentioned before that the folk fairy tale, as distinct from more recently invented fairy tales, is the result of a story being shaped and reshaped by being told millions of times, by different adults to all kinds of other adults and children. Each narrator, as he told the story, dropped and added elements to make it more meaningful to himself and to the listeners, whom he knew well. When talking to a child, the adult responded to what he surmised from the child's reactions. Thus the narrator let his unconscious understanding of what the story told be influenced by that of the child. Successive narrators adapted the story according to the questions the child asked, the delight and fear he expressed openly or indicated by the way he snuggled up against the adult. Slavishly sticking to the way a fairy story is printed robs it of much of its value. The telling of the story to a child, to be most effective, has to be an interpersonal event, shaped by those who participate in it.

There is no getting around the possibility that this also contains some pitfalls. A parent not attuned to his child, or too beholden to what goes on in his own unconscious, may choose to tell fairy tales on the basis of *his* needs—rather than those of the child. But even if he does, all is not lost. The child will better understand what moves his parent, and this is of great interest and value to him in comprehending the motives of those most important in his life.

An example of this occurred when a father was about to leave his much more competent wife and his five-year-old son, both of whom he had failed to support for some time. He worried that his son would be entirely in the power of his wife, whom he thought of as a domineering woman, when he was no longer around. One evening the boy requested that the father tell him a bedtime story. His father chose "Hansel and Gretel"; and when the narrative reached the point where Hansel had been put into the cage and was being fattened to be eaten by the witch, the father began to yawn and said he felt too tired to continue; he left the boy, went to bed, and fell asleep. Thus Hansel was left in the power of the devouring witch without any support—as the father thought that he was about to leave his son in the power of his dominant wife.

Although only five years old, the boy understood that his father was about to abandon him, and that his father thought his mother a threatening person, but that he nonetheless saw no way to protect or to rescue his son. While the boy may have had a bad night, he decided that since there seemed to be no hope of his father's taking good care of him, he would have to come to terms with the situation he faced with his mother. The next day he told his mother what had happened, and spontaneously added that even if Father were not around, he knew that Mother would always take good care of him.

Fortunately, children not only know how to deal with such parental distortions of fairy tales, but they also have their own ways of dealing with story elements which run counter to their emotional needs. They do this by changing the story around and remembering it differently from its original version, or by adding details to it. The fantastic ways in which the stories unfold encourage such spontaneous changes; stories which deny the irrational in us do not as easily permit such variations. It is fascinating to view the changes which even the most widely known stories undergo in the minds of individuals, notwithstanding the fact that the story's events are such common knowledge.

One boy reversed the story of Hansel and Gretel so that it was Gretel who was put in the cage, and Hansel who conceived of the idea of using a bone to fool the witch, and who pushed her into the oven, thereby freeing Gretel. To add some female distortions of fairy tales which made them conform to individual needs: a girl remembered "Hansel and Gretel" with the change that it was the father who insisted that the children had to be cast out, despite his wife's entreaties not to do so, and that the father did his evil deed behind his wife's back.

A young lady remembered "Hansel and Gretel" mainly as a story depicting Gretel's dependency on her older brother, and objected to its "male chauvinistic" character. As far as her recollection of the story went—and she claimed to remember it very vividly—it was Hansel who managed to escape by his own wits and who pushed the witch into the oven and thus rescued Gretel. On rereading the story, she was much surprised by the way her memory had distorted it, but realized that all through her childhood she had relished her dependence on a somewhat older brother and, as she put it, "I have been unwilling to accept my own strength and the responsibilities that go along with that awareness." There was another reason why in early adolescence this distortion was strongly reinforced. While her brother had been abroad, her mother had died and she had had to make the arrangements for the cremation. Therefore, even on rereading the fairy tale as an adult she felt revulsion at the idea that it was Gretel who was responsible for the witch being burned to death; it reminded her too painfully of the cremation of her mother. Unconsciously she had understood the story well, especially the degree to which the witch represented the bad mother about whom we all harbor negative feelings, but feel guilty about them. Another girl recalled with rich detail how Cinderella's going to the ball was made possible by her father, despite the stepmother's objections.

I mentioned before that, ideally, the telling of a fairy story should be an interpersonal event into which adult and child enter as equal partners, as can never be the case when a story is read to a child. A story of Goethe's childhood illustrates this.

Long before Freud spoke about id and superego, Goethe from his own experience divined that they were the building blocks of personality. Fortunately for him, in his life each of the two was represented by a parent. "From father I got my bearings, the seriousness in life's pursuits; from mother the enjoyment of life, and love of spinning fantasies."[49] Goethe knew that to be able to enjoy life, to make the hard work of it palatable, we need a rich fantasy life. The account of how Goethe gained some of this ability and self-confidence through his mother's telling him fairy tales illustrates how fairy tales ought to be told, and how they can bind parent and child together by each making his own contributions. Goethe's mother recounted in her old age:

"Air, fire, water and earth I presented to him as beautiful princesses, and everything in all nature took on a deeper meaning," she reminisced. "We invented roads between stars, and what great minds we would encounter. . . . He devoured me with his eyes; and if the fate of one of his favorites did not go as he wished, this I could see from the anger in his face, or his efforts not to break out in tears. Occasionally he interfered by saying: 'Mother, the princess will *not* marry the miserable tailor, even if he slays the giant,' at which I stopped and postponed the catastrophe until the next evening. So my imagination often was replaced by his; and when the following morning I arranged fate according to his suggestions and said, 'You guessed it, that's how it came out,' he was all excited, and one could see his heart beating."[50]

Not every parent can invent stories as well as Goethe's mother—who during her lifetime was known as a great teller of fairy stories. She told the stories in line with her listeners' inner feelings of how things should proceed in the tale, and this was considered the right way to tell these stories. Unfortunately, many modern parents were never themselves told fairy tales as children; and, having thus been deprived of the intense pleasure, and enrichment of the inner life, that these stories give to a child, even the best of parents cannot be spontaneous in providing his child with what was absent from his own experience. In that case, an intellectual understanding of how meaningful a fairy tale can be for his child, and why, must replace direct empathy based on recollections of one's own childhood.

When speaking here of an intellectual understanding of the meaning of a fairy tale, it should be emphasized that it will not do to approach the telling of fairy tales with didactic intentions. When in various contexts throughout this book it is mentioned that a fairy tale helps the child to understand himself, guides him to find solutions to the problems that beset him, etc., this is always meant metaphorically.

If listening to a fairy tale permits a child to achieve this for himself, that he may be able to do so was not the conscious intention either of those who in the dim past invented a story, or of those who in retelling it hand it down the generations. The purpose in telling a fairy story ought to be that of Goethe's mother: a shared experience of enjoying the tale, although what makes for this enjoyment may be quite different for child and adult. While the child enjoys the fantasy, the adult may well derive his pleasure from the child's enjoyment; while the child may be elated because he now understands something about himself better, the adult's delight in telling the story may derive from the child's experiencing a sudden shock of recognition.

A fairy tale is most of all a work of art, about which Goethe said in his prologue to *Faust*, "Who offers many things will offer some to many a one."[51] This implies that any deliberate attempt to offer something specific to a particular person cannot be the purpose of a work of art. Listening to a fairy tale and taking in the images it presents may be compared to a scattering of seeds, only some of which will be implanted in the mind of the child. Some of these will be working in his conscious mind right away; others will stimulate processes in his unconscious. Still others will need to rest for a long time until the child's mind has reached a state suitable for their germination, and many will never take root at all. But those seeds which have fallen on the right soil will grow into beautiful flowers and sturdy trees—that is, give validity to important feelings, promote insights, nourish hopes, reduce anxieties—and in doing so enrich the child's life at the moment and forever after. Telling a fairy tale with a particular purpose other than that of enriching the child's experience turns the fairy story into a cautionary tale, a fable, or some other didactic experience which at best speaks to the child's conscious mind, while reaching the child's unconscious directly also is one of the greatest merits of this literature.

If the parent tells his child fairy tales in the right spirit—that is, with feelings evoked in himself both through remembering the meaning the story had for him when he was a child, and through its different present meaning to him; and with sensitivity for the reasons why his child may also derive some personal meaning from hearing the tale —then, as he listens, the child feels understood in his most tender longings, his most ardent wishes, his most severe anxieties and feelings of misery, as well as in his highest hopes. Since what the parent tells him in some strange way happens also to enlighten him about what goes on in the darker and irrational aspects of his mind, this shows the child that he is not alone in his fantasy life, that it is shared by the person he needs and loves most. In such favorable conditions, fairy tales subtly offer suggestions on how to deal constructively with these inner experiences. The fairy story communicates to the child an intuitive, subconscious understanding of his own nature and of what his future may hold if he develops his positive potentials. He senses from fairy tales that to be a human being in this world of ours means having to accept difficult challenges, but also encountering wondrous adventures.

One must never "explain" to the child the meanings of fairy tales. However, the narrator's understanding of the fairy tale's message to the child's preconscious mind is important. The narrator's comprehension of the tale's many levels of meaning facilitates the child's deriving from the story clues for understanding himself better. It furthers the adult's sensitivity to selection of those stories which are most appropriate to the child's state of development, and to the specific psychological difficulties he is confronted with at the moment.

Fairy tales describe inner states of the mind by means of images and actions. As a child recognizes unhappiness and grief when a person is crying, so the fairy tale does not need to enlarge on somebody's being unhappy. When Cinderella's mother dies, we are not told that Cinderella grieved for her mother or mourned the loss and felt lonely, deserted, desperate, but simply that "every day she went out to her mother's grave and wept."

In fairy tales, internal processes are translated into visual images. When the hero is confronted by difficult inner problems which seem to defy solution, his psychological state is not described; the fairy story shows him lost in a dense, impenetrable wood, not knowing which way to turn, despairing of finding the way out. To everybody who has heard fairy tales, the image and feeling of being lost in a deep, dark forest are unforgettable.

Unfortunately, some moderns reject fairy tales because they apply to this literature standards which are totally inappropriate. If one takes these stories as descriptions of reality, then the tales are indeed outrageous in all respects—cruel, sadistic, and whatnot. But as symbols of psychological happenings or problems, these stories are quite true.

That is why it depends largely on the narrator's feelings about a fairy tale whether it falls flat or is cherished. The loving grandmother who tells the tale to a child who, sitting on her lap, listens to it enraptured will communicate something very different than a parent who, bored by the story, reads it to several children of quite different ages out of a sense of duty. The adult's sense of active participation in telling the story makes a vital contribution to, and greatly enriches, the child's experience of it. It entails an affirmation of his personality through a particular shared experience with another human being who, though an adult, can fully appreciate the feelings and reactions of the child.

If, as we tell the story, the agonies of sibling rivalry do not reverberate in us, as well as the desperate feeling of rejection the child has when he doesn't feel he is thought the best; his feelings of inferiority when his body fails him; his dismal sense of inadequacy if he or others expect the performance of tasks that seem Herculean; his anxiety about the "animal" aspects of sex; and how all this and so much more can be transcended—then we fail the child. In this failure we also fail to give the child the conviction that after all his labors a wonderful future is awaiting him—and only this belief can give him the strength to grow up well, securely, with self-confidence and self-respect.

Part Two
IN FAIRY LAND

"HANSEL AND GRETEL"

"Hansel and Gretel" begins realistically. The parents are poor, and they worry about how they will be able to take care of their children. Together at night they discuss their predicament, and how they can deal with it. Even taken on this surface level, the folk fairy tale conveys an important, although unpleasant, truth: poverty and deprivation do not improve man's character, but rather make him more selfish, less sensitive to the sufferings of others, and thus prone to embark on evil deeds.

The fairy tale expresses in words and actions the things which go on in children's minds. In terms of the child's dominant anxiety, Hansel and Gretel believe that their parents are talking about a plot to desert them. A small child, awakening hungry in the darkness of the night, feels threatened by complete rejection and desertion, which he experiences in the form of fear of starvation. By projecting their inner anxiety onto those they fear might cut them off, Hansel and Gretel are convinced that their parents plan to starve them to death! In line with the child's anxious fantasies, the story tells that until then the parents had been able to feed their children, but had now fallen upon lean times.

The mother represents the source of all food to the children, so it is she who now is experienced as abandoning them, as if in a wilderness. It is the child's anxiety and deep disappointment when Mother is no longer willing to meet all his oral demands which leads him to believe that suddenly Mother has become unloving, selfish, rejecting. Since the children know they need their parents desperately, they attempt to return home after being deserted. In fact, Hansel succeeds in finding their way back from the forest the first time they are abandoned. Before a child has the courage to embark on the voyage of finding himself, of becoming an independent person through meeting the world, he can develop initiative only in trying to return to passivity, to secure for himself eternally dependent gratification. "Hansel and Gretel" tells that this will not work in the long run.

The children's successful return home does not solve anything. Their effort to continue life as before, as if nothing had happened, is to no avail. The frustrations continue, and the mother becomes more shrewd in her plans for getting rid of the children.

By implication, the story tells about the debilitating consequences of trying to deal with life's problems by means of regression and denial, which reduce one's ability to solve problems. The first time in the forest Hansel used his intelligence appropriately by putting down white pebbles to mark the path home. The second time he did not use his intelligence as well—he, who lived close to a big forest, should have known that birds would eat the bread crumbs. Hansel might instead have studied landmarks on the way in, to find his way back out. But having engaged in denial and regression—the return home— Hansel has lost much of his initiative and ability to think clearly. Starvation anxiety has driven him back, so now he can think only of food as offering a solution to the problem of finding his way out of a serious predicament. Bread stands here for food in general, man's "life line"—an image which Hansel takes literally, out of his anxiety. This shows the limiting effects of fixations to primitive levels of development, engaged in out of fear.

The story of "Hansel and Gretel" gives body to the anxieties and learning tasks of the young child who must overcome and sublimate his primitive incorporative and hence destructive desires. The child must learn that if he does not free himself of these, his parents or society will force him to do so against his will, as earlier his mother had stopped nursing the child when she felt the time had come to do so. This tale gives symbolic expression to these inner experiences directly linked to the mother. Therefore, the father remains a shadowy and ineffectual figure throughout the story, as he appears to the child during his early life when Mother is all-important, in both her benign and her threatening aspects.

Frustrated in their ability to find a solution to their problem in reality because reliance on food for safety (bread crumbs to mark the path) fails them, Hansel and Gretel now give full rein to their oral regression. The gingerbread house represents an existence based on the most primitive satisfactions. Carried away by their uncontrolled craving, the children think nothing of destroying what should give shelter and safety, even though the birds' having eaten the crumbs should have warned them about eating up things.

By devouring the gingerbread house's roof and window, the children show how ready they are to eat somebody out of house and home, a fear which they had projected onto their parents as the reason for their desertion. Despite the warning voice which asks, "Who is nibbling at my little house?" the children lie to themselves and blame it on the wind and "[go] on eating without disturbing themselves."

The gingerbread house is an image nobody forgets: how incredibly appealing and tempting a picture this is, and how terrible the risk one runs if one gives in to the temptation. The child recognizes that, like Hansel and Gretel, he would wish to eat up the gingerbread house, no matter what the dangers. The house stands for oral greediness and how attractive it is to give in to it. The fairy tale is the primer from which the child learns to read his mind in the language of images, the only language which permits understanding before intellectual maturity has been achieved. The child needs to be exposed to this language, and must learn to be responsive to it, if he is to become master of his soul.

The preconscious content of fairy-tale images is much richer than even the following simple illustrations convey. For example, in dreams as well as in fantasies and the child's imagination, a house, as the place in which we dwell, can symbolize the body, usually the mother's. A gingerbread house, which one can "eat up," is a symbol of the mother, who in fact nurses the infant from her body. Thus, the house at which Hansel and Gretel are eating away blissfully and without a care stands in the unconscious for the good mother, who offers her body as a source of nourishment. It is the original all-giving mother, whom every child hopes to find again later somewhere out in the world, when his own mother begins to make demands and to impose restrictions. This is why, carried away by their hopes, Hansel and Gretel do not heed the soft voice that calls out to them, asking what they are up to—a voice that is their externalized conscience. Carried away by their greediness, and fooled by the pleasures of oral satisfaction which seem to deny all previous oral anxiety, the children "thought they were in heaven."

But, as the story tells, such unrestrained giving in to gluttony threatens destruction. Regression to the earliest "heavenly" state of being —when on the mother's breast one lived symbiotically off her—does away with all individuation and independence. It even endangers one's very existence, as cannibalistic inclinations are given body in the figure of the witch.

The witch, who is a personification of the destructive aspects of orality, is as bent on eating up the children as they are on demolishing her gingerbread house. When the children give in to untamed id impulses, as symbolized by their uncontrolled voraciousness, they risk being destroyed. The children eat only the symbolic representation of the mother, the gingerbread house; the witch wants to eat the children themselves. This teaches the hearer a valuable lesson: dealing in symbols is safe when compared with acting on the real thing. Turning the tables on the witch is justified also on another level: children who have little experience and are still learning self-control are not to be measured by the same yardstick as older people, who are supposed to be able to restrain their instinctual desires better. Thus, the punishment of the witch is as justified as the children's rescue.

The witch's evil designs finally force the children to recognize the dangers of unrestrained oral greed and dependence. To survive, they must develop initiative and realize that their only recourse lies in intelligent planning and acting. They must exchange subservience to the pressures of the id for acting in accordance with the ego. Goal-directed behavior based on intelligent assessment of the situation in which they find themselves must take the place of wish-fulfilling fantasies: the substitution of the bone for the finger, tricking the witch to climb into the oven.

Only when the dangers inherent in remaining fixed to primitive orality with its destructive propensities are recognized does the way to a higher stage of development open up. Then it turns out that the good, giving mother was hidden deep down in the bad, destructive one, because there are treasures to be gained: the children inherit the witch's jewels, which become valuable to them after their return home—that is, after they can again find the good parent. This suggests that as the children transcend their oral anxiety, and free themselves of relying on oral satisfaction for security, they can also free themselves of the image of the threatening mother—the witch—and rediscover the good parents, whose greater wisdom—the shared jewels— then benefit all.

On repeated hearing of "Hansel and Gretel," no child remains unaware of the fact that birds eat the bread crumbs and thus prevent the children from returning home without first meeting their great adventure. It is also a bird which guides Hansel and Gretel to the gingerbread house, and thanks only to another bird do they manage to get back home. This gives the child—who thinks differently about animals than older persons do—pause to think: these birds must have a purpose, otherwise they would not first prevent Hansel and Gretel from finding their way back, then take them to the witch, and finally provide passage home.

Obviously, since all turns out for the best, the birds must have known that it is preferable for Hansel and Gretel not to find their way directly back home out of the forest, but rather to risk facing the dangers of the world. In consequence of their threatening encounter with the witch, not only the children but also their parents live much more happily ever afterward. The different birds offer a clue to the path the children must follow to gain their reward.

After they have become familiar with "Hansel and Gretel," most children comprehend, at least unconsciously, that what happens in the parental home and at the witch's house are but separate aspects of what in reality is one total experience. Initially, the witch is a perfectly gratifying mother figure, as we are told how "she took them both by the hand, and led them into her little house. Then good food was set before them, milk and pancakes with sugar, apples, and nuts. Afterwards two pretty little beds were covered with clean white linen, and Hansel and Gretel lay down in them, and thought they were in heaven." Only on the following morning comes a rude awakening from such dreams of infantile bliss. "The old woman had only pretended to be so kind; she was in reality a wicked witch. . . ."

This is how the child feels when devastated by the ambivalent feelings, frustrations, and anxieties of the oedipal stage of development, as well as his previous disappointment and rage at failures on his mother's part to gratify his needs and desires as fully as he expected. Severely upset that Mother no longer serves him unquestioningly but makes demands on him and devotes herself ever more to her own interests—something which the child had not permitted to come to his awareness before—he imagines that Mother, as she nursed him and created a world of oral bliss, did so only to fool him—like the witch of the story.

Thus, the parental home "hard by a great forest" and the fateful house in the depths of the same woods are on an unconscious level but the two aspects of the parental home: the gratifying one and the frustrating one.

The child who ponders on his own the details of "Hansel and Gretel" finds meaning in how it begins. That the parental home is located at the very edge of the forest where everything happens suggests that what is to follow was imminent from the start. This is again the fairy tale's way to express thoughts through impressive images which lead the child to use his own imagination to derive deeper understanding. Mentioned before was how the behavior of the birds symbolizes that the entire adventure was arranged for the children's benefit. Since early Christian times the white dove has symbolized superior benevolent powers. Hansel claims to be looking back at a white dove that is sitting on the roof of the parental home, wanting to say goodbye to him. It is a snow-white bird, singing delightfully, which leads the children to the gingerbread house and then settles on its roof, suggesting that this is the right place for them to arrive at. Another white bird is needed to guide the children back to safety: their way home is blocked by a "big water" which they can cross only with the help of a white duck.

The children do not encounter any expanse of water on their way in. Having to cross one on their return symbolizes a transition, and a new beginning on a higher level of existence (as in baptism). Up to the time they have to cross this water, the children have never separated. The school-age child should develop consciousness of his personal uniqueness, of his individuality, which means that he can no longer share everything with others, has to live to some degree by himself and stride out on his own. This is symbolically expressed by the children not being able to remain together in crossing the water. As they arrive there, Hansel sees no way to get across, but Gretel spies a white duck and asks it to help them cross the water. Hansel seats himself on its back and asks his sister to join him. But she knows better: this will not do. They have to cross over separately, and they do.

The children's experience at the witch's house has purged them of their oral fixations; after having crossed the water, they arrive at the other shore as more mature children, ready to rely on their own intelligence and initiative to solve life's problems. As dependent children they had been a burden to their parents; on their return they have become the family's support, as they bring home the treasures they have gained. These treasures are the children's new-won independence in thought and action, a new self-reliance which is the opposite of the passive dependence which characterized them when they were deserted in the woods.

It is females—the stepmother and the witch—who are the inimical forces in this story. Gretel's importance in the children's deliverance reassures the child that a female can be a rescuer as well as a destroyer. Probably even more important is the fact that Hansel saves them once and then later Gretel saves them again, which suggests to children that as they grow up they must come to rely more and more on their age mates for mutual help and understanding. This idea reinforces the story's main thrust, which is a warning against regression, and an encouragement of growth toward a higher plane of psychological and intellectual existence.

"Hansel and Gretel" ends with the heroes returning to the home from which they started, and now finding happiness there. This is psychologically correct, because a young child, driven into his adventures by oral or oedipal problems, cannot hope to find happiness outside the home. If all is to go well in his development, he must work these problems out while still dependent on his parents. Only through good relations with his parents can a child successfully mature into adolescence.

Having overcome his oedipal difficulties, mastered his oral anxieties, sublimated those of his cravings which cannot be satisfied realistically, and learned that wishful thinking has to be replaced by intelligent action, the child is ready to live happily again with his parents. This is symbolized by the treasures Hansel and Gretel bring home to share with their father. Rather than expecting everything good to come from the parents, the older child needs to be able to make some contribution to the emotional well-being of himself and his family.

As "Hansel and Gretel" begins matter-of-factly with the worries of a poor woodcutter's family unable to make ends meet, it ends on an equally down-to-earth level. Although the story tells that the children brought home a pile of pearls and precious stones, nothing further suggests that their economic way of life was changed. This emphasizes the symbolic nature of these jewels. The tale concludes: "Then all worries ended, and they lived together in perfect joy. My tale is ended; there runs a mouse, who catches it may make himself a big fur cap out of it." Nothing has changed by the end of "Hansel and Gretel" but inner attitudes; or, more correctly, all has changed because inner attitudes have changed. No more will the children feel pushed out, deserted, and lost in the darkness of the forest; nor will they seek for the miraculous gingerbread house. But neither will they encounter or fear the witch, since they have proved to themselves that through their combined efforts they can outsmart her and be victorious. Industry, making something good even out of unpromising material (such as by using the fur of a mouse intelligently for making a cap), is the virtue and real achievement of the school-age child who has fought through and mastered the oedipal difficulties.

"Hansel and Gretel" is one of many fairy tales where two siblings cooperate in rescuing each other and succeed because of their combined efforts. These stories direct the child toward transcending his immature dependence on his parents and reaching the next higher stage of development: cherishing also the support of age mates. Cooperating with them in meeting life's tasks will eventually have to replace the child's single-minded reliance on his parents only. The child of school age often cannot yet believe that he ever will be able to meet the world without his parents; that is why he wishes to hold on to them beyond the necessary point. He needs to learn to trust that someday he will master the dangers of the world, even in the exaggerated form in which his fears depict them, and be enriched by it.

The child views existential dangers not objectively, but fantastically exaggerated in line with his immature dread—for example, personified as a child-devouring witch. "Hansel and Gretel" encourages the child to explore on his own even the figments of his anxious imagination, because such fairy tales give him confidence that he can master not only the real dangers which his parents told him about, but even those vastly exaggerated ones which he fears exist.

A witch as created by the child's anxious fantasies will haunt him; but a witch he can push into her own oven and burn to death is a witch the child can believe himself rid of. As long as children continue to believe in witches—they always have and always will, up to the age when they no longer are compelled to give their formless apprehensions humanlike appearance—they need to be told stories in which children, by being ingenious, rid themselves of these persecuting figures of their imagination. By succeeding in doing so, they gain immensely from the experience, as did Hansel and Gretel.

"LITTLE RED RIDING HOOD"

A charming, "innocent" young girl swallowed by a wolf is an image which impresses itself indelibly on the mind. In "Hansel and Gretel" the witch only planned to devour the children; in "Little Red Riding Hood" both grandmother and child are actually swallowed up by the wolf. Like most fairy tales, "Little Red Riding Hood" exists in many different versions. The most popular is the Brothers Grimm's story, in which Little Red Cap and the grandmother are reborn and the wolf is meted out a well-deserved punishment.

But the literary history of this story begins with Perrault.[52] It is by his title, "Little Red Riding Hood," that the tale is best known in English, though the title it was given by the Brothers Grimm, "Little Red Cap," is more appropriate. However, Andrew Lang, one of the most erudite and astute students of fairy tales, remarks that if all variants of "Little Red Riding Hood" ended the way Perrault concluded his, we might as well dismiss it.*[53] This would probably have been its fate if the Brothers Grimm's version had not made it into one of the most popular fairy tales. But since this story's known history starts with Perrault, we shall consider—and dismiss—his rendering first.

Perrault's story begins like all other well-known versions, telling how the grandmother had made her granddaughter a little red riding hood (or cap), which led to the girl's being known by that name. One day her mother sent Little Red Riding Hood to take goodies to her grandmother, who was sick. The girl's way led her through a forest, where she met up with the wolf. The wolf did not dare to eat her up then because there were woodcutters in the forest, so he asked Little Red Riding Hood where she was going, and she told him. The wolf asked exactly where Grandmother lived, and the girl gave the information. Then the wolf said that he would go visit Grandmother too, and he took off at great speed, while the girl dallied along the way.

The wolf gained entrance at the grandmother's home by pretending to be Little Red Riding Hood, and immediately swallowed up the old woman. In Perrault's story the wolf does not dress up as Grandmother, but simply lies down in her bed. When Little Red Riding Hood arrived, the wolf asked her to join him in bed. Little Red Riding Hood undressed and got into bed, at which moment, astonished at how Grandmother looked naked, she exclaimed, "Grandmother, what big arms you have!" to which the wolf answered: "To better embrace you!" Then Little Red Riding Hood said: "Grandmother, what big legs you have!" and received the reply: "To be better able to run." These two exchanges, which do not occur in the Brothers Grimm's version, are then followed by the well-known questions

*Interestingly enough, it is the Perrault version Andrew Lang chose to include in his *Blue Fairy Book*. Perrault's story ends with the wolf victorious; thus it is devoid of escape, recovery, and consolation; it is not—and was not intended by Perrault to be—a fairy tale, but a cautionary story which deliberately threatens the child with its anxiety-producing ending. It is curious that even Lang, despite his severe criticisms of it, preferred to reproduce Perrault's version. It seems that many adults think it better to scare children into good behavior than to relieve their anxieties as a true fairy tale does.

about Grandmother's big ears, eyes, and teeth. To the last question the wolf answers, "To better eat you." "And, in saying these words, the bad wolf threw himself on Little Red Riding Hood and ate her up."

There Lang's translation ends, as do many others. But Perrault's original rendering continues with a little poem setting forth the moral to be drawn from the story: that nice girls ought not to listen to all sorts of people. If they do, it is not surprising that the wolf will get them and eat them up. As for wolves, these come in all variations; and among them the gentle wolves are the most dangerous of all, particularly those who follow young girls into the streets, even into their homes. Perrault wanted not only to entertain his audience, but to teach a specific moral lesson with each of his tales. So it is understandable that he changed them accordingly.* Unfortunately, in doing so, he robbed his fairy stories of much of their meaning. As he tells the story, nobody warned Little Red Riding Hood not to dally on the way to Grandmother's house, or not to stray off the proper road. Also, in Perrault's version it does not make sense that the grandmother, who has done nothing wrong at all, should end up destroyed.

Perrault's "Little Red Riding Hood" loses much of its appeal because it is so obvious that his wolf is not a rapacious beast but a metaphor, which leaves little to the imagination of the hearer. Such simplifications and a directly stated moral turn this potential fairy tale

*When Perrault published his collection of fairy tales in 1697, "Little Red Riding Hood" already had an ancient history, with some elements going very far back in time. There is the myth of Cronos swallowing his children, who nevertheless return miraculously from his belly; and a heavy stone was used to replace the child to be swallowed. There is a Latin story of 1023 (by Egbert of Lièges, called *Fecunda ratis*) in which a little girl is found in the company of wolves; the girl wears a red cover of great importance to her, and scholars tell that this cover was a red cap. Here, then, six centuries or more before Perrault's story, we find some basic elements of "Little Red Riding Hood": a little girl with a red cap, the company of wolves, a child being swallowed alive who returns unharmed, and a stone put in place of the child.

There are other French versions of "Little Red Riding Hood," but we do not know which of them influenced Perrault in his retelling of the story. In some of them the wolf makes Little Red Riding Hood eat of Grandmother's flesh and drink of her blood, despite warning voices which tell her not to.[54] If one of these stories was Perrault's source, one can well understand that he eliminated such vulgarity as unseemly, since his book was designed for perusal at the court of Versailles. Perrault not only prettified his stories, he also used affectation, such as the pretense that his stories were written by his ten-year-old son, who dedicated the book to a princess. In Perrault's asides and the morals appended to the stories, he speaks as if he were winking at the adults over the heads of the children.

into a cautionary tale which spells everything out completely. Thus the hearer's imagination cannot become active in giving the story a personal meaning. Captive to a rationalistic interpretation of the story's purpose, Perrault makes everything as explicit as possible. For example, when the girl undresses and joins the wolf in bed and the wolf tells her that his strong arms are for embracing her better, nothing is left to the imagination. Since in response to such direct and obvious seduction Little Red Riding Hood makes no move to escape or fight back, either she is stupid or she wants to be seduced. In neither case is she a suitable figure to identify with. With these details Little Red Riding Hood is changed from a naïve, attractive young girl, who is induced to neglect Mother's warnings and enjoy herself in what she consciously believes to be innocent ways, into nothing but a fallen woman.

It destroys the value of a fairy tale for the child if someone details its meaning for him; Perrault does worse—he belabors it. All good fairy tales have meaning on many levels; only the child can know which meanings are of significance to him at the moment. As he grows up, the child discovers new aspects of these well-known tales, and this gives him the conviction that he has indeed matured in understanding, since the same story now reveals so much more to him. This can happen only if the child has not been told didactically what the story is supposed to be about. Only when discovery of the previously hidden meanings of a fairy tale is the child's spontaneous and intuitive achievement does it attain full significance for him. This discovery changes a story from something the child is being given into something he partially creates for himself.

The Brothers Grimm recount two versions of this story, which is very unusual for them.* In both, the story and the heroine are called "Little Red Cap" because of the "little cap of red velvet which suited her so well that she would not wear anything else."

The threat of being devoured is the central theme of "Little Red Riding Hood," as it is of "Hansel and Gretel." The same basic psychological constellations which recur in every person's development can lead to the most diverse human fates and personalities, depending on what the individual's other experiences are and how he interprets them to himself. Similarly, a limited number of basic themes depict in fairy stories quite different aspects of the human experience; all

---

*Their collection of fairy stories, which contained "Little Red Cap," appeared first in 1812—more than one hundred years after Perrault published his version.

depends on how such a motif is elaborated and in what context events happen. "Hansel and Gretel" deals with the difficulties and anxieties of the child who is forced to give up his dependent attachment to the mother and free himself of his oral fixation. "Little Red Cap" takes up some crucial problems the school-age girl has to solve if oedipal attachments linger on in the unconscious, which may drive her to expose herself dangerously to the possibility of seduction.

In both these fairy tales the house in the woods and the parental home are the same place, experienced quite differently because of a change in the psychological situation. In her own home Little Red Cap, protected by her parents, is the untroubled pubertal child who is quite competent to cope. At the home of her grandmother, who is herself infirm, the same girl is helplessly incapacitated by the consequences of her encounter with the wolf.

Hansel and Gretel, subjects of their oral fixation, think nothing of eating the house that symbolically stands for the bad mother who has deserted them (forced them to leave home), and they do not hesitate to burn the witch to death in an oven as if she were food to be cooked for eating. Little Red Cap, who has outgrown her oral fixation, no longer has any destructive oral desires. Psychologically, the distance is enormous between oral fixation symbolically turned into cannibalism, which is the central theme of "Hansel and Gretel," and how Little Red Cap punishes the wolf. The wolf in "Little Red Cap" is the seducer, but as far as the overt content of the story goes, the wolf doesn't do anything that does not come naturally—namely, it devours to feed itself. And it is common for man to kill a wolf, although the method used in this story is unusual.

Little Red Cap's home is one of abundance, which, since she is way beyond oral anxiety, she gladly shares with her grandmother by bringing her food. To Little Red Cap the world beyond the parental home is not a threatening wilderness through which the child cannot find a path. Outside Red Cap's home there is a well-known road, from which, her mother warns, one must not stray.

While Hansel and Gretel have to be pushed out into the world, Little Red Cap leaves her home willingly. She is not afraid of the outside world, but recognizes its beauty, and therein lies a danger. If this world beyond home and duty becomes too attractive, it may induce a return to proceeding according to the pleasure principle—which, we assume, Little Red Cap had relinquished due to her parents' teachings in favor of the reality principle—and then destructive encounters may occur.

This quandary of standing between reality principle and pleasure principle is explicitly stated when the wolf says to Little Red Cap: "See how pretty the flowers are which are all around you. Why don't you look about? I believe you don't even hear how beautifully the little birds are singing. You walk along with singlemindedness and concentration as if you were going to school, while everything out here in the woods is merry." This is the same conflict between doing what one likes to do and what one ought to do which Red Cap's mother had warned her about at the outset, as she admonished her daughter to "walk properly and don't run off the road. . . . And when you come to Grandmother's place, do not forget to wish her a 'Good morning,' and don't look into all the corners as soon as you arrive." So her mother is aware of Little Red Cap's proclivity for straying off the beaten path, and for spying into corners to discover the secrets of adults.

The idea that "Little Red Cap" deals with the child's ambivalence about whether to live by the pleasure principle or the reality principle is borne out by the fact that Red Cap stops gathering flowers only "when she had collected so many that she could not carry any more." At that moment Little Red Cap "once more remembered Grandmother and set out on the way to her." That is, only when picking flowers is no longer enjoyable does the pleasure-seeking id recede and Red Cap become aware of her obligations.*

Little Red Cap is very much a child already struggling with pubertal problems for which she is not yet ready emotionally because she has not mastered her oedipal conflicts. That Little Red Cap is more mature than Hansel and Gretel is shown by her questioning attitude toward what she encounters in the world. Hansel and Gretel do not wonder about the gingerbread house, or explore what the witch is all about. Little Red Cap wishes to find out things, as her mother's cau-

*Two French versions quite different from Perrault's make it even more obvious that Little Red Riding Hood chose to follow the path of pleasure, or at least of greater ease, although the path of duty was also brought to her attention. In these renderings of the story Little Red Riding Hood encounters the wolf at a fork in the road—that is, a place where an important decision has to be made: which road to follow. The wolf asks: Which road will you take, that of the needles or that of the pins? Little Red Riding Hood chooses the road of the pins because, as one version explains, it is easier to fasten things together with pins, while it is much harder labor to sew them together with needles.[55] At a time when sewing was very much a work task expected of young girls, taking the easy way of using pins instead of needles was readily understood as behaving in accordance with the pleasure principle, where the situation would require acting according to the reality principle.

tioning her not to peek indicates. She observes that something is wrong when she finds her grandmother "looking very strange," but is confused by the wolf's having disguised himself in the old woman's attire. Little Red Cap tries to understand, when she asks Grandmother about her big ears, observes the big eyes, wonders about the large hands, the horrible mouth. Here is an enumeration of the four senses: hearing, seeing, touching, and tasting; the pubertal child uses them all to comprehend the world.

"Little Red Cap" in symbolic form projects the girl into the dangers of her oedipal conflicts during puberty, and then saves her from them, so that she will be able to mature conflict-free. The maternal figures of mother and witch which were all-important in "Hansel and Gretel" have shrunk to insignificance in "Little Red Cap," where neither mother nor grandmother can do anything—neither threaten nor protect. The male, by contrast, is all-important, split into two opposite forms: the dangerous seducer who, if given in to, turns into the destroyer of the good grandmother and the girl; and the hunter, the responsible, strong, and rescuing father figure.

It is as if Little Red Cap is trying to understand the contradictory nature of the male by experiencing all aspects of his personality: the selfish, asocial, violent, potentially destructive tendencies of the id (the wolf); the unselfish, social, thoughtful, and protective propensities of the ego (the hunter).

Little Red Cap is universally loved because, although she is virtuous, she is tempted; and because her fate tells us that trusting everybody's good intentions, which seems so nice, is really leaving oneself open to pitfalls. If there were not something in us that likes the big bad wolf, he would have no power over us. Therefore, it is important to understand his nature, but even more important to learn what makes him attractive to us. Appealing as naïveté is, it is dangerous to remain naïve all one's life.

But the wolf is not just the male seducer, he also represents all the asocial, animalistic tendencies within ourselves. By giving up the school-age child's virtues of "walking singlemindedly," as her task demands, Little Red Cap reverts to the pleasure-seeking oedipal child. By falling in with the wolf's suggestions, she has also given the wolf the opportunity to devour her grandmother. Here the story speaks to some of the oedipal difficulties which remained unresolved in the girl, and the wolf's swallowing Little Red Cap is the merited punishment for her arranging things so that the wolf can do away with a mother figure. Even a four-year-old cannot help wondering what

Little Red Cap is up to when, answering the wolf's question, she gives the wolf specific directions on how to get to her grandmother's house. What is the purpose of such detailed information, the child wonders to himself, if not to make sure that the wolf will find the way? Only adults who are convinced that fairy tales do not make sense can fail to see that Little Red Cap's unconscious is working overtime to give Grandmother away.

Grandmother, too, is not free of blame. A young girl needs a strong mother figure for her own protection, and as a model to imitate. But Red Cap's grandmother is carried away by her own needs beyond what is good for the child, as we are told: "There was nothing she would not have given the child." It would not have been the first or last time that a child so spoiled by a grandmother runs into trouble in real life. Whether it is Mother or Grandmother—this mother once removed—it is fatal for the young girl if this older woman abdicates her own attractiveness to males and transfers it to the daughter by giving her a too attractive red cloak.

All through "Little Red Cap," in the title as in the girl's name, the emphasis is on the color red, which she openly wears. Red is the color symbolizing violent emotions, very much including sexual ones. The red velvet cap given by Grandmother to Little Red Cap thus can be viewed as a symbol of a premature transfer of sexual attractiveness, which is further accentuated by the grandmother's being old and sick, too weak even to open a door. The name "Little Red Cap" indicates the key importance of this feature of the heroine in the story. It suggests that not only is the red cap little, but also the girl. She is too little, not for wearing the cap, but for managing what this red cap symbolizes, and what her wearing it invites.

Little Red Cap's danger is her budding sexuality, for which she is not yet emotionally mature enough. The person who is psychologically ready to have sexual experiences can master them, and grow because of it. But a premature sexuality is a regressive experience, arousing all that is still primitive within us and that threatens to swallow us up. The immature person who is not yet ready for sex but is exposed to an experience which arouses strong sexual feelings falls back on oedipal ways for dealing with it. The only way such a person believes he can win out in sex is by getting rid of the more ex-perienced competitors—hence Little Red Cap's giving specific in-structions to the wolf on how to get to Grandmother's house. In doing this, however, she also shows her ambivalence. In directing the wolf to Grandmother, she acts as if she were telling the wolf, "Leave me alone; go to Grandmother, who is a mature woman; she should be able to cope with what you represent; I am not."

This struggle between her conscious desire to do the right thing and the unconscious wish to win out over her (grand)mother is what endears the girl and the story to us and makes her so supremely human. Like many of us when we were children and caught in inner ambivalences that, despite our best efforts, we could not master, she tries to push the problem onto somebody else: an older person, a parent or parent substitute. But by thus trying to evade a threatening situation, she nearly gets destroyed by it.

As mentioned before, the Brothers Grimm also present an important variation of "Little Red Riding Hood," which essentially consists of only an addition to the basic story. In the variation, we are told that at a later time, when Little Red Cap is again taking cakes to her grandmother, another wolf tries to entice her to stray from the direct path (of virtue). This time the girl hurries to Grandmother and tells her all about it. Together they secure the door so that the wolf cannot enter. In the end, the wolf slips from the roof into a trough filled with water and drowns. The story ends, "But Little Red Cap went gaily home, and nobody did any harm to her."

This variation elaborates on what the hearer of the story feels convinced of—that after her bad experience the girl realizes that she is by no means mature enough to deal with the wolf (the seducer), and she is ready to settle down to a good working alliance with her mother. This is symbolically expressed by her rushing to Grandmother as soon as danger threatens, rather than her thinking nothing of it, as she did in her first encounter with the wolf. Little Red Cap works with her (grand)mother and follows her advice—in the continuation, Grandmother tells Red Cap to fill the trough with water that smells of sausages which had been cooked in it, and the smell attracts the wolf so that he falls into the water—and together the two easily overcome the wolf. The child thus needs to form a strong working alliance with the parent of the same sex, so that through identification with the parent and conscious learning from him, the child will grow successfully into an adult.

Fairy stories speak to our conscious and our unconscious, and therefore do not need to avoid contradictions, since these easily coexist in our unconscious. On a quite different level of meaning, what happens with and to Grandmother may be seen in a very different light. The hearer of the story rightly wonders why the wolf does not devour

Little Red Cap as soon as he meets her—that is, at the first opportunity. Typically for Perrault, he offers a seemingly rational explanation: the wolf would have done so were it not afraid of some woodcutters who were close by. Since in Perrault's story the wolf is all along
a male seducer, it makes sense that an older man might be afraid to
seduce a little girl in the sight and hearing of other men.

Things are quite different in the Brothers Grimm's tale, where we
are given to understand that the wolf's excessive greed accounts for
the delay: "The wolf thought to itself, 'That young tender thing, what
a fat mouthful, it'll taste much better than the old one: you have to
proceed craftily so that you catch both.'" But this explanation does
not make sense, because the wolf could have gotten hold of Little Red
Cap right then and there, and later tricked the grandmother just as
it happens in the story.

The wolf's behavior begins to make sense in the Brothers Grimm's
version if we assume that to get Little Red Cap, the wolf first has to
do away with Grandmother. As long as the (grand)mother is around,
Little Red Cap will not become his.* But once the (grand)mother is
out of the way, the road seems open for acting on one's desires, which
had to remain repressed as long as Mother was around. The story on
this level deals with the daughter's unconscious wish to be seduced by
her father (the wolf).

With the reactivation in puberty of early oedipal longings, the girl's
wish for her father, her inclination to seduce him, and her desire to
be seduced by him, also become reactivated. Then the girl feels she
deserves to be punished terribly by the mother, if not the father also,
for her desire to take him away from Mother. Adolescent reawakening of early emotions which were relatively dormant is not restricted
to oedipal feelings, but includes even earlier anxieties and desires
which reappear during this period.

On a different level of interpretation, one could say that the wolf
does not devour Little Red Cap immediately upon meeting her because he wants to get her into bed with him first: a sexual meeting of
the two has to precede her being "eaten up." While most children do
not know about those animals of which one dies during the sex act,
these destructive connotations are quite vivid in the child's conscious
and unconscious mind—so much so that most children view the sexual
act primarily as an act of violence which one partner commits on the

---

*It is not all that long since, in certain peasant cultures, when the mother died, the
oldest daughter took her place in all respects.

other. I believe it is the child's unconscious equation of sexual excitement, violence, and anxiety which Djuna Barnes alludes to when she writes: "Children know something they can't tell; they like Red Riding Hood and the wolf in bed!"[56] Because this strange coincidence of opposite emotions characterizing the child's sexual knowledge is given body in "Little Red Riding Hood," the story holds a great unconscious attraction to children, and to adults who are vaguely reminded by it of their own childish fascination with sex.

Another artist has given expression to these same underlying feelings. Gustave Doré, in one of his famous illustrations to fairy tales, shows Little Red Riding Hood and the wolf in bed together.[57] The wolf is depicted as rather placid. But the girl appears to be beset by powerful ambivalent feelings as she looks at the wolf resting beside her. She makes no move to leave. She seems most intrigued by the situation, attracted and repelled at the same time. The combination of feelings her face and body suggest can best be described as fascination. It is the same fascination which sex, and everything surrounding it, exercises over the child's mind. This, to return to Djuna Barnes's statement, is what children feel about Red Riding Hood and the wolf and their relation, but can't tell—and is what makes the story so captivating.

It is this "deathly" fascination with sex—which is experienced as simultaneously the greatest excitement and the greatest anxiety— that is bound up with the little girl's oedipal longings for her father, and with the reactivation of these same feelings in different form during puberty. Whenever these emotions reappear, they evoke memories of the little girl's propensity for seducing her father, and with it other memories of her desire to be seduced by him also.

While in Perrault's rendering the emphasis is on sexual seduction, the opposite is true for the Brothers Grimm's story. In it, no sexuality is directly or indirectly mentioned; it may be subtly implied, but, essentially, the hearer has to supply the idea to help his understanding of the story. To the child's mind, the sexual implications remain preconscious, as they should. Consciously a child knows that there is nothing wrong with picking flowers; what is wrong is disobeying Mother when one has to carry out an important mission serving the legitimate interest of the (grand)parent. The main conflict is between what seem justified interests to the child and what he knows his parent wants him to do. The story implies that the child doesn't know how dangerous it may be to give in to what he considers his innocuous desires, so he must learn of this danger. Or rather, as the story warns, life will teach it to him, at his expense.

"Little Red Cap" externalizes the inner processes of the pubertal child: the wolf is the externalization of the badness the child feels when he goes contrary to the admonitions of his parents and permits himself to tempt, or to be tempted, sexually. When he strays from the path the parent has outlined for him, he encounters "badness," and he fears that it will swallow up him and the parent whose confidence he betrayed. But there can be resurrection from "badness," as the story proceeds to tell.

Very different from Little Red Cap, who gives in to the temptations of her id and in doing so betrays mother and grandmother, the hunter does not permit his emotions to run away with him. His first reaction on finding the wolf sleeping in the grandmother's bed is, "Do I find you here, you old sinner? I have been looking for you for a long time" —and his immediate inclination is to shoot the wolf. But his ego (or reason) asserts itself despite the proddings of the id (anger at the wolf), and the hunter realizes that it is more important to try to rescue Grandmother than to give in to anger by shooting the wolf outright. The hunter restrains himself, and instead of shooting the animal dead, he carefully cuts open the wolf's belly with scissors, rescuing Little Red Cap and her grandmother.

The hunter is a most attractive figure, to boys as well as girls, because he rescues the good and punishes the bad. All children encounter difficulties in obeying the reality principle, and they easily recognize in the opposite figures of wolf and hunter the conflict between the id and the ego-superego aspects of their personality. In the hunter's action, violence (cutting open the belly) is made to serve the highest social purpose (rescuing the two females). The child feels that nobody appreciates that his violent tendencies seem constructive to him, but the story shows that they can be.

Little Red Cap has to be cut out of the wolf's stomach as if through a Caesarean operation; thus the idea of pregnancy and birth is intimated. With it, associations of a sexual relation are evoked in the child's unconscious. How does a fetus get into the mother's womb? wonders the child, and decides that it can happen only through the mother having swallowed something, as the wolf did.

Why does the hunter speak of the wolf as an "old sinner" and say that he has been trying to find him for a long time? As the seducer is called a wolf in the story, so the person who seduces, particularly when his target is a young girl, is popularly referred to as an "old sinner" today as in olden times. On a different level, the wolf also represents the unacceptable tendencies within the hunter; we all refer on occasion to the animal within us, as a simile for our propensity for acting violently or irresponsibly to gain our goals.

While the hunter is all-important for the denouement, we do not know where he comes from, nor does he interact with Little Red Cap —he rescues her, that's all. All through "Little Red Cap" no father is mentioned, which is most unusual for a fairy story of this kind. This suggests that the father is present, but in hidden form. The girl certainly expects her father to rescue her from all difficulties, and particularly those emotional ones which are the consequence of her wish to seduce him and to be seduced by him. What is meant here by "seduction" is the girl's desire and efforts to induce her father to love her more than anybody else, and her wish that he should make all efforts to induce her to love him more than anybody else. Then we may see that the father is indeed present in "Little Red Cap" in two opposite forms: as the wolf, which is an externalization of the dangers of overwhelming oedipal feelings, and as the hunter in his protective and rescuing function.

Despite the hunter's immediate inclination to shoot the wolf dead, he does not do so. After her rescue, it is Little Red Cap's own idea to fill the wolf's belly with stones, "and as it woke up, it tried to jump away, but the stones were so heavy that it collapsed and fell to its death." It has to be Little Red Cap who spontaneously plans what to do about the wolf and goes about doing it. If she is to be safe in the future, she must be able to do away with the seducer, be rid of him. If the father-hunter did this for her, Red Cap could never feel that she had really overcome her weakness, because she had not rid herself of it.

It is fairy-tale justice that the wolf should die of what he tried to do: his oral greediness is his own undoing. Since he tried to put something into his stomach nefariously, the same is done to him.*

There is another excellent reason why the wolf should not die from having his belly cut open to free those he swallowed up. The fairy tale protects the child from unnecessary anxiety. If the wolf should die when his belly is opened up as in a Caesarean operation, those hearing the story might come to fear that a child coming out of the mother's body kills her. But if the wolf survives the opening up of his belly and

*In some other renderings Little Red Cap's father happens to come on the scene, cuts the wolf's head off, and thus rescues the two females.[58] Maybe the shift from cutting open the stomach to cutting off the head was made because it was Little Red Cap's father who did it. A father's manipulating a stomach in which his daughter temporarily dwells comes too close for comfort in suggesting a father in a sexual activity connected with his daughter.

dies only because heavy stones were sewn into it, then there is no reason for anxiety about childbirth.

Little Red Cap and her grandmother do not really die, but they are certainly reborn. If there is a central theme to the wide variety of fairy tales, it is that of a rebirth to a higher plane. Children (and adults, too) must be able to believe that reaching a higher form of existence is possible if they master the developmental steps this requires. Stories which tell that this is not only possible but likely have a tremendous appeal to children, because such tales combat the ever-present fear that they won't be able to make this transition, or that they'll lose too much in the process. That is why, for example, in "Brother and Sister" the two do not lose each other after their transformation but have a better life together; why Little Red Cap is a happier girl after her rescue; why Hansel and Gretel are so much better off after their return home.

Many adults today tend to take literally the things said in fairy tales, whereas they should be viewed as symbolic renderings of crucial life experiences. The child understands this intuitively, though he does not "know" it explicitly. An adult's reassurance to a child that Little Red Cap did not "really" die when the wolf swallowed her is experienced by the child as a condescending talking down. This is just the same as if a person is told that in the Bible story Jonah's being swallowed by the big fish was not "really" his end. Everybody who hears this story knows intuitively that Jonah's stay in the fish's belly was for a purpose—namely, so that he would return to life a better man.

The child knows intuitively that Little Red Cap's being swallowed by the wolf—much like the various deaths other fairy-tale heroes experience for a time—is by no means the end of the story, but a necessary part of it. The child also understands that Little Red Cap really "died" as the girl who permitted herself to be tempted by the wolf; and that when the story says "the little girl sprang out" of the wolf's belly, she came to life a different person. This device is necessary because, while the child can readily understand one thing being replaced by another (the good mother by the evil stepmother), he cannot yet comprehend inner transformations. So among the great merits of fairy tales is that through hearing them, the child comes to believe that such transformations are possible.

The child whose conscious and unconscious mind has become deeply involved in the story understands that what is meant by the wolf's swallowing grandmother and girl is that because of what happened, the two were temporarily lost to the world—they lost the ability to be in contact and to influence what goes on. Therefore somebody from the outside must come to their rescue; and where a mother and child are concerned, who could that be but a father?

Little Red Cap, when she fell in with the wolf's seduction to act on the basis of the pleasure principle instead of the reality principle, implicitly returned to a more primitive, earlier form of existence. In typical fairy-story fashion, her return to a more primitive level of life is impressively exaggerated as going all the way to the prebirth existence in the womb, as the child thinks in extremes.

But why must the grandmother experience the same fate as the girl? Why is she both "dead" and reduced to a lower state of existence? This detail is in line with the way the child conceives of what death means—that this person is no longer available, is no longer of any use. Grandparents must be of use to the child—they must be able to protect him, teach him, feed him; if they are not, then they are reduced to a lower form of existence. As unable to cope with the wolf as Little Red Cap is, the grandmother is reduced to the same fate as the girl.*

The story makes it quite clear that the two have not died by being swallowed. This is made obvious by Little Red Cap's behavior when liberated. "The little girl sprang out crying: 'Ah, how frightened I have been; how dark it was inside the wolf's body!' " To have been frightened means that one has been very much alive, and signifies a state opposite to death, when one no longer thinks or feels. Little Red Cap's fear was of the darkness, because through her behavior she had lost her higher consciousness, which had shed light on her world. Or as the child who knows he has done wrong, or who no longer feels well protected by his parents, feels the darkness of night with its terrors settle on him.

Not just in "Little Red Cap" but throughout the fairy-tale literature, death of the hero—different from death of old age, after life's fulfillment—symbolizes his failure. Death of the unsuccessful—such as those who tried to get to Sleeping Beauty before the time was ripe, and perished in the thorns—symbolizes that this person was not mature enough to master the demanding task which he foolishly (prema-

*That this interpretation is justified is borne out by the second version of the story presented by the Brothers Grimm. It tells how the second time around Grandmother protects Little Red Cap against the wolf, and successfully plans his demise. This is how a (grand)parent is supposed to act; if he does, neither (grand)parent nor child needs to fear the wolf, however clever it may be.

turely) undertook. Such persons must undergo further growth experiences, which will enable them to succeed. Those predecessors of the hero who die in fairy stories are nothing but the hero's earlier immature incarnations.

Little Red Cap, having been projected into inner darkness (the darkness inside the wolf), becomes ready and appreciative of a new light, a better understanding of the emotional experiences she has to master, and those others which she has to avoid because as yet they overwhelm her. Through stories such as "Little Red Cap" the child begins to understand—at least on a preconscious level—that only those experiences which overwhelm us arouse in us corresponding inner feelings with which we cannot deal. Once we have mastered those, we need not fear any longer the encounter with the wolf.

This is reinforced by the story's concluding sentence, which does not have Little Red Cap say that she will never again risk encountering the wolf, or go alone in the woods. On the contrary, the ending implicitly warns the child that withdrawal from all problematic situations would be the wrong solution. The story ends: "But Little Red Cap thought 'as long as you live, you won't run off the path into the woods all by yourself when mother has forbidden you to do so.' " With such inner dialogue, backed up by a most upsetting experience, Little Red Cap's encounter with her own sexuality will have a very different outcome, when she is ready—at which time her mother will approve of it.

Deviating from the straight path in defiance of mother and superego was temporarily necessary for the young girl, to gain a higher state of personality organization. Her experience convinced her of the dangers of giving in to her oedipal desires. It is much better, she learns, not to rebel against the mother, nor try to seduce or permit herself to be seduced by the as yet dangerous aspects of the male. Much better, despite one's ambivalent desires, to settle for a while longer for the protection the father provides when he is not seen in his seductive aspects. She has learned that it is better to build father and mother, and their values, deeper and in more adult ways into one's superego, to become able to deal with life's dangers.

There are many modern counterparts to "Little Red Cap." The profundity of fairy tales when compared to much of today's children's literature becomes apparent when one parallels them. David Riesman, for example, has compared "Little Red Riding Hood" with a modern children's story, *Tootle the Engine*, a Little Golden Book which some twenty years ago sold in the millions.[59] In it, an anthropomorphically depicted little engine goes to engine school to learn to become a big streamliner. Like Little Red Riding Hood, Tootle has been told to move only on the tracks. It, too, is tempted to stray off them, since the little engine delights in playing among the pretty flowers in the fields. To stop Tootle from going astray, the townspeople get together and conceive of a clever plan, in which they all participate. Next time Tootle leaves the tracks to wander in its beloved meadows, it is stopped by a red flag wherever it turns, until it promises never to leave the tracks again.

Today we could view this as a story which exemplifies behavior modification through adverse stimuli: the red flags. Tootle reforms, and the story ends with Tootle having mended its ways and indeed going to grow up to be a big streamliner. *Tootle* seems to be essentially a cautionary tale, warning the child to stay on the narrow road of virtue. But how shallow it is when compared with the fairy tale.

"Little Red Cap" speaks of human passions, oral greediness, aggression, and pubertal sexual desires. It opposes the cultured orality of the maturing child (the nice food taken to Grandmother) to its earlier cannibalistic form (the wolf swallowing up Grandmother and the girl). With its violence, including that which saves the two females and destroys the wolf by cutting open its belly and then putting stones into it, the fairy tale does not show the world in a rosy light. The story ends as all figures—girl, mother, grandmother, hunter, and wolf—"do their own thing": the wolf tries to run away and falls to its death, after which the hunter skins the wolf and takes its pelt home; Grandmother eats what Little Red Cap has brought her; and the girl has learned her lesson. There is no conspiracy of adults which forces the story's hero to mend her way as society demands—a process which denies the value of inner-directedness. Far from others doing it for her, Little Red Cap's experience moves her to change herself, as she promises herself that "as long as you live, you won't run off the path into the woods. . . ."

How much truer both to the reality of life and to our inner experiences is the fairy tale when compared with *Tootle*, which uses realistic elements as stage props: trains running on tracks, red flags stopping them. The trappings are real enough, but everything essential is unreal, since the entire population of a town does not stop what it is doing, to help a child mend his ways. Also, there was never any real danger to Tootle's existence. Yes, Tootle is helped to mend its ways; but all that is involved in the growth experience is to become a bigger and faster train—that is, an externally more successful and useful adult. There is no recognition of inner anxieties, nor of the dangers of temptation to our very existence. To quote Riesman, "there is none of the grimness of Little Red Riding Hood," which has been replaced by "a fake which the citizens put on for Tootle's benefit." Nowhere in *Tootle* is there an externalization onto story characters of inner processes and emotional problems pertaining to growing up, so that the child may be able to face the first and thus solve the latter.

We can fully believe it when at the end of *Tootle* we are told that Tootle has forgotten it ever did like flowers. Nobody with the widest stretch of imagination can believe that Little Red Riding Hood could ever forget her encounter with the wolf, or will stop liking flowers or the beauty of the world. Tootle's story, not creating any inner conviction in the hearer's mind, needs to rub in its lesson and predict the outcome: the engine will stay on the tracks and become a streamliner. No initiative, no freedom there.

The fairy tale carries within itself the conviction of its message; therefore it has no need to peg the hero to a specific way of life. There is no need to tell what Little Red Riding Hood will do, or what her future will be. Due to her experience, she will be well able to decide this herself. The wisdom about life, and about the dangers which her desires may bring about, is gained by every listener.

Little Red Riding Hood lost her childish innocence as she encountered the dangers residing in herself and the world, and exchanged it for wisdom that only the "twice born" can possess: those who not only master an existential crisis, but also become conscious that it was their own nature which projected them into it. Little Red Riding Hood's childish innocence dies as the wolf reveals itself as such and swallows her. When she is cut out of the wolf's belly, she is reborn on a higher plane of existence; relating positively to both her parents, no longer a child, she returns to life a young maiden.

"JACK AND THE BEANSTALK"

Fairy tales deal in literary form with the basic problems of life, particularly those inherent in the struggle to achieve maturity. They caution against the destructive consequences if one fails to develop higher levels of responsible selfhood, setting warning examples such as the older brothers in "The Three Feathers," the stepsisters in "Cinderella," the wolf in "Little Red Cap." To the child, these tales subtly suggest why he ought to strive for higher integration, and what is involved in it.

These same stories also intimate to a parent that he ought to be aware of the risks involved in his child's development, so that he may be alert to them and protect the child when necessary to prevent a catastrophe; and that he ought to support and encourage his child's personal and sexual development when and where this is appropriate.

The tales of the Jack cycle are of British origin; from there they became diffused throughout the English-speaking world.[60] By far the best-known and most interesting story of this cycle is "Jack and the Beanstalk." Important elements of this fairy tale appear in many stories all over the world: the seemingly stupid exchange which provides something of magic power; the miraculous seed from which a tree grows that reaches into heaven; the cannibalistic ogre that is outwitted and robbed; the hen that lays golden eggs or the golden goose; the musical instrument that talks. But their combination into a story which asserts the desirability of social and sexual self-assertion in the pubertal boy, and the foolishness of a mother who belittles this, is what makes "Jack and the Beanstalk" such a meaningful fairy tale.

One of the oldest stories of the Jack cycle is "Jack and His Bargains." In it the original conflict is not between a son and his mother who thinks him a fool, but a battle for dominance between son and father. This story presents some problems of the social-sexual development of the male in clearer form than "Jack and the Beanstalk," and the underlying message of the latter can be understood more readily in the light of this earlier tale.

In "Jack and His Bargains" we are told that Jack is a wild boy, of no help to his father. Worse, because of Jack the father has fallen on hard times and must meet all kinds of debts. So he has sent Jack with one of the family's seven cows to the fair, to sell it for as much money as he can get for it. On the way to the fair Jack meets a man who asks him where he is headed. Jack tells him, and the man offers to swap the cow for a wondrous stick: all its owner has to say is "Up stick and at it" and the stick will beat all enemies senseless. Jack makes the exchange. When he comes home, the father, who has expected to receive money for his cow, gets so furious that he fetches a stick to beat Jack with. In self-defense Jack calls on *his* stick, which beats the father until he cries for mercy. This establishes Jack's ascendancy over his father in the home, but does not provide the money they need. So Jack is sent to the next fair to sell another cow. He meets the same man and exchanges the cow for a bee that sings beautiful songs. The need for money increases, and Jack is sent to sell a third cow. Once more he meets the man, and exchanges this cow for a fiddle which plays marvelous tunes.

Now the scene shifts. The king who rules in this part of the world has a daughter who is unable to smile. Her father promises to marry her to the man who can make her merry. Many princes and rich men try in vain to amuse her. Jack, in his ragged clothes, gets the better of all the highborn competitors, because the princess smiles when she hears the bee sing and the fiddle play so beautifully. She laughs outright as the stick beats up all the mighty suitors. So Jack is to marry her.

Before the marriage is to take place, the two are to spend a night in bed together. There Jack lies stock still and makes no move toward the princess. This greatly offends both her and her father; but the king soothes his daughter, and suggests that Jack may be scared of her and the new situation in which he finds himself. So on the following night another try is made, but the night passes as did the first. When on a third try Jack still does not move toward the princess in bed, the angry king has him thrown into a pit full of lions and tigers. Jack's stick beats these wild animals into submission, at which the princess marvels at "what a proper man he was." They get married "and had baskets full of children."

The story is somewhat incomplete. For example, while the number three is emphasized repeatedly—three encounters with the man, three exchanges of a cow for a magic object, three nights with the princess without Jack's "turning to her"—it remains unclear why seven cows are mentioned at the beginning and then we hear no more about the four cows remaining after three have been exchanged for the magic objects. Secondly, while there are many other fairy tales in which a man remains unresponsive to his love for three consecutive days or nights, usually this is explained in some fashion;* Jack's behavior in this regard, however, is left quite unexplained, and so we have to rely on our imagination for its meaning.

The magic formula "Up stick and at it" suggests phallic associations,

*For example, in the Brothers Grimm's tale "The Raven," a queen's daughter turned into a raven can be freed from her enchantment if the hero awaits her fully awake on the following afternoon. The raven warns him that to remain awake he must not eat or drink of anything an old woman will offer him. He promises, but on three consecutive days permits himself to be induced to take something and in consequence falls asleep at the appointed time when the raven-princess comes to meet him. Here it is an old woman's jealousy and a young man's selfish cupidity which explain his falling asleep when he should be wide awake for his beloved.

as does the fact that only this new acquisition permits Jack to hold his own in relation to his father, who up to now has dominated him. It is this stick which gains him victory in the competition with all suitors —a competition which is a sexual contest, since the prize is marrying the princess. It is the stick that finally leads to sexual possession of the princess, after it has beaten the wild animals into submission. While the lovely singing of the bee and the beautiful tunes of the fiddle make the princess smile, it is the stick's beating up the pretentious suitors, and thus making a shambles of what we may assume was their masculine posturing, that makes her laugh.* But if these sexual connotations were all there was to this story, it would not be a fairy tale, or not a very meaningful one. For its deeper significance we have to consider the other magic objects, and the nights during which Jack rests unmovingly beside the princess as if he himself were a stick.

Phallic potency, the story implies, is not enough. In itself it does not lead to better and higher things, nor does it make for sexual maturity. The bee—a symbol of hard work and sweetness, as it gives us honey, hence its delightful songs—stands for work and its enjoyment. Constructive labor as symbolized by the bee is a stark contrast to Jack's original wildness and laziness. After puberty, a boy must find constructive goals and work for them to become a useful member of society. That is why Jack is first provided with the stick, before he is given the bee and fiddle. The fiddle, the last present, symbolizes artistic achievement, and with it the highest human accomplishment. To win the princess, the power of the stick and what it symbolizes sexually is not sufficient. The power of the stick (sexual prowess) must become controlled, as suggested by the three nights in bed during which Jack does not move. By such behavior he demonstrates his self-control; with it he no longer rests his case on the display of phallic masculinity; he does not wish to win the princess by overpowering her. Through his subjugation of the wild animals Jack shows that he uses his strength to control those lower tendencies—the ferocity of

*There are many fairy tales in which an all-too-serious princess is won by the man who can make her laugh—that is, free her emotionally. This is frequently achieved by the hero's making persons who normally command respect look ridiculous. For example, in the Brothers Grimm's story "The Golden Goose," Simpleton, the youngest of three sons, because of his kindness to an old dwarf is given a goose with golden feathers. Cupidity induces various people to try to pull a feather off, but for this they get stuck to the goose, and to each other. Finally a parson and a sexton get stuck, too, and have to run after Simpleton and his goose. They look so ridiculous that on seeing this procession, the princess laughs.

lion and tiger, his wildness and irresponsibility which had piled up debts for his father—and with it becomes worthy of princess and kingdom. The princess recognizes this. Jack at first has made her only laugh, but at the end when he has demonstrated not only (sexual) power but also (sexual) self-control, he is recognized by her as a proper man with whom she can be happy and have many children.*

"Jack and His Bargains" begins with adolescent phallic self-assertion ("Up stick and at it") and ends with personal and social maturity as self-control and valuation of the higher things in life are achieved. The much-better-known "Jack and the Beanstalk" story starts and ends considerably earlier in a male's sexual development. While loss of infantile pleasure is barely hinted at in the first story with the need to sell the cows, this is a central issue in "Jack and the Beanstalk." We are told that the good cow Milky White, which until then had supported child and mother, has suddenly stopped giving milk. Thus the expulsion from an infantile paradise begins; it continues with the mother's deriding Jack's belief in the magic power of his seeds. The phallic beanstalk permits Jack to engage in oedipal conflict with the ogre, which he survives and finally wins, thanks only to the oedipal mother's taking his side against her own husband. Jack relinquishes his reliance on the belief in the magic power of phallic self-assertion as he cuts down the beanstalk; and this opens the way toward a development of mature masculinity. Thus, both versions of the Jack story together cover the entire male development.

Infancy ends when the belief in an unending supply of love and nutriment proves to be an irrealistic fantasy. Childhood begins with an equally irrealistic belief in what the child's own body in general, and specifically one aspect of it—his newly discovered sexual equipment—can achieve for him. As in infancy the mother's breast was symbol of all the child wanted of life and seemed to receive from her, so now his body, including his genitals, will do all that for the child, or so he wishes to believe. This is equally true for boys and girls; that is why "Jack and the Beanstalk" is enjoyed by children of both sexes.

*The Brothers Grimm's story "The Raven" may serve as a comparison to support the idea that three-times-repeated self-control over instinctual tendencies demonstrates sexual maturity, while its absence indicates an immaturity that prevents the gaining of one's true love. Unlike Jack, the hero in "The Raven," instead of controlling his desire for food and drink and for falling asleep, succumbs three times to the temptation by accepting the old woman's saying "One time is no time"—that is, it doesn't count—which shows his moral immaturity. He thus loses the princess. He finally gains her only after many errands through which he grows.

The end of childhood, as suggested before, is reached when such childish dreams of glory are given up and self-assertion, even against a parent, becomes the order of the day.

Every child can easily grasp the unconscious meaning of the tragedy when the good cow Milky White, who provided all that was needed, suddenly stops giving milk. It arouses dim memories of that tragic time when the flow of milk ceased for the child, when he was weaned. That is the time when the mother demands that the child must learn to make do with what the outside world can offer. This is symbolized by Jack's mother sending him out into the world to arrange for something (the money he is expected to get for the cow) that will provide sustenance. But Jack's belief in magic supplies has not prepared him for meeting the world realistically.

If up until now Mother (the cow, in fairy-tale metaphor) has supplied all that was needed and she now no longer does so, the child will naturally turn to his father—represented in the story by the man encountered on the way—expecting Father to supply magically to the child all he needs. Deprived of the "magic" supplies which up to then have been assured, and which he has felt were his unquestionable "rights," Jack is more than ready to exchange the cow for any promise of a magic solution to the impasse in living in which he finds himself.

It is not just Mother who tells Jack to sell the cow because it no longer gives milk; Jack also wants to get rid of this no-good cow that disappoints him. If Mother, in the form of Milky White, deprives and makes it imperative to change things, then Jack is going to exchange the cow not for what Mother wants, but for what seems more desirable to him.

To be sent out to encounter the world means the end of infancy. The child then has to begin the long and difficult process of turning himself into an adult. The first step on this road is relinquishing reliance on oral solutions to all of life's problems. Oral dependency has to be replaced by what the child can do for himself, on his own initiative. In "Jack and His Bargains" the hero is handed all three magic objects and only by means of them gains his independence; these objects do everything for him. His only contribution, while it shows self-control, is a rather passive one: he does nothing while in bed with the princess. When he is thrown into a pit with the wild animals, he is rescued not by his courage or intelligence, but only by the magic power of his stick.

Things are very different in "Jack and the Beanstalk." This story tells that while belief in magic can help in daring to meet the world on our own, in the last analysis we must take the initiative and be willing to run the risks involved in mastering life. When Jack is given the magic seeds, he climbs the beanstalk on his own initiative, not because somebody else suggested it. Jack uses his body's strength skillfully in climbing the beanstalk, and risks his life three times to gain the magic objects. At the end of the story he cuts down the beanstalk and in this way makes secure his possession of the magic objects which he has gained through his own cunning.

Giving up oral dependency is acceptable only if the child can find security in a realistic—or, more likely, a fantastically exaggerated—belief in what his body and its organs will do for him. But a child sees in sexuality not something based on a relation between a man and a woman, but something that he can achieve all by himself. Disappointed in his mother, a little boy is not likely to accept the idea that to achieve his masculinity he requires a woman. Without such (unrealistic) belief in himself, the child is not able to meet the world. The story tells that Jack looked for work, but didn't succeed in finding it; he is not yet able to manage realistically; this the man who gives him the magic seeds understands, although his mother does not. Only trust in what his own body—or, more specifically, his budding sexuality—can achieve for him permits the child to give up reliance on oral satisfaction; this is another reason why Jack is ready to exchange cow for seeds.

If his mother would accept Jack's wish to believe that his seeds and what they eventually may grow into are as valuable now as cow milk was in the past, then Jack would have less need to take recourse to fantasy satisfactions, such as the belief in magic phallic powers as symbolized by the huge beanstalk. Instead of approving of Jack's first act of independence and initiative—exchanging the cow for seeds—his mother ridicules what he has done, is angry with him for it, beats him, and, worst of all, falls back on the exercise of her depriving oral power: as punishment for having shown initiative, Jack is sent to bed without being given any food.

There, while he is in bed, reality having proven so disappointing, fantasy satisfaction takes over. The psychological subtlety of fairy stories which gives what they tell the ring of truth is shown once more in the fact that it is during the night that the seeds grow into the huge beanstalk. No normal boy could during the day exaggerate so fantastically the hopes which his newly discovered masculinity evokes in him. But during the night, in his dreams, it appears to him in extravagant images, such as the beanstalk on which he will climb to the gates of heaven. The story tells that when Jack awakes, his room is partly dark, the beanstalk shutting off the light. This is another hint that all that takes place—Jack's climbing into the sky on the beanstalk, his encounters with the ogre, etc.—is but dreams, dreams which give a boy hope for the great things he will one day accomplish.

The fantastic growth of the humble but magic seeds during the night is understood by children as a symbol of the miraculous power and of the satisfactions Jack's sexual development can bring about: the phallic phase is replacing the oral one; the beanstalk has replaced Milky White. On this beanstalk the child will climb into the sky to achieve a higher existence.

But, the story warns, this is not without its great dangers. Getting stuck in the phallic phase is little progress over fixation on the oral phase. Only when the relative independence acquired due to the new social and sexual development is used to solve the old oedipal problems will it lead to true human progress. Hence Jack's dangerous encounters with the ogre, as the oedipal father. But Jack also receives help from the ogre's wife, without which he would be destroyed by the ogre. How insecure Jack in "Jack and the Beanstalk" is about his newly discovered masculine strength is illustrated by his "regression" to orality whenever he feels threatened: he hides twice in the oven, and finally in a "copper," a large cooking vessel. His immaturity is further suggested by his stealing the magic objects which are the ogre's possessions, which he gets away with only because the ogre is asleep.* Jack's essential unreadiness to trust his newly found masculinity is indicated by his asking the ogre's wife for food because he is so hungry.

In fairy-tale fashion, this story depicts the stages of development a boy has to go through to become an independent human being, and shows how this is possible, even enjoyable, despite all dangers, and most advantageous. Giving up relying on oral satisfactions—or rather having been forced out of it by circumstances—and replacing them with phallic satisfaction as solution to all of life's problems are not enough: one has also to add, step by step, higher values to the ones already achieved. Before this can happen, one needs to work through the oedipal situation, which begins with deep disappointment in the mother and involves intense competition with and jealousy of the

*How different is the behavior of Jack in "Jack and His Bargains," who trusts his newly gained strength. He does not hide or get things on the sly; on the contrary, when in a dangerous situation, whether with his father, his competitors for the princess, or the wild beasts, he openly uses the power of his stick to gain his goals.

father. The boy does not yet trust Father enough to relate openly to
him. To master the difficulties of this period, the boy needs a mother's
understanding help: only because the ogre's wife protects and hides
Jack can he acquire the ogre-father's powers.

On his first trip Jack steals a bag filled with gold. This gives him and
his mother the resources to buy what they need, but eventually they
run out of money. So Jack repeats his excursion, although he now
knows that in doing so he risks his life.*

On his second trip Jack gains the hen that lays the golden eggs: he
has learned that one runs out of things if one cannot produce them
or have them produced. With the hen Jack could be content, since
now all physical needs are permanently satisfied. So it is not necessity
which motivates Jack's last trip, but the desire for daring and adventure—the wish to find something better than mere material goods.
Thus, Jack next attains the golden harp, which symbolizes beauty, art,
the higher things in life. This is followed by the last growth experience, in which Jack learns that it will not do to rely on magic for
solving life's problems.

As Jack gains full humanity by striving for and gaining what the
harp represents, he is also forcefully made aware—through the ogre's
nearly catching him—that if he continues to rely on magic solutions,
he will end up destroyed. As the ogre pursues him down the beanstalk, Jack calls out to his mother to get the ax and cut the beanstalk.

*On some level, climbing up the beanstalk symbolizes not only the "magic" power
of the phallus to rise, but also a boy's feelings connected with masturbation. The child
who masturbates fears that if he is found out, he will suffer terrible punishment, as
symbolized by the ogre's doing away with him if he should discover what Jack is up
to. But the child also feels as if he is, in masturbating, "stealing" some of his parent's
powers. The child who, on an unconscious level, understands this meaning of the
story derives reassurance that his masturbation anxieties are invalid. His "phallic"
excursion into the world of the grown-up giant-ogres, far from leading to his destruction, gains him advantages he is able to enjoy permanently.

Here is another example of how the fairy tale permits the child to understand and
be helped on an unconscious level without his having to become aware on a conscious
level of what the story is dealing with. The fairy tale represents in images what goes
on in the unconscious or preconscious of the child: how his awakening sexuality seems
like a miracle that happens in the darkness of the night, or in his dream. Climbing
up the beanstalk, and what it symbolizes, creates the anxiety that at the end of this
experience he will be destroyed for his daring. The child fears that his desire to
become sexually active amounts to stealing parental powers and prerogatives, and
that therefore this can be done only on the sly, when the adults are unable to see what
goes on. After the story has given body to these anxieties, it assures the child that the
ending will be a good one.

The mother brings the ax as told, but on seeing the giant's huge legs coming down the beanstalk, she freezes into immobility; she is unable to deal with phallic objects. On a different level, the mother's freezing signifies that while a mother may protect her boy against the dangers involved in striving for manhood—as the ogre's wife did in hiding Jack —she cannot gain it for him; only he himself can do that. Jack grabs the ax and cuts off the beanstalk, and with it brings down the ogre, who perishes from his fall. In doing so, Jack rids himself of the father who is experienced on the oral level: as a jealous ogre who wants to devour.

But in cutting down the beanstalk Jack not only frees himself from a view of the father as a destructive and devouring ogre; he also thus relinquishes his belief in the magic power of the phallus as the means for gaining him all the good things in life. In putting the ax to the beanstalk, Jack forswears magic solutions; he becomes "his own man." He no longer will take from others, but neither will he live in mortal fear of ogres, nor rely on Mother's hiding him in an oven (regressing to orality).

As the story of "Jack and the Beanstalk" ends, Jack is ready to give up phallic and oedipal fantasies and instead try to live in reality, as much as a boy his age can do so. The next development may see him no longer trying to trick a sleeping father out of his possessions, nor fantasizing that a mother figure will for his sake betray her husband, but ready to strive openly for his social and sexual ascendency. This is where "Jack and His Bargains" begins, which sees its hero attain such maturity.

This fairy tale, like many others, could teach parents much as it helps children grow up. It tells mothers what little boys need to solve their oedipal problems: Mother must side with the boy's masculine daring, surreptitious though it may still be, and protect him against the dangers which might be inherent in masculine assertion, particularly when directed against the father.

The mother in "Jack and the Beanstalk" fails her son because, instead of supporting his developing masculinity, she denies its validity. The parent of the other sex ought to encourage a child's pubertal sexual development, particularly as he seeks goals and achievements in the wider world. Jack's mother, who thought her son utterly foolish for the trading he had done, stands revealed as the foolish one because she failed to recognize the development from child to adolescent which was taking place in her son. If she had had her way, Jack would have remained an immature child, and neither he nor his mother would have escaped their misery. Jack, motivated by his budding manhood, undeterred by his mother's low opinion of him, gains great fortune through his courageous actions. This story teaches—as do many other fairy tales, such as "The Three Languages"—that the parents' error is basically the lack of an appropriate and sensitive response to the various problems involved in a child's maturing personally, socially, and sexually.

The oedipal conflict within the boy in this fairy tale is conveniently externalized onto two very distant figures who exist somewhere in a castle in the sky: the ogre and his wife. It is many a child's experience that most of the time, when Father—like the ogre in the tale—is out of the home, the child and his mother have a good time together, as do Jack and the ogre's wife. Then suddenly Father comes home, asking for his meal, which spoils everything for the child, who is not made welcome by his father. If a child is not given the feeling that his father is happy to find him home, he will be afraid of what he fantasized while Father was away, because it didn't include Father. Since the child wants to rob Father of his most prized possessions, how natural that he should fear being destroyed in retaliation.

Given all the dangers of regressing to orality, here is another implied message of the Jack story: it was not at all bad that Milky White stopped giving milk. Had this not happened, Jack would not have gotten the seeds out of which the beanstalk grew. Orality thus not only sustains—when hung on to too long, it prevents further development; it even destroys, as does the orally fixated ogre. Orality can be left safely behind for masculinity if Mother approves and continues to offer protection. The ogre's wife hides Jack in a safe, confined place, as Mother's womb had provided safety against all dangers. Such a short regression to a previous stage of development provides the security and strength needed for the next step in independence and self-assertion. It permits the little boy to enjoy fully the advantages of the phallic development he is now entering. And if the bag of gold and, even more, the hen that lays the golden eggs stand for anal ideas of possession, the story assures that the child will not get stuck in the anal stage of development: he will soon realize that he must sublimate such primitive views and become dissatisfied with them. He will then settle for nothing less than the golden harp and what it symbolizes.*

*Unfortunately, "Jack and the Beanstalk" is often reprinted in a form that contains many changes and additions, mostly the result of efforts to provide moral justification for Jack's robbing the giant. These changes, however, destroy the story's poetic impact and rob it of its deeper psychological meaning. In this bowdlerized version,

THE JEALOUS QUEEN
IN "SNOW WHITE"
AND THE MYTH OF OEDIPUS

Since fairy tales deal imaginatively with the most important developmental issues in all our lives, it is not surprising that so many of them
center in some way on oedipal difficulties. But so far the fairy tales
discussed have focused on the problems of the child and not those of
the parent. In actuality, as the relation of a child to his parent is full
of problems, so is that of a parent to his child, so many fairy tales touch
also on the parents' oedipal problems. While the child is encouraged
to believe that he is quite able to find his way out of his oedipal
difficulties, the parent is warned against the disastrous consequences
for him if he permits himself to get caught up in them.*

In "Jack and the Beanstalk" a mother's unreadiness to permit her

---

a fairy tells Jack that the giant's castle and the magic objects were once the possessions
of Jack's father, which the giant took after killing him; and that Jack is therefore to
slay the giant and gain rightful possession of the magic objects. This makes all that
happens to Jack a moral tale of retribution rather than a story of manhood achieved.

The original "Jack and the Beanstalk" is the odyssey of a boy striving to gain
independence from a mother who thinks little of him, and on his own achieving
greatness. In the bowdlerized version, Jack does only what another powerful older
female, the fairy, orders him to do.

One last example of how those who think they are improving on a traditional fairy
tale actually do the opposite. In both versions, when Jack seizes the magic harp, it
cries out "Master, Master," awakening the ogre, who then pursues Jack with the
intention of killing him. That a talking harp arouses its rightful master when being
stolen makes good fairy-tale sense. But what is the child to think of a magic harp
which was not only stolen from its rightful master, but stolen by the man who vilely
killed him, and which in the process of being regained by his rightful master's son
nevertheless arouses the thief and murderer? Changing such details robs the story of
its magic impact, as it deprives the magic objects—and everything else that happens
in the story—of their symbolic meaning as external representations of inner processes.

*As with wishing, the fairy tale has full understanding that the child cannot help
being subjected to the oedipal predicaments, and hence is not punished if he acts in
line with them. But the parent who permits himself to act out *his* oedipal problems
on the child suffers severely for it.

son to become independent was hinted at. "Snow White" tells how a parent—the queen—gets destroyed by jealousy of her child who, in growing up, surpasses her. In the Greek tragedy of Oedipus, who is of course undone by oedipal entanglements, not only is his mother, Jocasta, also ruined, but first of all to fall is Oedipus' father, Laius, whose fear that his son will replace him eventually leads to the tragedy that undoes them all. The queen's fear that Snow White will excel her is the theme of the fairy tale which carries the wronged child's name, as does the story of Oedipus. It may be useful, therefore, to consider briefly this famous myth which, through psychoanalytic writings, has become the metaphor by which we refer to a particular emotional constellation within the family—one that can cause the most severe impediments to growing up into a mature, well-integrated person, while being, on the other hand, the potential source of the richest personality development.

In general, the less a person has been able to resolve his oedipal feelings constructively, the greater the danger that he may be beset by them again when he becomes a parent. The male parent who has failed to integrate in the process of maturation his childish wish to possess his mother and his irrational fear of his father is likely to be anxious about his son as a competitor, and may even act destructively out of this fear, as we are told King Laius did. Nor does the child's unconscious fail to respond to such feelings in a parent, if they are part of his relation to his child. The fairy story permits the child to comprehend that not only is he jealous of his parent, but that the parent may have parallel feelings—an insight that can not only help to bridge the gap between parent and child, but may also permit dealing constructively with difficulties in relating which otherwise would not be accessible to resolution. Even more important, the fairy tale reassures the child that he need not be afraid of parental jealousy where it may exist, because he will survive successfully, whatever complications these feelings may create temporarily.

Fairy tales do not tell *why* a parent may be unable to enjoy his child's growing up and surpassing him, but becomes jealous of the child. We do not know why the queen in "Snow White" cannot age gracefully and gain satisfaction from vicariously enjoying her daughter's blooming into a lovely girl, but something must have happened in her past to make her vulnerable so that she hates the child she should love. How the sequence of the generations can account for a parent's fear of his child is illustrated in the cycle of myths of which the story of Oedipus is the central part.[61]

This mythic cycle, which ends with *The Seven Against Thebes*, begins with Tantalus, who as a friend of the gods tried to test their ability to know everything by having his son Pelops slain and served to the gods as dinner. (The queen in "Snow White" orders that her daughter be killed, and eats what she believes to be part of Snow White's body.) The myth tells that it was Tantalus' vanity which motivated his evil deed, as it is vanity which spurs the queen to commit her villainy. The queen, who wanted to remain fairest forever, is punished by having to dance to her death, in red-hot shoes. Tantalus, who tried to fool the gods with his son's body as food, suffers eternally in Hades, by being tempted to satisfy his unending thirst and hunger with water and fruits which seem within his grasp but recede as soon as he tries to seize them. Thus, punishment does fit the crime in myth and fairy tale.

In both stories also, death does not necessarily signify the end of life, as Pelops is restored by the gods, and Snow White regains her consciousness. Death is rather a symbol that this person is wished away —just as the oedipal child does not really wish to see his parent-competitor die, but simply wants him removed from the child's way of winning his other parent's complete attention. The child's expectation is that, much as he has wished a parent out of the way at one moment, the parent should be very much alive and at the child's service in the next. Accordingly, in the fairy tale a person is dead or turned into stone at one moment, and comes to life in the next.

Tantalus was a father ready to risk his son's well-being to feed his vanity, and this was destructive to him, and also to his son. Pelops, having been used thus by his father, later does not hesitate to kill a father to gain his goals. King Oenomaus of Elis selfishly wished to keep his beautiful daughter, Hippodamia, all to himself, and he devised a scheme by which he disguised this desire while making sure that his daughter would never leave him. Any suitor for Hippodamia had to compete with King Oenomaus in a chariot race; if the suitor won, he could marry Hippodamia; if he lost, the king gained the right to kill him, which he always did. Pelops surreptitiously replaced the brass bolts in the king's chariot with wax ones, and in this deceitful way he won the race, in which the king was killed.

So far the myth indicates that the consequences are equally tragic if a father misuses his son for his own purposes, or if a father should, out of an oedipal attachment to his daughter, try to deprive her of a life of her own, and her suitors of their very lives. Next the myth tells of the terrible consequences of "oedipal" sibling rivalry. Pelops had two legitimate sons, Atreus and Thyestes. Out of jealousy, Thyestes, the younger of the two, stole Atreus' ram, which had a fleece of gold. As retribution, Atreus slaughtered Thyestes' two sons, and fed them to Thyestes in a big banquet.

This was not the only instance of sibling rivalry in the house of Pelops. He also had an illegitimate son, Chrysippus. Laius, Oedipus' father, as a youth found protection and a home at the court of Pelops. Despite Pelops' kindness to him, Laius wronged Pelops by abducting —or ravishing—Chrysippus. We may assume that Laius did this out of his jealousy of Chrysippus, who was preferred to him by Pelops. In punishment for such acted-out rivalry, the oracle at Delphi told Laius he would be killed by his own son. As Tantalus had destroyed, or tried to destroy, his son, Pelops, and as Pelops had arranged for the death of his father-in-law, Oenomaus, so Oedipus would come to kill his father, Laius. In the normal course of events, a son replaces his father —so we may read all these stories as telling about the son's wish to do this and the father's trying to forestall it. But this myth relates that oedipal acting-out on the part of the fathers precedes oedipal acting-out on the part of the children.

To prevent his son from killing him, Laius on Oedipus' birth had the infant's ankles pierced and his feet tied together. Laius ordered a shepherd to take the child Oedipus and leave him in the wilderness to die. But the shepherd—like the hunter in "Snow White"—took pity on the child; he pretended to have deserted Oedipus, but gave the boy over to the care of another shepherd. This shepherd took Oedipus to his king, who raised Oedipus as his son.

As a young man, Oedipus consulted the oracle of Delphi and was told that he would slay his father and wed his mother. Thinking that the royal pair who had raised him were his parents, Oedipus did not return home but wandered off, to prevent such horror. At a crossroads he slew Laius, unaware that he was his father. On his wanderings Oedipus came to Thebes, solved the riddle of the Sphinx, and thus delivered the city. As reward, Oedipus married the queen—his widowed mother, Jocasta. Thus the son replaced his father as king and husband; the son fell in love with his mother, and the mother had sexual relations with her son. When the truth of it all was finally discovered, Jocasta committed suicide and Oedipus blinded himself; he destroyed his eyes in punishment for not having seen what he was doing.

But the tragic story does not end there. Oedipus' twin sons, Eteocles and Polynices, did not support him in his misery, and only his daughter Antigone stayed with and by him. Time passed, and in the war of the Seven Against Thebes, Eteocles and Polynices killed each other in combat. Antigone buried Polynices against King Creon's orders, and was killed for it. Not only does intense sibling rivalry devastate, as shown by the fate of the two brothers, but over-intense sibling attachment is equally fatal, as we learn from Antigone's fate.

To sum up the variety of death-bringing relations in these myths: instead of lovingly accepting his son, Tantalus sacrifices him to his own ends; so does Laius in respect to Oedipus; and both fathers end up destroyed. Oenomaus dies because he tries to keep his daughter all to himself, as does Jocasta, who attaches herself too closely to her son: sexual love for the child of the other sex is as destructive as acted-out fear that the child of the same sex will replace and surpass the parent. Doing away with the parent of the same sex is Oedipus' undoing, as it is that of his sons who desert him in his distress. Sibling rivalry kills Oedipus' sons. Antigone, who does not forsake her father, Oedipus, but on the contrary shares his misery, dies because of her too great devotion to her brother.

But still this does not conclude the story. Creon, who as king condemns Antigone to die, does so against the entreaties of his son, Haemon, who loves Antigone. In destroying Antigone, Creon also destroys his son; once more, here is a father who cannot give up ruling his son's life. Haemon, in despair over Antigone's death, tries to kill his father and, failing to do so, commits suicide; so does his mother, Creon's wife, in consequence of her son's death. The only one to survive in the family of Oedipus is Ismene, Antigone's sister, who has not attached herself too deeply to either of her parents, nor any of her siblings, and with whom no member of the immediate family had become deeply involved. According to the myth, there seems to be no way out: whoever by chance or his own desires remains too deeply entangled in an "oedipal" relation is destroyed.

Nearly all types of incestuous attachment are found in this cycle of myths, and all types are intimated also in fairy tales. But in fairy tales the hero's story shows how these potentially destructive infantile relations can be, and are, integrated in developmental processes. In the myth, oedipal difficulties are acted out and in consequence all ends in total destruction, whether the relations are positive or negative. The message is clear enough: when a parent cannot accept his child as such and be satisfied that he will have to be replaced by him eventually, deepest tragedy results. Only an acceptance of the child as child— neither as a competitor nor as a sexual love object—permits good relations between parents and children, and between the siblings.

How different are the ways the fairy tale and this classic myth present oedipal relations and their consequences. Despite her step-mother's jealousy, Snow White not only survives but finds great happiness, as does Rapunzel, whose parents had given her up because satisfying their own cravings had been more important to them than keeping their daughter, and whose foster mother tried to hold on to her for too long. Beauty in "Beauty and the Beast" is loved by her father, and she loves him equally deeply. Neither of them is punished for their mutual attachment: on the contrary, Beauty saves her father and the Beast by transferring her attachment from father to lover. Cinderella, far from being destroyed by her siblings' jealousy as were Oedipus' sons, emerges victorious.

It is thus in all fairy tales. The message of *these* stories is that oedipal entanglements and difficulties may seem to be unsolvable, but by courageously struggling with these emotional familial complexities, one can achieve a much better life than those who are never beset by severe problems. In the myth there is only insurmountable difficulty and defeat; in the fairy tale there is equal peril, but it is successfully overcome. Not death and destruction, but higher integration—as symbolized by victory over the enemy or competitor, and by happiness—is the hero's reward at the end of the fairy tale. To gain it, he undergoes growth experiences that parallel those necessary for the child's development toward maturity. This gives the child the courage not to become dismayed by the difficulties he encounters in his struggle to become himself.

"SNOW WHITE"

"Snow White" is one of the best-known fairy tales. It has been told for centuries in various forms in all European countries and languages; from there it was disseminated to the other continents. More often than not, the story's title is simply the name "Snow White," although there are many variations.* "Snow White and the Seven Dwarfs," the

*For example, one Italian version is called *"La Ragazza di Latte e Sangue"* ("The Girl of Milk and Blood"), which finds its explanation in the fact that in many Italian renderings the three drops of blood which the queen sheds do not fall on snow, which is very rare in most parts of Italy, but instead on milk, white marble, or even white cheese.

name by which the tale is now widely known, is a bowdlerization
which unfortunately emphasizes the dwarfs, who, failing to develop
into mature humanity, are permanently arrested on a pre-oedipal
level (dwarfs have no parents, nor do they marry or have children)
and are but foils to set off the important developments taking place
in Snow White.

Some versions of "Snow White" begin: "A count and a countess
drove by three mounds of white snow which made the count say, 'I
wish I had a girl as white as this snow.' A short while later they came
to three holes full of red blood, at which he said, 'I wish I had a girl
with cheeks as red as this blood.' Finally three black ravens flew by,
at which moment he desired a girl 'with hair as black as these ravens.'
As they drove on, they encountered a girl as white as snow, as red as
blood, and with hair as black as the raven; and she was Snow White.
The count immediately made her sit in the coach and loved her, but
the countess did not like it and thought only about how she could get
rid of her. Finally she dropped her glove and ordered Snow White to
look for it; in the meantime the coachman had to drive on with great
speed."

A parallel version differs only in the detail that the couple drive
through a forest and Snow White is asked to descend to gather a bunch
of beautiful roses which grow there. As she does so, the queen orders
the coachman to drive on, and Snow White is deserted.[62]

In these renderings of the story, the count and countess or king and
queen are thinly disguised parents, and the girl so admired by a father
figure and found by chance is a surrogate daughter. The oedipal
desires of a father and daughter, and how these arouse the mother's
jealousy which makes her wish to get rid of the daughter, are much
more clearly stated here than in more common versions. The now
widely accepted form of "Snow White" leaves the oedipal entanglements to our imagination rather than forcing them on our conscious
mind.*[63]

*Some elements of one of the earliest versions of the "Snow White" motif found
in Basile's "The Young Slave" make it clear that the heroine's persecution is due to
a (step)mother's jealousy, the cause of which is not just the young girl's beauty, but
rather the real or imagined love of the (step)mother's husband for the girl. The girl,
whose name is Lisa, dies temporarily from a comb that gets stuck in her hair. Like
Snow White, she is buried in a casket of crystal in which she continues to grow as the
coffin grows with her. After she has spent seven years in the coffin, her uncle goes
away. This uncle, who is her foster father really, is the only father she has ever had,
since her mother was magically impregnated by the leaf of a rose which she had
swallowed. His wife, insanely jealous because of what she views as her husband's love

Whether openly stated or only hinted at, oedipal difficulties and how the individual solves them are central to the way his personality and human relations unfold. By camouflaging the oedipal predicaments, or by only subtly intimating the entanglements, fairy stories permit us to draw our own conclusions when the time is propitious for our gaining a better understanding of these problems. Fairy stories teach by indirection. In the versions just mentioned, Snow White is not the count's and countess' child, deeply desired and loved though she is by the count, and jealous though the countess is of her. In the well-known story of Snow White, the jealous older female is not her mother but her stepmother, and the person for whose love the two are in competition is not mentioned. So the oedipal problems—source of the story's conflict—are left to our imagination.

While, physiologically speaking, the parents create the child, it is the arrival of the child which causes these two people to become parents. Thus, it is the child who creates the parental problems, and with these come his own. Fairy tales usually begin when the child's life in some manner has reached an impasse. In "Hansel and Gretel" the children's presence creates hardships for the parents, and because of this, life turns problematic for the children. In "Snow White" it is not any external difficulty such as poverty, but the relations between her and her parents which create the problematic situation.

As soon as the position of the child within the family becomes a problem to him or to his parents, the process of the child's struggle to escape the triadic existence has begun. With it, he enters the often desperately lonely course to find himself—a struggle in which others serve mainly as foils who facilitate or impede this process. In some fairy tales the hero has to search, travel, and suffer through years of a lonely existence before he is ready to find, rescue, and join one other person in a relation which gives permanent meaning to both their lives. In "Snow White" it is the years Snow White spends with the dwarfs which stand for her time of troubles, of working through problems, her period of growth.

Few fairy tales help the hearer to distinguish between the main phases of childhood development as neatly as does "Snow White." The earliest, entirely dependent pre-oedipal years are hardly men-

for Lisa, shakes her out of the coffin; the comb drops out of her hair, and she awakes. The jealous (step)mother turns her into a slave; hence the story's title. At the end, the uncle finds out that the young slave girl is Lisa. He restores her and drives away his wife, who, out of jealousy for his love for Lisa, has nearly destroyed her.[64]

tioned, as is true of most fairy tales. The story deals essentially with the oedipal conflicts between mother and daughter; with childhood; and finally with adolescence, placing major emphasis on what constitutes a good childhood, and what is needed to grow out of it.

The Brothers Grimm's story of "Snow White" begins: "Once upon a time, in the middle of winter when the snow flakes fell like feathers from the sky, a queen sat at a window which had a frame of black ebony. And as she was sewing while looking at the snow, she pricked her finger with the needle and three drops of blood fell on the snow. The red looked so beautiful on the white snow that she thought to herself, 'I wish I had a child as white as snow, as red as the blood, and with hair as black as the wood of the window frame.' Soon after she got a little daughter who was as white as snow, as red as blood, and had hair as black as ebony, and she was therefore called Snow White. And when the child had been born, the queen died. After a year had passed, the king took himself another wife. . . ."

The story begins with Snow White's mother pricking her finger so that three drops of red blood fall upon the snow. Here the problems the story sets out to solve are intimated: sexual innocence, whiteness, is contrasted with sexual desire, symbolized by the red blood. Fairy tales prepare the child to accept what is otherwise a most upsetting event: sexual bleeding, as in menstruation and later in intercourse when the hymen is broken. Listening to the first few sentences of "Snow White," the child learns that a small amount of bleeding— three drops of blood (three being the number most closely associated in the unconscious with sex[65])—is a precondition for conception, because only after this bleeding is the child born. Here, then, (sexual) bleeding is closely connected with a "happy" event; without detailed explanations the child learns that without bleeding no child—not even he—could have been born.

Although we are told that her mother died when she was born, during her first years nothing bad happens to Snow White, despite the fact that her mother is replaced by a stepmother. The latter turns into the "typical" fairy-tale stepmother only *after* Snow White reaches the age of seven and starts to mature. Then the stepmother begins to feel threatened by Snow White and becomes jealous. The stepmother's narcissism is demonstrated by her seeking reassurance about her beauty from the magic mirror long before Snow White's beauty eclipses hers.

The queen's consulting the mirror about her worth—i.e., beauty— repeats the ancient theme of Narcissus, who loved only himself, so much that he became swallowed up by his self-love. It is the narcissis-

tic parent who feels most threatened by his child's growing up, because that means the parent must be aging. As long as the child is
totally dependent, he remains, as it were, *part* of the parent; he does
not threaten the parent's narcissism. But when the child begins to
mature and reaches for independence, then he is experienced as a
menace by such a parent, as happens to the queen in "Snow White."

Narcissism is very much part of the young child's make-up. The
child must gradually learn to transcend this dangerous form of self-
involvement. The story of Snow White warns of the evil consequences
of narcissism for both parent and child. Snow White's narcissism
nearly undoes her as she gives in twice to the disguised queen's entice-
ments to make her look more beautiful, while the queen is destroyed
by her own narcissism.

As long as she remained home, Snow White did nothing; we hear
nothing about her life before her expulsion. We are told nothing about
her relation to her father, although it is reasonable to assume that it
is competition for him which sets (step)mother against daughter.

The fairy tale views the world and what happens in it not objectively, but from the perspective of the hero, who is always a person
in development. Since the hearer identifies with Snow White, he sees
all events through her eyes, and not through those of the queen. To
the girl child, her love for her father is the most natural thing in the
world, and so is his love for her. She cannot conceive of this being a
problem—short of his not loving her enough, in preference to everybody else. Much as the child wants the father to love her more than
her mother, she cannot accept that this may create jealousy of her in
the mother. But on a preconscious level, the child knows quite well
how jealous she is of the attention one parent pays to the other, when
the child feels she should get that attention. Since the child wants to
be loved by both parents—a fact which is well known, but in discussion of the oedipal situation is frequently neglected because of the
nature of the problem—it is much too threatening for the child to
imagine that love for him by one parent may create jealousy in the
other. When this jealousy—as is true for the queen in "Snow White"
—cannot be overlooked, then some other reason must be found to
explain it, as in the story it is ascribed to the child's beauty.

In the normal course of events, the relations of parents to each other
are not threatened by the love of one or both parents for their child.
Unless the marital relations are quite bad, or a parent is very narcissistic, jealousy of a child favored by one parent remains small and well
controlled by the other parent.

Matters are quite different for the child. First, he cannot find solace for the pangs of jealousy in a good relation such as that his parents have with each other. Second, all children are jealous, if not of their parents, then of the privileges the parents enjoy as adults. When the tender, loving care of the parent of the same sex is not strong enough to build up ever more important positive ties in the naturally jealous oedipal child, and with it set the process of identification working against this jealousy, then the latter dominates the child's emotional life. Since a narcissistic (step)mother is an unsuitable figure to relate to or identify with, Snow White, if she were a real child, could not help being intensely jealous of her mother and all her advantages and powers.

If a child cannot permit himself to feel his jealousy of a parent (this is very threatening to his security), he projects his feelings onto this parent. Then "I am jealous of all the advantages and prerogatives of Mother" turns into the wishful thought: "Mother is jealous of me." The feeling of inferiority is defensively turned into a feeling of superiority.

The prepubertal or adolescent child may say to himself, "I do not compete with my parents, I am already better than they are; it's they who are competing with me." Unfortunately, there are also parents who try to convince their adolescent children that they are superior to them—which the parents may well be in some respects, but for the sake of their children's ability to become secure, they ought to keep this fact to themselves. Worse, there are parents who maintain that they are in all ways as good as their adolescent child: the father who attempts to keep up with the youthful strength and sexual prowess of his son; the mother who tries in looks, dress, and behavior to be as youthfully attractive as her daughter. The ancient history of stories such as "Snow White" suggests that this is an age-old phenomenon. But competition between a parent and his child makes life unbearable for parent and child. Under such conditions the child wants to free himself and be rid of the parent, who forces him either to compete or to buckle under. The wish to be rid of the parent arouses great guilt, justified though it may be when the situation is viewed objectively. So in a reversal which eliminates the guilt feeling, this wish, too, is projected onto the parent. Thus, in fairy tales there are parents who try to rid themselves of their child, as happens in "Snow White."

In "Snow White," as in "Little Red Riding Hood," a male who can be viewed as an unconscious representation of the father appears—the hunter who is ordered to kill Snow White, but instead saves her life.

Who else but a father substitute would seem to acquiesce to the stepmother's dominance and nevertheless, for the child's sake, dare to go against the queen's will? This is what the oedipal and adolescent girl wishes to believe about her father: that even though he does as the mother bids him, he would side with his daughter if he were free to, tricking the mother as he did so.

Why are rescuing male figures so often cast in the role of hunters in fairy tales? While hunting may have been a typically masculine occupation when fairy stories came into being, this is much too easy an explanation. At that time princes and princesses were as rare as they are today, and fairy tales simply abound with them. But when and where these stories originated, hunting was an aristocratic privilege, which supplies a good reason to see the hunter as an exalted figure like a father.

Actually, hunters appear frequently in fairy tales because they lend themselves so well to projections. Every child at some time wishes that he were a prince or a princess—and at times, in his unconscious, the child believes he is one, only temporarily degraded by circumstances. There are so many kings and queens in fairy tales because their rank signifies absolute power, such as the parent seems to hold over his child. So the fairy-tale royalty represent projections of the child's imagination, as does the hunter.

The ready acceptance of the hunter figure as a suitable image of a strong and protective father figure—as opposed to the many ineffectual fathers such as the one in "Hansel and Gretel"—must relate to associations which attach themselves to this figure. In the unconscious the hunter is seen as the symbol of protection. In this connection we must consider the animal phobias of which no child is entirely free. In his dreams and daydreams the child is threatened and pursued by angry animals, creations of his fear and guilt. Only the parent-hunter, so he feels, can scare these threatening animals away, keep them permanently from the child's door. Hence the hunter of fairy tales is not a figure who kills friendly creatures, but one who dominates, controls, and subdues wild, ferocious beasts. On a deeper level, he represents the subjugation of the animal, asocial, violent tendencies in man. Since he seeks out, tracks down, and defeats what are viewed as lower aspects of man—the wolf—the hunter is an eminently protective figure who can and does save us from the dangers of our violent emotions and those of others.

In "Snow White" the pubertal girl's oedipal struggle is not repressed, but acted out around the mother as competitor. In Snow

White's story the father-huntsman fails to take a strong and definite stand. He neither does his duty to the queen, nor meets his moral obligation to Snow White to make her safe and secure. He does not kill her outright, but he deserts her in the forest, expecting her to be killed by wild animals. The hunter tries to placate both the mother, by seemingly executing her order, and the girl, by merely not killing her. Lasting hatred and jealousy of the mother are the consequence of the father's ambivalence, which in "Snow White" are projected onto the evil queen, who therefore continues to reappear in Snow White's life.

A weak father is as little use to Snow White as he was to Hansel and Gretel. The frequent appearance of such figures in fairy tales suggests that wife-dominated husbands are not exactly new to this world. More to the point, it is such fathers who either create unmanageable difficulties in the child or fail to help him solve them. This is another example of the important messages fairy tales contain for parents.

Why is the mother outright rejecting in these fairy tales while the father is often only ineffectual and weak? The reason the (step)mother is depicted as evil and the father as weak has to do with what the child expects of his parents. In the typical nuclear family setting, it is the father's duty to protect the child against the dangers of the outside world, and also those that originate in the child's own asocial tendencies. The mother is to provide nurturing care and the general satisfaction of immediate bodily needs required for the child's survival. Therefore, if the mother fails the child in fairy tales, the child's very life is in jeopardy, as happens in "Hansel and Gretel" when the mother insists that the children must be gotten rid of. If the father out of weakness is negligent in meeting his obligations, then the child's life as such is not so directly endangered, although a child deprived of the father's protection must shift for himself as best he can. So Snow White must fend for herself when she is abandoned by the hunter in the forest.

Only loving care combined with responsible behavior on the part of both parents permits the child to integrate his oedipal conflicts. If he is deprived of either by one or both parents, the child will not be able to identify with them. If a girl cannot form a positive identification with her mother, not only does she get stuck in oedipal conflicts, but regression sets in, as it always does when the child fails to attain the next higher stage of development for which she is chronologically ready.

The queen, who is fixated to a primitive narcissism and arrested on the oral incorporative stage, is a person who cannot positively relate, nor can anybody identify with her. The queen orders the hunter not only to kill Snow White, but to return with her lungs and liver as evidence. When the hunter brings the queen the lungs and liver of an animal to prove he has executed her command, "The cook had to cook them in salt, and the bad woman ate them and thought she had eaten Snow White's lungs and liver." In primitive thought and custom, one acquires the powers or characteristics of what one eats. The queen, jealous of Snow White's beauty, wanted to incorporate Snow White's attractiveness, as symbolized by her internal organs.

This is not the first story of a mother's jealousy of her daughter's budding sexuality, nor is it all that rare that a daughter in her mind accuses her mother of such jealousy. The magic mirror seems to speak with the voice of a daughter rather than that of a mother. As the small girl thinks her mother is the most beautiful person in the world, this is what the mirror initially tells the queen. But as the older girl thinks she is much more beautiful than her mother, this is what the mirror says later. A mother may be dismayed when looking into the mirror; she compares herself to her daughter and thinks to herself: "My daughter is more beautiful than I am." But the mirror says: "She is a thousand times more beautiful"—a statement much more akin to an adolescent's exaggeration which he makes to enlarge his advantages and silence his inner voice of doubt.

The pubertal child is ambivalent in his wish to be much better than his parent of the same sex because the child fears that if this were actually so, the parent, still much more powerful, would take terrible revenge. It is the child who fears destruction because of his imagined or real superiority, not the parent who wishes to destroy. The parent may suffer pangs of jealousy if he, in his turn, has not succeeded in identifying with his child in a very positive way, because only then can he take vicarious pleasure in his child's accomplishments. It is essential that the parent identify strongly with his child of the same sex for the child's identification with him to prove successful.

Whenever the oedipal conflicts are revived in the pubertal child, he finds life with his family unbearable because of his violently ambivalent feelings. To escape his inner turmoil, he dreams of being the child of different and better parents with whom he would have none of these psychological difficulties. Some children even go beyond such fantasizing and actually run away in search of this ideal home. Fairy tales, however, implicitly teach the child that it exists only in an imaginary country, and that when found, it often turns out to be far from satisfying. This is true for Hansel and Gretel and also for Snow White. While Snow White's experience with a home away from home is less scary than Hansel's and Gretel's, it does not work out too well either. The dwarfs are unable to protect her, and her mother continues to have power over her which Snow White cannot help giving her —as symbolized by Snow White's permitting the queen (in her various disguises) entry into the house, despite the dwarfs' warnings to beware of the queen's tricks and not let anybody in.

One cannot free oneself from the impact of one's parents and one's feelings about them by running away from home—although that seems the easiest way out. One succeeds in gaining independence only by working through one's inner conflicts, which children usually try to project onto their parents. At first every child wishes that it would be possible to evade the difficult work of integration, which, as Snow White's story also shows, is fraught with great dangers. For a time it seems feasible to escape this task. Snow White lives a peaceful existence for a while, and under the guidance of the dwarfs she grows from a child helpless to deal with the difficulties of the world into a girl who learns to work well, and to enjoy it. This is what the dwarfs request of her for living with them: she can remain with them and lack nothing if "you will take care of our household, cook, make the beds, wash, sew and knit, and will keep everything clean and in good order." Snow White becomes a good housekeeper, as is true of many a young girl who, with mother away, takes good care of her father, the house, and even her siblings.

Even before she meets the dwarfs, Snow White shows that she can control her oral cravings, great as they are. Once in the dwarfs' house, though very hungry, she eats just a little from each of the seven plates, and drinks just a drop from each of the seven glasses, so as to rob none of them too much. (How different from Hansel and Gretel, the orally fixated children, who disrespectfully and voraciously eat up the gingerbread house!)

After having satisfied her hunger, Snow White tries out all seven beds, but one is too long, another too short, until finally she falls asleep in the seventh bed. Snow White knows that these are all some other persons' beds, and that each bed's owner will want to sleep in his bed, despite Snow White's lying in it. Her exploration of every bed suggests she is dimly aware of this risk, and she tries to settle into one where no such risk is involved. And she is right. The dwarfs on coming home are very much taken with her beauty, but the seventh dwarf, in whose bed she is sleeping, does not claim it but instead "slept with his companions, one hour with each, until the night had passed."

Given the popular view of Snow White's innocence, the notion that she may have subconsciously risked being in bed with a man seems outrageous. But Snow White shows, by permitting herself to be tempted three times by the queen in disguise, that, like most humans —and, most of all, adolescents—she is quite easily tempted. However, Snow White's inability to resist temptation makes her all the more human and attractive, without the hearer of the story becoming consciously aware of this. On the other hand, her behavior in restraining herself in eating and drinking, her resisting sleeping in a bed that is not just right for her shows that she also has learned to control to some degree her id impulses and to subject them to superego requirements. We find that her ego too has matured, since now she works hard and well, and shares with others.

Dwarfs—these diminutive men—have different connotations in various fairy tales.[66] Like the fairies themselves, they can be good or bad; in "Snow White" they are of the helpful variety. The first thing we learn about them is that they have returned home from working as miners in the mountains. Like all dwarfs, even the unpleasant ones, they are hard-working and clever at their trade. Work is the essence of their lives; they know nothing of leisure or recreation. Although the dwarfs are immediately impressed by Snow White's beauty and moved by her tale of misfortune, they make it clear right away that the price of living with them is engaging in conscientious work. The seven dwarfs suggest the seven days of the week—days filled with work. It is this working world Snow White has to make her own if she is to grow up well; this aspect of her sojourn with the dwarfs is easily understood.

Other historical meanings of dwarfs may serve to explain them further. European fairy tales and legends were often residuals of pre-Christian religious themes which became unacceptable because Christianity would not brook pagan tendencies in open form. In a fashion, Snow White's perfect beauty seems distantly derived from the sun; her name suggests the whiteness and purity of strong light. According to the ancients, seven planets circle the sun, hence the seven dwarfs. Dwarfs or gnomes, in Teutonic lore, are workers of the earth, extracting metals, of which only seven were commonly known in past times—another reason why these miners are seven in number. And each of these seven metals was related to one of the planets in ancient natural philosophy (gold to the sun, silver to the moon, etc.). These connotations are not readily available to the modern child.

But the dwarfs evoke other unconscious associations. There are no female dwarfs. While all fairies are female, wizards are their male counterparts, and there are both sorcerers and sorceresses, or witches. So dwarfs are eminently male, but males who are stunted in their development. These "little men" with their stunted bodies and their mining occupation—they skillfully penetrate into dark holes—all suggest phallic connotations. They are certainly not men in any sexual sense—their way of life, their interest in material goods to the exclusion of love, suggest a pre-oedipal existence.*

At first sight it may seem strange to identify a figure that symbolizes a phallic existence as also representing childhood before puberty, a period during which all forms of sexuality are relatively dormant. But the dwarfs are free of inner conflicts, and have no desire to move beyond their phallic existence to intimate relations. They are satisfied with an identical round of activities; their life is a never-changing circle of work in the womb of the earth, as the planets circle endlessly in a never-changing path in the sky. This lack of change or of any desire for it is what makes their existence parallel that of the prepubertal child. And this is why the dwarfs do not understand or sympathize with the inner pressures which make it impossible for Snow White to resist the queen's temptations. Conflicts are what make us dissatisfied with our present way of life and induce us to find other solutions; if we were free of conflicts, we would never run the risks involved in moving on to a different and, we hope, higher form of living.

The peaceful pre-adolescent period Snow White has while living with the dwarfs before the queen again disturbs her gives her the strength to move into adolescence. Thus she enters once more a time of troubles—now no longer as a child who must passively suffer what Mother inflicts on her, but as a person who must take part in and responsibility for what happens to her.

Snow White and the queen's relations are symbolic of some severe difficulties which may occur between mother and daughter. But they

*Giving each dwarf a separate name and a distinctive personality—in the fairy tale they are all identical—as in the Walt Disney film, seriously interferes with the unconscious understanding that they symbolize an immature pre-individual form of existence which Snow White must transcend. Such ill-considered additions to fairy tales, which seemingly increase the human interest, actually are apt to destroy it because they make it difficult to grasp the story's deeper meaning correctly. The poet understands the meaning of fairy-tale figures better than a film maker and those who follow his lead in retelling the story. Anne Sexton's poetic rendering of "Snow White" suggests their phallic nature, since she refers to them as "the dwarfs, those little hot dogs."[67]

are also projections onto separate figures of tendencies which are incompatible within one person. Often these inner contradictions originate in a child's relationships with his parents. Thus, the fairy-tale projection of one side of an inner conflict onto a parental figure also represents a historical truth: this is where it originated. This is suggested by what happens to Snow White when her quiet and uneventful life with the dwarfs is interrupted.

Nearly destroyed by the early pubertal conflict and competition with her stepmother, Snow White tries to escape back into a conflict-free latency period, where sex remains dormant and hence adolescent turmoils can be avoided. But neither time nor human development remains static, and returning to a latency existence to escape the troubles of adolescence cannot succeed. As Snow White becomes an adolescent, she begins to experience the sexual desires which were repressed and dormant during latency. With this the stepmother, who represents the consciously denied elements in Snow White's inner conflict, reappears on the scene, and shatters Snow White's inner peace.

The readiness with which Snow White repeatedly permits herself to be tempted by the stepmother, despite the warnings of the dwarfs, suggests how close the stepmother's temptations are to Snow White's inner desires. The dwarfs' admonition to let nobody enter the house —or, symbolically, Snow White's inner being—is to no avail. (The dwarfs have an easy time preaching against adolescent dangers because, being fixated to the phallic stage of development, they are not subjected to them.) The ups and downs of adolescent conflicts are symbolized by Snow White's twice being tempted, endangered, and rescued by returning to her previous latency existence. Snow White's third experience with temptation finally ends her efforts to return to immaturity when encountering adolescent difficulties.

While we are not told how long Snow White lived with the dwarfs before her stepmother reappeared in her life, it is the attraction of stay-laces which induces Snow White to let the queen, disguised as a peddler woman, enter the dwarfs' dwelling. This makes it clear that Snow White is by now a well-developed adolescent girl and, in line with the fashion of times past, in need of, and interested in, laces. The stepmother laces Snow White so tightly that she falls down as if she were dead.*

Now, if the queen's purpose was to kill Snow White, she could easily

*Depending on the custom of time or place, it is not stay-laces but another piece of clothing which tempts Snow White—in some versions it is a shirt or a cloak which the queen wraps so tightly around Snow White that she collapses.

have done so at this moment. But if the queen's goal was to prevent her daughter from surpassing her, reducing her to immobility is sufficient for a time. The queen, then, stands for a parent who temporarily succeeds in maintaining his dominance by arresting his child's development. On another level the meaning of this episode is to suggest Snow White's conflicts about her adolescent desire to be well laced because it makes her sexually attractive. Her collapsing unconscious symbolizes that she became overwhelmed by the conflict between her sexual desires and her anxiety about them. Since it is Snow White's own vanity which seduces her into letting herself be laced, she and the vain stepmother have much in common. It seems that Snow White's adolescent conflicts and desires are her undoing. But the fairy tale knows better, and it continues to teach the child a more significant lesson: without having experienced and mastered those dangers which come with growing up, Snow White would never be united with her prince.

On their return from work, the good dwarfs find Snow White unconscious and unlace her. She comes to life again; she retreats temporarily into latency. The dwarfs warn her once more, and more seriously, against the tricks of the evil queen—that is, against the temptations of sex. But Snow White's desires are too strong. When the queen, disguised as an old woman, offers to fix Snow White's hair— "Now I will comb you properly for once"—Snow White is again seduced and lets her do it. Snow White's conscious intentions are overwhelmed by her desire to have a beautiful coiffure, and her unconscious wish is to be sexually attractive. Once more this wish is "poisonous" to Snow White in her early, immature adolescent state, and she again loses consciousness. Again the dwarfs rescue her. The third time Snow White gives in to temptation, she eats of the fateful apple which the queen, dressed up as a peasant woman, hands to her. The dwarfs can no longer help her then, because regression from adolescence to a latency existence has ceased to be a solution for Snow White.

In many myths as well as fairy tales, the apple stands for love and sex, in both its benevolent and its dangerous aspect. An apple given to Aphrodite, the goddess of love, showing she was preferred to chaste goddesses, led to the Trojan War. It was the Biblical apple with which man was seduced to forswear his innocence in order to gain knowledge and sexuality. While it was Eve who was tempted by male masculinity, as represented by the snake, not even the snake could do it all by itself—it needed the apple, which in religious iconography also symbolizes the mother's breast. On our mother's breast we were all first attracted to form a relation, and find satisfaction in it. In "Snow White" mother and daughter share the apple. That which is symbolized by the apple in "Snow White" is something mother and daughter have in common which runs even deeper than their jealousy of each other—their mature sexual desires.

To overcome Snow White's suspicion of her, the queen cuts the apple in half, eating the white part herself, while Snow White accepts the red, "poisonous" half. Repeatedly we have been told of Snow White's double nature: she was as white as snow and as red as blood —that is, her being has both its asexual and its erotic aspect. Eating the red (erotic) part of the apple is the end of Snow White's "innocence." The dwarfs, the companions of her latency existence, can no longer bring her back to life; Snow White has made her choice, which is as necessary as it is fateful. The redness of the apple evokes sexual associations like the three drops of blood which led to Snow White's birth, and also menstruation, the event which marks the beginning of sexual maturity.

As she eats of the red part of the apple, the child in Snow White dies, and is buried in a transparent coffin made of glass. There she rests for a long time, visited not only by the dwarfs but also by three birds: first an owl, then a raven, and last a dove. The owl symbolizes wisdom; the raven—as in the Teutonic god Woden's raven—probably mature consciousness; and the dove stands traditionally for love. These birds suggest that Snow White's deathlike sleep in the coffin is a period of gestation which is her final period of preparing for maturity.*

Snow White's story teaches that just because one has reached physical maturity, one is by no means intellectually and emotionally ready for adulthood, as represented by marriage. Considerable growth and time are needed before the new, more mature personality is formed and the old conflicts are integrated. Only then is one ready for a partner of the other sex, and the intimate relation with him which is

*This period of inertness may further explain Snow White's name, which stresses only one of the three colors that account for her beauty. White frequently symbolizes purity, innocence, the spiritual. But by emphasizing the connection with snow, inertness is also symbolized. When snow covers the earth, all life seems to stop, as Snow White's life seems to have stopped while she is lying in her coffin. Then her eating of the red apple was premature; she had overreached herself. Experiencing sexuality too soon, the story warns, can lead to nothing good. But when it is followed by a prolonged period of inertia, then the girl can recuperate fully from her premature and hence destructive experiences with sexuality.

needed for the achievement of mature adulthood. Snow White's partner is the prince, who "carries her off" in her coffin—which causes her
to cough up or spit out the poisonous apple and come to life, ready
for marriage. Her tragedy began with oral incorporative desires: the
queen's wish to eat Snow White's internal organs. Snow White's spit-
ting out of the suffocating apple—the bad object she had incorporated
—marks her final freedom from primitive orality, which stands for all
her immature fixations.

Like Snow White, each child in his development must repeat the
history of man, real or imagined. We are all expelled eventually from
the original paradise of infancy, where all our wishes seemed to be
fulfilled without any effort on our part. Learning about good and evil
—gaining knowledge—seems to split our personality in two: the red
chaos of unbridled emotions, the id; and the white purity of our
conscience, the superego. As we grow up, we vacillate between being
overcome by the turmoil of the first and the rigidity of the second (the
tight lacing, and the immobility enforced by the coffin). Adulthood
can be reached only when these inner contradictions are resolved and
a new awakening of the mature ego is achieved, in which red and
white coexist harmoniously.

But before the "happy" life can begin, the evil and destructive
aspects of our personality must be brought under our control. The
witch is punished for her cannibalistic desires in "Hansel and Gretel"
by being burned in the oven. In "Snow White" the vain, jealous, and
destructive queen is forced to put on red-hot shoes, in which she must
dance until she dies. Untrammeled sexual jealousy, which tries to ruin
others, destroys itself—as symbolized not only by the fiery red shoes
but by death from dancing in them. Symbolically, the story tells that
uncontrolled passion must be restrained or it will become one's undoing. Only the death of the jealous queen (the elimination of all outer
and inner turbulence) can make for a happy world.

Many fairy-tale heroes, at a crucial point in their development, fall
into deep sleep or are reborn. Each reawakening or rebirth symbolizes the reaching of a higher stage of maturity and understanding. It
is one of the fairy tale's ways to stimulate the wish for higher meaning
in life: deeper consciousness, more self-knowledge, and greater
maturity. The long period of inactivity before reawakening makes the
hearer realize—without consciously verbalizing it—that this rebirth
requires a time of rest and concentration in both sexes.

Change signifies the need to give up something one had enjoyed up
to then, such as Snow White's existence before the queen became

jealous, or her easy life with the dwarfs—difficult and painful growing-up experiences which cannot be avoided. These stories also convince the hearer that he need not be afraid of relinquishing his childish position of depending on others, since after the dangerous hardships of the transitional period, he will emerge on a higher and better plane, to enter upon a richer and happier existence. Those who are reluctant to risk such a transformation, such as the two older brothers in "The Three Feathers," never gain the kingdom. Those who got stuck in the pre-oedipal stage of development, such as the dwarfs, will never know the happiness of love and marriage. And those parents who, like the queen, act out parental oedipal jealousies nearly destroy their child and certainly destroy themselves.

"GOLDILOCKS AND THE THREE BEARS"

This story lacks some of the most important features of true fairy tales: at its end there is neither recovery nor consolation; there is no resolution of conflict, and thus no happy ending. But it is a very meaningful tale because it deals symbolically with some of the most important growing-up problems of the child: the struggle with the oedipal predicaments; the search for identity; and sibling rivalry.

In its present form this story is of recent origin, although it is derived from an ancient tale. Its short modern history illustrates the development over time of a cautionary tale as it acquires fairy-story characteristics, becoming ever more popular and meaningful. Its history demonstrates that a fairy tale's appearance in print does not preclude its being revised in later editions. But when such altering occurs, the changes—in contrast to the time when fairy tales were only perpetuated orally—reflect more than just the personal idiosyncrasies of the storyteller.

Unless he is an original artist, an author recasting a fairy tale for a new printing is rarely guided mainly by his unconscious feeling for the story, nor does he have a particular child in mind whom he wishes to entertain and enlighten or help with a pressing problem. Such changes are instead most often instituted on the basis of what the author thinks a "general" reader wishes to be told. Designed to satisfy the desires or moral scruples of an unknown reader, the tale is often recounted in ways which are trite and commonplace.

When a story exists only in oral tradition, it is largely the teller's unconscious that determines what story he relates, and what of it he remembers. In doing so, he is motivated not only by his conscious and unconscious feelings for the story, but also by the nature of his emotional involvement with the child to whom he tells it. In many such oral repetitions of a story, over many years, by various persons to different listeners, a version is finally reached which is so convincing to the conscious and unconscious of many people that no further change seems appropriate. With this, the story has attained its "classic" form.

There is general agreement that the original source of "Goldilocks" is an ancient Scottish tale of three bears which are intruded upon by a she-fox.[68] The bears devour the trespasser—a cautionary tale warning us to respect others' property and privacy. In a small homemade book written by Eleanor Muir in 1831 as a birthday gift for a little boy and discovered again only in 1951, she told the story with an angry old woman as the intruder. It is possible that in doing so she mistook the "vixen" of the original to mean not a female fox, but a shrewish woman. Whether this alteration was a case of mistaken identity, a "Freudian" slip, or deliberate, it was the change which began the transition of an old cautionary tale into a fairy story. In 1894 another probably quite old rendering of the story became known from the oral tradition, in which the intruder helps herself to milk, sits in the chairs, and rests in the beds of the bears, which, in this version, live in a castle in the woods. In both these stories the intruder is most severely punished by the bears, which try to throw her into the fire, drown her, or drop her from a church steeple.

We do not know whether Robert Southey, who published the story for the first time in printed form in 1837 in his book *The Doctor*, was familiar with any of these older tales. But he made an important change, since for the first time the intruder jumped out of the window and her further fate remained unknown. His story ends: "Out the little woman jumped; and whether she broke her neck in the fall; or ran into the wood and was lost there; or found her way out of the wood, and was taken up by the constable for a vagrant as she was, I cannot tell. But the Three Bears never saw anything more of her." There was immediate positive response to this published version of the story.

The next alteration was made by Joseph Cundall, as he explains in a dedicatory note of 1849 to the *Treasury of Pleasure Books for Young Children,* which appeared in 1856: he made the intruder into a little girl and called her "Silver-Hair" ("Silver-Hair" or "Silver-Locks" became in 1889 "Golden-Hair" and finally, in 1904, "Goldilocks"). The tale attained great popularity only after two more important changes. In *Mother Goose's Fairy Tales* of 1878, "Great Huge Bear," "Middle Bear," and "Little Small Wee Bear" became "Father Bear," "Mother Bear," and "Baby Bear"; and the heroine simply disappears out of the window—no longer is any bad ending for her anticipated or told about.

With this spelled-out designation of the bears as forming a family, the story unconsciously came to relate much more closely to the oedipal situation. While it is acceptable that a tragedy should project destructive results of oedipal conflicts, a fairy tale cannot. The story could become popular only because the outcome was left to our imagination. The reason such uncertainty is acceptable is that the intruder is seen to interfere with the integration of the basic family constellation, and thus is threatening the family's emotional security. From a stranger who invades privacy and takes property she changed into one who endangers the family's emotional well-being and security. It is this psychological underpinning which explains the sudden great popularity of the story.

The relative shortcomings of a rather recently invented fairy tale as compared with an ancient, many-times-retold folk tale appear when one views "Goldilocks" in relation to "Snow White," from which some details were lifted and modified to improve the original "Three Bears." In both tales a young girl, lost in the woods, finds an inviting little house that is temporarily deserted by its inhabitants. In "Goldilocks" we are not told how or why the girl got lost in the forest, why she needed to seek refuge, or where her home is. We do not know the overt or the more important underlying reasons for her being lost.* Thus, from its inception "Goldilocks" raises questions which

*In some modern bowdlerizations Goldilocks' being lost is explained by saying that her mother sent her on an errand, and that she lost her way in the forest. This adaptation reminds us of how Little Red Cap was sent out by her mother; but she did not get lost—she permitted herself to be tempted to stray away from a well-known path, so what happened to Red Cap was to a large degree her own doing. Hansel and Gretel's and Snow White's getting lost was not their doing but that of their parents. Even the young child knows that one does not get lost in the woods without reason; this is why all true fairy stories tell what the reason was. As suggested before, being lost in a forest is an ancient symbol for the need to find oneself. This meaning is seriously interfered with if it is all due to pure chance.

remain unanswered, while the greatest merit of a fairy story is that it gives answers, fantastic though these may overtly be, even to questions of which we are unaware because they perturb us only in our unconscious.

Despite the historical vicissitudes which changed the intruder from a vixen to a nasty old woman to a young, attractive girl, she is and remains an outsider who never becomes an insider. Maybe the reason that this tale became so immensely popular at the turn of the century was that more and more persons came to feel like outsiders. We are made to feel for the bears whose privacy had been invaded, and we feel for poor, beautiful, and charming Goldilocks, who comes from nowhere and has no place to go to. There are no villains in the story, although Baby Bear is robbed of his food and has his chair broken. Unlike the dwarfs, the bears are not taken with Goldilocks' beauty. Nor are they moved by a tale of woe, as the dwarfs are on hearing Snow White's story. But then Goldilocks has no story to tell; her entering is as enigmatic as her leaving.

"Snow White" starts with a mother who deeply desires a daughter. But the idealized mother of infancy disappears, and is replaced by a jealous stepmother who not only ejects Snow White from her home, but threatens her very life. Sheer need to survive forces Snow White to risk the dangers of the wild forest, where she learns to make a go of life on her own. The oedipal jealousy between mother and daughter is sketched clearly enough for a child to comprehend intuitively the emotional conflicts and inner pressures underlying the plot.

The contrast in "Goldilocks" is between the well-integrated family represented by the bears, and the outsider in search of himself. The happy but naïve bears have no identity problems: each knows exactly where he stands in relation to the other family members, a fact made more obvious by naming them Father, Mother, and Baby Bear. While each has his individuality, they function as a threesome. Goldilocks tries to find out who she is, what role is appropriate to her. Snow White is the older child struggling with a particular phase of her unresolved oedipal conflicts: the ambivalent relation to the mother. Goldilocks is the pre-adolescent who attempts to cope with all aspects of the oedipal situation.

This is symbolized in the significant role the number three plays in the story. The three bears form a happy family, where things proceed in such unison that no sexual or oedipal problems exist for them. Each is happy in his place; each has his own distinct dish, chair, bed. Goldilocks, on her part, is utterly confused as to which of the three will fit her. But in her behavior the number three appears long before Goldilocks encounters the three dishes, beds, chairs—for three separate efforts mark her entrance into the bears' dwelling. In the Southey rendering, the old woman "first . . . looked in at the window, and then she peeped in at the keyhole; and seeing nobody in the house, she lifted the latch." Some later versions have Goldilocks do the same; in others she knocks three times at the door before entering.

Peeping through window and keyhole before lifting the latch suggests an anxious and avid curiosity about what goes on behind the closed door. What child is not curious about what adults do behind their closed door and would not wish to find out? What child would not delight in the temporary absence of the parents, which permits a chance to pry into their secrets? With Goldilocks having replaced the old woman as the main figure of the story, it becomes much easier to associate with her behavior a child's peeping to discover the mysteries of adult life.

Three is a mystical and often a holy number, and was so long before the Christian doctrine of the Holy Trinity. It is the threesome of snake, Eve, and Adam which, according to the Bible, makes for carnal knowledge. In the unconscious, the number three stands for sex, because each sex has three visible sex characteristics: penis and the two testes in the male; vagina and the two breasts in the female.

The number three stands in the unconscious for sex also in a quite different way, as it symbolizes the oedipal situation with its deep involvement of three persons with one another—relations which, as the story of "Snow White" among many others shows, are more than tinged with sexuality.

The relation to the mother is the most important in every person's life; more than any other it conditions our early personality development, affecting to a large degree what our outlook on life and ourselves will be—whether optimistic or pessimistic, for example.* But as far as the infant is concerned, no choice is involved: the mother and her attitude to him are a great "given." So, of course, are the father and one's siblings. (And so are the economic and social conditions of the family; but these influence the young child only through the impact on his parents and their behavior toward him.)

The child begins to feel himself as a person, as a significant and meaningful partner in a human relation, when he begins to relate to

*Erikson speaks about the fact that these experiences will determine all through life whether we approach each event with trust or mistrust—a basic attitude which cannot help shaping how these events unfold, and what their impact on us will be.[69]

the father. One becomes a person only as one defines oneself against another person. Since the mother is the first and for a time the only person in one's life, some very rudimentary self-definition begins with defining oneself in regard to her. But because of his deep dependency on the mother, the child cannot move out into self-definition unless he can lean on some third person. It is a necessary step toward independence to learn "I can also lean, rely, on some person other than Mother" before one can believe that one can manage without leaning on *somebody*. After the child has established a close relationship to one other person, he can begin to feel that if he now prefers Mother to this other person, it is his decision—no longer something about which he feels he has no freedom.

The number three is central in "Goldilocks"; it refers to sex, but not in terms of the sexual act. On the contrary, it relates to something that must precede mature sexuality by far: namely, finding out who one is biologically. Three also stands for the relations within the nuclear family, and efforts to ascertain where one fits in there. Thus, three symbolizes a search for who one is biologically (sexually), and who one is in relation to the most important persons in one's life. Broadly put, three symbolizes the search for one's personal and one's social identity. From his visible sex characteristics and through his relations to his parents and siblings, the child must learn with whom he ought to identify as he grows up, and who is suitable to become his life's companion, and with it also his sexual partner.

This search for identity is clearly alluded to in "Goldilocks" with its three dishes, chairs, and beds. The most direct image for a need to search is that something which has been lost must be found. If the search is for ourselves, then the most convincing symbol for this is that we have gotten lost. In fairy tales, being lost in the forest symbolizes not a need to be found, but rather that one must find or discover oneself.

Goldilocks' embarkation on her voyage of self-discovery begins with her trying to peek into the bears' house. This evokes associations to the child's desire to find out the sexual secrets of adults in general, and of the parents in particular. This curiosity often has much more to do with the child's need to gain knowledge about what is involved in his own sexuality than with a wish to know exactly what his parents are doing with each other in bed.

Once inside the house, Goldilocks explores three different sets of objects—dishes of porridge, chairs, and beds—in regard to their suitability. She tries them always in the same sequence: first Father's, then Mother's, and finally the child's. One might view this as suggesting that Goldilocks investigates both which sex role fits her best, and which of the family positions: that of father, mother, or child. Goldilocks' search for her self and role in the family begins with eating, as every person's first conscious experience is being fed, and his relating to another person begins around being fed by Mother. But Goldilocks' choice of Father Bear's dish suggests that she wishes to be like him (male), or that she desires most to relate to him, as does her choosing first his chair and bed, although her experience with the porridge and the chair should have taught her that what belongs to him is not fitting for her. It is hard to come closer to a girl's oedipal wishes than by suggesting that Goldilocks tries to share bed and board with a father figure.

But, as the story tells, whether it is a wish to be male or to sleep in Father's bed, this does not work. The reasons are that Father's porridge is "too hot" and his chair "too hard." So, disappointed that a male identity, or intimacy with Father, is not available to her, or is too threatening—one might get burned—and too hard to manage, Goldilocks, like every girl experiencing deep oedipal disappointment in the father, turns back to the original relation to the mother. But this does not work out either. What had once been a warm relationship is now found too cold for comfort (the porridge is too cold). And while Mother's chair is not too hard to sit in, it is found to be too soft; maybe it envelops as Mother envelops the infant, and Goldilocks rightly does not wish to return to that.

As for the beds, Goldilocks finds Father Bear's bed too high at the head, and Mother Bear's too high at the foot, showing that both their roles and intimacy with them are out of reach for Goldilocks. Only Baby Bear's things fit her "just right." So nothing seems left to her but the role of the child. But not quite: as Goldilocks sits in Baby Bear's chair, which we are told "was neither too hard, nor too soft, but just right, the bottom of the chair came out, and down came hers, plump upon the ground." So, obviously, she has outgrown the small child's chair. The bottom indeed dropped out of her life because she could not find success in being or relating to, first, Father and, second, Mother; but it did so only when after these failures Goldilocks reluctantly tried to return to an infantile, babylike existence. For Goldilocks there is no happy ending—from her failure to find what is fitting for her, she awakes as if from a bad dream, and runs away.

Goldilocks' story illustrates the meaning of the difficult choice the child must master: is he to be like father, like mother, or like child?

To decide who he wants to be in respect to these basic human positions is indeed a tremendous psychological battle, an ordeal every human being has to undergo. But while the child is not yet ready to be in Father's or Mother's place, just accepting that of the child is no solution—this is why the three tests are not sufficient. For growth, realization that one is still a child must be coupled with another recognition: that one has to become oneself, something different from either parent, or from being merely their child.

In folk fairy tales, as distinct from an invented one such as "Goldilocks," things do not end after three efforts. At the end of "Goldilocks" no resolution of the identity problem is projected, no self-discovery, no becoming a new and independent person. Still, Goldilocks' experience in the bears' house at least teaches her that regression to infantilism offers no escape from the difficulties of growing up. Becoming oneself, the story suggests, is a process begun by sorting out what is involved in one's relations to one's parents.

The bears in "Goldilocks" do not provide help; on the contrary, they are appalled and critical that a little girl should try to fit herself into Papa's bed and try to take Mama's place. The opposite happens in "Snow White": the dwarfs, far from finding fault with Snow White for tasting from their seven plates and glasses and trying seven beds, admire the little heroine. While the bears awaken Goldilocks with their dismay, the dwarfs make sure that Snow White's sleep remains undisturbed, even if they have to inconvenience themselves. Much as the dwarfs are taken with Snow White's beauty, they tell her right from the start that if she wants to remain with them, she has to accept obligations: if she wants to become a person, she has to act maturely. The dwarfs warn her of the dangers which growing up may entail, but even when Snow White goes against their advice, they repeatedly help her out of her troubles.

Goldilocks receives no help with her growing-up problems from the bears, so all she can do is to run away, scared by her own daring, defeated in her efforts to find herself. Running away from a difficult developmental task hardly encourages a child to pursue the hard labor of solving, one at a time, the problems which growing up presents to him. Further, Goldilocks' story does not end with any promise of future happiness awaiting those who have mastered their oedipal situation as a child, and again as an adolescent when these old difficulties recur, now to be solved in more mature ways. "Goldilocks" is sadly lacking in this respect, since only great hopes for the future provide a child with the courage which enables him to go on struggling until he achieves selfhood.

Despite the shortcomings of "Goldilocks" when compared to other folk fairy tales, it has considerable merit, otherwise it would not have gained such popularity. The story deals with the difficulties in achieving sexual identity, and the problems created by oedipal desires and efforts to gain first one and then the other parent's undivided love.

Because "Goldilocks" is an ambiguous story, much depends on how it is told. The parent who, for his own reasons, delights in the idea that children should be scared off from peeping into adults' secrets will tell it with a different emphasis than a parent who has empathy with a child's desire to do so. One person will be in sympathy with Goldilocks' difficulties in making her peace with being a girl; another will not. Some people will feel more deeply for Goldilocks' frustration when she must accept that she is still a child, but also that she must grow out of childhood, though she may wish not to do so.

The story's ambiguity permits telling it with emphasis on sibling rivalry—its other main motif. Here much depends on how, for example, the incident with the broken chair is told. It can be told with empathy for Goldilocks' shock when the chair which seemed so fitting suddenly breaks down; or in the opposite way, with glee either about Goldilocks' pratfall or the fact that she broke Baby Bear's chair.

When the story is told from the perspective of Baby Bear, Goldilocks is the intruder who suddenly comes from nowhere, as did the next younger sibling, and usurps—or tries to usurp—a place in a family which, to Baby Bear, was complete without her. This nasty intruder takes away his food, ruins his chair, even tries to drive him out of his bed—and, by extension, to take away his place in his parents' love. Then it is understandable that it is not the parents' but Baby Bear's voice that "was so sharp, and so shrill, that it awakened her at once. Up she started . . . and ran to the window." It is Baby Bear— the child—who wants to get rid of the newcomer, wants her to go back where she came from, never to see "anything more of her." Thus the story gives imaginative body to the fears and wishes a child has about an imagined or real new arrival in the family.

If, seen from the viewpoint of Goldilocks, Baby Bear is the sibling, then we can empathize with her wish to take away his food, destroy his toy (the chair), and occupy his bed so that he will no longer have any place in the family. Interpreted thus, the story becomes again a cautionary tale, now warning against giving in to sibling rivalry to the degree that one acts destructively against the sibling's possessions. If one does this, one might find oneself left out in the cold, with nowhere to go.

The great popularity of "Goldilocks" with children and adults alike derives partly from its manifold meanings on many different levels. The young child may respond mainly to the motif of sibling rivalry, delighted that Goldilocks must go back from whence she came, as so many children wish the new baby would do. An older child will be enthralled by Goldilocks' experimentation with adult roles. Children will enjoy her peeping and entering; some adults may like to remind their children that Goldilocks is expelled for it.

The story is particularly timely because it depicts the outsider, Goldilocks, in such appealing form. This makes it as attractive to some as it is to others because the insiders, the bears, win. Thus, whether one feels like an outsider or an insider, the story can be equally enchanting. The change in title over time shows how a story protecting the property and psychological rights of insiders—the bears— became one which concentrates attention on the outsider. What was once called "The Three Bears" is now known mainly as "Goldilocks." Further, the story's ambiguity, which is so much in line with the temper of the times, may also account for its popularity, while the clear-cut solutions of the traditional fairy tale seem to point to a happier age when things were believed to permit definite solutions.

Even more important in this respect is the story's greatest appeal, which at the same time is its greatest weakness. Not only in modern times, but all through the ages, running away from a problem—which in the unconscious means denying or repressing it—seems the easiest way out when confronted with what seems to be too difficult or unsolvable a predicament. This is the solution with which we are left in "Goldilocks." The bears seem unmoved by her appearance in and sudden disappearance from their lives. They act as if nothing had happened but an interlude without consequences; all is solved by her jumping out of the window. As far as Goldilocks is concerned, her running away suggests that no solution of the oedipal predicaments or of sibling rivalry is necessary. Contrary to what happens in traditional fairy tales, the impression is that Goldilocks' experience in the bears' house made as little change in her life as it did in that of the bear family; we hear nothing more about it. Despite her serious exploration of where she fits in—by implication, of who she is—we are not told that it led to any higher selfhood for Goldilocks.

Parents would like their daughters to remain eternally their little girls, and the child would like to believe that it is possible to evade the struggle of growing up. That is why the spontaneous reaction to "Goldilocks" is: "What a lovely story." But it is also why this story does not help the child to gain emotional maturity.

"THE SLEEPING BEAUTY"

Adolescence is a period of great and rapid change, characterized by periods of utter passivity and lethargy alternating with frantic activity, even dangerous behavior to "prove oneself" or discharge inner tension. This back-and-forth adolescent behavior finds expression in some fairy tales by the hero's rushing after adventures and then suddenly being turned to stone by some enchantment. More often, and psychologically more correctly, the sequence is reversed: Dummy in "The Three Feathers" does nothing until he is well into adolescence; and the hero of "The Three Languages," pushed by his father to go abroad to develop himself, spends three years in passive learning before his adventures begin.

While many fairy tales stress great deeds the heroes must perform to become themselves, "The Sleeping Beauty" emphasizes the long, quiet concentration on oneself that is also needed. During the months before the first menstruation, and often also for some time immediately following it, girls are passive, seem sleepy, and withdraw into themselves. While no equally noticeable state heralds the coming of sexual maturity in boys, many of them experience a period of lassitude and of turning inward during puberty which equals the female experience. It is thus understandable that a fairy story in which a long period of sleep begins at the start of puberty has been very popular for a long time among girls and boys.

In major life changes such as adolescence, for successful growth opportunities both active and quiescent periods are needed. The turning inward, which in outer appearance looks like passivity (or sleeping one's life away), happens when internal mental processes of such importance go on within the person that he has no energy for outwardly directed action. Those fairy tales which, like "The Sleeping Beauty," have the period of passivity for their central topic, permit the budding adolescent not to worry during his inactive period: he learns that things continue to evolve. The happy ending assures the child that he will not remain permanently stuck in seemingly doing nothing, even if at the moment it seems as if this period of quietude will last for a hundred years.

After the period of inactivity which typically occurs during early puberty, adolescents become active and make up for the period of passivity; in real life and in fairy tales they try to prove their young manhood or womanhood, often through dangerous adventures. This is how the symbolic language of the fairy tale states that after having gathered strength in solitude they now have to become themselves. Actually, this development *is* fraught with dangers: an adolescent must leave the security of childhood, which is represented by getting lost in the dangerous forest; learn to face up to his violent tendencies and anxieties, symbolized by encounters with wild animals or dragons; get to know himself, which is implied in meeting strange figures and experiences. Through this process the adolescent loses a previous innocence suggested by their having been "Simpletons," considered dumb and lowly, or merely somebody's child. The risks involved in bold adventures are obvious, as when Jack meets the ogre. "Snow White" and "The Sleeping Beauty" encourage the child not to be afraid of the dangers of passivity. Ancient as "The Sleeping Beauty" is, in many ways it has a more important message for today's youth than many other tales. Presently many of our young people—and their parents—are fearful of quiet growth, when nothing seems to happen, because of a common belief that only doing what can be seen achieves goals. "The Sleeping Beauty" tells that a long period of quiescence, of contemplation, of concentration on the self, can and often does lead to highest achievement.

Recently it has been claimed that the struggle against childhood dependency and for becoming oneself in fairy tales is frequently described differently for the girl than for the boy, and that this is the result of sexual stereotyping. Fairy tales do not render such one-sided pictures. Even when a girl is depicted as turning inward in her struggle to become herself, and a boy as aggressively dealing with the external world, these two *together* symbolize the two ways in which one has to gain selfhood: through learning to understand and master the inner as well as the outer world. In this sense the male and female heroes are again projections onto two different figures of two (artificially) separated aspects of one and the same process which *everybody* has to undergo in growing up. While some literal-minded parents do not realize it, children know that, whatever the sex of the hero, the story pertains to their own problems.

Male and female figures appear in the same roles in fairy tales; in "The Sleeping Beauty" it is the prince who observes the sleeping girl, but in "Cupid and Psyche" and the many tales derived from it, it is Psyche who apprehends Cupid in his sleep and, like the prince, marvels at the beauty she beholds. This is just one example. Since there are thousands of fairy tales, one may safely guess that there are probably equal numbers where the courage and determination of females rescue males, and vice versa. This is as it should be, since fairy tales reveal important truths about life.

"The Sleeping Beauty" is best known today in two different versions: Perrault's, and that of the Brothers Grimm.[70] To explain the difference, it may be best to consider briefly the form the story took in Basile's *Pentamerone*, where its title is "Sun, Moon, and Talia."*[71]

On the birth of his daughter Talia, a king asked all the wise men and seers to tell her future. They concluded that she would be exposed to great danger from a splinter of flax. To prevent any such accident, the king ordered that no flax or hemp should ever come into his castle. But one day when Talia had grown up, she saw an old woman who was spinning pass by her window. Talia, who had never seen anything like it before, "was therefore delighted with the dancing of the spindle." Made curious, she took the distaff in her hand and began to draw out the thread. A splinter of hemp "got under her fingernail and she immediately fell dead upon the ground." The king left his lifeless daughter seated on a velvet chair in the palace, locked the door, and departed forever, to obliterate the memory of his sorrow.

Some time after, another king was hunting. His falcon flew into a window of the empty castle and did not return. The king, trying to find the falcon, wandered in the castle. There he found Talia as if asleep, but nothing would rouse her. Falling in love with her beauty, he cohabited with her; then he left and forgot the whole affair. Nine months later Talia gave birth to two children, all the time still asleep. They nursed from her breast. "Once when one of the babies wanted to suck, it could not find the breast, but got into its mouth instead the finger that had been pricked. This the baby sucked so hard that it drew out the splinter, and Talia was roused as if from deep sleep."

One day the king remembered his adventure and went to see Talia. He was delighted to find her awake with the two beautiful children, and from then on they were always on his mind. The king's wife found out his secret, and on the sly sent for the two children in the king's name. She ordered them cooked and served to her husband. The cook hid the children in his own home and prepared instead some goat

*By that time it was already an old motif, as there are French and Catalan renderings from the fourteenth to the sixteenth centuries which served as Basile's models, if he did not rely on folk tales of his own time as yet unknown to us.[72]

kids, which the queen served to the king. A while later the queen sent for Talia and planned to have her thrown into the fire because she was the reason for the king's infidelity. At the last minute the king arrived, had his wife thrown into the fire, married Talia, and was happy to find his children, whom the cook had saved. The story ends with the verses:

> Lucky people, so 'tis said,
> Are blessed by Fortune whilst in bed.*

Perrault, by adding on his own the story of the slighted fairy who utters the curse, or by using this familiar fairy-tale motif, explains why the heroine falls into deathlike sleep and thus enriches the story, since in "Sun, Moon, and Talia" we are given no reason why this should be her fate.

In Basile's story Talia is the daughter of a king who loved her so much that he could not remain in his castle after she fell into a deathlike sleep. We hear nothing more about him after he left Talia ensconced on her thronelike chair "under an embroidered canopy," not even after she reawakened, married her king, and lived happily with him and her beautiful children. One king replaces another king in the same country; one king replaces another in Talia's life—the father king is replaced by the lover king. Might these two kings not be substitutes for each other at different periods in the girl's life, in different roles, in different disguises? We encounter here again the "innocence" of the oedipal child, who feels no responsibility for what she arouses or wishes to arouse in the parent.

Perrault, the academician, doubly distances his story from Basile's. He was, after all, a courtier who told stories for the perusal of princes, pretending that they were invented by his little son to please a princess. The two kings are changed into a king and a prince, the latter somebody who obviously is not yet married and has no children. And

---

*Since Talia's children are called the sun and moon, there is the possibility that Basile was influenced by the story of Leto, one of the many loves of Zeus, who bore him Apollo and Artemis, the sun god and the moon goddess. If so, we may assume that, as Hera was jealous of those whom Zeus loved, the queen in this tale is a distant memory of Hera and her jealousies.

Most fairy tales of the Western world have at some time included Christian elements, so much so that an account of those underlying Christian meanings would make another book. In this tale Talia, who does not know that she has had intercourse or that she has conceived, has done so without pleasure and without sin. This she has in common with the Virgin Mary, as she, like the Virgin, in such manner becomes the mother of God(s).

the presence of the king is separated from the prince by a sleep of one hundred years, so that we can feel certain that the two have nothing in common. Interestingly enough, Perrault does not quite manage to extricate himself from the oedipal connotations: in his story the queen is not insanely jealous because of the betrayal by her husband, but she appears as the oedipal mother who is so jealous of the girl her son the prince falls in love with that she seeks to destroy her. But while the queen in Basile's tale is convincing, Perrault's queen is not. His story falls into two incongruous parts: a first which ends with the prince's awakening Sleeping Beauty and marrying her; followed by a second part in which we are suddenly told that the mother of Prince Charming is really a child-devouring ogress who wishes to eat her own grandchildren.

In Basile, the queen wishes to feed his children to her husband—the most terrible punishment for preferring Sleeping Beauty to her that she can think of. In Perrault, she wants to eat them herself. In Basile, the queen is jealous because her husband's mind and love are entirely taken up with Talia and her children. The king's wife tries to burn Talia in the fire—the king's "burning" love for Talia having aroused the queen's "burning" hatred for her.

There is no explanation for the cannibalistic hatred of the queen in Perrault's tale but that she is an ogress who "whenever she saw little children passing by, . . . had all the difficulty in the world to avoid falling upon them." Also, Prince Charming keeps his marriage to Sleeping Beauty a secret for two years, until his father dies. Only then does he bring Sleeping Beauty and her two children, called Morning and Day, to his castle. And although he knows that his mother is an ogress, when he leaves to go to war he puts her in charge, entrusting his kingdom and wife and children to her. Perrault's story ends with the king returning at the moment when his mother is just about to have Sleeping Beauty thrown into a pit full of vipers. On his arrival the ogress, who sees her plans spoiled, jumps into the pit herself.

It can easily be understood that Perrault did not feel it appropriate to tell at the French court a story in which a married king ravishes a sleeping maiden, gets her with child, forgets it entirely, and remembers her after a time only by chance. But a fairy prince who keeps his marriage and fatherhood a secret from his father-king—shall we assume because he fears the king's oedipal jealousy if the son also becomes a father—is unconvincing, if for no other reason than that oedipal jealousy of mother and father in regard to the same son in the same tale is overdoing it, even in a fairy story. Knowing his mother is an ogress, the prince does not bring his wife and child home as long as his good father may exercise a restraining influence, but only after his death, when such protection is no longer available. The reason for all this is not that Perrault was lacking in artistry, but that he did not take his fairy stories seriously and was most intent on the cute or moralistic verse ending he appended to each.*

With two such incongruous parts to this story, it is understandable that in oral telling—and often also in printed form—the story ends with the happy union of the prince and Sleeping Beauty. It is this form that the Brothers Grimm heard and recorded, and which was then and is now most widely known. Still, something got lost which was present in Perrault. To wish death to a newborn child only because one is not invited to the christening or is given inferior silverware is the mark of an evil fairy. Thus, in Perrault, as in the Brothers Grimm's version, at the very beginning of the story we find the (fairy god)-mother(s) split into the good and the evil aspects. The happy ending requires that the evil principle be appropriately punished and done away with; only then can the good, and with it happiness, prevail. In Perrault, as in Basile, the evil principle is done away with, and thus fairy-story justice is done. But the Brothers Grimm's version, which will be followed from here on, is deficient because the evil fairy is not punished.

However great the variations in detail, the central theme of all versions of "The Sleeping Beauty" is that, despite all attempts on the part of parents to prevent their child's sexual awakening, it will take place nonetheless. Furthermore, parents' ill-advised efforts may post-

*Perrault, speaking to the courtiers he had in mind as his readers, made fun of the fairy stories he told. For example, he specifies that the queen-ogress wishes to have the children served her "with Sauce Robert." He thus introduces details which detract from the fairy-story character, as when he tells that on her awakening Sleeping Beauty's dress was recognized as old-fashioned: "she was dressed as my great-grandmother, and had a point band peeping over a high collar; she looked not a bit the less beautiful and charming for all that." As if fairy-tale heroes would not live in a world where fashions do not change.

Such remarks, in which Perrault indiscriminately mixes petty rationality with fairy-story fantasy, grossly detract from his work. The dress detail, for example, destroys that mythical, allegorical, and psychological time which is suggested by the hundred years of sleep by making it a specific chronological time. It makes it all frivolous—not like the legends of saints who awake from a hundred years of sleep, recognize how the world has changed, and immediately turn into dust. By such details, which were meant to amuse, Perrault destroyed the feeling of timelessness that is an important element in the effectiveness of fairy tales.

pone the reaching of maturity at the proper time, as symbolized by Sleeping Beauty's hundred years of sleep, which separate her sexual awakening from her being united with her lover. Closely related to this is a different motif—namely, that to have to wait even a long time for sexual fulfillment does not at all detract from its beauty.

Perrault's and the Brothers Grimm's versions begin by indicating that one may have to wait a long time to find sexual fulfillment, as indicated by having a child. For a very long time, we are told, the king and his queen wished for a child in vain. In Perrault, the parents behave like his contemporaries: "They went to all the waters in the world; vows, pilgrimages, everything was tried and nothing came of it. At last, however, the Queen was with child." The Brothers Grimm's beginning is much more fairy-tale-like: "Once upon a time was a king and a queen who said every day 'Oh, if we only had a child!' but they never got one. Once when the queen sat in the bath, it happened that a frog crawled out of the water on the land and told her 'Your wish will be fulfilled; before a year is over, you'll bring a daughter into the world.' " The frog's saying that the queen will give birth before a year is over puts the time of waiting close to the nine months of pregnancy. This, plus the queen's being in her bath, is reason to believe that conception took place on the occasion of the frog's visit to the queen. (Why in fairy tales the frog often symbolizes sexual fulfillment is discussed later, in connection with the story "The Frog King.")

The parents' long wait for a child which finally arrives conveys that there is no need to hurry toward sex; it loses none of its rewards if one has to wait a long time for it. The good fairies and their wishes at the christening actually have little to do with the plot, except to contrast with the curse of the fairy who feels slighted. This may be seen from the fact that the number of fairies varies from country to country, from three to eight to thirteen.* The good fairies' gifts of endowment to the child also differ in the different versions, while the curse of the evil one is always the same: the girl (in the Brothers Grimm's story

*In the *Anciennes Chroniques de Perceforest* of the fourteenth century (printed for the first time in France in 1528) three goddesses are invited to the celebration of the birth of Zellandine. Lucina confers health on her; Themis, angry because there is no knife beside her plate, utters the curse that while spinning Zellandine will pull a thread off the distaff and push it into her finger; she will have to sleep until it is pulled out. Venus, the third goddess, promises to arrange for the rescue to happen. In Perrault, there are seven invited fairies and one uninvited, who utters the well-known curse. In the Brothers Grimm's story there are twelve benevolent fairies and one malevolent one.

when she is fifteen) will prick her finger on a distaff (of a spinning wheel) and die. The last good fairy is able to change this threat of death into a hundred years' sleep. The message is similar to that of "Snow White": what may seem like a period of deathlike passivity at the end of childhood is nothing but a time of quiet growth and preparation, from which the person will awaken mature, ready for sexual union. It must be stressed that in fairy tales this union is as much one of the minds and souls of two partners as it is one of sexual fulfillment.

In times past, fifteen was often the age at which menstruation began. The thirteen fairies in the Brothers Grimm's story are reminiscent of the thirteen lunar months into which the year was once, in ancient times, divided. While this symbolism may be lost on those not familiar with the lunar year, it is well known that menstruation typically occurs with the twenty-eight-day frequency of lunar months, and not with the twelve months which our year is divided into. Thus, the number of twelve good fairies plus a thirteenth evil one indicates symbolically that the fatal "curse" refers to menstruation.

It is very much to the point that the king, the male, does not understand the necessity of menstruation and tries to prevent his daughter from experiencing the fatal bleeding. The queen, in all versions of the story, seems unconcerned with the prediction of the angry fairy. In any case, she knows better than to try to prevent it. The curse centers on the distaff, a word which in English has come to stand for female in general. While the same is not true for the French (Perrault) or German (Brothers Grimm) word for distaff, until fairly recently spinning and weaving were considered as characteristically "woman's" occupations.

All the king's painstaking efforts to forestall the "curse" of the malicious fairy fail. Removing all the distaffs from the kingdom cannot prevent the girl's fateful bleeding once she reaches puberty, at fifteen, as the evil fairy predicted. Whatever precautions a father takes, when the daughter is ripe for it, puberty will set in. The temporary absence of both parents when this event occurs symbolizes all parents' incapacity to protect their child against the various growing-up crises which every human being has to undergo.

As she becomes an adolescent, the girl explores the formerly inaccessible areas of existence, as represented by the hidden chamber where an old woman is spinning. At this point the story abounds in Freudian symbolism. As she approaches the fateful place, the girl ascends a circular staircase; in dreams such staircases typically stand for sexual experiences. At the top of this staircase she finds a small door and in its lock a key. As she turns the key, the door "springs open" and the girl enters a small room in which an old woman spins. A small locked room often stands in dreams for the female sexual organs; turning a key in a lock often symbolizes intercourse.

Seeing the old woman spinning, the girl asks: "What kind of thing is this that jumps about so funnily?" It does not take much imagination to see the possible sexual connotations in the distaff; but as soon as the girl touches it, she pricks her finger, and falls into sleep.

The main associations this tale arouses in the child's unconscious are to menstruation rather than intercourse. In common language, referring also to its Biblical origin, menstruation is often called the "curse"; and it is a female's—the fairy's—curse that causes the bleeding. Second, the age at which this curse is to become effective is about the age at which, in past times, menstruation most frequently set in. Finally, the bleeding comes about through an encounter with an old woman, not a man; and according to the Bible, the curse is inherited by woman from woman.

Bleeding, as in menstruation, is for the young girl (and for the young man too, in a different manner) an overwhelming experience if she is not emotionally ready for it. Overcome by the experience of sudden bleeding, the princess falls into a long sleep, protected against all suitors—i.e., premature sexual encounters—by an impenetrable wall of thorns. While the most familiar version stresses in the name "The Sleeping Beauty" the long sleep of the heroine, the titles of other variants give prominence to the protective wall, such as the English "Briar Rose."*

Many princes try to reach Sleeping Beauty before her time of maturing is over; all these precocious suitors perish in the thorns. This is a warning to child and parents that sexual arousal before mind and body are ready for it is very destructive. But when Sleeping Beauty has finally gained both physical and emotional maturity and is ready for love, and with it for sex and marriage, then that which had seemed impenetrable gives way. The wall of thorns suddenly turns into a wall of big, beautiful flowers, which opens to let the prince enter. The implied message is the same as in many other fairy tales: don't worry and don't try to hurry things—when the time is ripe, the impossible problem will be solved, as if all by itself.

The long sleep of the beautiful maiden has also other connotations.

*The German name of girl and tale, *"Dornröschen,"* emphasizes both the hedge of thorns and the (hedge) rose. The diminutive form of "rose" in the German name stresses the girl's immaturity, which must be protected by the wall of thorns.

Whether it is Snow White in her glass coffin or Sleeping Beauty on her bed, the adolescent dream of everlasting youth and perfection is just that: a dream. The alteration of the original curse, which threatened death, to one of prolonged sleep suggests that the two are not all that different. If we do not want to change and develop, then we might as well remain in a deathlike sleep. During their sleep the heroines' beauty is a frigid one; theirs is the isolation of narcissism. In such self-involvement which excludes the rest of the world there is no suffering, but also no knowledge to be gained, no feelings to be experienced.

Any transition from one stage of development to the next is fraught with dangers; those of puberty are symbolized by the shedding of blood on touching the distaff. A natural reaction to the threat of having to grow up is to withdraw from a world and life which impose such difficulties. Narcissistic withdrawal is a tempting reaction to the stresses of adolescence, but, the story warns, it leads to a dangerous, deathlike existence when it is embraced as an escape from the vagaries of life. The entire world then becomes dead to the person; this is the symbolic meaning, and warning, of the deathlike sleep into which everybody surrounding Sleeping Beauty falls. The world becomes alive only to the person who herself awakens to it. Only relating positively to the other "awakens" us from the danger of sleeping away our life. The kiss of the prince breaks the spell of narcissism and awakens a womanhood which up to then has remained undeveloped. Only if the maiden grows into woman can life go on.

The harmonious meeting of prince and princess, their awakening to each other, is a symbol of what maturity implies: not just harmony within oneself, but also with the other. It depends on the listener whether the arrival of the prince at the right time is interpreted as the event which causes sexual awakening or the birth of a higher ego; the child probably comprehends both these meanings.

Awakening from a long sleep will be understood differently by the child depending on his age. The younger child will see in it mainly an awakening to his selfhood, the achievement of concordance between what had been his inner chaotic tendencies—that is, as an attaining of inner harmony between his id, ego, and superego.

After the child has experienced this meaning until he reaches puberty, in adolescence he will gain additional understanding of the same fairy tale. Then it becomes also an image of achieving harmony with the other, as represented by a person of the other sex, so that the two, as told at the end of "The Sleeping Beauty," may live enjoyably together till their end. This, the most desirable goal of life, seems to be the most significant communication which fairy stories transmit to the older child. It is symbolized by an ending in which the prince and princess find each other "and they lived happily until their death." Only after one has attained inner harmony within oneself can one hope to find it in relations with others. A preconscious understanding of the connection between the two stages is gained by the child through his own developmental experiences.

The story of Sleeping Beauty impresses every child that a traumatic event—such as the girl's bleeding at the beginning of puberty, and later, in first intercourse—does have the happiest consequences. The story implants the idea that such events must be taken very seriously, but that one need not be afraid of them. The "curse" is a blessing in disguise.

One more look at the earliest known form of the motif of "The Sleeping Beauty" in *Perceforest* some six hundred years ago: it is Venus, the goddess of love, who arranges for the sleeping girl's awakening by having her baby suck the splinter out of her finger, and the same happens in Basile's story. Full self-fulfillment of the female does not come with menstruation. Female completeness is not achieved when falling in love, not even in intercourse, nor in childbirth, since the heroines in *Perceforest* and in Basile's story sleep all through it. These are necessary steps on the way to ultimate maturity; but complete selfhood comes only with having given life, and with nurturing the one whom one has brought into being: with the baby sucking from the mother's body. Thus, these stories enumerate experiences which pertain only to the female; she must undergo them all before she reaches the summit of femininity.

It is the infant's sucking the splinter out from under the mother's nail which brings her back to life—a symbol that her child is not just the passive recipient of what the mother gives to him, but that he also actively renders her great service. Her nurturing permits him to do so; but it is his nursing from her which reawakens her to life—a being reborn, which, as always in fairy tales, symbolizes the achievement of a higher mental state. Thus, the fairy tale tells parent and child alike that the infant not only receives from his mother, but also gives to her. While she gives him life, he adds a new dimension to her life. The self-involvement which was suggested by the heroine's long-lasting sleep comes to an end as she gives to the infant and he, by taking from her, restores her to the highest level of existence: a mutuality in which the one who receives life also gives life.

In "The Sleeping Beauty" this is further emphasized because not only she but her entire world—her parents, all inhabitants of the castle—returns to life the moment she does. If we are insensitive to the world, the world ceases to exist for us. When Sleeping Beauty fell asleep, so did the world for her. The world awakens anew as a child is nurtured into it, because only in this way can humanity continue to exist.

This symbolism got lost in the story's later forms which end with the awakening of Sleeping Beauty, and with it her world, to a new life. Even in the shortened form in which the tale came down to us, in which Sleeping Beauty is awakened by the kiss of the prince, we feel —without it being spelled out as in the more ancient versions—that she is the incarnation of perfect femininity.

"CINDERELLA"

By all accounts, "Cinderella" is the best-known fairy tale, and probably also the best-liked.[73] It is quite an old story; when first written down in China during the ninth century A.D., it already had a history.[74] The unrivaled tiny foot size as a mark of extraordinary virtue, distinction, and beauty, and the slipper made of precious material are facets which point to an Eastern, if not necessarily Chinese, origin.* The modern hearer does not connect sexual attractiveness and beauty in general with extreme smallness of the foot, as the ancient Chinese did, in accordance with their practice of binding women's feet.

"Cinderella," as we know it, is experienced as a story about the agonies and hopes which form the essential content of sibling rivalry; and about the degraded heroine winning out over her siblings who abused her. Long before Perrault gave "Cinderella" the form in which it is now widely known, "having to live among the ashes" was a symbol of being debased in comparison to one's siblings, irrespective of sex. In Germany, for example, there were stories in which such an ash-boy later becomes king, which parallels Cinderella's fate. "Aschenputtel" is the title of the Brothers Grimm's version of the tale.

*Artistically made slippers of precious material were reported in Egypt from the third century on. The Roman emperor Diocletian in a decree of A.D. 301 set maximum prices for different kinds of footwear, including slippers made of fine Babylonian leather, dyed purple or scarlet, and gilded slippers for women.[75]

The term originally designated a lowly, dirty kitchenmaid who must tend to the fireplace ashes.

There are many examples in the German language of how being forced to dwell among the ashes was a symbol not just of degradation, but also of sibling rivalry, and of the sibling who finally surpasses the brother or brothers who have debased him. Martin Luther in his *Table Talks* speaks about Cain as the God-forsaken evildoer who is powerful, while pious Abel is forced to be his ash-brother *(Aschebrüdel)*, a mere nothing, subject to Cain; in one of Luther's sermons he says that Esau was forced into the role of Jacob's ash-brother.[76] Cain and Abel, Jacob and Esau are Biblical examples of one brother being suppressed or destroyed by the other.

The fairy tale replaces sibling relations with relations between step-siblings—perhaps a device to explain and make acceptable an animosity which one wishes would not exist among true siblings. Although sibling rivalry is universal and "natural" in the sense that it is the negative consequence of being a sibling, this same relation also generates equally as much positive feeling between siblings, highlighted in fairy tales such as "Brother and Sister."

No other fairy tale renders so well as the "Cinderella" stories the inner experiences of the young child in the throes of sibling rivalry, when he feels hopelessly outclassed by his brothers and sisters. Cinderella is pushed down and degraded by her stepsisters; her interests are sacrificed to theirs by her (step)mother; she is expected to do the dirtiest work and although she performs it well, she receives no credit for it; only more is demanded of her. This is how the child feels when devastated by the miseries of sibling rivalry. Exaggerated though Cinderella's tribulations and degradations may seem to the adult, the child carried away by sibling rivalry feels, "That's me; that's how they mistreat me, or would want to; that's how little they think of me." And there are moments—often long time periods—when for inner reasons a child feels this way even when his position among his siblings may seem to give him no cause for it.

When a story corresponds to how the child feels deep down—as no realistic narrative is likely to do—it attains an emotional quality of "truth" for the child. The events of "Cinderella" offer him vivid images that give body to his overwhelming but nevertheless often vague and nondescript emotions; so these episodes seem more convincing to him than his life experiences.

The term "sibling rivalry" refers to a most complex constellation of feelings and their causes. With extremely rare exceptions, the emotions aroused in the person subject to sibling rivalry are far out of proportion to what his real situation with his sisters and brothers would justify, seen objectively. While all children at times suffer greatly from sibling rivalry, parents seldom sacrifice one of their children to the others, nor do they condone the other children's persecuting one of them. Difficult as objective judgments are for the young child—nearly impossible when his emotions are aroused—even he in his more rational moments "knows" that he is not treated as badly as Cinderella. But the child often feels mistreated, despite all his "knowledge" to the contrary. That is why he believes in the inherent truth of "Cinderella," and then he also comes to believe in her eventual deliverance and victory. From her triumph he gains the exaggerated hopes for his future which he needs to counteract the extreme misery he experiences when ravaged by sibling rivalry.

Despite the name "sibling rivalry," this miserable passion has only incidentally to do with a child's actual brothers and sisters. The real source of it is the child's feelings about his parents. When a child's older brother or sister is more competent than he, this arouses only temporary feelings of jealousy. Another child being given special attention becomes an insult only if the child fears that, in contrast, he is thought little of by his parents, or feels rejected by them. It is because of such an anxiety that one or all of a child's sisters or brothers may become a thorn in his flesh. Fearing that in comparison to them he cannot win his parents' love and esteem is what inflames sibling rivalry. This is indicated in stories by the fact that it matters little whether the siblings actually possess greater competence. The Biblical story of Joseph tells that it is jealousy of parental affection lavished on him which accounts for the destructive behavior of his brothers. Unlike Cinderella's, Joseph's parent does not participate in degrading him, and, on the contrary, prefers him to his other children. But Joseph, like Cinderella, is turned into a slave, and, like her, he miraculously escapes and ends by surpassing his siblings.

Telling a child who is devastated by sibling rivalry that he will grow up to do as well as his brothers and sisters offers little relief from his present feelings of dejection. Much as he would like to trust our assurances, most of the time he cannot. A child can see things only with subjective eyes, and comparing himself on this basis to his siblings, he has no confidence that he, on his own, will someday be able to fare as well as they. If he could believe more in himself, he would not feel destroyed by his siblings no matter what they might do to him, since then he could trust that time would bring about a desired reversal of fortune. But since the child cannot, on his own, look forward with confidence to some future day when things will turn out all right for him, he can gain relief only through fantasies of glory—a domination over his siblings—which he hopes will become reality through some fortunate event.

Whatever our position within the family, at certain times in our lives we are beset by sibling rivalry in some form or other. Even an only child feels that other children have some great advantages over him, and this makes him intensely jealous. Further, he may suffer from the anxious thought that if he did have a sibling, his parents would prefer this other child to him. "Cinderella" is a fairy tale which makes nearly as strong an appeal to boys as to girls, since children of both sexes suffer equally from sibling rivalry, and have the same desire to be rescued from their lowly position and surpass those who seem superior to them.

On the surface, "Cinderella" is as deceptively simple as the story of Little Red Riding Hood, with which it shares greatest popularity. "Cinderella" tells about the agonies of sibling rivalry, of wishes coming true, of the humble being elevated, of true merit being recognized even when hidden under rags, of virtue rewarded and evil punished—a straightforward story. But under this overt content is concealed a welter of complex and largely unconscious material, which details of the story allude to just enough to set our unconscious associations going. This makes a contrast between surface simplicity and underlying complexity which arouses deep interest in the story and explains its appeal to the millions over centuries. To begin gaining an understanding of these hidden meanings, we have to penetrate behind the obvious sources of sibling rivalry discussed so far.

As mentioned before, if the child could only believe that it is the infirmities of his age which account for his lowly position, he would not have to suffer so wretchedly from sibling rivalry, because he could trust the future to right matters. When he thinks that his degradation is deserved, he feels his plight is utterly hopeless. Djuna Barnes's perceptive statement about fairy tales—that the child knows something about them which he cannot tell (such as that he likes the idea of Little Red Riding Hood and the wolf being in bed together)—could be extended by dividing fairy tales into two groups: one group where the child responds only unconsciously to the inherent truth of the story and thus cannot tell about it; and another large number of tales where the child preconsciously or even consciously knows what the "truth" of the story consists of and thus could tell about it, but does not want to let on that he knows.[77] Some aspects of "Cinderella" fall into the latter category. Many children believe that Cinderella probably deserves her fate at the beginning of the story, as they feel they would, too; but they don't want anyone to know it. Despite this, she is worthy at the end to be exalted, as the child hopes he will be too, irrespective of his earlier shortcomings.

Every child believes at some period of his life—and this is not only at rare moments—that because of his secret wishes, if not also his clandestine actions, he deserves to be degraded, banned from the presence of others, relegated to a netherworld of smut. He fears this may be so, irrespective of how fortunate his situation may be in reality. He hates and fears those others—such as his siblings—whom he believes to be entirely free of similar evilness, and he fears that they or his parents will discover what he is really like, and then demean him as Cinderella was by her family. Because he wants others—most of all, his parents—to believe in his innocence, he is delighted that "everybody" believes in Cinderella's. This is one of the great attractions of this fairy tale. Since people give credence to Cinderella's goodness, they will also believe in his, so the child hopes. And "Cinderella" nourishes this hope, which is one reason it is such a delightful story.

Another aspect which holds large appeal for the child is the vileness of the stepmother and stepsisters. Whatever the shortcomings of a child may be in his own eyes, these pale into insignificance when compared to the stepsisters' and stepmother's falsehood and nastiness. Further, what these stepsisters do to Cinderella justifies whatever nasty thoughts one may have about one's siblings: they are so vile that anything one may wish would happen to them is more than justified. Compared to their behavior, Cinderella is indeed innocent. So the child, on hearing her story, feels he need not feel guilty about his angry thoughts.

On a very different level—and reality considerations coexist easily with fantastic exaggerations in the child's mind—as badly as one's parents or siblings seem to treat one, and much as one thinks one suffers because of it, all this is nothing compared to Cinderella's fate. Her story reminds the child at the same time how lucky he is, and how much worse things could be. (Any anxiety about the latter possibility is relieved, as always in fairy tales, by the happy ending.)

The behavior of a five-and-a-half-year-old girl, as reported by her father, may illustrate how easily a child may feel that she is a "Cinderella." This little girl had a younger sister of whom she was very jealous. The girl was very fond of "Cinderella," since the story offered her material with which to act out her feelings, and because without the story's imagery she would have been hard pressed to comprehend and express them. This little girl had used to dress very neatly and liked pretty clothes, but she became unkempt and dirty. One day when she was asked to fetch some salt, she said as she was doing so, "Why do you treat me like Cinderella?"

Almost speechless, her mother asked her, "Why do you think I treat you like Cinderella?"

"Because you make me do all the hardest work in the house!" was the little girl's answer. Having thus drawn her parents into her fantasies, she acted them out more openly, pretending to sweep up all the dirt, etc. She went even further, playing that she prepared her little sister for the ball. But she went the "Cinderella" story one better, based on her unconscious understanding of the contradictory emotions fused into the "Cinderella" role, because at another moment she told her mother and sister, "You shouldn't be jealous of me just because I am the most beautiful in the family."[78]

This shows that behind the surface humility of Cinderella lies the conviction of her superiority to mother and sisters, as if she would think: "You can make me do all the dirty work, and I pretend that I am dirty, but within me I know that you treat me this way because you are jealous of me because I am so much better than you." This conviction is supported by the story's ending, which assures every "Cinderella" that eventually she will be discovered by her prince.

Why does the child believe deep within himself that Cinderella deserves her dejected state? This question takes us back to the child's state of mind at the end of the oedipal period. Before he is caught in oedipal entanglements, the child is convinced that he is lovable, and loved, if all is well within his family relationships. Psychoanalysis describes this stage of complete satisfaction with oneself as "primary narcissism." During this period the child feels certain that he is the center of the universe, so there is no reason to be jealous of anybody.

The oedipal disappointments which come at the end of this developmental stage cast deep shadows of doubt on the child's sense of his worthiness. He feels that if he were really as deserving of love as he had thought, then his parents would never be critical of him or disappoint him. The only explanation for parental criticism the child can think of is that there must be some serious flaw in him which accounts for what he experiences as rejection. If his desires remain unsatisfied and his parents disappoint him, there must be something wrong with him or his desires, or both. He cannot yet accept that reasons other than those residing within him could have an impact on his fate. In his oedipal jealousy, wanting to get rid of the parent of the same sex had seemed the most natural thing in the world, but now the child realizes that he cannot have his own way, and that maybe this is so because the desire was wrong. He is no longer so sure that he is preferred to his siblings, and he begins to suspect that this may be due to the fact that *they* are free of any bad thoughts or wrongdoing such as his.

All this happens as the child is gradually subjected to ever more critical attitudes as he is being socialized. He is asked to behave in ways which run counter to his natural desires, and he resents this. Still he must obey, which makes him very angry. This anger is directed against those who make demands, most likely his parents; and this is another reason to wish to get rid of them, and still another reason to feel guilty about such wishes. This is why the child also feels that he deserves to be chastised for his feelings, a punishment he believes he can escape only if nobody learns what he is thinking when he is angry. The feeling of being unworthy to be loved by his parents at a time when his desire for their love is very strong leads to the fear of rejection, even when in reality there is none. This rejection fear compounds the anxiety that others are preferred and also maybe preferable—the root of sibling rivalry.

Some of the child's pervasive feelings of worthlessness have their origin in his experiences during and around toilet training and all other aspects of his education to become clean, neat, and orderly. Much has been said about how children are made to feel dirty and bad because they are not as clean as their parents want or require them to be. As clean as a child may learn to be, he knows that he would much prefer to give free rein to his tendency to be messy, disorderly, and dirty.

At the end of the oedipal period, guilt about desires to be dirty and disorderly becomes compounded by oedipal guilt, because of the child's desire to replace the parent of the same sex in the love of the other parent. The wish to be the love, if not also the sexual partner, of the parent of the other sex, which at the beginning of the oedipal development seemed natural and "innocent," at the end of the period is repressed as bad. But while this wish as such is repressed, guilt about it and about sexual feelings in general is not, and this makes the child feel dirty and worthless.

Here again, lack of objective knowledge leads the child to think that he is the only bad one in all these respects—the only child who has such desires. It makes every child identify with Cinderella, who is relegated to sit among the cinders. Since the child has such "dirty" wishes, that is where he also belongs, and where he would end up if his parents knew of his desires. This is why every child needs to believe that even if he were thus degraded, eventually he would be rescued from such degradation and experience the most wonderful exaltation—as Cinderella does.

For the child to deal with his feelings of dejection and worthlessness aroused during this time, he desperately needs to gain some grasp on what these feelings of guilt and anxiety are all about. Further, he needs assurance on a conscious and an unconscious level that he will be able to extricate himself from these predicaments. One of the greatest merits of "Cinderella" is that, irrespective of the magic help Cinderella receives, the child understands that essentially it is through her own efforts, and because of the person she is, that Cinderella is able to transcend magnificently her degraded state, despite what appear as insurmountable obstacles. It gives the child confidence that the same will be true for him, because the story relates so well to what has caused both his conscious and his unconscious guilt.

Overtly "Cinderella" tells about sibling rivalry in its most extreme form: the jealousy and enmity of the stepsisters, and Cinderella's sufferings because of it. The many other psychological issues touched upon in the story are so covertly alluded to that the child does not become consciously aware of them. In his unconscious, however, the child responds to these significant details which refer to matters and experiences from which he consciously has separated himself, but which nevertheless continue to create vast problems for him.

In the Western world the history of "Cinderella" in print begins with Basile's story "The Cat Cinderella."[79] In it, we are told of a widowed prince who loves his daughter so much "that he saw with no other eyes but hers." This prince marries an evil woman who hates his daughter—we may assume out of jealousy—and "threw sour looks on her, enough to make her jump with fright." The girl complains about this to her beloved governess, saying that she wishes the prince had married the governess instead. The governess, tempted by this possibility, tells the girl, named Zezolla, to ask her stepmother to fetch some clothes out of a big chest so that as the woman is bending into the chest, Zezolla can slam the lid on her head and thus break her neck. Zezolla follows this advice and kills her stepmother.[80] Then she persuades her father to marry the governess.

Within days after the marriage, the new wife begins to promote her own six daughters, whom she has kept hidden up till now. She turns the father's heart against Zezolla, who is "brought to such a pass that she fell from the salon to the kitchen, from the canopy to the grate, from splendid silks and gold to dish-clouts, from scepter to spits; not only did she change her state, but also her name, and was no longer Zezolla, but 'Cat Cinderella.'"

One day when the prince is about to go on a trip, he asks all his daughters what they want him to bring back to them. The stepdaughters ask for various expensive things; Zezolla requests only that he recommend her to the dove of the fairies and beg them to send her something. The fairies send Zezolla a date tree with materials for planting and cultivating it. Soon after Cat Cinderella has planted and tended the tree with great care, it grows to the size of a woman. A fairy comes out of it and asks Cat Cinderella what she wants. All she wishes is to be able to leave the house without her stepsisters knowing.

On the day of a great feast, the stepsisters dress fancily and go to the feast. As soon as they have left, Cat Cinderella "ran to the plant and uttered the words the fairy had taught her, and at once she was decked out like a queen." The country's king, who happens to come to the feast, is bewitched by Cat Cinderella's extraordinary loveliness. To find out who she is, he orders one of his servants to follow her, but she manages to elude him. The same events occur on the next feast day. During a third celebration, events again repeat themselves, but this time, while being pursued by a servant, Cat Cinderella lets slip from her foot "the richest and prettiest patten you could imagine." (In Basile's time Neapolitan ladies wore high-heeled overshoes, called pattens, when they went out.) To find the beautiful girl to whom the shoe belongs, the king orders all the females in the kingdom to come to a party. At its end, when the king orders all females to try on the lost patten, "the moment it came near Zezolla's foot, it darted forward of itself to shoe her." So the king makes Zezolla his queen, and "the sisters, livid with envy, crept quietly home to their mother."

The motif of a child killing a mother or stepmother is very rare.* Zezolla's temporary degradation is so inadequate a punishment for murder that we have to look for some explanation, particularly since her debasement to being "Cat Cinderella" is not retaliation for this

*In one story of the "Brother and Sister" type, "La Mala Matrè," the children kill an evil mother on the advice of a female teacher and, as in Basile's story, ask their father to marry the teacher.[81] This tale, like Basile's, is of South Italian origin, so it seems likely that one served as a model for the other.

evil deed, or at least not directly so. Another unique feature of this story is the duplication of stepmothers. In "Cat Cinderella" we are told nothing about her true mother, who is mentioned in most "Cinderella" stories; and it is not a symbolic representation of the original mother who provides her mistreated daughter with the means for meeting her prince, but a fairy in the form of a date tree.

It is possible that in "Cat Cinderella," real mother and first stepmother are one and the same person at different developmental periods; and her murder and replacement are an oedipal fantasy rather than a reality. If so, it makes good sense that Zezolla is not punished for crimes she only imagined. Her degradation in favor of her siblings may also be a fantasy of what might happen to her if she would act on her oedipal wishes. Once Zezolla has outgrown the oedipal age and is ready to have good relations with her mother once again, the mother returns in the form of the fairy in the date tree and enables her daughter to gain sexual success with the king, a non-oedipal object.

That Cinderella's position is the consequence of an oedipal relation is suggested by many versions in this cycle of fairy tales. In stories which are diffused all over Europe, Africa, and Asia—in Europe, for example, in France, Italy, Austria, Greece, Ireland, Scotland, Poland, Russia, Scandinavia—Cinderella flees from a father who wants to marry her. In another group of widely distributed tales she is exiled by her father because she does not love him as much as he requires, although she loves him well enough. So there are many examples of the "Cinderella" theme in which her degradation—often without any (step)mother and (step)sisters being part of the story—is the consequence of oedipal entanglement of father and daughter.

M. R. Cox, who has made a comprehensive study of 345 "Cinderella" stories, divides them into three broad categories.[82] The first group contains only the two features which are essential to all: an ill-treated heroine, and her recognition by means of a slipper. Cox's second main group contains two more essential features: what Cox in her Victorian manner calls an "unnatural father"—that is, a father who wants to marry his daughter—and another feature which is a consequence of this—the heroine's flight, which eventually makes her into a "Cinderella." In Cox's third large grouping, the two additional features of the second are replaced by what Cox calls a "King Lear Judgment": a father's extracting from his daughter a declaration of love which he deems insufficient, so that she is therefore banished, which forces her into the "Cinderella" position.

Basile's is one of the very few "Cinderella" stories in which the heroine's fate is clearly her own creation, the result of her plotting and misdeed. In practically all other versions, she is on the surface entirely innocent. She does nothing to arouse her father's wish to marry her; she does not fail to love her father, although he banishes her because he thinks she does not love him enough. In the stories now best known, Cinderella does nothing that would warrant her debasement in favor of her stepsisters.

In most "Cinderella" stories, except Basile's, Cinderella's innocence is stressed; her virtue is perfect. Unfortunately, in human relations it is rare that one of the partners is innocence incarnate while the other is the sole guilty party. In a fairy tale this is of course possible; it is no greater miracle than those performed by fairy godmothers. But when we identify with a story's heroine, we do so for our own reasons, and our conscious and unconscious associations enter into it. A girl's thoughts about this story may be strongly influenced by what she wishes to believe about her father's relation to her, and what she desires to dissemble about her feelings toward him.[83]

The many stories in which innocent Cinderella is claimed by her father as his marital partner, a fate from which she can save herself only through flight, could be interpreted as conforming to and expressing universal childish fantasies in which a girl wishes her father would marry her and then, out of guilt because of these fantasies, denies doing anything to arouse this parental desire. But deep down a child who knows that she does want her father to prefer her to her mother feels she deserves to be punished for it—thus her flight or banishment, and degradation to a Cinderella existence.

The other stories in which Cinderella is expelled by her father because she does not love him enough may be viewed as a projection of a little girl's wish that her father should want her to love him beyond reason, as she wants to love him. Or the father's expulsion of Cinderella because she does not love him enough could equally well be regarded as giving body to paternal oedipal feelings for a daughter, in this way making an appeal to the unconscious and by now deeply repressed oedipal feelings of both father and child.

In Basile's story Cinderella is innocent in relation to her stepsisters and the governess turned stepmother, although she is guilty of murdering her first stepmother. Neither in Basile's story nor in the much more ancient Chinese tale is there any mention of Cinderella being mistreated by her siblings, nor of any debasement other than being forced by a (step)mother to perform menial tasks in tattered clothes.

She is not deliberately excluded from attending the feast. Sibling rivalry, so dominant in the presently known versions of "Cinderella," hardly plays a role in these early stories. For example, when the sisters in Basile's story are envious of Cinderella becoming queen, this seems no more than a natural reaction at losing out to her.

Matters are quite different in the "Cinderella" stories known today, where the siblings actively participate in Cinderella's mistreatment and are appropriately punished. Even so, nothing untoward happens to the stepmother, although she is very much an accessory to what the stepsisters inflict on Cinderella. It is as if the story implies that abuse by the (step)mother was somehow deserved, but not that by the stepsisters. What Cinderella may have done or wished to do which could justify the (step)mother's mistreatment can only be surmised from stories such as Basile's, or those others where she arouses so much love in the father that he wants to marry her.

Given these early "Cinderella" stories in which sibling rivalry plays only an insignificant role while oedipal rejections are central—a daughter flees from her father because of his sexual desires for her; a father rejects his daughter because she does not love him sufficiently; a mother rejects her daughter because the husband loves her too much; and the rare case where a daughter wishes to replace her father's wife with a choice of her own—one might think that, originally, thwarted oedipal desires account for the heroine's degradation. But there is no clear historical sequence in regard to these fairy stories forming one cycle, if for no other reason that, in oral tradition, ancient versions exist side by side with more recent ones. The lateness of the period when fairy stories were finally collected and published makes any sequential ordering of them before this happened highly speculative.

But while there are great variations in less important details, all versions of this story are alike in regard to the essential features. For example, in all stories the heroine at first enjoyed love and high esteem, and her fall from this favored position to utter degradation occurs as suddenly as her return to a much more exalted position at the story's end. The denouement comes about by her being recognized by the slipper which fits only her foot. (Occasionally another object, such as a ring, takes the slipper's place.[84]). The one crucial point of difference—in terms of which (as discussed) various groups of the stories are distinguished—lies in the *cause* of Cinderella's degradation.

In one group, the father plays a central role as Cinderella's antagonist. In the second group, the (step)mother *cum* stepsisters are the antagonists; in these stories, mother and daughters are so closely identified with each other that one gets the feeling that they are one unit split into different figures. In the first group, too much love of a father for his daughter causes Cinderella's tragic condition. In the other, the hatred of a (step)mother and her daughters due to sibling competition accounts for it.

If we trust the clues provided by Basile's story, then we may say that inordinate love of a father for his daughter and hers for him came first, and her reduction to the Cinderella role by mother *cum* sisters is the consequence. This situation parallels the oedipal development of a girl. She first loves her mother—the original good mother, who later in the story reappears as fairy godmother. Later she turns from her mother to her father, loving him and wanting to be loved by him; at this point the mother—and all her siblings, real and imagined, most of all the female ones—become her competitors. At the end of the oedipal period the child feels cast out, all alone; then when all goes well in puberty, if not sooner, the girl finds her way back to the mother, now as a person not to be loved exclusively, but as one with whom to identify.

The hearth, the center of the home, is a symbol for the mother. To live so close to it that one dwells among the ashes may then symbolize an effort at holding on to, or returning to, the mother and what she represents. All little girls try to return to the mother from the disappointment inflicted on them by the father. This attempted return to Mother, however, no longer works—because she is no longer the all-giving mother of infancy, but a mother who makes demands of the child. Seen in this light, at the story's beginning Cinderella mourns not only the loss of the original mother, but grieves also at the loss of her dreams about the wonderful relation she was going to have with Father. Cinderella has to work through her deep oedipal disappointments to return to a successful life at the story's end, no longer a child, but a young maiden ready for marriage.

Thus, the two groups of "Cinderella" stories which differ so greatly on the surface, in regard to what causes her misfortune, are not at all contrary on a deeper level. They simply render separately some main aspects of the same phenomenon: the girl's oedipal desires and anxieties.

Things are considerably more complex in the "Cinderella" stories now popular, which may go a long way to explain why these superseded some of the older versions, such as Basile's. The oedipal desires for the father are repressed—except for the expectation that he will give her a magic present. The present her father brings Cinderella, such as the date tree in "Cat Cinderella," gives her the opportunity to meet her prince and gain his love, which leads to his replacing the father as the man she loves most in the world.

Cinderella's wish to eliminate Mother is completely repressed in the modern versions and replaced by a displacement and a projection: it is not Mother who overtly plays a crucial role in the girl's life, but a stepmother; Mother is displaced by a substitute. And it is not the girl who wants to debase Mother so that she will be able to play a much bigger role in her father's life, but, in a projection, it is the stepmother who wants to see the girl replaced. One more displacement further assures that the true desires remain hidden: it is her siblings who want to take the heroine's rightful place away from her.

In those versions, sibling rivalry takes the place of an oedipal involvement that has been repressed, as the center of the plot. In real life, positive and negative oedipal relations, and guilt about these relations often remain hidden behind sibling rivalry. However, as happens frequently with complex psychological phenomena which arouse great guilt, all that the person consciously experiences is anxiety due to the guilt, and not the guilt itself, or what caused it. Thus, "Cinderella" tells only about the misery of being degraded.

In the best fairy-tale tradition, the anxiety Cinderella's pitiful existence evokes in the hearer is soon relieved by the happy ending. By feeling deeply for Cinderella, the child (implicitly and without its coming to conscious awareness) deals in some fashion with oedipal anxiety and guilt, and also with the desires which underlie it. The child's hope of being able to disentangle herself from her oedipal predicament by finding a love object to whom she can give herself without guilt or anxiety is turned into confidence, because the story assures that entering the lower depths of existence is but a necessary step toward becoming able to realize one's highest potentials.

It must be stressed that it would be impossible, upon hearing the story of Cinderella in one of its presently popular forms, to recognize consciously that her unhappy state is due to oedipal involvements on her part, and that by insisting on her unrivaled innocence the story is covering up her oedipal guilt. The well-known "Cinderella" stories consistently obscure what is oedipal, and offer no hints to cast doubt on Cinderella's innocence. On a conscious level, the evilness of stepmother and stepsisters is sufficient explanation for what happens to Cinderella. The modern plot centers on sibling rivalry; the stepmother's degrading Cinderella has no cause other than the wish to advance her own daughters; and the stepsisters' nastiness is due to their being jealous of Cinderella.

But "Cinderella" cannot fail to activate in us those emotions and unconscious ideas which, in our inner experience, are connected with our feelings of sibling rivalry. From his own experience with it, the child might well understand—without "knowing" anything about it—the welter of inner experiences connected with Cinderella. Recalling, if she is a girl, her repressed wishes to get rid of Mother and have Father all to herself, and now feeling guilty about such "dirty" desires, a girl may well "understand" why a mother would send her daughter out of sight to reside among the cinders, and prefer her other children. Where is the child who has not wished to be able to banish a parent at some time, and who does not feel that in retaliation he merits the same fate? And where is the child who has not wanted to wallow to his heart's desire in dirt or mud; and, being made to feel dirty by parental criticism in consequence, become convinced that he deserves nothing better than to be relegated to a dirty corner?

The purpose of elaborating on "Cinderella's" oedipal background was to show that the story offers the hearer a deeper understanding of that which is behind his own feelings of sibling rivalry. If the hearer permits his unconscious understanding to "swing" along with what his conscious mind is being told, he gains a much deeper understanding of what accounts for the complex emotions which his siblings arouse. Sibling rivalry, both in its overt expression and in its denial, is very much part of our lives well into maturity, as is its counterpart, our positive attachments to our siblings. But because the latter rarely lead to emotional difficulties, and the former does, greater understanding of what is psychologically involved in sibling rivalry could help us deal with this important and difficult problem in our lives.

Like "Little Red Cap," "Cinderella" is known today mainly in two different forms, one which derives from Perrault, the other from the Brothers Grimm—and the two versions are considerably at variance.[85]

As with all of Perrault's stories, the trouble with his "Cinderella" is that he took fairy-tale material—either Basile's or some other "Cinderella" story known to him from oral tradition, or a combination of both sources—freed it of all content he considered vulgar, and refined its other features to make the product suitable to be told at court. Being an author of great skill and taste, he invented details and changed others to make the story conform to his aesthetic concepts.

It was, for example, his invention that the fateful slipper was made of glass, which is in no other versions but those derived from his.

There is quite a controversy about this detail. Since in French the word *vair* (which means variegated fur) and *verre* (glass) are sometimes pronounced similarly, it was assumed that Perrault, on having heard the story, mistakenly substituted *verre* for *vair* and thus changed a fur slipper into one made of glass. Although this explanation is often repeated, there seems no doubt that the glass slipper was Perrault's deliberate invention. But because of it he had to drop an important feature of many earlier versions of "Cinderella," which tell how the stepsisters mutilated their feet to make them fit the slipper. The prince fell for this deception until he was made aware by the songs of birds that there was blood in the shoe. This detail would have been immediately obvious had the slipper been made of glass. For example, in "Rashin Coatie" (a Scottish version) the stepmother forces the slipper onto her daughter's foot by cutting off her heel and toes. On the way to church a bird sings:

> "Minched fit, and pinched fit
> Beside the king she rides,
> But braw fit, and bonny fit
> In the kitchen neuk she hides."[86]

The bird's song brings to the prince's attention that the stepsister is not the right bride. But such coarse mutilation would not have fitted in with the polite way in which Perrault wished to retell his story.

Perrault's story and those directly based on it depict the character of the heroine quite differently from all other versions. Perrault's Cinderella is sugar-sweet and insipidly good, and she completely lacks initiative (which probably accounts for Disney's choosing Perrault's version of "Cinderella" as the basis for his rendering of the story). Most other Cinderellas are much more of a person. To mention only some of the differences, in Perrault it is Cinderella's choice to sleep among the cinders: "When she had done her work, she went to the corner of the chimney and sat down among the cinders," which led to her name. There is no such self-debasement in the Brothers Grimm's story; as they tell it, Cinderella *had* to bed down among the ashes.

When it comes to dressing the stepsisters for the ball, Perrault's Cinderella all on her own "advised them the best way in the world, and offered herself to do their hair," while in the Brothers Grimm's version the stepsisters order her to comb their hair and brush their shoes; she obeys but weeps while doing so. As for getting to the ball, Perrault's Cinderella takes no action; it is her fairy godmother who tells her that she wishes to go. In the Brothers Grimm's story Cinderella asks her stepmother to let her go to the ball, persists in her request although turned down, and performs the impossible tasks demanded of her so that she can go. At the ball's end she leaves of her own accord and hides from the pursuing prince. Perrault's Cinderella does not depart because she considers it right to do so, but simply obeys a command of her fairy godmother not to remain one moment after midnight because otherwise the coach will again become a pumpkin, etc.

When it comes to the trying on of the slipper, in Perrault it is not the prince who searches for its owner, but a gentleman sent to look for the girl it fits. Before Cinderella is to meet the prince, her godmother appears and equips her with beautiful clothes. Thus, an important detail in the Brothers Grimm's and most other versions gets lost —namely, that the prince remains undismayed by Cinderella's appearance in rags because he recognizes her inherent qualities, apart from her outer appearance. Thus, the contrast between the materialistic stepsisters, who rely on externals, and Cinderella, who cares little about them, is reduced.

In Perrault's version it does not make all that much difference whether one is vile or virtuous. In his story the stepsisters are considerably more abusive of Cinderella than in that of the Brothers Grimm; nevertheless, at the end Cinderella embraces those who have vilified her and tells them that she loves them with all her heart and desires them always to love her. From the story, however, it is incomprehensible why she would care for their love, or how they could love her after all that has happened. Even after her marriage to the prince, Perrault's Cinderella "gave her two sisters lodging in the palace, and married them the same day to two great lords of the court."

In the Brothers Grimm's version the ending is quite different, as it is in all other renderings of the tale. First, the sisters mutilate their feet to make the slipper fit. Second, they come on their own to Cinderella's wedding to ingratiate themselves and have a share in her good fortune. But as they walk to the church, the pigeons—probably the same birds which had helped Cinderella earlier to meet the impossible tasks set her—pick out one eye from each, and as they return from church, the other. The story ends: "And thus for their wickedness and falsehood they were punished with blindness for the rest of their days."

Of the many other differences in these two versions, only two more will be mentioned. In Perrault's tale the father plays no role to speak of. All we learn about him is that he married a second time and that Cinderella "did not dare to complain to her father because he would only have scolded her, because he was entirely run by his wife." Also, we hear nothing about the fairy godmother until she suddenly appears from nowhere to provide Cinderella with her coach, horses, and dress.

Since "Cinderella" is the most popular of all fairy tales and is distributed worldwide, it may be appropriate to consider the important motifs woven into the story which, in their combination, make for its great conscious and unconscious appeal and its deep significance. Stith Thompson, who has made the most complete analysis of folk-tale motifs, enumerates those appearing in the Brothers Grimm's "Cinderella" as follows: an ill-treated heroine; her having to live by the hearth; the gift she asks of her father; the hazel branch she plants on her mother's grave; the tasks demanded of the heroine; the animals which help her perform them; the mother, transformed into the tree Cinderella grew on her grave, who provides her with beautiful clothes; the meeting at the ball; and Cinderella's threefold flight from it; her hiding first in a pigeon house and second in a pear tree, which are cut down by her father; the pitch trap and the lost shoe; the shoe test; the sisters' mutilation of their feet and acceptance as (false) brides; the animals which reveal the deception; the happy marriage; the nemesis wreaked on the villains.[87] My discussion of these story elements also includes some remarks on the better-known details of Perrault's "Cinderella" which are not part of the Brothers Grimm's tale.

Cinderella's mistreatment as a consequence of sibling rivalry, the story's main motif in its modern form, has already been dealt with. This is what makes the most immediate impact on the hearer and arouses his empathy. It leads him to identify with the heroine, and sets the stage for all that follows.

Cinderella's living among the ashes—from which she derives her name—is a detail of great complexity.* On the surface, it signifies

---

*It is unfortunate that "Cinderella" became known by this name in English, an all-too-facile and incorrect translation of the French *"Cendrillon,"* which, like the German name of the heroine, stresses her living among ashes. "Ashes" and not "cinders" is the correct translation of the French *cendre*, which is derived from the Latin term for ashes, *cinerem*. The *Oxford English Dictionary* makes a special point of noting that "cinders" is not connected etymologically with the French word *"cen-*

abuse, and degradation from the fortunate position she enjoyed before the beginning of the story. But it is not without reason that Perrault has her choose to dwell among the ashes. We are so accustomed to thinking of living as a lowly servant among the ashes of the hearth as an extremely degraded situation that we have lost any recognition that, in a different view, it may be experienced as a very desirable, even exalted position. In ancient times, to be the guardian of the hearth—the duty of the Vestal Virgins—was one of the most prestigious ranks, if not the most exalted, available to a female. To be a Vestal Virgin was to be much envied in ancient Rome. A girl was selected for this honor when she was between six and ten years old —roughly the age of Cinderella as we imagine her during her years of servitude. In the Brothers Grimm's story Cinderella plants a twig and cultivates it with her tears and prayers. Only after it has grown into a tree does it provide her with what she needs to go to the ball —thus, several years must have passed between the planting and the ball. Six to ten years old is also the age of children on whom this story makes the deepest impression, and it often stays with them and sustains them for the rest of their lives.

Speaking of Cinderella's years of servitude: only at later times did it become customary for Vestal Virgins to serve for thirty years before they gave up office and could marry. Originally they remained priestesses for only five years: that is, until they reached marriageable age. This is about the amount of time one imagines Cinderella's sufferings to last. To be a Vestal Virgin meant both to be a guardian of the hearth and to be absolutely pure. After they had performed well in the role, these women made prestigious marriages, as does Cinderella. Thus, innocence, purity, and being guardian of the hearth go together in ancient connotations.* It is possible that with the rejection of pagan-

---

dres." This is important in regard to the connotations that attach themselves to the name of "Cinderella," since ashes are the very clean powdery substance which is the residue of complete combustion; cinders, to the contrary, are the quite dirty remnants of an incomplete combustion.

*The purity of the priestess responsible for the sacred fire, and fire itself, which purifies, evoke appropriate connotations also to ashes. In many societies ashes were used for ablutions, as a means of cleansing oneself. This was one of the connotations of ashes, although today it is no longer widespread.

The other connotation of ashes is to mourning. Sprinkling ashes over the head, as on Ash Wednesday, is still a sign of bereavement as it was in ancient times. Sitting among the ashes as a reaction to, and a sign of, mourning is mentioned in the *Odyssey*, and was practiced among many peoples.[88] By making Cinderella sit among cinders, and basing her name on it, these connotations to purity and to deep mourning which

ism, what had been a highly desirable role became devalued in the Christian era to be the meanest. The Vestal Virgins served the sacred hearth and Hera, the mother goddess. With the change to a father god, the old maternal deities were degraded and devalued, as was a place close to the hearth. In this sense, Cinderella might also be viewed as the degraded mother goddess who at the end of the story is reborn out of the ashes, like the mythical bird phoenix. But these are connections of a historical nature which the average hearer of "Cinderella" will not readily establish in his mind.

There are other, equally positive associations to living by the hearth which are available to every child. Children love to spend time in the kitchen, watching and participating in the preparation of food. Before central heating, a seat close to the hearth was the warmest and often the coziest place in the house. The hearth evokes in many children happy memories of the time they spent there with their mothers.

Children also like to get themselves good and dirty; to be able to do so is a symbol of instinctual freedom to them. Thus, being a person who stirs around in the ashes, the original meaning of the name Aschenbrödel, has also very positive connotations for the child. Making oneself "good and dirty" is both pleasurable and guilt-producing today, as it was in times past.

Finally, Cinderella mourns her dead mother. "Ashes to ashes" is not the only saying which establishes close connection between the dead and ashes. To cover oneself with ashes is a symbol of mourning; living in dirty rags is a symptom of depression. Thus, dwelling among the ashes may symbolize both lovely times with Mother in proximity to the hearth, and also our state of deep mourning for this intimate closeness to Mother which we lost as we grew up, symbolized by the "death" of Mother. Because of this combination of images, the hearth evokes strong feelings of empathy, reminding us all of the paradise in which we once dwelt, and how radically our lives changed when we were forced to give up the simple and happy existence of the very young child, to cope with all the ambivalences of adolescence and adulthood.

As long as the child is little, his parents protect him against the ambivalences of his siblings and the demands of the world. In retro-

---

are connected with her original name in the Italian story (which by far antedates Perrault's tale), as much as with her French and German names, have become changed in English to the exact opposite connotations, referring to blackness and dirtiness.

spect this seems to have been a paradisal time. Then, suddenly, these older siblings seem to take advantage of the now less-protected child; they make demands; they and Mother become critical of what the child does. The references to his disorderliness, if not dirty habits, make him feel rejected and dirty; and the siblings seem to live in splendor. But their good behavior, the child believes, is a sham, a pretense, and a falsehood. And this is the image of the stepsisters in "Cinderella." The young child lives in extremes: at one moment he feels himself vile and dirty, full of hate; in the next he is all innocence, and the others are evil creatures.

Whatever the external conditions, during these years of sibling rivalry the child experiences an inner period of suffering, privation, even want; and he experiences misunderstandings, even malice. Cinderella's years among the ashes tell the child that nobody can escape this. There are times when it seems that only hostile forces exist, that no helpful ones are about. If the child being told the story of Cinderella did not come to feel that she had to endure a considerable stretch of such bad times, her relief would be incomplete when finally the helpful forces overcame the hostile ones. The child's misery at moments is so deep that it seems to last a very long time. Therefore no fleeting period in Cinderella's life would seem comparable to this. Cinderella must suffer as much and as long as the child believes he does, for her delivery to carry conviction and give him the certitude that the same thing will happen in his life.

After we have felt compassion for Cinderella's dejected state, the first positive development in her life occurs. "It once happened that the father wanted to go to a fair, so he asked the two stepdaughters what he should bring them. 'Beautiful clothes,' said one. 'Pearls and gems,' said the other. 'What about you, Aschenputtel,' he said, 'what do you want?' 'Father, the first twig that pushes against your hat on your return trip, break it off for me.'" He acts accordingly; a hazel branch not only pushes against his hat, but knocks it off. This branch he brings home to Aschenputtel. "She thanked him, went to her mother's grave and planted the branch on it; she wept so much that her tears fell on it and watered it. It grew and became a beautiful tree. There she went three times a day and wept and prayed; and each time a white bird lighted on the tree, and when she expressed a wish, the bird threw down what she had wished for."

Cinderella's asking her father for the twig she planned to plant on her mother's grave, and his meeting her desire, is a first tentative re-establishment of a positive relation between the two. From the story we assume that Cinderella must have been very disappointed in her father, if not also angry that he married such a shrew. But to the young child, his parents are all-powerful. If Cinderella is to become master of her own fate, her parents' authority must be diminished. This diminution and transfer of power could be symbolized by the branch knocking the father's hat off his head, and also the fact that the same branch grows into a tree that has magic powers for Cinderella. Therefore, that which diminished the father (the branch of the hazel tree) is used by Cinderella to increase the power and prestige of the archaic (dead) mother. Since her father gives Cinderella the twig which enhances the memory of the mother, it seems to be a sign that he approves of her returning from her heavy involvement with him to the original unambivalent relation to the mother. This diminution of the father's emotional importance in Cinderella's life prepares the way for her transferring her childish love for him eventually into a mature love for the prince.

The tree which Cinderella plants on her mother's grave and waters with her tears is one of the most poetically moving and psychologically significant features of the story. It symbolizes that the memory of the idealized mother of infancy, when kept alive as an important part of one's internal experience, can and does support us even in the worst adversity.

This is told even more clearly in other versions of the story where the figure into which the good mother becomes transformed is not a tree but a helpful animal. For example, in the earliest recorded Chinese rendering of the "Cinderella" motif, the heroine has a tame fish which grows from two inches to ten feet under her devoted care. The evil stepmother discovers the importance of the fish, and cunningly kills and eats it. The heroine is desolate until a wise man tells her where the fish's bones are buried and advises her to collect and keep them in her room. He tells her that if she prays to these bones, she will obtain whatever she wishes. In many European and Eastern variations it is a calf, cow, goat, or some other animal into which the dead mother is transformed to become the heroine's magic helper.

The Scottish tale of "Rashin Coatie" is older than either Basile's or Perrault's "Cinderella," since it is mentioned as early as 1540.[89] A mother, before her death, bequeaths her daughter, Rashin Coatie, a little red calf, which gives her whatever she asks for. The stepmother finds out about this and orders the calf butchered. Rashin Coatie is desperate, but the dead calf tells her to pick up its bones and bury them under a gray stone. She does and henceforth receives what she desires by going to the stone and telling the calf. At Yuletide, when everybody puts on their best clothes to go to the church, Rashin Coatie is told by her stepmother that she is too dirty to join them in church. The dead calf provides Rashin Coatie with beautiful clothes; in church a prince falls in love with her; on their third meeting she loses a slipper, etc.

In many other "Cinderella" stories the helpful animal also nourishes the heroine. For example, in an Egyptian tale a stepmother and step-siblings mistreat two children, who beg, "O cow, be kind to us, as our mother was kind to us." The cow gives them good food. The step-mother finds out and has the cow butchered. The children burn the cow's bones and bury the ashes in a clay pot, from which a tree grows and bears fruits for the children, and this provides happiness for them.[90] So there are stories of the "Cinderella" type in which the animal and the tree representing the mother are combined, showing how one can stand for the other. These tales also illustrate the sym-bolic replacement of the original mother by an animal that gives us milk—the cow or, in Mediterranean countries, the goat. This reflects the emotional and psychological connection of early feeding experi-ences which provide security in later life.

Erikson speaks of "a sense of *basic trust*, which," he says, "is an attitude toward oneself and the world derived from the experience of the first year of life."[91] Basic trust is instilled in the child by the good mothering he experiences during the earliest period of his life. If all goes well then, the child will have confidence in himself and in the world. The helpful animal or the magic tree is an image, embodiment, external representation of this basic trust. It is the heritage which a good mother confers on her child which will stay with him, and pre-serve and sustain him in direst distress.

The stories where the stepmother kills the helpful animal but does not succeed in depriving Cinderella of what gives her inner strength indicate that for our managing or coping with life, what exists in reality is less important than what goes on in our mind. What makes life bearable even in the worst circumstances is the image of the good mother which we have internalized, so that the disappearance of the external symbol does not matter.[92]

One of the main overt messages of the various "Cinderella" stories is that we are mistaken if we think we must hold on to something in the external world to succeed in life. All efforts of the stepsisters to gain their goal through externals are in vain—their carefully selected and prepared clothes, the fraud through which they try to make their feet fit the shoe. Only being true to oneself, as Cinderella is, succeeds in the end. The same idea is conveyed by the mother's or the helpful animal's presence not being required. This is psychologically correct, because for one's inner security and feeling of self-worth, no externals are necessary once one has developed basic trust—nor can externals compensate for not having attained basic trust in infancy. Those so unfortunate as to have lost out on basic trust at the beginning of life can achieve it, if at all, only through changes in the inner structure of their mind and personality, never through things that look good.

The image conveyed by the tree growing from a twig or the calf's bones or ashes is that of something different developing out of the original mother, or the experience of her. The image of the tree is particularly pertinent because growth is involved, whether it is Cat Cinderella's date tree or Cinderella's hazel branch. This indicates that simply to retain the internalized image of the mother of a past period is not enough. As the child grows up, this internalized mother must undergo changes, too, as he does. This is a process of dematerialization, similar to that in which the child sublimates the real good mother into an inner experience of basic trust.

In the Brothers Grimm's "Cinderella," all of this is refined even more. Cinderella's inner processes begin with her desperate mourning for her mother, as symbolized by her existence among the ashes. If she remained stuck there, no internal development would occur. Mourning as a temporary transition to continuing life without the loved person is necessary; but for survival it must eventually be turned into something positive: the erection of an internal representation of what has been lost in reality. Such an inner object will always remain inviolate within us, whatever happens in reality. Cinderella's weeping over the planted twig shows that the memory of her dead mother is kept alive; but as the tree grows, so does the internalized mother grow inside Cinderella.

Cinderella's prayers, also said over the tree, bespeak the hopes she cultivates. Prayers ask for something that we trust will happen: basic trust reasserts itself after the shock of adversity has worn off; this trust restores in us the hope that eventually things will again go well for us, as they have in our past. The little white bird which comes in answer to Cinderella's prayers is the messenger of Ecclesiastes: "A bird of the air shall carry the voice, and that which has wings shall tell the matter." The white bird is easily recognized as the mother's spirit conveyed to her child through the good mothering she gives him; it is the spirit which originally became implanted in the child as basic trust. As such, it becomes the child's own spirit, which sustains him in all hardships, giving him hope for the future, and the strength to create a good life for himself.

Whether or not we recognize consciously the full significance of that which is symbolically expressed through the image of Cinderella's asking for the twig, planting it, cultivating it with her tears and prayers, and finally through the little white bird alighting on it whenever Cinderella needs it, this feature of "Cinderella" touches us all, and we respond, at least preconsciously, to the meaning. It is a beautiful and effective image, even more meaningful and instructive to the child who is just beginning to internalize what his parents mean to him. It is as significant to boys as it is to girls because the internalized mother—or basic trust—is a crucially important mental phenomenon, whatever a person's sex. By eliminating the tree and replacing it with a fairy godmother who appears suddenly and unexpectedly out of nowhere, Perrault has robbed the story of some of its deepest meaning.

The Brothers Grimm's "Cinderella" conveys ever so subtly to the child that, miserable as he may feel at the moment—because of sibling rivalry or any other reason—by sublimating his misery and sorrow, as Cinderella does by planting and cultivating the tree with her emotions, the child on his very own can arrange things so that his life in the world will also become a good one.

In the Brothers Grimm's "Cinderella," right after we have been told about the tree and the little white bird that fulfills Cinderella's wishes, we learn that the king has ordered a three-day festival so that his son may select a bride. Cinderella begs to be permitted to go. Despite denials, she persists in her entreaties. Finally the stepmother tells her that she has emptied a dish of lentils into the ashes; if Cinderella picks them out within two hours, she may go to the ball.

This is one of the seemingly impossible tasks which fairy-tale heroes have to perform. In Eastern versions of "Cinderella," she has to do some spinning; in some Western stories, sift grain.[93] On the surface, this is another example of her being abused. But when this demand is made of Cinderella—after the radical change in her fortunes, since she has gained a magic helper in the white bird which fulfills her wishes, and just before she is to go to the ball—this suggests that hard and difficult tasks must be performed well before Cinderella is worthy of a happy ending. Thanks to the birds she calls in as helpers, Cinderella is able to finish the sorting task, only to have the stepmother repeat her demand with doubly increased difficulties: the second time she is required to sort two dishes of lentils spilled into the ashes and to do so in only one hour. Again with the aid of the birds Cinderella succeeds, but the stepmother still will not allow her to go to the ball, despite her two promises to do so.

The task demanded of Cinderella seems senseless: why drop lentils into the ashes only to have them picked out again? The stepmother is convinced that this is impossible, degrading, meaningless. But Cinderella knows that something good can be gained from whatever one does if one is able to endow it with meaning, even from stirring around in the ashes. This detail of the story encourages the child in his conviction that to dwell in lowly places—to play in and with dirt —can be of great value, if one knows how to extract it. Cinderella calls on the birds to help her, telling them to pick out the good lentils and put them in the pot, but to do away with the bad ones by eating them.

The stepmother's falseness in twice reneging on her promises is thus opposed to Cinderella's recognition that what is needed is a sorting out of good from evil. After Cinderella has spontaneously turned the task into a moral problem of good versus bad, and eliminated the bad, she proceeds to her mother's grave and asks the tree to "scatter gold and silver" over her. The bird throws down a gold-and-silver dress and, the first and second times, slippers decorated with silk and silver. The last time the slippers are made of gold.

In Perrault's tale, too, Cinderella has to accomplish a task before she can go to the ball. After the fairy godmother has told Cinderella that she is to go, she orders Cinderella to bring her a pumpkin from the garden. Although Cinderella does not understand the meaning of this, she does as she is told. It is the godmother, and not Cinderella, who scoops out the pumpkin and turns it into a coach. Then the godmother tells Cinderella to open a mousetrap, and she changes the six mice found there into horses. One rat is similarly transformed into a coachman. Finally Cinderella is to fetch six lizards, which become footmen. Her rags are made into beautiful clothes, and she is given glass slippers. So equipped, Cinderella leaves for the ball, but not before she is ordered to return before midnight because at that moment all will return to its original form.

The glass slippers, the pumpkin made into a coach—these are all Perrault's invention: there is no trace of them in any other version but his and those dependent on his. Marc Soriano sees in these details Perrault's mockery of the hearer who takes the story seriously, but also the irony with which he treats his subject: if Cinderella can be changed into the most beautiful princess, then mice and a rat can become horses and a coachman.*

Irony is in part the result of unconscious thoughts; and the wide acceptance of Perrault's details can be explained only by their touching a responsive chord in the hearer. The obligation to hold on to the best in one's past; to cultivate one's sense of morality; to remain true to one's values despite adversity; not to permit oneself to be defeated by the malice or nastiness of others—all this is so obvious in "Cinderella" that Perrault cannot have remained untouched by it. The conclusion must be that he deliberately defends himself against it. His irony invalidates the demand inherent in the story that we transform ourselves through an inner process. It ridicules the idea that striving for the highest goals permits us to transcend the lowly conditions of our external existence.[95] Perrault reduces "Cinderella" to a nice fantasy with no implications for ourselves. And this is how many people want to look at the story, which accounts for the widespread acceptance of his version of it.

While this may explain Perrault's manner of reworking the old tale, it does not account for the specific details which he invented according to both his conscious and his unconscious understanding of the story, and which we accept for the same reason. Contrary to all versions in which Cinderella is forced to live among the ashes, only Perrault tells that she *chose* to do so. This makes her the prepubertal child who has not yet repressed her desire to get herself good and dirty; and who has not yet acquired an aversion to furtive little animals like rats, mice, and lizards; and who scoops out a pumpkin and imagines it to be a beautiful coach. Mice and rats inhabit dark and dirty corners and steal food, all things the child also likes to do. Unconsciously, they also arouse associations to the phallus, indicating the coming of sexual interest and maturation. Irrespective of their phallic connotations, to transform such lowly if not disgusting animals into horses, coachman, and footmen represents a sublimation. So this detail seems correct on at least two levels: it signifies the company Cinderella kept while living among the ashes in her lowly stage, if not also her phallic interests; and it seems fitting that such interests must be sublimated as she matures—i.e., prepares herself for the prince.

Perrault's rendering makes his "Cinderella" more acceptable to our

---

*As for the lizards, Soriano reminds us of the French expression "lazy as a lizard," which explains why Perrault may have chosen these animals to be transformed into footmen, whose laziness was a matter for jokes.[94]

conscious and unconscious understanding of what the story is all about. Consciously we are willing to accept the irony which reduces the story to a nice fantasy without serious content, since it relieves us of the otherwise implied obligation to come to terms with the problem of sibling rivalry, and of the task of internalizing our early objects and living up to their moral requirements. Unconsciously the details he adds seem convincing on the basis of our own buried childhood experiences, since they appear to indicate that to become mature we must transform and sublimate our early fascination with instinctual behavior, whether it is the attraction of dirt or of phallic objects.

Perrault's Cinderella, who goes to the ball in a coach driven by six horses attended by six footmen—as if the ball would take place at Louis XIV's Versailles—must depart before midnight, when she will be returned to her mean attire. On the third night, however, she fails to pay sufficient attention to the passage of time, and in her hurry to get away before the magic spell expires, she loses one of her glass slippers. "The guards at the gates of the palace were asked if they had not seen a princess leaving; they said that they had seen nobody leave but a young girl very badly dressed, who looked much more like a country wench than a lady."

In the Brothers Grimm's story Cinderella can stay at the ball as long as she likes. When she leaves, she does so for a purpose and not because she must. When she does leave, the prince tries to accompany her, but she slips away, hiding from him on the first night. "The son of the king waited till the father came and told him that a strange girl had jumped into the dovecote. The old man thought, 'Could it be Aschenputtel?' and they had to bring him an ax and a pick so that he could break the dovecote into two; but nobody was in it." In the meantime Cinderella has made her escape and changed back into her dirty clothes. The following day, things repeat themselves, with the exception that Cinderella hides in a pear tree. On the third day the prince has the stairs coated with pitch, so when Cinderella again slips away, one of her slippers gets stuck there.

There are variations of the story in which Cinderella takes the initiative to be recognized, not waiting passively. In one of them the prince gives her a ring, which she bakes into a cake served to him; he will marry no other girl than the one on whose finger the ring fits.

Why does Cinderella go three times to the ball to meet the prince, only to run away from him to return to her degraded position? As it often does, the three-times-repeated behavior reflects the child's position in regard to his parents, and his reaching for his true selfhood as he works through his early conviction that he is the most important element in the threesome, and his later fear that he is the least significant. True selfhood is gained not through the three repetitions, but through something else that these lead up to—the fitting of the shoe.

On the overt level, Cinderella's evading the prince tells that she wants to be chosen for the person she really is, and not for her splendid appearance. Only if her lover has seen her in her degraded state and still desires her will she be his. But, for that, a single appearance and losing the slipper the first night would do. On a deeper level, repeating her visits to the ball symbolizes the ambivalence of the young girl who wants to commit herself personally and sexually, and at the same time is afraid to do so. It is an ambivalence which is also reflected in the father, who wonders whether the beautiful girl is his daughter Cinderella, but does not trust his feelings. The prince, as if recognizing that he cannot win Cinderella as long as she remains emotionally tied to her father in an oedipal relation, does not pursue her himself, but asks the father to do it for him. Only if the father first indicates his readiness to release his daughter from her ties to him can she feel good about transferring her heterosexual love from its immature object (the father) to its mature object—her future husband. The father's demolishing Cinderella's hiding places—chopping down the dovecote and the pear tree—shows his readiness to hand her over to the prince. But his efforts do not have the desired result.

On a quite different level, the dovecote and the pear tree stand for the magic objects which have sustained Cinderella up to this point. The first is the living place of the helpful birds which sorted out the lentils for Cinderella—substitutes for the white bird on the tree which provided her with her pretty clothes, including the fateful slippers. And the pear tree reminds us of that other tree which had grown on the mother's grave. Cinderella must relinquish her belief in and reliance on the help of magic objects if she is to live well in the world of reality. The father seems to understand this, and so he cuts down her hiding places: no more hiding among the ashes, but also no more seeking refuge from reality in magic places. From now on Cinderella will exist neither far below her true status nor way above it.

Cox, following Jacob Grimm, mentions the ancient German custom of the groom giving a shoe to his bride as sign of betrothal.[96] But this does not explain why the fit of a golden shoe decides who is the right bride in the ancient Chinese tale, and in Perrault's tale, a glass slipper. For the test to work, the shoe must be a slipper that does not stretch, or it would fit some other girl, such as the stepsisters. Perrault's subtlety is shown in his saying the shoe was made of glass, a material that does not stretch, is extremely brittle and easily broken.

A tiny receptacle into which some part of the body can slip and fit tightly can be seen as a symbol of the vagina. Something that is brittle and must not be stretched because it would break reminds us of the hymen; and something that is easily lost at the end of a ball when one's lover tries to keep his hold on his beloved seems an appropriate image for virginity, particularly when the male sets a trap—the pitch on the stairs—to catch her. Cinderella's running away from this situation could be seen as her effort to protect her virginity.

The godmother's order that Cinderella must be home by a certain hour or things will go very wrong, in Perrault's story, is similar to the parent's request that his daughter must not stay out too late at night because of his fear of what may happen if she does. The many "Cinderella" stories in which she flees to evade being ravished by an "unnatural" father support the notion that her running away from the ball is motivated by the wish to protect herself against being violated, or carried away by her own desires. It also forces the prince to seek her in her father's house, thus paralleling the groom coming to ask for the hand of his bride. While in Perrault's "Cinderella" a gentleman of the court tries the slipper on, and in the Brothers Grimm's tale the prince only hands it to Cinderella and she herself puts it on her foot, in many stories it is the prince who slips the shoe on. This might be likened to the groom's putting the ring on the finger of the bride as an important part of the marriage ceremony, a symbol of their being tied together henceforth.

All this is easily understood. On hearing the story one senses that the fitting on of the slipper is a betrothal, and it is quite clear that Cinderella is a virginal bride. Every child knows that marriage is connected with sex. In past times, when more children grew up close to animals, they knew that sex has something to do with the male putting his organ into the female, and the modern child is told as much by his parents. However, in view of the story's major topic, sibling rivalry, there are other possible symbolic meanings for the fitting of the precious slipper onto the appropriate foot.

Sibling rivalry is the topic of "Cinderella," as it is of many fairy tales. In these other fairy tales the rivalry nearly always exists among children of the same sex. But in real life, more often than not, the sharpest rivalry among the children of one family is between sister and brother.

The discrimination which females suffer when compared with

males is an age-old story now being challenged. It would be strange if this discrimination did not also create jealousy and envy between sisters and brothers within the family. Psychoanalytic publications are full of examples of girls being envious of boys' sexual apparatus; the "penis envy" of the female has been a familiar concept for quite some time. Less well recognized is that this envy is by no means a one-way street; boys are also quite jealous of what girls possess: breasts, and the ability to bear children.[97]

Each sex is jealous of what the other has which it lacks, much though either sex may like and be proud of what belongs to it—be it status, social role, or sexual organs. While this can be readily observed and is undoubtedly a correct view of the matter, unfortunately it is not yet widely recognized and accepted. (To some degree this is due to early psychoanalysis' one-sidedly stressing the so-called penis envy of girls, which probably occurred because at that time most treatises were written by males who did not examine their own envy of females. This is somewhat paralleled today in writings of militantly proud females.)

"Cinderella," the story which more than any other fairy tale deals with the topic of sibling rivalry, would be strangely deficient if in some fashion it did not also give expression to the rivalry of boys and girls due to their physical differences. Behind this sexual envy lies sexual fear, the so-called "castration anxiety" that some part of one's anatomy is missing. *Overtly* "Cinderella" tells only about sibling rivalry of girls; but might there not be some *covert* allusions to these other, deeper-reaching, and much more repressed emotions?

While girls and boys suffer equally severely from "castration anxiety," the feelings they suffer are not the same. Both the terms "penis envy" and "castration anxiety" stress only one of many and complex psychological aspects of the phenomena they name. According to Freudian theory, the girl's castration complex centers on her imagining that originally all children had penises and that girls somehow lost theirs (possibly as punishment for misbehavior) and on the consequent hope that it may grow back. The boy's parallel anxiety is that since all girls lack penises, this can be explained only by their having lost them, and he fears the same thing may happen to him. The girl subject to castration anxiety uses many and varied defenses to protect her self-esteem from such imagined deficiency; among these are unconscious fantasies that she, too, has similar equipment.

To understand the unconscious thoughts and feelings which may have led to the invention of a beautiful, tiny slipper as a central feature of "Cinderella," and, more important, the unconscious responses to this symbol which make it so convincing that "Cinderella" is one of the best-loved tales, one must accept that many different, even contradictory psychological attitudes may have become connected with the shoe as a symbol.

A very strange incident which takes place in most versions of "Cinderella" is the stepsisters' mutilation of their feet to make them fit the tiny slipper. Although Perrault excluded this event from his story, according to Cox it is common to all "Cinderella" stories except those derived from Perrault and a few others. This incident may be viewed as a symbolic expression of some aspects of the female castration complex.

The sisters' devious foot-mutilation is the final barrier to the happy ending; it immediately precedes the prince's finding Cinderella. For the last time the stepsisters, with the active help of the stepmother, try to cheat Cinderella out of what rightly belongs to her. Trying to fit their feet into the shoe, the stepsisters mutilate them. In the Brothers Grimm's story the oldest stepsister cannot enter the shoe with her big toe. So her mother hands her a knife and tells her to cut off the toe, because once she is a queen, she will no longer need to walk. The daughter does as she is told, forces her foot into the shoe, and goes to the prince, who rides off with her. As they pass Cinderella's mother's grave and the hazel tree, two white pigeons sitting on it call, "Look, there is blood in the shoe: the shoe is too small; the right bride still sits at home." The prince looks at the shoe and sees blood oozing out. He returns the stepsister to her home. The other stepsister tries to put on the shoe, but her heel is too big. Again the mother tells her to cut it off, and the same sequence of events occurs. In other versions where there is only one impostor bride, she cuts off either her toe or her heel, or both. In "Rashin Coatie" it is the mother who performs the operation.

This episode reinforces the impression created previously of how gross the stepsisters are, proving that they stop at nothing to cheat Cinderella and gain their goals. Overtly the stepsisters' behavior contrasts them sharply with Cinderella, who does not wish to gain happiness through anything but her true self. She refuses to be chosen on the basis of an appearance created by magic, and arranges things so that the prince has to see her in her ragged clothes. The stepsisters rely on deception, and their falsehood leads to their mutilation—a topic which is taken up again at the story's end when two white birds pick out their eyes. But it is a detail of such extraordinary crudeness and cruelty that it must have been invented for some specific, although probably unconscious reason. Self-mutilations are rare in fairy tales, as contrasted to mutilations by others, which are by no means infrequent as punishment or for some other reason.

When "Cinderella" was invented, the common stereotype contrasted the bigness of the male with the smallness of the female, and Cinderella's small feet would make her especially feminine. To have such big feet that they don't fit the slipper makes the stepsisters more masculine than Cinderella—therefore less desirable. Desperate to gain the prince, the stepsisters do not shy away from doing anything possible to make themselves into dainty females.

The stepsisters' efforts to trick the prince through self-mutilation are discovered by their bleeding. They tried to make themselves more female through cutting off a part of their body; bleeding is a consequence of it. They engaged in symbolic self-castration to prove their femininity; bleeding from the place on the body where this self-castration occurred may be another demonstration of their femininity, as it may stand for menstruation.

Whether or not self-mutilation or mutilation by the mother is an unconscious symbol of castration to get rid of an imagined penis; whether or not the bleeding is a symbol of menstruation, the story tells that the stepsisters' efforts do not succeed. The birds reveal the bleeding which shows that neither of the stepsisters is the right bride. Cinderella is the virginal bride; in the unconscious, the girl who does not yet menstruate is more clearly virginal than one who already does. And the girl who permits her bleeding to be seen, particularly by a man—as the stepsisters with their bleeding feet cannot help doing—is not only coarse, but certainly less virginal than one who does not bleed. Thus it seems that this episode, on another level of unconscious understanding, contrasts the virginity of Cinderella with the absence of it in the stepsisters.

The slipper, a central feature of the "Cinderella" story and that which decides her fate, is a most complex symbol. It was probably invented out of a variety of somewhat contradictory unconscious thoughts, and hence evokes a diversity of unconscious reponses in the hearer.

To the conscious mind, an object such as a slipper is just that—while symbolically in the unconscious it may in this story represent the vagina, or ideas connected with it. Fairy tales proceed on both a conscious and an unconscious level, which makes them more artistic, captivating, and convincing. Thus the objects used in them must be appropriate on the overt, conscious level while also calling forth associations quite different from their overt significance. The tiny slipper and the foot that fits it, and another mutilated one that does not, are images which make good sense to our conscious mind.

In "Cinderella" the pretty, tiny foot exercises an unconscious sexual appeal, but in conjunction with a beautiful, precious (for example, golden) slipper into which the foot fits snugly. This element of the "Cinderella" story also exists all by itself as a complete fairy tale, one reported by Strabo, much older than the ancient Chinese "Cinderella." This tale tells of an eagle that absconds with a sandal of the beautiful courtesan Rhodope, which it drops on the pharaoh. The pharaoh is so taken with the sandal that all of Egypt is searched for the original owner so that she may become his wife.[98] This story suggests that in ancient Egypt, as today, in certain circumstances the female slipper, as a symbol for that which is most desirable in a woman, arouses love in the male for definite but deeply unconscious reasons.

Since for over two thousand years—as Strabo's story shows—all over the world in much loved stories the female slipper has been accepted as a fairy-tale solution to the problem of finding the right bride, there must be good reasons for it. The difficulty in analyzing the unconscious meaning of the slipper as a symbol for the vagina is that although both males and females respond to this symbolic meaning, they do not do so in the same ways.* This is the subtlety but also the complexity and ambiguity of this symbol, and why it makes a strong emotional appeal to both sexes, although for different reasons. This is hardly surprising since the vagina and what it stands for in the unconscious means something different to the male and to the female; and this is particularly so until such time as both have attained full personal and sexual maturity, which is rather late in life.

In the story the prince's selection of Cinderella as his bride is based on the slipper. If the basis of his choice had been her looks or personality or any other quality, he could never have been deceived by the stepsisters. But they fooled him to the degree that he was riding off

*A wide variety of folklore data supports the notion that the slipper can serve as a symbol for the vagina. Rooth, quoting Jameson, reports that among the Manchu a bride is expected to present gifts of slippers to her husband's brothers, who, since group marriage is practiced, become her sexual partners through her marriage. These slippers are ornamented with *"lien hua,"* which is a vulgar term for the female genitals.[99]

Jameson cites several instances of the slipper used as a sexual symbol in China, and Aigremont supplies examples of this from Europe and the East.[100]

first with one, then the other of them, as his bride. The birds had to tell him that neither was the right bride because blood was oozing out of her shoe. So it was not so much the fit of the slipper which decided who was the right bride, but rather that bleeding from the foot into the slipper indicated who were the wrong choices. This was something the prince seemed unable to observe on his own, although one would think it had to be quite visible. He recognized it only after it was forced on his attention.

The prince's inability to observe the blood in the shoe suggests another part of castration anxiety, that connected with bleeding in menstruation. The blood oozing out of the slipper is but another symbolic equation of slipper-vagina, but now with the vagina bleeding as in menstruation. The prince's remaining unaware of it suggests his need to defend himself against the anxieties this arouses in him.

Cinderella is the right bride because she frees the prince of these anxieties. Her foot slips easily into the beautiful slipper, which shows that something that is dainty can be hidden within it. She does not need to mutilate herself; she does not bleed from any part of her body. Her repeated withdrawal shows that, contrary to her sisters, she is not aggressive in her sexuality but waits patiently to be chosen. But once she is chosen, she is not at all reluctant. By putting the slipper on her foot and not waiting until the prince does it, she shows her initiative and her ability to arrange her own fate. The prince had great anxiety in respect to the stepsisters, so much so that he could not see what was going on. But he has great security with Cinderella. Since she can provide this security for him, this makes her the right bride for him.

But what about Cinderella, who is, after all, the heroine of the story? Since the prince cherishes her slipper, this tells her in symbolic form that he loves her femininity as represented by the symbol of the vagina. However Cinderella may have felt about dwelling among the ashes, she knew that a person who lives thus appears to others as being dirty and uncouth. There are females who feel this way about their sexuality, and others who fear that males feel this way about it. That is why Cinderella made sure that the prince saw her in this state also before he chose her. By handing her the slipper to put her foot into, the prince symbolically expresses that he accepts her the way she is, dirty and degraded.

Here we must remember that the golden shoe was borrowed from the bird which represents the spirit of the dead mother, which Cinderella had internalized and which sustained her in her trials and tribulations. The prince, by presenting the slipper to her, finally makes the slipper and his kingdom truly hers. He symbolically offers her femininity in the form of the golden slipper-vagina: male acceptance of the vagina and love for the woman is the ultimate male validation of the desirability of her femininity. But nobody, not even a fairy-tale prince, can hand such acceptance to her—not even his love can do it. Only Cinderella herself can finally welcome her femininity, although she is helped by the prince's love. This is the deeper meaning of the story's telling that "she drew her foot out of the heavy wooden shoe and put it into the slipper, which fitted her to perfection."

At this moment, what had been a borrowed appearance of beauty while at the ball becomes Cinderella's true self; it is she who changes from the wooden shoe, which belongs to her existence among the ashes, into the golden one.

In the slipper ceremony, which signifies the betrothal of Cinderella and the prince, he selects her because in symbolic fashion she is the uncastrated woman who relieves him of his castration anxiety, which would interfere with a happy marital relationship. She selects him because he appreciates her in her "dirty" sexual aspects, lovingly accepts her vagina in the form of the slipper, and approves of her desire for a penis, symbolized by her tiny foot fitting within the slipper-vagina. That is why the prince brings the beautiful slipper to Cinderella and why she puts her tiny foot into it—only as she does so is she recognized as the right bride. But as she slips her foot into the slipper she asserts that she, too, will be active in their sexual relationship; she will do things, too. And she also gives the assurance that she is not and never was lacking in anything; she has everything that fits, as her foot snugly fits into the slipper.

A reflection on a universally accepted part of the wedding ceremony may lend support to this idea. The bride stretches out one of her fingers for the groom to slip a ring onto it. Pushing one finger through a circle made out of the thumb and index finger of the other hand is a vulgar expression for intercourse. But in the ring ceremony something entirely different is symbolically expressed. The ring, a symbol for the vagina, is given by the groom to his bride; she offers him in return her outstretched finger, so that he may complete the ritual.

Many unconscious thoughts are expressed in this ceremony. Through the ritual exchange of rings the male expresses his desire for, and acceptance of, the vagina—something about which the female may have worried—as well as of the wish she may have for a penis of her own. By having the ring put onto her finger, the bride acknowledges that from now on, her husband to some degree will have possession of her vagina, and she of his penis; with it she will no longer feel deprived by not having one—which symbolizes the end of her castration anxiety; as his ended with his making his own, and wearing from then on, his wedding ring. The *golden* slipper that the prince hands to Cinderella to slip her foot into may be seen as but another form of this ritual, which we take so much for granted that we give little thought to its symbolic meaning, although it is with this act that the groom takes the bride for his wife.

"Cinderella" is the story of sibling rivalry and jealousy, and of how victory over them can be achieved. The greatest envy and jealousy are aroused by the sex characteristics which the one possesses and which the other lacks. Not just sibling rivalry but sexual rivalry, too, is integrated and transcended as the story of Cinderella ends. What started as utter deprivation because of jealousy ends in great happiness because of a love which understands the sources of this jealousy, accepts them, and in doing so eliminates them.

Cinderella receives from her prince that which she thought was lacking in her, as he assures her in symbolic form that she is not lacking in any respect, and that she will receive what she has wished to possess. The prince receives from Cinderella the assurance he needed most: that while all along she had a wish for a penis, she accepts that only he can satisfy it. It is an act which symbolizes that she was not castrated of her desires, and does not wish to castrate anybody; so he need not fear that this may happen to him. She receives from him what she needs most for herself; he receives from her what he needs most for himself. The slipper motif serves to pacify unconscious anxieties in the male, and to satisfy unconscious desires in the female. This permits both to find the most complete fulfillment in their sexual relation in marriage. By means of this motif, the story enlightens the hearer's unconscious about what is involved in sex and marriage.

The child whose unconscious responds to the hidden meaning of the story, whether girl or boy, will understand better what lies behind his jealous feelings and his anxiety that he may end up the deprived one. He also will gain some inkling of the irrational anxiety which may stand in his way to forming a happy sexual relation, and what is required to achieve such a relation. But the story also assures the child that, as the heroes of the story do, so will he be able to master his anxieties and, despite all trials, there will be a happy ending.

The happy ending would be incomplete without the punishment of the antagonists. But it is neither Cinderella nor the prince who inflicts the punishment. The birds, who had helped Cinderella to sort out good from bad by picking out the lentils, now complete the destruction which the stepsisters themselves had begun: they pick out the stepsisters' eyes. Being blinded is a symbolic statement of their blindness in thinking they could elevate themselves by degrading others; trusting their fate to outward appearances; most of all, believing that sexual happiness could be achieved by (self-)castration.

To probe into the unconscious significance of some of this best-loved fairy tale's features, the sexual connotations must be considered. In discussing them I fear I have gone against the poet's advice, "Tread softly because you tread on my dreams."[101] But dreams began to reveal their meaning and importance only when Freud dared probe into the manifold, often uncouth, and grossly sexual unconscious thoughts which are hidden behind apparently innocent surfaces. With Freud's influence, our dreams have become much more problematic to us—more upsetting and difficult to deal with. But they are also the royal road to the unconscious mind, and they permit us to form a new and richer view of ourselves and the nature of our humanity.

The child who enjoys "Cinderella" will respond mainly to one or another of the surface meanings most of the time. But at various moments in his development toward self-understanding, depending on what is problematic to him, the child's unconscious will be enlightened by one of the story's hidden meanings, indicated by some important detail.[102]

Overtly the story helps the child to accept sibling rivalry as a rather common fact of life and promises that he need not fear being destroyed by it; on the contrary, if these siblings were not so nasty to him, he could never triumph to the same degree at the end. Further, it tells the child that if he was once considered dirty and uncouth, this was a temporary stage with no adverse consequences for the future. There are also obvious moral lessons: that surface appearances tell nothing about the inner worth of a person; that if one is true to oneself, one wins out over those who pretend to be what they are not; and that virtue will be rewarded, evil punished.

Openly stated, but not as readily recognized, are the lessons that to develop one's personality to the fullest, one must be able to do hard work and be able to separate good from evil, as in the sorting of the lentils. Even out of lowly matter like ashes, things of great value can be gained, if one knows how to do it.

Just below the surface and quite accessible to the child's conscious mind is the importance of keeping faith with what was good in one's past, of keeping alive basic trust gained from the relation to the good mother. This faith permits achieving what is best in life; and if one finds one's way back to the values of the good mother, these help win the victory.

Regarding a child's relation not just to his mother but to his parents in general, "Cinderella" offers both parents and children important insights which no other well-known fairy tale expresses as well. These insights are of such significance that their consideration has been saved for the end of this discussion. Being so clearly inherent in the story that they cannot fail to make an impression, these messages make a greater impact just because we do not consciously spell out to ourselves what they are. Without our "knowing" it, the lessons become part of our understanding about life when we make this fairy tale part of ourselves.

In no other popular fairy tale are the good and the bad mother put so clearly into juxtaposition. Even in "Snow White," which tells about one of the worst stepmothers, the stepmother does not set impossible tasks for her daughter, or demand hard work of her. Nor does she reappear at the end in the form of the original good mother, to arrange for her child's happiness. But hard work and seemingly impossible tasks are what Cinderella's stepmother requires of her. On the overt level the story tells all about how Cinderella finds her prince *despite* what the stepmother does to her. But in the unconscious, particularly for the young child, "despite" is often tantamount to "because of."

Without having first been forced to become a "Cinderella," the heroine would never have become the bride of the prince; the story makes this quite obvious. In order to achieve personal identity and gain self-realization on the highest level, the story tells us, both are needed: the original good parents, and later the "step"-parents who seem to demand "cruelly" and "insensitively." The two together make up the "Cinderella" story. If the good mother did not for a time turn into the evil stepmother, there would be no impetus to develop a separate self, to discover the difference between good and evil, develop initiative and self-determination. Witness the fact that the stepsisters, to whom the stepmother remains the good mother throughout the story, never achieve any of this; they remain empty shells. When the slipper does not fit the stepsisters, it is not they who take action, but their mother who tells them to. All this is given emphasis by the sisters' remaining blind—i.e., insensitive—for the rest of their lives, a symbol, but also the logical consequence of having failed to develop a personality of their own.

For the possibility of a development toward individuation to exist, a firm basis is needed—"basic trust," which we can gain only from the relationship between the infant and the good parents. But for the process of individuation to become possible and necessary—and unless it becomes unavoidable we do not engage in it, for it is much too painful—the good parents have to appear for a period as bad, persecuting ones who send the child out to wander for years in his personal desert, demanding seemingly "without respite" and without consideration for the child's comfort. But if the child responds to these hardships by developing his self in an independent way, then as if by miracle the good parents reappear. This is similar to the parent who does not make any sense to his adolescent child until after the adolescent has achieved maturity.

"Cinderella" sets forth the steps in personality development required to reach self-fulfillment, and presents them in fairy-tale fashion so that every person can understand what is required of him to become a full human being. This is hardly surprising, since the fairy tale, as I have tried to show throughout this book, represents extremely well the workings of our psyche: what our psychological problems are, and how these can best be mastered. Erikson, in his model of the human life-cycle, suggests that the ideal human being develops through what he calls "phase-specific psychosocial crises" if he achieves the ideal goals of each phase in succession. These crises in their sequence are: First, basic trust—represented by Cinderella's experience with the original good mother, and what this firmly implanted in her personality. Second, autonomy—as Cinderella accepts her unique role and makes the best of it. Third, initiative—Cinderella develops this as she plants the twig and makes it grow with the expression of her personal feelings, tears and prayers. Fourth, industry—represented by Cinderella's hard labors, such as sorting out the lentils. Fifth, identity—Cinderella escapes from the ball, hides in the dovecote and tree, and insists that the prince see and accept her in her negative identity as "Cinderella" before she assumes her positive identity as his bride, because any true identity has its negative as well as its positive aspects. According to Erikson's scheme, having ideally solved these psychosocial crises by having achieved the personality attributes just enumerated, one becomes ready for true intimacy with the other.[103]

The difference between what happens to the stepsisters, who remain tied to their "good parents" without inner development, and the hardships and significant developments Cinderella has to undergo when her original good parents are replaced by step-parents, permits every child and parent to understand that, in the child's best interests, for a time he needs to see even the best of parents as rejecting and demanding "step"-parents. If "Cinderella" makes an impression on parents, it can help them accept that as an inescapable step in their child's development toward true maturity, they must seem for a time to have turned into bad parents. The story also tells that when the child has attained his true identity, the good parents will be resuscitated in his mind, prove much more powerful, and replace permanently the image of the bad parents.

Thus, "Cinderella" offers parents much-needed comfort, for it can teach them why and for what good purposes they are seen temporarily in a bad light by their child. The child learns from "Cinderella" that to gain his kingdom he must be ready to undergo a "Cinderella" existence for a time, not just in regard to the hardships this entails, but also in regard to the difficult tasks he must master on his own initiative. Depending on the child's stage of psychological development, this kingdom which Cinderella achieves will be one either of unlimited gratification or of individuality and unique personal achievement.

Unconsciously, children and adults also respond to the other assurances "Cinderella" offers: that despite the seemingly devastating oedipal conflicts which caused Cinderella's dejected state, the disappointment in the parent of the other sex and the good mother turned stepmother, Cinderella will have a good life, even a better one than her parents. Further, the story tells that even castration anxiety is only a figment of the child's anxious imagination: in a good marriage everyone will find the sexual fulfillment even of what seemed impossible dreams: he will gain a golden vagina, she a temporary penis.

"Cinderella" guides the child from his greatest disappointments— oedipal disillusionment, castration anxiety, low opinion of himself because of the imagined low opinion of others—toward developing his autonomy, becoming industrious, and gaining a positive identity of his own. Cinderella, at the story's end, is indeed ready for a happy marriage. But does she love the prince? Nowhere does the story say so. It takes Cinderella up to the moment of engagement as the prince hands her the golden slipper, which might as well be the golden wedding ring (as indeed it is a ring in some "Cinderella" stories).[104]

But what else must Cinderella learn? What other experiences are needed to show the child what it means to be truly in love? The answer to this question is provided in the last cycle of stories we shall consider in this book, that of the animal groom.

THE ANIMAL-GROOM CYCLE
OF FAIRY TALES

THE STRUGGLE FOR MATURITY

Snow White is carried off by the prince, inert in her coffin; it is by chance that she coughs up the poisonous piece of apple stuck in her throat and thus comes back to life. Sleeping Beauty awakens only because her lover kisses her. Cinderella's time of degradation ends when the slipper fits her. In each of these stories—as in so many others —the rescuer demonstrates his love for his future bride in some form. We are left in the dark about the feelings of the heroines, however. The way the Brothers Grimm tell these stories, we hear nothing about Cinderella being in love, although we may draw some conclusions from the fact that she goes to the ball three times to meet her prince. About Sleeping Beauty's feelings we learn only that she looks "in a friendly fashion" at the man who frees her from her enchantment. Similarly, all we are told is that Snow White "felt friendly" toward the man who brought her back to life. It seems as if these stories deliberately avoid stating that the heroines are in love; one gets the impression that even fairy tales put little stock in love at first sight. Instead, they suggest that much more is involved in loving than being awakened or chosen by some prince.

The rescuers fall in love with these heroines because of their beauty, which symbolizes their perfection. Being in love, the rescuers have to become active and prove that they are worthy of the woman they love—something quite different from the heroine's passive acceptance of being loved. In "Snow White" the prince declares he cannot live without Snow White, he offers the dwarfs whatever they want for her, and is finally permitted to carry her off. In penetrating the wall of thorns to reach Sleeping Beauty, her suitor risks his life. The prince in "Cinderella" devises an ingenious scheme to trap her, and when he catches not her but only her slipper, he searches for her far and wide. The stories seem to imply that falling in love is something that happens; being in love demands much more. But since the male rescuers in these stories have only supporting roles, nothing more specific can be learned from their behavior about what developments are involved in loving somebody, what the nature of the commitment "being in love" entails.

All the stories considered so far convey that if one wishes to gain selfhood, achieve integrity, and secure one's identity, difficult developments must be undergone: hardships suffered, dangers met, victories won. Only in this way can one become master of one's fate and win one's kingdom. What happens to the heroes and heroines in fairy tales can be likened—and has been compared—to initiation rites which the novice enters naïve and unformed, and which dismiss him at their end on a higher level of existence undreamed of at the start of this sacred voyage through which he gains his reward or salvation. Having truly become himself, the hero or heroine has become worthy of being loved.

But meritorious as such self-development is, and while it may save our soul, it is still not enough for happiness. For this, one must go beyond one's isolation and form a bond with the other. On however high a plane his life may proceed, the *I* without the *Thou* lives a lonely existence. The happy endings to fairy tales, in which the hero is united with his life's partner, tell this much. But they do not teach what the individual must do to transcend his isolation after he has won his selfhood. Neither in "Snow White" nor in "Cinderella" (the Brothers Grimm's versions) are we told anything about their life after they are married; nothing is said about their living happily with their partner. These stories, while they take the heroine up to the threshold of true love, do not tell what personal growth is required for union with the beloved other.

Laying the groundwork for achieving full consciousness and relatedness would not be complete if fairy tales did not prepare the child's mind for the transformation demanded by, and brought about by, being in love. There are many fairy stories which start where those like "Cinderella" or "Snow White" end, and they communicate that, charming as it is to be loved, not even being loved by a prince guarantees happiness. To find fulfillment through and in love requires one more transition. Merely being oneself is not enough, even when it is selfhood won through struggles as difficult as those of Snow White or Cinderella.

One becomes a complete human being who has achieved all his potentialities only if, in addition to being oneself, one is at the same time able and happy to be oneself with another. To achieve this state involves the deepest layers of our personality. Like any transmutation which touches our innermost being, it has dangers which must be met with courage and presents problems which must be mastered. The message of these fairy stories is that we must give up childish attitudes and achieve mature ones if we wish to establish that intimate bond with the other which promises permanent happiness for both.

Fairy tales prepare for doing that in ways which permit the child to gain a preconscious comprehension of matters which would greatly perturb him if they were forced into his conscious attention. But these ideas, imbedded in his preconscious or unconscious mind, become available when the time is ripe for the child to build his understanding on them. Since all is expressed in symbolic language in fairy tales, the child can disregard what he is not ready for by responding only to what he has been told on the surface. But he is also enabled to peel off, layer by layer, some of the meaning hidden behind the symbol as he becomes gradually ready and able to master and profit from it.

In such manner, fairy tales are an ideal way for the child to learn about sex in a fashion appropriate to his age and developmental understanding. Any sex education which is more or less direct, even when put in the language of the child and in terms he can comprehend, leaves the child no alternative but to accept it although he is not ready for it and then be greatly perturbed or confused by it. Or else the child can protect himself against being overwhelmed by information he is not yet ready to master by distorting or repressing what he is told—with most pernicious consequences at the moment and in the future.

Fairy tales suggest that eventually there comes a time when we must learn what we have not known before—or, to put it psychoanalytically, to undo the repression of sex. What we had experienced as dangerous, loathsome, something to be shunned, must change its appearance so that it is experienced as truly beautiful. It is love which permits this to happen. While the undoing of repressions and the change in the experience of sex are parallel processes in reality, fairy tales deal with them separately. Only rarely does this happen suddenly; more often it is a long process of evolution which leads to the recognition that sex can seem very different from the way we have viewed it before. So there are some fairy tales which familiarize us with the sudden shock of happy recognition, while others convey that a long struggle is necessary to reach the point where this unexpected revelation can take place.

In many fairy tales the intrepid hero slays dragons, battles giants and monsters, witches and sorcerers. Eventually the intelligent child begins to wonder what these heroes are out to prove. If they have no feelings for their own security, how can they offer it to the maiden they rescue? What have they done with their natural feelings of anxiety and why? Knowing his own fear and trembling, but also how often he tries to deny them, the child concludes that for some reason these heroes need to convince everybody—including themselves—that they are free of anxiety.

Oedipal fantasies of glory are given body in tales where the heroes slay dragons and rescue maidens. But these stories are simultaneously denials of oedipal anxieties, very much including sexual ones. By repressing all feelings of anxiety so that they appear absolutely fearless, these heroes protect themselves from discovering exactly what they are anxious about. Sometimes sexual anxieties surface behind fantasies of outlandish courage: after the dauntless hero has won the princess, he avoids her, as if his courage would enable him to do battle, but not to love. In one such story, the Brothers Grimm's "The Raven," the hero falls asleep on three consecutive days at the time his princess has promised to visit him. In other tales (the Brothers Grimm's "The Two King's Children," "The Drummer") the hero lies fast asleep all night while his beloved calls for him at the threshold of his bedroom, awakening only at the third try. In "Jack and His Bargains" one interpretation of Jack's lying stock still in bed beside his bride was offered; and on another level Jack's not moving toward the princess symbolizes his sexual anxiety. What looks like an absence of feelings is actually the void left by their repression, and this repression must be undone before marital bliss, requiring sexual happiness, becomes possible.

"THE FAIRY TALE OF ONE WHO WENT FORTH TO LEARN FEAR"

There are fairy tales which tell about the need to be able to feel fear. A hero may survive hair-raising adventures without any anxiety, but he can find satisfaction in life only after the ability to feel fear is restored to him. In a few fairy stories the hero recognizes this lack of fear as a deficiency in the beginning. This is the case with the Brothers Grimm's story "The Fairy Tale of One Who Went Forth to Learn Fear." When challenged by his father to make something of himself, the hero replies, "I'd like to learn shuddering; that is something I don't comprehend at all." In order to do this, the hero exposes himself to terrifying adventures, but he fails to feel anything. With superhuman strength and with what would be superhuman courage if he felt fear, the hero then disenchants a king's castle. The king tells him that as reward he will get to marry the king's daughter. " 'That's all very fine,' the hero replied, 'but I still do not know what it means to shudder.' " This answer implies a recognition that as long as he is unable to feel fear, the hero is not ready to marry. This is further emphasized by the story's telling that, fond though the hero was of his wife, he continued to say, "If I only could shudder." He finally learns how to shudder in his marital bed. His wife teaches him one night when she pulls off his covers and pours a pail of cold water full of gudgeons (little fish like minnows) over him. As the little fish wriggle all over him, he cries, "Oh, how I shudder, dear wife. Yes, now I know what it is to shudder!"

Thanks to his wife, in their marital bed the hero of this story finds what had been missing in his life. To the child even more than to the adult, it seems clear that one can find something only where one lost it in the first place. On a subconscious level the story suggests that the fearless hero lost his ability to shudder so that he would not have to face the feelings which overcome him in the marital bed—that is, sexual emotions. But without these feelings, as he asserts all along, he is not a full person; he does not even want to marry as long as he is unable to shudder.

The hero of this story could not shudder due to repression of all sexual feelings—as demonstrated by the fact that once sexual fear was restored to him, he could be happy. There is a subtlety in this story that is easy to overlook consciously, although it does not fail to make an unconscious impression. The story's title tells us that the hero went forth to learn fear. But throughout the story reference is made mostly to shuddering; the hero states that it is an art that remains beyond his comprehension. Sexual anxiety is experienced most often in the form of repugnance; the sexual act makes the person who is anxious about it shudder, but does not usually arouse active fear.

Whether or not the hearer of this story recognizes that it was sexual anxiety that led to the hero's inability to shudder, that which finally makes him shudder suggests the irrational nature of some of our most pervasive anxieties. Because it is a fear of which only his wife is able to cure him at night in bed, this is a sufficient hint of the underlying nature of the anxiety.

To the child, who is most fearful at night in his bed, but eventually comes to realize how irrational his anxieties have been, this tale offers on an overt level the idea that behind a boastful absence of anxiety may be hidden very immature, even childish fears which are denied coming to awareness.

However the story is experienced, it tells that marital happiness requires that feelings must become accessible to a person which up to the time of marriage were not available to him. It further tells that it is the female partner who finally brings out the humanity in the male—because to feel fear is human; not being able to feel it is inhuman. This tale reveals, in fairy-story fashion, that in the last transition needed for achieving mature humanity, repressions must be undone.

THE ANIMAL GROOM

Much more popular and numerous are tales which—without any reference to repression which causes a negative attitude to sex—simply teach that for love, a radical change in previously held attitudes about sex is absolutely necessary. What must happen is expressed, as always in fairy tales, through a most impressive image: a beast is turned into a magnificent person. Different as these stories are, a common feature to them all is the sexual partner first experienced as an animal; hence, in the literature on fairy tales this cycle has become known as that of the "animal groom" or "animal husband." (For the stories, at present somewhat less well known, where the future female partner is first an animal, the cycle is that of the "animal bride."*) The best-known of

*That in these fairy tales nearly as often the animal groom is rescued through the love of the female as the animal bride is disenchanted through the devotion of the male offers another example that the same fairy-tale motif applies equally to females and to males. In languages where the structure permits it, the names of the central characters are ambiguous, so that the hearer is at liberty to picture them as of either of the two sexes.

In Perrault's stories the names of the main figures are such that they can be viewed as masculine or feminine. For example, the title of "Bluebeard" is *"La Barbe Bleue"*; here the name of a clearly masculine figure is so constructed that it takes the feminine article. The French name of Cinderella, *Cendrillon*, has a masculine ending; the feminine form would have to be something like *La Cendrouse*. Little Red Riding Hood is called *Le Petit Chaperon Rouge* because in French *chaperon* is not only a masculine piece of wearing apparel, but because of it the girl's name requires the masculine article. Sleeping Beauty, *La Belle au bois dormant*, takes the feminine article, but *dormant* is a form which applies equally to male and female persons. (Soriano, *op. cit.*)

In German many of the main characters are of neuter sex, as is the child himself

these tales today is "Beauty and the Beast."[105] This motif is so popular worldwide that probably no other fairy-tale theme has so many variations.[106]

There are three typical features to the stories of the animal-groom cycle. First, it remains unknown how and why the groom was changed into an animal; and this although most fairy tales provide such information. Second, it is a sorceress who did this deed; but she is not punished for her evil doings. Third, it is the father who causes the heroine to join the Beast; she does it because of her love for or obedience to her father; overtly the mother plays no significant role.

Applying insights of depth psychology to these three facets of the stories, one begins to see the subtle meaning of what at first appear as serious shortcomings. We do not learn why the groom was forced to take on the form of an ugly animal, or why this harm inflicted on him remains unpunished. This suggests that the change from the "natural" or beautiful appearance took place in the unfathomable past when we did not know why something happened to us, even when it had the most far-reaching consequences. Shall we say that repression of sex occurred so early that it cannot be recalled? None of us can remember at what moment in our life sex first took on the form of something animal-like, something to be afraid of, to hide, to shun; it usually is tabooed much too early. We might recall that not long ago many middle-class parents told their children that when they got married, then was the time to understand what sex was all about. It is hardly surprising in the light of this that in "Beauty and the Beast" the former Beast tells Beauty: "A wicked fairy had condemned me to remain under that shape until a beautiful virgin should consent to marry me." Only marriage made sex permissible, changed it from something animal-like into a bond sanctified by the sacrament of marriage.

Since our mothers—or nurses—were our earliest educators, it is likely that they first tabooed sex in some fashion; hence it is a female who turns the future groom into an animal. At least in one story of the animal bride we are told that it is the child's naughtiness which causes the change into an animal, and that it is the mother who does it. The Brothers Grimm's "The Raven" begins: "Once upon a time there was a queen who had a daughter, so little that she was still a babe in arms. At one time the child was naughty, would not give peace, the mother

---

(Das Kind). Thus it is *Das Schneewittchen* (Snow White), *Das Dornröschen* (Sleeping Beauty), *Das Rotkäppchen* (Little Red Riding Hood), *Das Aschenputtel* (Cinderella).

might say what she liked. Then the mother got impatient, and as ravens flew around the castle, she opened the window and said, 'I wish you were a raven and flew away, then I had some peace.' No sooner had she said it, the child was changed into a raven. . . ." It does not seem farfetched to think that it was unmentionable, unacceptable, instinctual sexual behavior which the child would not stop and which so disturbed the mother that she subconsciously felt the little girl was like an animal and thus might as well become one. If the child had only fussed or cried, the story might have told us so, or the mother would not have been so ready to give up on the child.

In animal-groom stories, by contrast, mothers are outwardly absent; they are present, however, in the guise of the sorceress who has caused the child to view sex as animal-like. Since nearly all parents taboo sex in some form or another, it is something so universal and, at least to some degree, unavoidable in the child's education that there is no reason to punish the person who made sex appear animal-like. This is the reason the sorceress who turned the groom into an animal is not punished at the story's end.

It is the heroine's affection and devotion that transform the beast. Only if she comes to love him truly will he be disenchanted. For the girl to love her male partner fully, she must be able to transfer to him her earlier, infantile attachment to her father. She can do this well if he, despite hesitation, agrees to her doing so—as the father in "Beauty and the Beast" does not at first want to accept her joining the Beast so that he may live, but permits himself to be convinced that she should do so. And the girl can transfer—and transform—this oedipal love for her father most freely and happily to her lover if, in sublimated fashion, it seems to offer a belated fulfillment of her childish love for her father, while at the same time it presents fulfillment of her mature love for an age-correct partner.

Beauty joins the Beast only out of love for her father, but as her love matures, it changes its main object—although not without difficulty, as the story tells. In the end, through her love both father and husband regain their lives. If any further corroboration of this interpretation of the story's meaning is necessary, it is provided by the detail of Beauty asking her father to bring her a rose, and he risking his life to comply with her wish. The wishing for a rose, the giving and receiving of it, are images of Beauty's continuing love for her father, and his for her—a symbol that this love had been kept alive by both. It is this love that never stopped blooming which permits such an easy transfer to the Beast.

Fairy tales speak to our unconscious mind and are experienced as telling us something important, irrespective of our sex and that of the story's protagonist. Still it is worth remarking that in most Western fairy tales the beast is male and can be disenchanted only by the love of a female. The nature of the beast changes from place to place according to the local situation. For example, in a Bantu (Kaffir) story a crocodile is restored to its human form by a maiden who licks its face.[107] In other tales the beast appears in the form of a pig, lion, bear, ass, frog, snake, etc., which is restored to human form by the love of a maiden.* One must assume that the inventors of these tales believed that to achieve a happy union, it is the female who has to overcome her view of sex as loathsome and animal-like. There are also Western fairy tales in which the female has been bewitched into animal form, and then it is she who must be disenchanted by the love and determined courage of a male. But in practically all examples of animal brides there is nothing dangerous or repugnant in their animal form; on the contrary, they are lovely. "The Raven" has already been mentioned. In another Brothers Grimm tale, "The Drummer," the girl has been changed into a swan. Thus, it seems that while fairy tales suggest that sex without love and devotion is animal-like, at least in the Western tradition its animal aspects are nonthreatening or even charming, as far as the female is concerned; only the male aspects of sex are beastly.

"SNOW-WHITE AND ROSE-RED"

While the animal groom is nearly always a disgusting or ferocious beast, in a few stories it is a tame animal, despite its savage nature. This is true in the Brothers Grimm's "Snow-White and Rose-Red," in

---

*The many stories of the animal-groom type from preliterate cultures suggest that living in intimacy with nature fails to change the view that sex is something animal-like which only love can transform into a human relation. Nor does it alter the fact that more often than not the male is unconsciously experienced as the more animal-like partner because of his more aggressive role in sex. It also does not change the preconscious realization that although the female role in intercourse is more passive-receptive, she, too, must activate herself in sex, must do something quite difficult, even uncouth—such as licking a crocodile's face—if love is to enrich a mere sexual bond.

In preliterate societies, stories of animal husbands and animal wives have not only fairy-tale-like but also totemistic features. For example, among the Lalang in Java it is believed that a princess took a dog for a husband and that the son who was born to this marriage is the ancestor of the tribe.[108] In a Yoruba fairy tale a turtle marries a girl and in this way introduces intercourse on earth, showing the close relation between the idea of the animal groom and intercourse.[109]

which it is a friendly bear, not at all scary or disgusting. But these bestial qualities are not absent from the story—they are represented by an uncouth dwarf who has bewitched the prince into a bear. In this story both protagonists have been split into doubles: there are two rescuing maidens, Snow-White and Rose-Red, and there are the gentle bear and the obnoxious dwarf. The two girls, encouraged by their mother, befriend the bear; and they help the dwarf in its troubles despite its nastiness. They rescue the dwarf from great danger twice by cutting off part of its beard, and the third and last time by tearing off part of its coat. In this story the girls have to rescue the dwarf three times before the bear can kill it and become disenchanted. So while the animal groom is friendly and tame, the female(s) still have to exorcise its nasty nature in the form of the dwarf for an animal-like relation to become a human one. This story implies that there are both friendly and disgusting aspects to our natures, and when we rid ourselves of the latter, all can be happiness. At the story's end the essential unity of the protagonists is restated by Snow-White's marrying the prince, and Rose-Red his brother.

The animal-groom stories convey that it is mainly the female who needs to change her attitude about sex from rejecting to embracing it, because as long as sex appears to her as ugly and animal-like, it remains animalistic in the male; i.e., he is not disenchanted. As long as one partner loathes sex, the other cannot enjoy it; as long as one partner views it as animal-like, the other remains partially an animal to himself and his partner.

"THE FROG KING"

Some fairy stories emphasize the long and difficult development which alone permits gaining control over what seems animalistic in us, while conversely other tales center on the shock of recognition when that which seemed animal suddenly reveals itself as the source of human happiness. The Brothers Grimm's story "The Frog King" belongs to the latter category.*

While it is not as ancient as some stories about animal grooms, a

*The full title of the story is "The Frog King, or Iron Henry," but Iron Henry is not part of most versions of this story. His extreme loyalty is added at the story's end like an afterthought made to compare his faithfulness to the original disloyalty of the princess. It does not add materially to the story's meaning and is therefore neglected here. (Iona and Peter Opie, for good reasons, dropped "Iron Henry" both from the title and from the story in their version.)[110]

version of "The Frog King" is mentioned as early as the thirteenth century. In the *Complaynt of Scotland* in 1540 a similar tale is called "The Well of the World's End."[111] A version of "The Frog King" printed by the Brothers Grimm in 1815 begins with three sisters. The two older ones are haughty and insensitive; only the youngest is ready to listen to the frog's entreaties. In the Grimm version presently best known, the heroine is also the youngest of sisters, but it is not specified of how many.

"The Frog King" begins with the youngest princess playing with her golden ball close by a well. The ball falls into it, and the girl is heartbroken. A frog appears, asking the princess what troubles her. It offers to restore the golden ball to her if she will accept it as the companion who will sit beside her, drink from her glass, eat from her plate, and sleep with her in her bed. She promises this, thinking to herself that no frog could ever be a person's companion. The frog then brings her the golden ball. When it asks to be taken home with her, she rushes away and soon forgets all about the frog.

But the next day when the royal court is eating dinner, the frog appears and asks to be let in. The princess closes the door on it. The king, who observes her distress, asks about its cause. She tells him, and he insists that her promises must be kept. So she opens the door to the frog, but still hesitates to lift it up to the table. Again the king tells her to keep her promise. The princess tries once more to renege when the frog asks to join her in bed, but the king now angrily tells her that those who have helped her when she was in need must not be despised. Once the frog joins the princess in her bed, she gets so disgusted that she hurls it against the wall, and then it turns into a prince. In most versions this happens after the frog has spent three nights with her. An original version is even more explicit: the princess must kiss the frog while it lies at her side in bed, and then it takes three weeks of sleeping together until the frog turns into a prince.[112]

In this story the process of maturing is enormously speeded up. At the beginning the princess is a beautiful little girl carelessly playing with a ball. (We are told that not even the sun had seen anything as beautiful as this girl.) Everything happens because of the ball. It is doubly a symbol of perfection: as a sphere, and because it is made out of gold, the most precious material. The ball stands for an as yet undeveloped narcissistic psyche: it contains all potentials, none yet realized. When the ball falls into the deep, dark well, naïveté is lost and Pandora's box is opened. The princess mourns the loss of her childish innocence as desperately as that of the ball. Only the ugly frog can restore perfection—the ball—to her out of the darkness into which the symbol of her psyche has fallen. Life has become ugly and complicated as it begins to reveal its darker sides.

Still beholden to the pleasure principle, the girl makes promises in order to gain what she wants, with no thought of the consequences. But reality asserts itself. She tries to evade it by slamming the door on the frog. But now the superego in the form of the king comes into play: the more the princess tries to go against the frog's demands, the more forcefully the king insists that she must keep her promises to the full. What started playfully becomes most serious: the princess must grow up as she is forced to accept the commitments she has made.

The steps toward intimacy with the other are clearly sketched: first the girl is all alone as she plays with her ball. The frog begins conversing with her when it asks what troubles her; it plays with her as it returns the ball. Then it comes to visit, sits by her, eats with her, joins her in her room and finally in her bed. The closer the frog comes to the girl physically, the more disgusted and anxious she gets, particularly about being touched by it. The awakening to sex is not free of disgust or of anxiety, even anger. Anxiety turns into anger and hatred as the princess hurls the frog against the wall. By thus asserting herself and taking risks in doing so—as opposed to her previous trying to weasel out and then simply obeying her father's commands—the princess transcends her anxiety, and hatred changes into love.

In a way this story tells that to be able to love, a person first has to become able to feel; even if the feelings are negative, that is better than not feeling. In the beginning the princess is entirely self-centered; all her interest is in her ball. She has no feelings when she plans to go back on her promise to the frog, gives no thought as to what this may mean for it. The closer the frog comes to her physically and personally, the stronger her feelings become, but with this she becomes more a person. For a long stretch of development she obeys her father, but feels ever more strongly; then at the end she asserts her independence in going against his orders. As she thus becomes herself, so does the frog; it turns into a prince.

On another level the story tells that we cannot expect our first erotic contacts to be pleasant, for they are much too difficult and fraught with anxiety. But if we continue, despite temporary repugnance, to permit the other to become ever more intimate, then at some moment we will experience a happy shock of recognition when complete closeness reveals sexuality's true beauty. In one version of "The Frog King," "after a night in bed, when awakening she saw by her side the handsomest gentleman."[113] Thus in this story the night spent together (and we may surmise what happened during this night) makes for the radically changed view of what has become the marital partner. The various other tales in which the timing of the events varies from the first night to three weeks all counsel patience: it takes time for closeness to turn into love.

The father, as in so many stories of the animal-groom cycle, is the person who brings his daughter and her future husband together in "The Frog King." It is only because of his insistence that the happy union comes about. Parental guidance which leads to superego formation—one must keep one's promises, ill-advised as these may have been—develops a responsible conscience. Such a conscience is necessary for a happy personal and sexual union, which without a mature conscience would be lacking in seriousness and permanence.

But what about the frog? It, too, has to mature before union with the princess can become possible. What happens to it shows that a loving, dependent relationship to a mother figure is the precondition for becoming human. Like every child, the frog desires an entirely symbiotic existence. What child has not wished to sit on Mother's lap, eat from her dish, drink from her glass, and has not climbed into Mother's bed, trying to sleep there with her? But after a time the child has to be denied the symbiosis with Mother, since it would prevent him from ever becoming an individual. Much as the child wants to remain in bed with Mother, she has to "throw" him out of it—a painful experience but inescapable if he is to gain independence. Only when forced by his parent to stop living in symbiosis does the child begin to be himself, as the frog, "thrown" out of the bed, becomes freed of bondage to an immature existence.

The child knows that, like the frog, he had to and still has to move from a lower to a higher state of being. This process is perfectly normal, since the child's life situation begins in a lower state, which is why there is no need to explain the hero's lowly animal form at the beginning of the animal-groom stories. The child knows his own situation is not due to some evil deed or a nefarious power; it is the natural order of the world. The frog emerges out of life in the water, as the child does at birth. Historically, fairy tales anticipate by centuries our knowledge of embryology, which tells how the human fetus undergoes various stages of development before birth, as the frog undergoes a metamorphosis in its development.

But why, of all animals, is the frog (or the toad, as in "The Three Feathers") a symbol for sexual relations? For example, a frog presaged

the conception of Sleeping Beauty. Compared to lions or other ferocious beasts, the frog (or the toad) does not arouse fear; it is an animal
which is not at all threatening. If it is experienced in a negative way,
the feeling is one of disgust, as in "The Frog King." It is difficult to
imagine a better way to convey to the child that he need not be afraid
of the (to him) repugnant aspects of sex than the way it is done in this
story. The story of the frog—how it behaves, what occurs to the princess in relation to it, and what finally happens to both frog and girl—
confirms the appropriateness of disgust when one is not ready for sex,
and prepares for its desirability when the time is ripe.

While according to psychoanalysis our sexual drives influence our
actions and behavior from the beginning of life, there is a world of
difference between the way these drives manifest themselves in the
child and in the adult. By using the frog as a symbol for sex, an animal
that exists in one form when young—as a tadpole—and in an entirely
different form when mature, the story speaks to the unconscious of
the child and helps him accept the form of sexuality which is correct
for his age, while also making him receptive to the idea that as he
grows up, his sexuality too must, in his own best interest, undergo a
metamorphosis.

There are also other, more direct associations between sex and the
frog which remain unconscious. Preconsciously the child connects the
tacky, clammy sensations which frogs (or toads) evoke in him with
similar feelings he attaches to the sex organs. The frog's ability to blow
itself out when excited arouses, again unconsciously, associations to
the penis' erectability.* Repulsive as the frog may be, as vividly described in "The Frog King," the story assures us that even an animal
so clammily disgusting turns into something very beautiful, provided
it all happens in the right way at the right time.

Children have a natural affinity to animals and often feel closer to
them than to adults, wishing to share what seems like an animal's easy
life of instinctual freedom and enjoyment. But with this affinity also
comes the child's anxiety that he might not be quite as human as he
ought to be. These fairy tales counteract this fear, by making the
animal existence a chrysalis from which a most attractive person
emerges.

Viewing sexual aspects of ourselves as animal-like has extremely

*Anne Sexton, with the poetic freedom and insights into the unconscious of the
artist, in her poem "The Frog Prince"—which is a retelling of the Brothers Grimm's
tale—writes, "At the feel of the frog / the touch-me-nots explode / like electric
slugs," and "Frog is my father's genitals."[114]

pernicious consequences, so much so that some people can never free their own—or others'—sexual experiences of this connotation. Therefore it must be conveyed to children that sex may seem disgustingly animal-like at first, but that once the right way is found to approach it, beauty will emerge from behind this repulsive appearance. Here the fairy tale, without ever mentioning or alluding to sexual experiences as such, is psychologically sounder than much of our conscious sex education. Modern sex education tries to teach that sex is normal, enjoyable, even beautiful, and certainly necessary for the survival of man. But since it does not start from an understanding that the child may find sex disgusting, and that this viewpoint has an important protective function for the child, modern sex education fails to carry conviction for him. The fairy tale, by agreeing with the child that the frog (or whatever other animal it may be) is disgusting, gains the child's confidence and thus can create in him the firm belief that, as the fairy tale tells, in due time this disgusting frog will reveal itself as life's most charming companion. And this message is delivered without ever directly mentioning anything sexual.

"CUPID AND PSYCHE"

In the best-known version of "The Frog King," the transformation brought about by love happens in an instant of violent self-assertion, due to a revulsion which arouses the deepest feelings. Once extremely stirred up, these feelings suddenly turn in the opposite direction. Other renderings of the story tell that it takes three nights or three weeks for love to work its wonder. In many stories of the animal-groom type, the achievement of true love requires years of endless travail. Contrary to the instantaneous effects achieved in "The Frog King," these stories warn that trying to rush things in sex and love— trying to find out in a hurry and on the sly what a person and love are all about—can have disastrous consequences.

The Western tradition of the animal-groom stories begins with Apuleius' story of Cupid and Psyche of the second century A.D., and he draws on even older sources.[115] This story is part of a larger work, *Metamorphoses,* which, as its title suggests, is concerned with initiations that cause such transformations. Although in "Cupid and Psyche" Cupid is a god, the story has important features in common with the tales of the animal groom. Cupid remains invisible to Psyche. Led astray by her two evil older sisters, Psyche believes her lover—

and with it sex—to be disgusting, "a huge serpent with a thousand coils." Cupid is a deity, and Psyche becomes one; a goddess, Aphrodite, out of her jealousy of Psyche, causes all the events. Today "Cupid and Psyche" is not known as a fairy tale, only as a myth. But since it influenced many Western tales of the animal-groom cycle, it needs to be considered here.

In this story a king has three daughters. Psyche, the youngest, is of such extraordinary beauty that she arouses Aphrodite's jealousy, so Aphrodite orders her son Eros to punish Psyche by making her fall in love with the most abominable of men. Psyche's parents, worried because she has not yet found a husband, consult the oracle of Apollo. The oracle says that Psyche must be set out on a high cliff to become the prey of a snakelike monster. Since this is tantamount to death, she is led to the assigned place in a funeral procession, ready to die. But a soft wind carries Psyche gently down the cliff and deposits her in an empty palace where all her wishes are fulfilled. There Eros, going against his mother's orders, keeps Psyche hidden away as his beloved. In the darkness of the night, in the disguise of a mysterious being, Eros joins Psyche in bed as her husband.

Despite all the comfort Psyche enjoys, she feels lonely during the day; moved by her entreaties, Eros arranges for her jealous sisters to visit Psyche. Out of their vile envy, the sisters persuade her that what she cohabits with and is pregnant by is "a huge serpent with a thousand coils," which, after all, is what the oracle seemed to predict. The sisters talk Psyche into cutting off the monster's head with a knife. Persuaded by them, against his orders never to try to see him, while Eros is asleep Psyche takes an oil lamp and a knife, planning to kill the beast. As light falls on Eros, Psyche discovers that he is a most beautiful youth. In her turmoil, Psyche's hand shakes, and a drop of hot oil scalds Eros; he awakes and departs. Heartbroken, Psyche tries to commit suicide, but is saved. Pursued by Aphrodite's anger and jealousy, Psyche has to suffer a series of terrible ordeals, including a descent into the underworld. (The evil sisters try to replace Psyche in the love of Eros and, hoping also to be wafted down by gentle winds, jump off the cliff and fall to their death.) Finally Eros, his wound healed, touched by Psyche's repentance, persuades Zeus to confer immortality on her. They get married on Olympus, and the child born to them is Pleasure.

Eros' arrows arouse uncontrollable sexual desires. Apuleius' tale uses his Latin name, Cupid, but in regard to sexual desires they stand for the same thing. Psyche is the Greek term for soul. In "Cupid and

Psyche" the neo-Platonist Apuleius turned what was probably an ancient Greek tale of a beautiful girl who was married to a snakelike monster into an allegory which, according to Robert Graves, symbolizes the progress of the rational soul toward intellectual love.[116] This is true, but this interpretation fails to do full justice to the richness of the story.

To begin with, the prediction that Psyche will be carried off by a horrible snake gives visual expression to the inexperienced girl's formless sexual anxieties. The funeral procession which leads Psyche to her destiny suggests the death of maidenhood, a loss not easily accepted. The readiness with which Psyche permits herself to be persuaded to kill Eros, with whom she cohabits, indicates the strong negative feelings which a young girl may harbor against him who has robbed her of her virginity. The being who has killed the innocent maiden in her deserves to some measure to be deprived of his virility—as she was of her virginity—and this is symbolized by Psyche's plan to cut off Eros' head.

Psyche's pleasant although boring life in the palace where she was deposited by the wind and where all her wishes are fulfilled suggests an essentially narcissistic life, and that, despite her name, consciousness has not yet entered her existence. Naïve sexual enjoyment is very different from mature love based on knowledge, experience, even suffering. Wisdom, the story tells, is not won by a life of easy pleasure. Psyche tries to reach for knowledge when—contrary to the warning she was given—she lets light fall on Eros. But the story warns that trying to reach for consciousness before one is mature enough for it or through short-cuts has far-reaching consequences; consciousness cannot be gained in one fell swoop. In desiring mature consciousness, one puts one's life on the line, as Psyche does when she tries to kill herself in desperation. The incredible hardships Psyche has to endure suggest the difficulties man encounters when the highest psychic qualities (Psyche) are to be wedded to sexuality (Eros). Not physical man, but spiritual man must be reborn to become ready for the marriage of sexuality with wisdom. This is represented by Psyche having to enter the underworld and return from it; wedding of the two aspects of man requires a rebirth.

One of the many meaningful details of this story might be mentioned here. Aphrodite does not just order her son to do her dirty work for her, she seduces him sexually to do so. And her jealousy reaches the highest pitch when she learns that Eros has not only gone against her wishes but—worse—has fallen in love with Psyche. The gods, the story tells, are not free of oedipal problems either; here is the oedipal love and possessive jealousy of a mother for her son. But Eros too has to grow if he is to become wedded to Psyche. Before he meets her, he is the most irrepressible and irresponsible of little gods. He strives for his independence when he goes against Aphrodite's orders. He reaches a higher state of consciousness only after he has been wounded by Psyche, and is moved by her ordeals.

"Cupid and Psyche" is a myth, not a fairy tale, although it contains some fairy-tale-like features. Of the two main figures, one is a god to begin with and the other becomes immortal, as no fairy-tale figure ever does. All through the story, gods take a hand in events, whether Psyche's suicide is prevented, ordeals are imposed on her, or she is given help in surviving them successfully. Unlike his counterparts in other animal-groom or animal-bride stories, Cupid is never anything but himself. Only Psyche, misguided by the oracle and her evil sisters —or her sexual anxiety—imagines him to be a beast.

However, this myth has influenced all later stories of the animal-groom type in the Western world. We encounter here for the first time the motif of two older sisters who are evil due to their jealousy of their youngest sister, who is more beautiful and virtuous than they. The sisters try to destroy Psyche, who nevertheless is victorious in the end, but only after she has undergone great hardships. Further, the tragic developments are the consequence of a bride who, ignoring her husband's warning not to try to gain knowledge of him (not to look at him, not to permit light to fall on him), acts contrary to his orders and then must wander all over the world to regain him.

More important even than these motifs is one very significant feature of the animal-groom cycle which appears here for the first time: the groom is absent during the day and present only in the darkness of night; he is believed to be animal during the day and to become human only in bed; in short, he keeps his day and night existences separate from each other. From what happens in the story it is not difficult to conclude that he wishes to keep his sex life separated from all else he is doing. The female, despite the ease and pleasure she enjoys, finds her life empty: she is unwilling to accept the separation and isolation of purely sexual aspects of life from the rest of it. She tries to force their unification. Little does she know that this can be achieved only through the hardest, most sustained moral and physical efforts. But once Psyche embarks on trying to wed the aspects of sex, love, and life into a unity, she does not falter, and in the end she wins.

If this were not a most ancient tale, one could be tempted to think that one of the messages inherent in fairy tales of this cycle is a most timely one: Despite all warnings about the dire consequences if she tries to find out, woman is not satisfied with remaining ignorant about sex and life. Comfortable as an existence in relative naïveté may be, it is an empty life which must not be accepted. Notwithstanding all the hardships woman has to suffer to be reborn to full consciousness and humanity, the stories leave no doubt that this is what she must do. Otherwise there would be no story: no fairy story worth telling, no worthwhile story to her life.

Once woman has overcome her view of sex as something beastly, she is not satisfied with being kept merely as a sex object or relegated to a life of leisure and relative ignorance. For the happiness of both partners they must have a full life in the world, and with each other as equals. That, these stories convey, is most difficult to achieve for both, but it cannot be avoided if they wish to find happiness in life, and with each other. This is the hidden message of many tales of the animal-groom cycle, and it can be seen more clearly from some other stories than from "Beauty and the Beast."

"THE ENCHANTED PIG"

"The Enchanted Pig" is a presently little-known Romanian fairy tale.[117] In it, a king has three daughters. The king must leave for war, so he entreats his daughters to behave well and look after everything in the house, warning them not to enter one back room, else harm will befall them. After his departure, for a while all goes well, but finally the eldest daughter suggests that they enter the forbidden room. The youngest daughter objects, but the second joins the oldest, who unlocks and opens the door. All they find in the room is a large table with an open book on it. First the eldest daughter reads what is written in the book: she will marry a prince from the East. The second turns the page and reads that she will marry a prince from the West. The youngest does not want to go against her father's order to find out her fate, but the other two force her; she learns that she will be married to a pig from the North.

The king returns, and eventually the two older sisters get married as predicted. Then an enormous pig comes from the North and asks to marry the youngest daughter. The king has to give in to the pig's wishes and advises his daughter to accept what is ordained, which she does. After the wedding, on their way home the pig gets into a bog and covers himself with mud. He then asks his wife to kiss him; obeying her father, the girl does so, after having wiped the pig's snout with her handkerchief. During their nights together she notices that in bed the pig changes into a man, but in the morning he is again a pig.

The girl asks a witch who happens to come by how to keep her husband from turning back into a pig. She is told to fasten a thread around her husband's leg at night; this will prevent him from becoming a pig again. She follows this recommendation, but her husband awakens and tells her that because she has tried to hurry things, he must leave her and that they shall not meet again "until you have worn out three pairs of iron shoes and blunted a steel staff in your search of me." He disappears, and her endless wanderings in search of him take her to the moon, the sun, and the wind. In each of these places she is given a chicken to eat and warned to save its bones; she is also told where to go from there. Finally, after she has worn out three pairs of iron shoes and even her steel staff has become blunted, she comes to a place high up, where she is told her husband dwells. She is helpless to get up there, until it occurs to her that the chicken bones she has carried faithfully might help. She puts one bone next to another, and they stick together. In this way the girl forms two long poles, and then constructs a ladder, on which she climbs up toward the high place. But she lacks a bone for the last rung, so she takes a knife and chops off her little finger, which, as the last step, permits her to reach her husband. In the meantime the spell of her husband's existence as a pig has ended. They inherit her father's kingdom, and "ruled as only kings rule who have suffered many things."

Trying to force the husband to give up his animalistic nature by tying him to his humanity with a string is a rare detail. Much more frequent is the motif of the female who is forbidden to shed light upon or see the secret of the male. In "Cupid and Psyche" it is an oil lamp which sheds light on that which is forbidden. In the Norwegian fairy tale "East of the Sun and West of the Moon" it is the light of a candle which shows the wife that her husband is not a white bear, as he appears during the day, but a beautiful prince who must now leave her.[118] The title suggests how far this wife's wanderings have to take her before she can be reunited with her husband. It is made clear in such stories that the husband would have regained his human form in the near future—the bear in "East of the Sun and West of the Moon" within a year's time, the enchanted pig in as little as three days —had the wife just restrained her curiosity.

Since in so many stories shedding light on the husband is the fatal mistake his young wife makes, one realizes that the wife wishes to find out about her husband's animal nature. This is not said directly, but is put into the mouth of some figure who induces the wife to go against her husband's warnings. In "Cupid and Psyche" the oracle and the sisters tell Psyche that Eros is a terrible dragon; in "East of the Sun and West of the Moon" it is her mother who tells the girl that the bear is likely to be a troll—with the clear implication that she had better look and find out. The witch who suggests tying a string around the husband's leg in "The Enchanted Pig" is an older female. Thus, the fairy tale subtly suggests that it is older women who give young girls the idea that males are beasts; that girls' sexual anxieties are the result not of their own experiences, but of what others have told them. The stories also imply that if girls listen and believe this, then their marital happiness will be in jeopardy. The enchantment of the animal husband is usually the work of some older female: Aphrodite, who actually wanted Psyche to be ravaged by an abominable beast; a stepmother who cast a spell on the white bear; a witch who enchanted the pig. This fact repeats the motif: it is older women who make males appear as beasts in the eyes of young girls.

Still, if the "animal husband" is a symbol of the girl's sexual anxieties, irrespective of whether these anxieties are her own creation or the consequence of what she has been told by older females, then one would expect the animal husband to be an animal at night in bed, and not during the day. What do the stories indicate by expressing that the animal husband is an animal during the day to the world, but lovely to behold to his wife at night in bed?

I think these tales reveal deep psychological insights. Many females who consciously or subconsciously experience sex as something "animal-like," and resent the male for depriving them of their virginity, feel quite differently while enjoying themselves with the man they love during the night. But once the man has left them, in bright daylight the old anxieties and resentments, including the jealousy of one sex for the other, reassert themselves. What seemed lovely at night looks different by day, particularly when the world with its critical attitude toward sexual enjoyment (the mother's warning that it might be a troll) reasserts itself. Similarly, there are many males who feel one way about their sexual experiences during them, and another way the next day when archaic anxieties and resentments are not subdued by the pleasure of the moment.

Stories about the animal husband assure children that their fear of sex as something dangerous and beastly is by no means unique to them; many people have felt the same way. But as the story characters discover that despite such anxiety their sexual partner is not an ugly creature but a lovely person, so will the child. On a preconscious level these tales convey to the child that much of his anxiety is implanted in him by what he has been told; and that matters may be quite different when one experiences them directly, from the way one sees them from the outside.

On another level, the stories seem to tell that throwing light on these matters, while it may demonstrate that one's anxiety was unfounded, does not solve the problem. This takes time—trying to do it prematurely only postpones it all—and, most of all, is hard work. To overcome sexual anxieties, one must grow as a person, and unfortunately much of this growth can be achieved only through suffering.

One obvious lesson of these stories may be less important today than in times past when the pattern was that the male had to woo the female—as the pig comes wooing from afar to win the princess, and the great white bear has to make all kinds of promises to win his bride. This, the stories tell, is not sufficient for a happy marriage. The female has to exert herself as much as the male; she has to pursue him actively as much as he pursues her, maybe even more so.

Other psychological subtleties of these stories may be lost on the hearer, but they may impress him subconsciously and thus make him sensitive to typical difficulties which, when not understood, may create hardships in the relations between people. For example, when the pig deliberately rolls itself in the mud and then asks its bride to kiss it, such behavior is typical of the person who fears that he is not acceptable and tests this by making himself appear worse than he is, because only when he is accepted under the worst appearance can he feel secure. Thus, in the stories of the animal husband the male's anxieties that his coarseness will turn off the female are juxtaposed with her anxieties about the bestial nature of sex.

Quite different is the detail which permits the bride of the enchanted pig to become reunited with her husband. To make the last step necessary for this, she has to cut off her little finger. It is her final, most personal sacrifice, her "key" to her happiness. Since nothing in the story suggests that her hand remained crippled or that she bled, hers is clearly a symbolic sacrifice, suggesting that in a successful marriage the relationship is more important even than the complete integrity of the body.[119]

This still leaves undiscussed the meaning of the secret room which must not be entered lest calamity result. This is best considered in connection with much more tragic consequences which follow from similar transgressions in other stories.

"BLUEBEARD"

Bluebeard is the most monstrous and beastly of all fairy-tale husbands. Actually this story is not a fairy tale, because with the single exception of the indelible blood on the key which gives away the fact that Bluebeard's bride has entered the forbidden room, there is nothing magical or supernatural in the story. More important, there is no development of any of the characters; although evil is punished in the end, this in itself makes neither for recovery nor for consolation. "Bluebeard" is a story invented by Perrault for which there are no direct antecedents in folk tales as far as we know.[120]

There are quite a few fairy tales with the central motif of a secret chamber which must not be entered, where previously killed women are preserved. In some Russian and Scandinavian tales of this sort it is an animal husband who forbids entering the room, suggesting a relation between the animal-groom stories and those of the "Bluebeard" type. Among the better known of these fairy tales are the English "Mr. Fox" and the Brothers Grimm's "Fitcher's Bird."[121]

In "Fitcher's Bird" a sorcerer carries off the eldest of three daughters. He tells her that she may enter all rooms of the house with the exception of one, which can be opened only by the smallest of the keys. This room she must avoid on pain of death. The sorcerer further entrusts the girl with an egg, which she is always to carry with her, because great misfortune will ensue should she lose it. The girl enters the forbidden room and finds it full of blood and dead people. In her fright she drops the egg, and the blood which gets on it cannot be wiped off. The egg gives her away on the return of the sorcerer, who then kills her like the others. Next he gets hold of the middle sister, whose fate is the same.

The youngest daughter is finally carried off by the wizard to his house. But she tricks him by putting the egg away carefully before she goes exploring. Positioning the limbs of her sisters together, she restores them to life. On his return, the sorcerer believes her to have been faithful and tells her that as a reward she will be his bride. She tricks him once more, this time into carrying her sisters and a lot of gold to her parents. Then she glues feathers all over her body so that she looks like a strange bird—hence the story's title—and in this way escapes. In the end the wizard and all his friends are burned to death. In fairy tales of this type there is full recovery of the victims, and the villain is not a human being.

"Bluebeard" and "Fitcher's Bird" are considered here because these stories present in the most extreme form the motif that as a test of trustworthiness, the female must not inquire into the secrets of the male. Carried away by her curiosity, she does so nevertheless, with calamitous consequences. In "The Enchanted Pig" the three daughters invade the forbidden room and find the book containing an account of their future. "The Enchanted Pig" has this feature in common with stories of the "Bluebeard" type, so we will consider these stories together, to help clarify the significance of this motif of the forbidden room.

In "The Enchanted Pig" knowledge about marriage is found in the book kept in the room which the sisters are told not to enter. That the forbidden information is about marriage suggests that it is carnal knowledge their father forbade them to acquire—as even today certain books containing sexual information are withheld from the young.

Whether it is Bluebeard or the sorcerer in "Fitcher's Bird," it seems clear that when the male gives the female a key to a room, while at the same time instructing her not to enter, it is a test of her faithfulness to his orders or, in a broader sense, to him. Then these males pretend to depart or do depart for a while, to test their partner's fidelity. Returning unexpectedly, they find that their confidence has been betrayed. The nature of the betrayal may be guessed by the punishment: execution. In certain parts of the world in times past, only one form of deception on the female's part was punishable by death inflicted by her husband: sexual infidelity.

With this thought, let us consider what gives the woman away. In "Fitcher's Bird" it is an egg, in "Bluebeard" a key. In both stories these are magic objects in the sense that once they are touched by blood, the blood cannot be washed off them. The motif of blood that cannot be washed off is an ancient one. Wherever it occurs, it is a sign that some evil deed, usually murder, was committed.* The egg is a symbol of female sexuality which, so it seems, the girls in "Fitcher's Bird" are to preserve unspoiled. The key that opens the door to a secret room suggests associations to the male sexual organ, particu-

*In the *Gesta Romanorum* of around 1300, blood which fell on a mother's hand when she murdered her child remains indelible. In Shakespeare, even if nobody else can see the blood on her hands, Lady Macbeth knows that it is there.

larly in first intercourse when the hymen is broken and blood gets on it. If this is one of the hidden meanings, then it makes sense that the blood cannot be washed away: defloration is an irreversible event.

In "Fitcher's Bird" the faithfulness of the girls is tested before they have gotten married. The sorcerer plans to marry the youngest daughter because she is able to fool him into believing that she has not disobeyed him. In Perrault's "Bluebeard" we are told that as soon as Bluebeard left for his pretended trip, a great festivity took place; visitors came who did not dare enter the house when its master was at home. It is left to our imagination what went on between the woman and her guests with Bluebeard away, but the story makes it clear that everybody had a high time. The blood on the egg and the key seems to symbolize that the woman had sexual relations. Therefore we can understand her anxious fantasy which depicts corpses of women who had been killed for having been similarly unfaithful.

On hearing any of these stories, it immediately becomes obvious that the female is strongly tempted to do what is forbidden to her. It is hard to imagine any more effective way to seduce a person than to tell her: "I am going away; in my absence you may inspect all rooms but one. Here is the key to the forbidden room, which you are not to use." Thus on one level which is easily obscured by the gruesome details of the story, "Bluebeard" is a tale about sexual temptation.

On another level which is much more obvious, "Bluebeard" is a tale about the destructive aspects of sex. But if one thinks over the story's events for a moment, strange discrepancies become apparent. For example, in Perrault's tale, after her gruesome discovery, Bluebeard's wife does not call for help from any of the many guests who, according to the story, must still be around. She does not confide in her sister Anne, nor seek her help; all she asks of Anne is to look out for her brothers, who are to come on that day. Finally, Bluebeard's wife does not choose what would seem the most obvious course of action: to run for safety, or hide, or disguise herself. This is exactly what happens in "Fitcher's Bird" and in a parallel fairy story of the Brothers Grimm, "The Robber Bridegroom," in which the girl first hides, then escapes, and finally tricks the murderous robbers into coming to a feast, during which they are unmasked. The behavior of Bluebeard's bride suggests two possibilities: that what she sees in the forbidden closet is the creation of her own anxious fantasies; or that she has betrayed her husband, but hopes he won't find out.

Whether or not these interpretations are valid, there is no doubt that "Bluebeard" is a story which gives body to two not necessarily related emotions which are by no means alien to the child: First, jealous love, when one wishes so badly to keep one's beloveds forever that one is even ready to destroy them so that they cannot change loyalties. And second, sexual feelings can be terribly fascinating and tempting, but also very dangerous.

It is easy to ascribe "Bluebeard's" popularity to the combination of crime and sex, or the fascination which sexual crimes hold. To the child, I believe part of the attraction of the story is that it confirms his idea that adults have terrible sexual secrets. It also states what the child knows only too well from his own experience: to find out about sexual secrets is so tempting that even adults are willing to run the greatest risks imaginable. Further, the person who so tempts others deserves a fitting punishment.

I believe that on a preconscious level the child understands from the indelible blood on the key and from other details that Bluebeard's wife has committed a sexual indiscretion. The story tells that although a jealous husband may believe a wife deserves to be severely punished —even killed—for this, he is absolutely wrong in such thoughts. To fall into temptation, the story clearly tells, is most human. And the jealous person who believes he can take things into his own hands and acts on this conviction deserves to be killed. Marital infidelity, symbolically expressed by the blood on the egg or the key, is something to be forgiven. If the partner does not understand this, it is he who will suffer for it.

Gruesome as the story is, this analysis suggests that "Bluebeard," like all fairy stories—although, as mentioned before, it does not really fall into this category—teaches deep down a higher morality or humanity. The person who seeks cruel revenge for infidelity is deservedly undone, as is one who experiences sex only in its destructive aspects. That this more humane morality which understands and forgives sexual transgressions is the most significant aspect of this story is, for once, expressed in the second "morality" which Perrault appended to it. He writes: "One can well see that this is a story of times past; there are no longer such terrible husbands who demand the impossible; even when they are dissatisfied or jealous, they act gently toward their wives."

However one interprets "Bluebeard," it is a cautionary tale which warns: Women, don't give in to your sexual curiosity; men, don't permit yourself to be carried away by your anger at being sexually betrayed. There is nothing subtle about it; most of all, no development toward higher humanity is projected. At the end, the protagonists, both Bluebeard and his wife, are exactly the same persons they were before. Earth-shaking events have taken place in the story and nobody is the better for them, except possibly the world because Bluebeard no longer exists in it.

How a true folk fairy tale elaborates the motif of the room one is forbidden to enter but which one opens despite such warning can be seen from a large group of tales—for example, the Brothers Grimm's "Our Lady's Child." When the girl is fourteen—the age of sexual maturation—she is given keys which unlock all rooms, but is told not to enter one of them. Tempted by her curiosity, she opens its door. Later she denies that she has done so, despite repeated questioning. As punishment she is robbed of the ability to speak, since she has misused it in lying. She suffers many severe trials, and finally she admits that she has lied. Her speech is restored to her and all is well again, because "whoever repents his sins and confesses will be forgiven."

"BEAUTY AND THE BEAST"

"Bluebeard" is a story about the dangerous propensities of sex, about its strange secrets and close connection with violent and destructive emotions; in short, about those dark aspects of sex which might well be kept hidden behind a permanently locked door, securely controlled. That which happens in "Bluebeard" has nothing whatsoever to do with love. Bluebeard, bent on having his will and possessing his partner, cannot love anybody, but neither can anyone love him.

Despite the title, there is nothing so beastly in the fairy tale of "Beauty and the Beast." Beauty's father is menaced by the Beast, but one knows right from the start that it is an empty threat, designed to gain first Beauty's company, eventually her love, and with it deliverance from an animal-like appearance. In this story all is gentleness and loving devotion to one another on the part of the three main characters: Beauty, her father, and the Beast. Cruel and destructive as the oedipal love of Aphrodite for her son is in the myth which begins the history of this fairy-tale cycle, the oedipal love of Beauty for her father, when transferred to her future husband, is wonderfully healing, in the fairy tale which is the final apotheosis of this cycle.

The following summary of "Beauty and the Beast" is based on Madame Leprince de Beaumont's rendering of the story published in 1757, which draws on an earlier French version of the motif by

Madame de Villeneuve. It is the version in which the tale is now best known.*[122]

Different from most renderings of "Beauty and the Beast," in Madame Leprince de Beaumont's story a rich merchant has not only the usual three daughters but in addition three sons, although they play hardly any role in the tale. All the girls are very good-looking, particularly the youngest, who has become known as "The little Beauty," which name makes her sisters very jealous. These sisters are vain and selfish, quite the opposite from Beauty, who is modest, charming, and sweet to everybody. Suddenly their father loses all his money, and the family is reduced to a mean existence which the sisters take very badly, but Beauty's character shines even more in these difficult circumstances.

The father then has to go on a trip, and asks his daughters what he should bring them. Since their hope is that on this trip the father will regain some of his wealth, the two sisters ask him to bring them expensive garments, while Beauty asks for nothing. Only when pressed by her father, Beauty asks him to bring her a rose. The hopes for regaining his wealth turn out to be empty, and the father has to return home as poor as he left. He gets lost in a large forest and nearly despairs; then he suddenly comes to a palace where he finds food and shelter, but nobody home. The next morning, about to depart, the father sees some beautiful roses and, remembering Beauty's request, gathers some for her. As he does so, a frightful Beast appears and berates him for stealing roses after it had received him so well in its castle. As a punishment, the Beast says, the father will have to die. The father pleads for his life, telling that he took the roses for his daughter. The Beast agrees to let him go if one of his daughters will take the father's place and suffer the fate the Beast had planned for him. But

*Perrault's *"Riquet à la Houppe"* is earlier than either of these two tales, and his original recasting of the ancient motif has no known precedent. He changes the beast into an ugly but brilliant man—misformed Riquet. A stupid princess who falls in love with him because of his character and brilliance no longer sees the deformities of his body, becomes blind to his physical defects. And she, because of his love for her, seems no longer stupid but full of intelligence. This is the magical transformation which love achieves: mature love and acceptance of sex make what was before repugnant, or seemed stupid, become beautiful and full of spirit. As Perrault points out, the moral of the story is that beauty, be it that of physical appearance or of the mind, lies in the eye of the beholder. But because Perrault tells a story with an explicit moral, it loses out as a fairy tale. While love changes all, there is really no development —there is no inner conflict that needs to be resolved, nor any struggle that lifts the protagonists to a higher level of humanity.

if none of the daughters will do so, the merchant must return within three months to die. On leaving, the Beast gives the father a chest filled with gold. The merchant has no intention of sacrificing one of his daughters, but accepts the three months' respite to see them again and bring them the gold.

On coming home, he gives Beauty the roses, but cannot help telling her what has happened. The brothers offer to find the Beast and slay it, but their father will not permit this, because they would only perish. Beauty insists on taking her father's place. Whatever he says to make her change her mind makes no impression on her; she will go with him anyway. The gold he brought back has permitted the two sisters to make fashionable marriages. After the three months the father, accompanied against his will by Beauty, sets out for the palace of the Beast. The Beast asks Beauty whether she has come of her own free will, and when she says "Yes," it bids the father leave, which he finally does with a heavy heart. Beauty is treated royally in the Beast's palace; all her wishes are met as if by magic. Each night, during supper, the Beast visits with her. Over time, Beauty comes to look forward to this, as it breaks her loneliness. The only thing which perturbs her is that at the end of their visits together the Beast regularly asks her to become its wife; when she ever so gently refuses, the Beast departs in great distress. Three months pass this way, and when she again refuses to become its wife, the Beast asks that at least she will promise to never leave it. She promises this, but asks to be permitted to visit her father since, from viewing in a mirror the events in other parts of the world, she knows he is pining away for her. The Beast gives her a week's time to do so, but warns her that it will die if she fails to return.

Next morning she finds herself home with her father, who is overjoyed. Her brothers are away serving in the army. Her sisters, who are unhappy in their marriages, plan out of jealousy to detain Beauty beyond the week, thinking that then the monster will come and destroy her. They succeed in persuading Beauty to remain another week; but during the tenth night she dreams of the Beast, and it reproaches her in a dying voice. She wishes herself back with it, and is immediately transported there. Beauty finds the Beast nearly dying of a broken heart because she did not keep her promise. During her stay at home Beauty realized how deeply she had become attached to the Beast; seeing it so helpless, she realizes her love for it and says that she can no longer live without it and wants to marry it. At this, the Beast turns into a prince; they are joined by her happy father and

the rest of her family. The evil sisters are turned into statues and have
to remain that way until they own up to their faults.

In "Beauty and the Beast" the Beast's form is left to our imagination. In a group of fairy tales found in many European countries, the
beast, in imitation of "Cupid and Psyche," is given the body of a snake.
Otherwise the events of these stories are quite similar to those just
mentioned, with one exception. When the male regains his human
form, he tells why he had been reduced to a snakelike existence: it was
his punishment for having seduced an orphan. He, who used a helpless victim to satisfy his sexual lust, could be redeemed only by an
unselfish love willing to sacrifice itself for the beloved. The prince had
been turned into a snake because, as a phallic animal, it is a symbol
for sexual lust which seeks satisfaction without benefit of a human
relation, and also because it uses its victim solely for its own purposes,
as did the snake in paradise. By giving in to its seduction, we lose our
state of innocence.

In "Beauty and the Beast," the fateful events are brought about by
a father's having stolen a rose to bring to his best-loved youngest
daughter. His doing so symbolizes both his love for her and also an
anticipation of her losing her maidenhood, as the broken flower—
particularly the broken rose—is a symbol for the loss of virginity. This
may seem to both father and daughter as if she would have to suffer
some "beastly" experience. But the story tells that their anxieties are
unfounded. What was feared to be a beastly experience turns out to
be one of deep humanity and love.

Considering "Bluebeard" in conjunction with "Beauty and the
Beast," one might say that the former presents those primitive, aggressive, and selfishly destructive aspects of sex which must be overcome if love is to bloom; while the latter tale depicts what true love
is all about. Bluebeard's behavior is in accordance with his ominous
appearance; the Beast, despite its looks, is as beautiful a person as
Beauty. This story, contrary to what the child's fears may be, assures
the listener that, although females and males look very different, they
are a perfect match when they are the right partners so far as their
personalities are concerned, and if they are tied together by love.
While "Bluebeard" conforms to the child's worst fears about sex,
"Beauty and the Beast" offers the child the strength to realize that his
fears are the creations of his anxious sexual fantasies; and that while
sex may at first seem beastlike, in reality love between woman and
man is the most satisfying of all emotions, and the only one which
makes for permanent happiness.

At various places in this book it has been mentioned that fairy tales help the child to understand the nature of his oedipal difficulties and offer hope that he will master them. "Cinderella" is a supreme statement of the devastating nature of a parent's unresolved and destructively acted-out oedipal jealousy of a child. No other well-known fairy tale makes it as obvious as "Beauty and the Beast" that a child's oedipal attachment to a parent is natural, desirable, and has the most positive consequences for all, if during the process of maturation it is transferred and transformed as it becomes detached from the parent and concentrated on the lover. Our oedipal attachments, far from being only the source of our greatest emotional difficulties (which they can be when they do not undergo proper development during our growing up), are the soil out of which permanent happiness grows if we experience the right evolution and resolution of these feelings.

This story suggests Beauty's oedipal attachment to her father not only by her asking him for a rose, but also by our being told in detail how her sisters went out enjoying themselves at parties and having lovers while Beauty always stayed home and told those who courted her that she was too young to marry and wanted "to stay with her father a few years longer." Since Beauty joins the Beast only out of love for her father, she wishes to have an asexual relation with it.

The Beast's palace in which all of Beauty's wishes are immediately fulfilled, a motif already discussed in "Cupid and Psyche," is a narcissistic fantasy typically engaged in by children. It is a rare child who has not at some time wished for an existence where nothing is demanded of him and all of his desires are met as soon as he expresses them. The fairy story tells that such a life, far from being satisfying, soon becomes empty and boring—so much so that Beauty comes to look forward to the evening visits of the Beast, which at first she dreaded.

If nothing happened to interrupt such a narcissistic dream life, there would be no story; narcissism, the fairy tale teaches, despite its seeming attractiveness, is not a life of satisfactions, but no life at all. Beauty comes to life when she learns that her father needs her. In some versions of the tale he has fallen seriously ill; in others he pines away for her, or in some other way is in great distress. This knowledge shatters Beauty's narcissistic non-existence; she begins to act and then she—and the story—come to life again.

Thrown into a conflict between her love for her father and the Beast's needs, Beauty deserts the beast to attend her father. But then she realizes how much she loves the Beast—a symbol of the loosening of ties to her father and transference of her love to the Beast. Only after Beauty decides to leave her father's house to be reunited with the Beast—that is, after she has resolved her oedipal ties to her father —does sex, which before was repugnant, become beautiful.

This foreshadows by centuries the Freudian view that sex must be experienced by the child as disgusting as long as his sexual longings are attached to his parent, because only through such a negative attitude toward sex can the incest taboo, and with it the stability of the human family, remain secure. But once detached from the parent and directed to a partner of more suitable age, in normal development, sexual longings no longer seem beastly—to the contrary, they are experienced as beautiful.

"Beauty and the Beast," in illustrating the positive aspects of a child's oedipal attachment while showing what must happen to it as he grows up, well deserves the praise Iona and Peter Opie bestow on it in their survey of *The Classic Fairy Tales*. They call it "the most symbolic of the fairy tales after Cinderella, and the most satisfying."

"Beauty and the Beast" begins with an immature view which posits man to have a dual existence as animal and as mind—symbolized by Beauty. In the process of maturation, these artificially isolated aspects of our humanity must become unified; that alone permits us to attain complete human fulfillment. In "Beauty and the Beast" there are no longer any sexual secrets which must remain unknown, the discovery of which necessitates a long and difficult voyage of self-discovery before the happy ending can be gained. On the contrary, in "Beauty and the Beast" there are no hidden secrets, and it is highly desirable that the Beast's true nature be revealed. Finding out what the Beast is really like or, to put it more correctly, what a kind and loving person he really is, leads right to the happy ending. The story's essence is not just the growth of Beauty's love for the Beast, or even her transferring her love for her father to the Beast, but her own growth in the process. From believing that she must choose between her love for her father and her love for the Beast, Beauty moves to the happy discovery that seeing these two loves in opposition is an immature view of things. By transferring her original oedipal love for her father to her future husband, Beauty gives her father the kind of affection most beneficial to him. This restores his failing health and provides him with a happy life in proximity to his beloved daughter. It also restores the Beast to his humanity, and then a life of marital bliss for him and Beauty becomes possible.

The marriage of Beauty to the former Beast is a symbolic expression of the healing of the pernicious break between the animal and the higher aspects of man—a separation which is described as a sickness, since, when separated from Beauty and what she symbolizes, first her father and then the Beast nearly die. It is also the end point of an evolution from a self-centered, immature (phallic-aggressive-destructive) sexuality to one that finds its fulfillment in a human relation of deep devotion: the Beast is about to die because of the separation from Beauty, who is both the beloved female and Psyche, our soul. This is an evolution from a primitive selfish-aggressive sexuality to one which finds its fulfillment as part of a loving relation freely engaged in. That is why the Beast accepts Beauty's substitution for her father only after she assures it that she voluntarily takes his place, and why it asks her repeatedly to marry it, but accepts without recrimination her rejection and makes no move toward her before she spontaneously declares her love for it.

Translating the poetic language of the fairy tale into the pedestrian language of psychoanalysis, the marriage of Beauty and the Beast is the humanization and socialization of the id by the superego. How apt, then, that in "Cupid and Psyche" the offspring of this union is Pleasure or Joy, an ego that provides us with the satisfactions we need for a good life. The fairy tale, unlike the myth, doesn't need to spell out the benefits of the union of the two protagonists. It uses a more impressive image: a world where the good live in happiness, and the evil ones—the sisters—are not beyond redemption.

Each fairy tale is a magic mirror which reflects some aspects of our inner world, and of the steps required by our evolution from immaturity to maturity. For those who immerse themselves in what the fairy tale has to communicate, it becomes a deep, quiet pool which at first seems to reflect only our own image; but behind it we soon discover the inner turmoils of our soul—its depth, and ways to gain peace within ourselves and with the world, which is the reward of our struggles.

The selection of stories to be considered was arbitrary, although guided to some degree by the popularity of the tales. As each story reflects some segment of the inner evolution of man, the second part of the book began with tales in which the child struggles for his independence: reluctantly and only when forced by his parents to do so against his will, as in "Hansel and Gretel," or more spontaneously, as in "Jack and the Beanstalk." Little Red Cap in the wolf's belly, and Sleeping Beauty, who in her castle experimented with the distaff, have prematurely exposed themselves to experiences for which they are not yet ready; they learn they must wait until they have matured, and how to do this. In "Snow White" and "Cinderella" the child can become himself only as the parent is defeated. If the book had ended with either of these two stories, it would have seemed that there is no happy solution to the generational conflict which, as these fairy tales show, is as old as man. But they also tell that where this conflict exists, it is due only to the self-centeredness of the parent and his lack of sensitivity to the child's legitimate needs. As a parent myself, I preferred to end with a fairy tale which tells that a parent's love for his child is also as old as man, as is the child's love for his parent. It is out of this tender affection that there grows a different love which, once the child is grown, will bind him to his beloved. Whatever may be true in reality, the child who listens to fairy tales comes to imagine and believe that out of love for him his parent is willing to risk his life to bring him the present he most desires. In his turn, such a child believes that he is worthy of such devotion, because he would be willing to sacrifice his life out of love for his parent. Thus the child will grow up to bring peace and happiness even to those who are so grievously afflicted that they seem like beasts. In doing so, a person will gain happiness for himself and his life's partner and, with it, happiness also for his parents. He will be at peace with himself and the world.

This is one of the manifold truths revealed by fairy tales, which can guide our lives; it is a truth as valid today as it was once upon a time.

NOTES

1. For Dickens' remarks about "Little Red Riding Hood" and his views of fairy tales, see Angus Wilson, *The World of Charles Dickens* (London: Secker and Warburg, 1970), and Michael C. Kotzin, *Dickens and the Fairy Tale* (Bowling Green: Bowling Green University Press, 1972).
2. Louis MacNeice, *Varieties of Parable* (New York: Cambridge University Press, 1965).
3. G. K. Chesterton, *Orthodoxy* (London: John Lane, 1909). C. S. Lewis, *The Allegory of Love* (Oxford: Oxford University Press, 1936).
4. "Jack the Giant Killer" and various other stories in the Jack cycle are printed in Katherine M. Briggs, *A Dictionary of British Folk Tales*, 4 volumes (Bloomington: Indiana University Press, 1970). British folk tales mentioned in this book can be found there. Another important collection of English fairy tales is that of Joseph Jacobs: *English Fairy Tales* (London: David Nutt, 1890) and *More English Fairy Tales* (London: David Nutt, 1895).
5. "The mighty hopes that make us men." A. Tennyson, *In Memoriam*, LXXXV.
6. The discussion of "The Fisherman and the Jinny" is based on Burton's translation of *The Arabian Nights' Entertainments*.

   "The Spirit in the Bottle" is one of the tales collected by the Brothers Grimm and published with the title *Kinder- und Hausmärchen*. This book has been translated many times, but only a few of these translations are true to the original. Among those which are acceptable are: *Grimm's Fairy Tales*, New York, Pantheon Books, 1944; and *The Grimm's German Folk Tales*, Carbondale, Southern Illinois University Press, 1960.

   All of the Brothers Grimm's fairy tales are discussed in respect to the origins of each story, its different versions all over the world, its relation to other legends and fairy tales, etc., in Johannes Bolte and Georg Polivka, *Anmerkungen zu den Kinder- und Hausmärchen der Brüder Grimm*, 5 vols., Hildesheim, Olms, 1963.

   "The Spirit in the Bottle" illustrates how parental attitudes induce a child to engage in fantasies about gaining powers which will make him superior to his father. The story's hero has had to leave school because of the family's poverty. He offers to help his poor woodcutter father with his work, but the father thinks little of his son's abilities and tells him: "That's too hard work for you; you are not accustomed to such strenuous labor; you can't bear it." After they have been working all morning, the father suggests that they rest and eat their noon meal. The son says that he prefers to walk about the forest and look for some birds' nests, at which the father exclaims, "Oh, you jackanapes, why do you want to run around? Afterwards you will be so tired you won't be able to lift your arm." Thus, the father belittles his son twice: first, by doubting his ability to do hard work; and, even after the son has displayed his stamina, by contemptuously dismissing his ideas about how to spend the resting time. After such an experience, what normal pubertal boy would not embark on daydreams about showing his father to be wrong, and proving that he is much better than his parent imagines?

The fairy tale makes this fantasy come true. As the son walks about looking for birds' nests, he hears a voice that says, "Let me out!" Thus he finds the spirit in the bottle, which, however, at first threatens to destroy him, in retaliation for having been incarcerated for so long. The boy cleverly induces the spirit to return into the bottle, much as the fisherman does in the *Arabian Nights* tale, and releases him only after being rewarded with a rag, one end of which heals all wounds, while the other changes everything rubbed by it into silver. By turning things into silver, the boy provides himself and his father with a good living, and because "he could heal all wounds, he became the most famous physician in the whole world."

The motif of the evil spirit locked up in a bottle goes back to very ancient Judean-Persian legends according to which King Solomon often imprisoned disobeying or heretic spirits in iron caskets, copper flasks, or wineskins, and dropped these into the sea. That "The Fisherman and the Jinny" is in part derived from this tradition is shown by the Jinny telling the fisherman of his rebellion against Solomon, who had as punishment shut him up in the bottle and thrown it into the sea.

In "The Spirit in the Bottle," this ancient motif has merged with two different traditions. One, though itself traceable ultimately to the legends of King Solomon, is a medieval account concerning the devil, who is similarly incarcerated by some holy man, or else freed by him and forced to serve his liberator. The second tradition originates in tales about a historical person: Theophrastus Bombastus Paracelsus von Hohenheim, a renowned German-Swiss physician of the sixteenth century whose allegedly miraculous cures stimulated the European imagination for centuries.

According to one of these stories, Paracelsus hears a voice coming out of a fir tree which calls his name. He recognizes it as the voice of the devil which, in the form of a spider, is locked in a tiny hole in the tree. Paracelsus offers to free the devil if it will give him medicine which cures all sickness, and a tincture which changes everything into gold. The devil complies, but then wants to rush off to destroy the holy man who had incarcerated it. To prevent this, Paracelsus doubts aloud that something as big as the devil could turn itself into something as small as a spider. The devil, to show that it can do so, changes back into a spider and is again locked up in the tree by Paracelsus. This story, in turn, goes back to a much older one about a sorcerer named Virgilius (Bolte and Polivka, *op. cit.*).

7. The most comprehensive enumerations of fairy-tale motifs, including that of the giant or spirit in the bottle, are those presented by Antti A. Aarne, *The Types of the Folktale* (Helsinki: Suomalainen Tiedeakatemia, 1961), and Stith Thompson, *Motif Index of Folk Literature*, 6 volumes (Bloomington: Indiana University Press, 1955).

   In Thompson's index, the spirit being tricked into making itself small to return into the bottle, etc., is motifs D1240, D2177.1, R181, K717, and K722. It would be tedious to give these data for all the fairy-tale motifs mentioned in this book, particularly since the distribution of a particular motif can be easily ascertained from these two reference works.

8. The discussion of the myth of Hercules and of all other Greek myths follows their rendering in Gustav Schwab, *Gods and Heroes: Myths and Epics of Ancient Greece* (New York: Pantheon Books, 1946).

9. Mircea Eliade, *Birth and Rebirth* (New York: Harper and Brothers, 1958); *Myth and Reality* (New York: Harper & Row, 1963). See also Paul Saintyves, *Les Contes de Perrault et les récits parallèles* (Paris, 1923), and Jan de Vries, *Betrachtungen zum Märchen, besonders in seinem Verhältnis zu Heldensage und Mythos* (Helsinki: Folklore Fellows Communications No. 150, 1954).

10. A collection of articles discussing fairy tales on a depth-psychological basis which has the merit of adequately representing the various schools of thought can be found in Wilhelm Laiblin, *Märchenforschung und Tiefenpsychologie* (Darmstadt: Wissenschaftliche Buchgesellschaft, 1969). It also contains a reasonably complete bibliography.

11. There is as yet no systematic discussion of fairy tales from a psychoanalytic viewpoint. Freud published two short articles in 1913 dealing with this topic: "The Occurrence in Dreams of Material from Fairy Tales" and "The Theme of the Three Caskets." The Brothers Grimm's "Little Red Cap" and "The Wolf and the Seven Little Kids" play an important role in Freud's famous "History of an Infantile Neurosis," which has become known as "The Wolf-Man." Sigmund Freud, *The Standard Edition of the Complete Psychological Works* (London: Hogarth Press, 1953 ff.), volumes 12, 17.

   Fairy tales are referred to in many other psychoanalytic writings, too numerous to enumerate here, but almost always only in cursory form, such as in Anna Freud, *The Ego and the Mechanisms of Defense* (New York: International Universities Press, 1946). From among the many papers dealing more specifically with fairy tales from a Freudian viewpoint, the following may be mentioned: Otto Rank, *Psychoanalytische Beiträge zur Mythenforschung* (Vienna: Deuticke, 1919); Alfred Winterstein, *"Die Pubertätsriten der Mädchen und ihre Spuren im Märchen,"* *Imago*, Vol. 14 (1928).

   In addition, a few fairy tales were discussed psychoanalytically—for example, Steff Bornstein, "The Sleeping Beauty," *Imago*, Vol. 19 (1933); J. F. Grant Duff, "Snow White," *ibid.*, vol. 20 (1934); Lilla Veszy-Wagner, "Little Red Riding Hood on the Couch," *The Psychoanalytic Forum*, vol. 1 (1966); Beryl Sandford, "Cinderella," *ibid.*, vol. 2 (1967). Erich Fromm, *The Forgotten Language* (New York: Rinehart, 1951), makes some references to fairy tales, particularly to "Little Red Riding Hood."

12. Fairy tales are treated much more comprehensively in the writings of Jung and Jungian analysts. Unfortunately, little of this vast literature has been translated into English. Typical for the approach of Jungian psychoanalysts to fairy tales is Marie Louise von Franz, *Interpretation of Fairy Tales* (New York: Spring Publications, 1970).

Probably the best example of the analysis of a famous fairy tale from the Jungian point of view is Erich Neumann, *Amor and Psyche* (New York: Pantheon, 1956).

The most complete discussion of fairy tales from a Jungian frame of reference is to be found in the three volumes of Hedwig von Beit, *Symbolik des Märchens* and *Gegensatz und Erneuerung im Märchen* (Bern: A. Francke, 1952 and 1956).

An intermediate position is taken by Julius E. Heuscher, *A Psychiatric Study of Fairy Tales* (Springfield: Charles Thomas, 1963).

13. For different versions of "The Three Little Pigs," see Briggs, *op. cit.* The discussion of this tale is based on its earliest published form, printed in J. O. Halliwell, *Nursery Rhymes and Nursery Tales* (London, c. 1843).

Only in some of the later renderings of the story do the two little pigs survive, which robs the tale of much of its impact. In some variations the pigs are given names, interfering with the child's ability to see them as representations of the three stages of development. On the other hand, some renderings spell out that it was the seeking of pleasure which prevented the littler ones from building more substantial and thus safer homes, as the littlest one builds his house out of mud because it feels so pleasant to wallow in it, while the second uses cabbage to build his abode because he loves eating it.

14. The quotation describing animistic thinking is from Ruth Benedict's article "Animism" in the *Encyclopedia of the Social Sciences* (New York: Macmillan, 1948).

15. For the various stages of animistic thinking in the child, and the dominance it exerts up to the age of twelve, see Jean Piaget, *The Child's Concept of the World* (New York: Harcourt, Brace, 1929).

16. "East of the Sun and West of the Moon" is a Norwegian fairy tale. A translation can be found in Andrew Lang, *The Blue Fairy Book* (London: Longmans, Green, c. 1889).

17. "Beauty and the Beast" is a very old story, existing in many different versions. Among the best known is that of Madame Leprince de Beaumont, to be found in Iona and Peter Opie, *The Classic Fairy Tales* (London: Oxford University Press, 1974).

"The Frog King" is one of the Brothers Grimm's stories.

18. A summarization of Piaget's theories can be found in J. H. Flavell, *The Developmental Psychology of Jean Piaget* (Princeton: Van Nostrand, 1963).

19. For a discussion of the goddess Nut, see Erich Neumann, *The Great Mother* (Princeton: Princeton University Press, 1955). "As vault of heaven she covers her creatures on earth like a hen sheltering her

chicks." How she was depicted can be seen on the lid of the Egyptian sarcophagus of Uresh-Nofer (XXX Dynasty) in the Metropolitan Museum in New York.

20. Michael Polanyi, *Personal Knowledge* (Chicago: University of Chicago Press, 1958).

21. Sigmund Freud, "From the History of an Infantile Neurosis," *op. cit.*

22. While I do not know of any studies showing how distracting the illustrations in fairy stories are, this is amply demonstrated for other reading matter. See, for example, S. J. Samuels, "Attention Process in Reading: The Effect of Pictures on the Acquisition of Reading Responses," *Journal of Educational Psychology*, vol. 58 (1967); and his review of many other studies of this problem: "Effects of Pictures on Learning to Read, Comprehension, and Attitude," *Review of Educational Research*, vol. 40 (1970).

23. J. R. R. Tolkien, *Tree and Leaf* (Boston: Houghton Mifflin, 1965).

24. There is considerable literature on the consequences of dream deprivation—for example, Charles Fisher, "Psychoanalytic Implications of Recent Research on Sleep and Dreaming," *Journal of the American Psychoanalytic Association*, vol. 13 (1965); and Louis J. West, Herbert H. Janszen, Boyd K. Lester, and Floyd S. Cornelison, Jr., "The Psychosis of Sleep Deprivation," *Annals of the New York Academy of Science*, vol. 96 (1962).

25. Chesterton, *op. cit.*

26. Sigmund Freud, "The Family Romance of the Neurotic," *op. cit.*, vol. 10.

27. "The Three Wishes" was originally a Scottish tale, reported by Briggs, *op. cit.* As mentioned, with appropriate variations the motif is found all over the world. For example, in an Indian tale a family is granted three wishes. The wife desires great beauty and uses the first wish to gain it, after which she elopes with a prince. The angry husband wishes her changed into a pig; the son must use the third and last wish to restore her as she was originally.

28. The same sequence of events could also be viewed as symbolically expressing that as the danger of giving in to id pressures decreases—the reduction of animal ferocity as represented by tiger and wolf to the tameness as symbolized by the deer—so the warning voices of ego and superego lose some of the power to control the id. But since in the tale brother tells sister in regard to his determination to drink from the third brook, "I must drink, whatever you say; my thirst is just too great," the interpretation given in the text seems closer to the underlying meaning of the story.

29. The discussion of "Sindbad the Sailor and Sindbad the Porter" follows Burton's translation of *The Arabian Nights' Entertainments*.

30. For the history of *The Arabian Nights' Entertainments* and particularly about the meaning of the number 1001, see von der Leyen, *Die Welt des Märchens*, 2 volumes (Düsseldorf: Eugen Diederich, 1953).

31. For the tale that forms the framework within which the 1001 stories are

put, see Emmanuel Cosquin, *"Le Prologue-Cadre des Mille et Une Nuits"* in his *Études Folkloriques* (Paris: Champion, 1922).

For the frame story of *Thousand and One Nights* I followed John Payne's translation in *The Book of the Thousand Nights and One Night* (London: Printed for Subscribers Only, 1914).

32. For the ancient Egyptian tale, see Emanuel de Rougé, "Notice sur un manuscrit égyptien," *Revue archéologique*, vol. 8 (1852); W. F. Petrie, *Egyptian Tales*, vol. 2 (1895); and Bolte and Polivka, *op. cit.*

33. The various renderings of the tale of "The Two Brothers" are discussed by Kurt Ranke, *"Die zwei Brüder,"* *Folk Lore Fellow Communications*, vol. 114 (1934).

34. It is quite unusual for a fairy tale to be so specific in regard to place names. Those who have studied this problem have come to the conclusion that when a place name is mentioned, this suggests that the tale is somehow connected with an event that actually took place. For example, in the city of Hameln at one time a group of children may have been abducted, which led to the story of the Pied Piper, which tells about the disappearance of children in this town. It is a morality tale, but hardly a fairy story, since it lacks a resolution and has no happy ending. But such a story with a historical reference exists essentially only in one form.

The wide distribution of the motif of "The Three Languages" and the many different versions in which it exists speak against a historical nucleus of this tale. On the other hand, it makes good sense that a story which begins in Switzerland stresses the importance of learning three different languages, and of the need to integrate them into a higher unit, since four language groups form the population of Switzerland: German, French, Italian, and Rhaeto-Romanic. Since one of these languages—in all likelihood German—was the native tongue of the hero, it makes good sense that he is sent to three different places and there learns other languages. What the Swiss listener to the story may overtly comprehend as the necessity of persons speaking different languages to form a higher unity—Switzerland—also refers on a covert level to the need for inner integration of the diverse tendencies residing within oneself.

35. For the custom of blowing a feather into the air to reach a decision on where to go, see Bolte and Polivka, *op. cit.*, vol. 2.

36. Tolkien, *op. cit.*

37. See, for example, the story of Joey in Bruno Bettelheim, *The Empty Fortress* (New York: Free Press, 1967).

38. Jean Piaget, *The Origins of Intelligence in Children* (New York: International Universities Press, 1952) and *The Construction of Reality in the Child* (New York: Basic Books, 1954).

39. Watty Piper, *The Little Engine That Could* (Eau Claire, Wisconsin: E. M. Hale, 1954).

40. A. A. Milne's poem "Disobedience" in *When We Were Very Young* (New York: E. P. Dutton, 1924).

41. The name of the horse Falada suggests an ancient origin of the tale. It

is derived from the name of Roland's horse, which in the *Chanson de Roland* is called Valantin, Valantis, Valatin, etc.

Even more ancient is the motif of the talking horse. Tacitus reported that among the Germans horses were presumed to be able to predict the future and were used as oracles. Among the Scandinavian nations, the horse is viewed in similar ways.

42. For "Roswal and Lillian," see Briggs, *op. cit.*

The motif of the true bride being supplanted by an evil usurper who is finally unmasked and punished, but not before the true bride has undergone severe trials which test her character, is worldwide. (See P. Arfert, *Das Motiv von der unterschobenen Braut in der internationalen Erzählungsliteratur* [Rostock: Dissertation, 1897].) Details vary both within a culture and between countries, as is true for fairy tales in general, since local features and customs are introduced into the basic motif.

43. A few lines from the same cycle testify once more to the formative impact of fairy tales on poets. Heine, recollecting fairy tales, writes:

> My old nurse's tales, how sweetly they ring,
> How dear are the thoughts they inspire!

and:

> When the song I recall, the remembrance too
> Of my dear old nurse never ceases.
> I see once more her swarthy face,
> With all its wrinkles and creases.

> In the district of Münster she was born,
> And knew, in all their glory,
> Many popular songs and wondrous tales,
> And many a wild ghost story.

The Poems of Heine (London: G. Bell and Sons, 1916).

44. For these other versions of "The Goose Girl," as for additional information on all other stories of the Brothers Grimm, see Bolte and Polivka, *op. cit.*

45. Tolkien, *op. cit.*

46. Mary J. Collier and Eugene L. Gaier, "Adult Reactions to Preferred Childhood Stories," *Child Development*, vol. 29 (1958).

47. Chesterton, *op. cit.*

Maurice Maeterlinck, *The Blue Bird* (New York: Dodd, Mead, 1911).

48. For the Turkish fairy tale, particularly the story of Iskender, see August Nitschke, *Die Bedrohung* (Stuttgart: Ernst Klett, 1972). This book discusses various other aspects of fairy tales, particularly how the threat is part of the striving for self-realization and with it for freedom; and the role of the helpful friend.

49.
> Vom Vater hab' ich die Statur,
> Des Lebens ernstes Führen,
> Vom Mütterchen die Frohnatur
> Und Lust zu fabulieren.
> Goethe, *Zahme Xenien*, VI.

50. The manner in which Goethe's mother told fairy tales to her son is described by Bettina von Arnim in *Goethe's Briefwechsel mit einem Kinde* (Jena: Diederichs, 1906).

51. *"Wer vieles bringt, wird manchem etwas bringen"*—Goethe, *Faust.*

52. Charles Perrault, *Histoires ou Contes du temps passé, avec des Moralitez* (Paris, 1697). The first English translation which appeared in print was by Robert Samber, *Histories or Tales of Past Times* (London, 1729). The best known of these tales have been reprinted in Iona and Peter Opie, *op. cit.* They can also be found in Andrew Lang's fairy books—"Little Red Riding Hood" is included among the tales of *The Blue Fairy Book, op. cit.*

53. There is a considerable literature dealing with Perrault and his fairy tales. The most useful work—comparable to what Bolte and Polivka did for the Brothers Grimm's tales—is Marc Soriano, *Les Contes de Perrault* (Paris: Gallimard, 1968).

    Andrew Lang, *Perrault's Popular Tales* (Oxford: At the Clarendon Press, 1888). There he writes: "If *Little Red Riding Hood* ended, in all variants, where it ends in Perrault, we might dismiss it, with the remark that the *machinery* of the story is derived from 'the time when beasts spoke,' or were believed to be capable of speaking. But it is well known that in the German form, *Little Red Cap* (Brothers Grimm 26), the tale by no means ends with the triumph of the wolf. Little Red Cap and her grandmother are resuscitated, 'the wolf it was that died.' This may either have been the original ending, omitted by Perrault because it was too wildly impossible for the nurseries of the time of Louis XIV, or children may have insisted on having the story 'turn out well.' In either case the German *Märchen* preserves one of the most widely spread mythical incidents in the world—the reappearance of living people out of the monster that has devoured them."

54. Two of these French versions of "Little Red Riding Hood" are published in *Melusine,* vol. 3 (1886–7) and vol. 6 (1892–3).

55. *Ibid.*

56. Djuna Barnes, *Nightwood* (New York: New Directions, 1937). T. S. Eliot, Introduction to *Nightwood, ibid.*

57. *Fairy Tales Told Again,* illustrated by Gustave Doré (London: Cassel, Petter and Galpin, 1872). The illustration is reprinted in Opie and Opie, *op. cit.*

58. For alternate versions of "Little Red Cap," see Bolte and Polivka, *op. cit.*

59. Gertrude Crampton, *Tootle the Engine* (New York: Simon and Schuster, 1946), a Little Golden Book.

60. For the various Jack stories, including the different versions of "Jack and the Beanstalk," see Briggs, *op. cit.*

61. For the various myths forming the cycle which begins with Tantalus, centers on Oedipus, and ends with *The Seven Against Thebes* and the death of Antigone, see Schwab, *op. cit.*

62. For the various versions of "Snow White," see Bolte and Polivka, *op. cit.*

63. The discussion of "Snow White" is based on its rendering by the Brothers Grimm.

64. "The Young Slave" is the Eighth Diversion of the Second Day of Basile's *Pentamerone*, which was first printed in 1636 (*The Pentamerone of Giambattista Basile* [London: John Lane the Bodley Head, 1932]).

65. For a discussion of why in the unconscious the number three often stands for sex, see p. 219 ff.

66. Dwarfs and their meaning in folklore is discussed in the article *"Zwerge und Riesen,"* and in many other articles found in Hans Bächtold-Stäubli, *Handwörterbuch des deutschen Aberglaubens* (Berlin: de Gruyter, 1927–42). It also contains interesting articles on fairy tales and on fairy-tale motifs.

67. Anne Sexton, *Transformations* (Boston: Houghton Mifflin, 1971).

68. For the first printed version of "The Three Bears," see Briggs, *op. cit.*

69. Erik H. Erikson, *Identity, Youth and Crisis* (New York: W. W. Norton, 1968).

70. For Perrault's *"La Belle au bois dormant,"* see Perrault, *op. cit.* English translations of "The Sleeping Beauty" are in Lang, *The Blue Fairy Book*, and Opie and Opie, *op. cit.* For the Brothers Grimm's tale "Dornröschen," see Brothers Grimm, *op. cit.*

71. Basile, *op. cit.* "Sun, Moon and Talia" is the Fifth Diversion of the Fifth Day of the *Pentamerone.*

72. For the precursors of "The Sleeping Beauty," see Bolte and Polivka, *op. cit.*, and Soriano, *op. cit.*

73. For the fact that "Cinderella" is the best known of all fairy tales, see *Funk and Wagnalls Dictionary of Folklore* (New York: Funk and Wagnalls, 1950). Also Opie and Opie, *op. cit.*
    For its being the best loved of fairy stories, see Collier and Gaier, *op. cit.*

74. For the earliest Chinese story of the "Cinderella" type, see Arthur Waley, "Chinese Cinderella Story," *Folk-Lore,* vol. 58 (1947).

75. For the history of footwear, including sandals and slippers, see R. T. Wilcox, *The Mode of Footwear* (New York, 1948).
    For an even more detailed discussion, including the edict of Diocletian, see E. Jaefert, *Skomod och skotillverkning fran medeltiden vara dagar* (Stockholm, 1938).

76. For the origin and meaning of "Aschenbrödel," and for many other details of the story, see Bolte and Polivka, *op. cit.*, and Anna B. Rooth, *The Cinderella Cycle* (Lund: Gleerup, 1951).

77. Barnes, *op. cit.*

78. B. Rubenstein, "The Meaning of the Cinderella Story in the Development of a Little Girl," *American Imago,* vol. 12 (1955).

79. *"La Gatta Cenerentola"* is the Sixth Diversion of the First Day of Basile's *Pentamerone, op. cit.*

80. The idea of letting the lid of a chest fall on a person's neck to kill him is extremely rare, although it appears in one of the Brothers Grimm's stories, "The Juniper Tree," in which an evil stepmother thus kills her

stepson. It probably is of historical origin. Gregory (St. Gregorius) of Tours in his *History of the Franks* (New York: Columbia University Press, 1916) tells that Queen Fredegund (who died in 597) tried to kill her own daughter Rigundis in this manner, but the daughter was saved by servants rushing to her aid. The reason Queen Fredegund tried to kill her daughter was that Rigundis asserted that she should be in her mother's place because she was "better"—that is, born as a king's daughter, while her mother had started life as a chambermaid. Thus, oedipal arrogance of a daughter—"I am better suited than my mother for her place"—leads to the mother's oedipal revenge by trying to eliminate the daughter who wished to replace her.

81. *"La mala matrè"* in A. de Nino, *Usi e costumi abruzzesi,* vol. 3: *Fiabe* (Florence, 1883–7).

82. Various tales in the center of which stands the Cinderella motif are discussed in Marian R. Cox, *Cinderella: Three Hundred and Forty-five Variants* (London: David Nutt, 1893).

83. This can be illustrated by a famous error which occurred during the early days of psychoanalysis. Freud, on the basis of what his female patients told him while in psychoanalysis—their dreams, free associations, recollections—concluded that as small children they all had been seduced by their fathers, and that this was the cause of their neuroses. Only when patients whose early life histories were well known to him had similar memories—although he knew that no such seduction had occurred in these cases—did Freud realize that paternal seduction could not possibly be as frequent as he had been led to believe. It then became apparent to him—and since then it has been corroborated in innumerable instances—that what his female patients recollected was not something that had happened, but what they wished would have happened. As young girls, during their oedipal period, they had desired that their fathers would be deeply in love with them and so wish to have them for wives, or at least lovers. They had wished it so passionately that they vividly imagined that it was so. Later, when they recalled the content of these fantasies, it was with such intensity of feeling that they were convinced that this could only be because of events which actually had taken place. They themselves had done nothing to provoke the paternal seduction, so they claimed and believed; it had been all their fathers' doing. In short, they had been as innocent as Cinderella.

After Freud had realized that these memories of seduction did not refer to things that had happened in reality, but only to fantasies, and therefore helped his patients to probe more deeply into their unconscious, then it became apparent that not only had a wish been taken for its having been fulfilled, but that the patients when little girls had been far from innocent. They had not only desired to be seduced and imagined that this was so, but also had tried to seduce their fathers in their childish ways—for example, by displaying themselves or in many other ways courting Father's love. (Sigmund Freud, "An Autobiographical

Study," *New Introductory Lectures to Psychoanalysis,"* etc., *op. cit.,* vols. 20, 22.)

84. For example in "Cap o' Rushes," Briggs, *op. cit.*
85. Perrault's "Cinderella" is reprinted in Opie and Opie, *op. cit.* Unfortunately, as in nearly all other English translations, the verses setting forth the story's moral are not included.
      For the Brothers Grimm's "Aschenputtel," see Grimm, *op. cit.*
86. "Rashin Coatie," Briggs, *op. cit.*
87. Stith Thompson, *Motif Index* ..., *op. cit.,* and *The Folk Tale* (New York: Dryden Press, 1946).
88. For the ritual meaning of ashes, and for the role of ashes in purifications and in mourning, see the article "Ashes" in James Hastings, *Encyclopedia of Religion and Ethics* (New York: Scribner, 1910). For the meaning and uses of ashes in folklore, and its role in fairy tales, see the article *"Asche"* in Bächtold-Stäubli, *op. cit.*
89. "Rashin Coatie," or a tale much like it, is mentioned in the *Complaynt of Scotland* (1540), edited by Murray (1872).
90. This Egyptian tale is reported in René Basset, *Contes populaires d'Afrique* (Paris: Guilmoto, 1903).
91. Erik H. Erikson, *Identity and the Life Cycle, Psychological Issues,* vol. 1 (1959) (New York: International Universities Press, 1959).
92. In an Icelandic "Cinderella" story, the dead mother appears to the mistreated heroine in a dream and provides her with a magic object which keeps her going until a prince finds her shoe, etc. Jon Arnason, *Folk Tales of Iceland* (Leipzig, 1862–4) and *Icelandic Folktales and Legends* (Berkeley: University of California Press, 1972).
93. For the various tasks asked of Cinderella, see Rooth, *op. cit.*
94. Soriano, *op. cit.*
95. This ridiculing of the Cinderella story he just told is highlighted by what Soriano calls "the bitter irony" of the second morality with which Perrault concludes his tale. In it he says that while it is advantageous to possess intelligence, courage, and other good qualities, these do not amount to much *("ce seront choses vaines")* if one does not have godfathers or godmothers to make them count.
96. Cox, *op. cit.*
97. Bruno Bettelheim, *Symbolic Wounds* (Glencoe: The Free Press, 1954).
98. The story of Rhodope is told by Strabo in *The Geography of Strabo,* Loeb Classical Library (London: Heinemann, 1932).
99. Rooth, *op. cit.*
100. Raymond de Loy Jameson, *Three Lectures on Chinese Folklore* (Peiping: Publications of the College of Chinese Studies, 1932).
      Aigremont, *"Fuss- und Schuh-Symbolik und Erotik,"* *Anthropopyteia,* vol. 5 (Leipzig, 1909).
101. "Tread softly because you tread on my dreams," from the poem "He Wishes for the Cloths of Heaven," in William Butler Yeats, *The Collected Poems* (New York: Macmillan, 1956).
102. One might rightly be worried, for example, if a child consciously recog-

nized that the golden slipper could be a symbol for the vagina, as one would be concerned if he consciously understood the sexual content of the well-known nursery rhyme:

> Cock a doodle do!
> My dame has lost her shoe;
> My master's lost his fiddle stick;
> And they don't know what to do!

And this although the slang meaning of the first word is by now quite well known even to children. In the rhyme the shoe is used in the same symbolic meaning as in "Cinderella." If the child understood what this nursery rhyme is all about, he would indeed "not know what to do!" And the same would be true if he understood—as no child does—all the hidden meanings of "Cinderella," only some of which I have tried to spell out, and even those only to a certain degree.

103. Erikson, *Identity and the Life Cycle, op. cit.; Identity, Youth, and Crisis, op. cit.*
104. "Cinderella" stories in which a ring and not a slipper leads to her recognition are (among others) "Maria Intaulata" and "Maria Intauradda," both in *Archivio per lo Studio delle Tradizioni Populari*, vol. 2 (Palermo, 1882), and "Les Souliers," in Auguste Dozon, *Contes Albanais* (Paris, 1881).
105. "Beauty and the Beast" is now best known in the version of Madame Leprince de Beaumont, first translated into English in *The Young Misses Magazine* in 1761. It is reprinted in Opie and Opie, *op. cit.*
106. The wide distribution of the motif of the animal groom is discussed in Lutz Röhrich, *Märchen und Wirklichkeit* (Wiesbaden: Steiner, 1974).
107. For the Kaffir story, see *Dictionary of Folklore, op. cit.*, and G. M. Teal, *Kaffir* (London: Folk Society, 1886).
108. *Die Märchen der Weltliteratur, Malaiische Märchen*, Paul Hambruch, editor (Jena: Diederichs, 1922).
109. Leo Frobenius, *Atlantis: Volksmärchen und Volksdichtungen aus Afrika* (Jena: Diederichs, 1921–8), vol. 10.
110. Opie and Opie, *op. cit.*
111. "The Well of the World's End" in Briggs, *op. cit.*
112. For the original version of "The Frog Prince" which the Brothers Grimm failed to publish, see Joseph Lefftz, *Märchen der Brüder Grimm: Urfassung* (Heidelberg: C. Winter, 1927).
113. Briggs, *op. cit.*
114. Sexton, *op. cit.*
115. For "Cupid and Psyche," see Erich Neumann, *Amor and Psyche, op. cit.* For the many versions of the story, see Ernst Tegethoff, *Studien zum Märchentypus von Amor und Psyche* (Bonn: Schroeder, 1922).

A good enumeration of fairy tales of this motif is presented in the discussion of the Brothers Grimm's tale "The Singing, Hopping Lark" in Bolte and Polivka, *op. cit.*

116. Robert Graves, *Apuleius Madaurensis: The Transformations of Lucius* (New York: Farrar, Straus & Young, 1951).
117. "The Enchanted Pig" in Andrew Lang, *The Red Fairy Book* (London: Longmans, Green, 1890), and "The Enchanted Pig" in Mite Kremnitz, *Rumänische Märchen* (Leipzig, 1882).
118. "East of the Sun and West of the Moon" in Andrew Lang, *The Blue Fairy Book, op. cit.*
119. Here we may recognize once more an allusion to the loss of the hymen, the sacrifice of a small part of the woman's body in her first experience with sex.

    The bones of chickens are such an unlikely magic object, and such a farfetched means of climbing a height, that they seem like a projection backward of the requirement to give up the little finger, or a device to make the idea of its being used to provide the last rung of the ladder more convincing. But, as mentioned in the discussion of "Cinderella," and one of the many symbolic meanings of the wedding ceremony, for finding complete fulfillment in marriage, the woman must relinquish the wish for a phallus of her own, and be satisfied with that of her husband. Cutting off her little finger, far from signifying symbolic self-castration, may suggest what fantasies the female must give up to be happy the way she is, so that she can be happy with her husband the way he is.
120. "Bluebeard," Perrault, *op. cit.* The first English translation is reprinted in Opie and Opie, *op. cit.*

    Long before Perrault there are tales in which entering a forbidden chamber has far-reaching consequences. This motif appears, for example, in the "Tale of the Third Calender" in *The Arabian Nights' Entertainments* and in the *Pentamerone*, where it is the Sixth Tale of the Fourth Day.
121. "Mr. Fox" in Briggs, *op. cit.*
122. For "Beauty and the Beast," see Opie and Opie, *op. cit.*

BIBLIOGRAPHY

The bibliographical information about the fairy tales and other literature mentioned in the book is given in the Notes and is *not* repeated here.

The fairy-tale literature is so vast that nobody has attempted to collect all the tales. Probably the most satisfactory and readily available collection in English is that edited by Andrew Lang and published in his twelve volumes titled: *The Blue, Brown, Crimson, Green, Grey, Lilac, Olive, Orange, Pink, Red, Violet,* and *Yellow Fairy Book.* Originally published by Longmans, Green, and Co., London, 1889 ff., these books have been recently republished by Dover Publications, New York, 1965 ff.

The most ambitious undertaking in this field is the German collection *Die Märchen der Weltliteratur.* Publication was begun in 1912 by Diederichs in Jena with Friedrich von der Leyen and Paul Zaunert as editors. So far, some seventy volumes have appeared. With very few exceptions, each volume is devoted to fairy tales of only one language or culture; hence only a very small selection of fairy tales of each culture is included. To give only one example, the collection made by Leo Frobenius, *Atlantis: Volksmärchen und Volksdichtungen aus Afrika* (Munich: Forschungsinstitut für Kulturmorphologie, 1921–8), consists of twelve volumes, and nonetheless contains only a quite limited selection of the fairy tales of that continent.

The literature *about* fairy tales is nearly as voluminous as that *of* fairy tales. Below, a few books are listed which seem of general interest, and some publications which were useful in the preparation of this volume without having been mentioned in the Notes.

AARNE, ANTTI A., *The Types of the Folktale.* Helsinki: Suomalainen Tiedeakatemia, 1961.

Archivio per lo Studio delle Tradizioni Populari. 28 vols. Palermo, 1890–1912.

ARNASON, JON, *Icelandic Folktales and Legends.* Berkeley: University of California Press, 1972.

BÄCHTOLD-STÄUBLI, HANS, ed., *Handwörterbuch des deutschen Aberglaubens.* 10 vols. Berlin: de Gruyter, 1927–42.

BASILE, GIAMBATTISTA, *The Pentamerone.* 2 vols. London: John Lane the Bodley Head, 1932.

BASSET, RENÉ, *Contes populaires Berbères.* 2 vols. Paris: Guilmoto, 1887.

BEDIERS, JOSEPH, *Les Fabliaux.* Paris: Bouillou, 1893.

BOLTE, JOHANNES, and GEORG POLIVKA, *Anmerkungen zu den Kinder- und Hausmärchen der Brüder Grimm.* 5 vols. Hildesheim: Olms, 1963.

BRIGGS, KATHERINE M., *A Dictionary of British Folk Tales.* 4 vols. Bloomington: Indiana University Press, 1970.

BURTON, RICHARD, *The Arabian Nights' Entertainments.* 13 vols. London: H. S. Nichols, 1894–7.

COX, MARIAN ROALFE, *Cinderella: Three Hundred and Forty-five Variants.* London: The Folk-Lore Society, David Nutt, 1893.

Folklore Fellows Communications. Ed. for the Folklore Fellows, Academia Scientiarum Fennica, 1910ff.

Funk and Wagnalls Dictionary of Folklore. 2 vols. New York: Funk and Wagnalls, 1950.

GRIMM, THE BROTHERS, *Grimm's Fairy Tales.* New York: Pantheon Books, 1944.

———, *The Grimm's German Folk Tales.* Carbondale, Ill.: Southern Illinios University Press, 1960.

HASTINGS, JAMES, *Encyclopedia of Religion and Ethics.* 13 vols. New York: Scribner's, 1910.

JACOBS, JOSEPH, *English Fairy Tales.* London: David Nutt, 1890.

———, *More English Fairy Tales.* London: David Nutt, 1895.

Journal of American Folklore. American Folklore Society, Boston, 1888ff.

LANG, ANDREW, ed., *The Fairy Books.* 12 vols. London: Longmans, Green, 1889ff.

———, *Perrault's Popular Tales.* Oxford: At the Clarendon Press, 1888.

LEFFTZ, J., *Märchen der Brüder Grimm: Urfassung.* Heidelberg, C. Winter, 1927.

LEYEN, FRIEDRICH VON DER, and PAUL ZAUNERT, eds., *Die Märchen der Weltliteratur.* 70 vols. Jena: Diederichs, 1912ff.

MACKENSEN, LUTZ, ed., *Handwörterbuch des deutschen Märchens.* 2 vols. Berlin: de Gruyter, 1930–40.

Melusine. 10 vols. Paris, 1878–1901.

OPIE, IONA and PETER, *The Classic Fairy Tales.* London: Oxford University Press, 1974.

PERRAULT, CHARLES, *Histoires ou Contes du temps passé.* Paris, 1697.

SAINTYVES, PAUL, *Les Contes de Perrault et les récits parallèles.* Paris: E. Nourry, 1923.

SCHWAB, GUSTAV, *Gods and Heroes: Myths and Epics of Ancient Greece.* New York: Pantheon Books, 1946.

SORIANO, MARC, *Les Contes de Perrault.* Paris: Gallimard, 1968.

STRAPAROLA, GIOVANNI FRANCESCO, *The Facetious Nights of Straparola.* 4 vols. London: Society of Bibliophiles, 1901.

THOMPSON, STITH, *Motif Index of Folk Literature.* 6 vols. Bloomington: Indiana University Press, 1955.

———, *The Folk Tale.* New York: Dryden Press, 1946.

INTERPRETATIONS

BAUSINGER, HERMANN, *"Aschenputtel: Zum Problem der Märchen-Symbolik,"* Zeitschrift für Volkskunde, vol. 52 (1955).

BEIT, HEDWIG VON, *Symbolik des Märchens* and *Gegensatz und Erneuerung im Märchen.* Bern: A. Francke, 1952 and 1956.

BILZ, JOSEPHINE, *"Märchengeschehen und Reifungsvorgänge unter tiefen-*

psychologischem Gesichtspunkt," in Bühler and Bilz, *Das Märchen und die Phantasie des Kindes.* München: Barth, 1958.

BITTNER, GUENTHER, *"Über die Symbolik weiblicher Reifung im Volksmärchen,"* Praxis der Kinderpsychologie und Kinderpsychiatrie, vol. 12 (1963).

BORNSTEIN, STEFF, *"Das Märchen vom Dornröschen in psychoanalytischer Darstellung,"* Imago, vol. 19 (1933).

BÜHLER, CHARLOTTE, *Das Märchen und die Phantasie des Kindes. Beihefte zur Zeitschrift für angewandte Psychologie,* vol. 17 (1918).

COOK, ELIZABETH, *The Ordinary and the Fabulous: An Introduction to Myths, Legends, and Fairy Tales for Teachers and Storytellers.* New York: Cambridge University Press, 1969.

DIECKMANN, HANNS, *Märchen und Träume als Helfer des Menschen.* Stuttgart: Adolf Bonz, 1966.

———, *"Wert des Märchens für die seelische Entwicklung des Kindes,"* Praxis der Kinderpsychologie und Kinderpsychiatrie, vol. 15 (1966).

HANDSCHIN-NINCK, MARIANNE, *"Ältester und Jüngster im Märchen,"* Praxis der Kinderpsychologie und Kinderpsychiatrie, vol. 5 (1956).

JOLLES, ANDRE, *Einfache Formen.* Darmstadt: Wissenschaftliche Buchgesellschaft, 1969.

KIENLE, G., *"Das Märchen in der Psychotherapie,"* Zeitschrift für Psychotherapie und medizinische Psychologie, 1959.

LAIBLIN, WILHELM, *"Die Symbolik der Erlösung und Wiedergeburt im deutschen Volksmärchen,"* Zentralblatt für Psychotherapie und ihre Grenzgebiete, 1943.

LEBER, GABRIELE, *"Über tiefenpsychologische Aspekte von Märchenmotiven,"* Praxis der Kinderpsychologie und Kinderpsychiatrie, vol. 4 (1955).

LEYEN, FRIEDRICH VON DER, *Das Märchen.* Leipzig: Quelle und Meyer, 1925.

LOEFFLER-DELACHAUX, M., *Le Symbolisme des contes de fées.* Paris, 1949.

LÜTHI, MAX, *Es war einmal—Vom Wesen des Volksmärchens.* Göttingen: Vandenhoeck & Ruprecht, 1962.

———, *Märchen.* Stuttgart: Metzler, 1962.

———, *Volksmärchen und Volkssage.* Bern: Francke, 1961.

MALLET, CARL-HEINZ, *"Die zweite und dritte Nacht im Märchen 'Das Gruseln,'"* Praxis der Kinderpsychologie und Kinderpsychiatrie, vol. 14 (1965).

MENDELSOHN, J., *"Das Tiermärchen und seine Bedeutung als Ausdruck seelischer Entwicklungsstruktur,"* Praxis der Kinderpsychologie und Kinderpsychiatrie, vol. 10 (1961).

———, *"Die Bedeutung des Volksmärchens für das seelische Wachstum des Kindes,"* Praxis der Kinderpsychologie und Kinderpsychiatrie, vol. 7 (1958).

OBENAUER, KARL JUSTUS, *Das Märchen, Dichtung und Deutung.* Frankfurt: Klostermann, 1959.

SANTUCCI, LUIGI, *Das Kind—Sein Mythos und sein Märchen.* Hanover: Schroedel, 1964.

TEGETHOFF, ERNST, *Studien zum Märchentypus von Amor und Psyche.* Bonn: Schroeder, 1922.

ZILLINGER, G. *"Zur Frage der Angst und der Darstellung psychosexueller Reifungsstufen im Märchen vom Gruseln," Praxis der Kinderpsychologie und Kinderpsychiatrie,* vol. 12 (1963).

INDEX

A NOTE ON THE TYPE

The text of this book was set, via computer-driven Cathode Ray Tube, in Video Gael, an adaptation of Caledonia, a type face originally designed by W. A. Dwiggins. It belongs to the family of printing types called "modern faces" by printers—a term used to mark the change in style of type letters that occurred about 1800. Caledonia borders on the general design of Scotch Modern, but is more freely drawn than that letter.

Composed, printed and bound by
The Haddon Craftsmen, Inc.,
Scranton, Pennsylvania

Designed by Earl Tidwell